THE TERADA'S
MAY / 96

COURTESY BCC.

Bukkyo Tozen*

A History of Jodo Shinshu Buddhism in Canada

1905 - 1995

Terry Watada

Afterword by Rev. Hoshu Y. Matsubayashi, Ed.D.
Bishop
Buddhist Churches of Canada

* the eastward movement of Buddhism

Bukkyo Tozen

The publishers gratefully acknowledge the financial assistance of the Toronto Buddhist Church, the Buddhist Churches of Canada, the Japanese Canadian Redress Foundation, the Buddha Dharma Kyokai, the Hastings Park Foundation and the Multicultural Programs of the Department of Canadian Heritage.

Edited by Dr. Irene Uchida
Cover design by Sandy Usami
Cover painting by Kazuo Hamasaki
Author photograph by Phil Doi
Japanese ideograms by Rev. Yasuo Izumi
Publication advice by Elaine Wyatt
Composition and page design by Kagami Images
Printed and bound in Canada by Webcom Limited

First Edition
1 2 3 4 5 00 99 98 97 96

Canadian Cataloguing in Publication Data
Watada, Terry
Bukkyo Tozen: a history of Jodo Shinshu Buddhism in Canada, 1905-1995
Includes bibliographical references.
ISBN: 0-9699502-0-9
1. Shin (Sect) - Canada - History - 20th Century.
1. Title.
BQ8712.9.C3W37 1996 294.3'926 C96-930060-3

Published by HpF Press and the Toronto Buddhist Church

Tozen no Buppi tokasu,
Canada-bare.

In the clear Canadian sky
The sun has risen high from the eastern horizon,
As if indicating ever-spreading the Light of Dharma
In the eastward direction.
Namu Amida Butsu

Rev. Enryo Shigefuji
Bishop BCA & BCC
1948 - 1958

Bukkyo Tozen

Table of Contents

Part Two: Restoration and the Movement East

Part Three: The Toronto Buddhist Church

Ohtani, Koshin
Monshu
Jodo Shinshu Hongwanji-ha

I wish to express my congratulations on the publication of **Bukkyo Tozen:** *A History of Jodo Shinshu Buddhism in Canada, 1905 - 1995,* written by Mr. Terry Watada in commemoration of the 50th anniversary of the Toronto Buddhist Church. This year is the 90th anniversary of the Shin Buddhist ministry in Canada, and this book has been published through the support of the Buddhist Churches of Canada, contributions from the special reparation to Japanese Canadians by the Canadian government, and the co-operation of many persons on the Toronto Buddhist Church History Committee. I express my deep esteem for the efforts and labour of all those involved.

This work records in detail the ninety-year history of the Canadian ministry down to the present. From a review of these nine decades, one can sense the prodigious endeavour and inexpressible hardships of ministers, members and the others who lent their support. At the same time, we can know that the aspirations of those who have made this ninety-year history have been carefully transmitted and embraced in the present. When we reflect on this, we realize that our lives as Buddhists today are not merely isolated events, but stand upon the aspirations and struggles of many who have gone before us.

The ministry in Canada was begun at the request of Japanese who had immigrated to Canada from Japan. Now, however, the teaching of the *Nembutsu* is spreading throughout the world, beyond the divisions of ethnic groups and national borders. This is because the *Nembutsu* teaching aspires for the genuine fulfilment of all living things. It is impossible to think of one's own life as separated from the lives of others. Those who are enclosed in the shell of the self, who cut off relations with their fellows, who think only of themselves and not of those around them - it is precisely for such persons that Amida Buddha made the Primal Vow, continuing now to call and summon them. We must reflect on ourselves and recognize that we human beings discriminate into groups, judge people as superior and inferior, and eventually fall into conflict with others. And we must, saying the *Nembutsu* as persons enabled to live in the wisdom and compassion of Amida Buddha, fulfil our responsibilities in the contexts in which we carry on our lives.

It is my deep hope that those who read this volume will take up the aspirations of our forebears, study Shinran Shonin's teaching within the context of the fundamental issues of their own lives, and in Canada and all places in the world, live lives of fulfilment together with all people of the *Nembutsu*.

September 1995

Hoshu Y. Matsubayashi, Ed.D.
Bishop
Buddhist Churches of Canada

The year of 1995 is a very significant year for both the Buddhist Churches of Canada and the Toronto Buddhist Church. For the BCC, this year marks the 90th Anniversary of its founding. In 1905, the first Jodo Shinshu minister, Rev. Senju Sasaki, arrived in Vancouver to begin the propagation of Jodo Shinshu Buddhism in Canada. The BCC history from 1905 to 1995 has not always been an easy one. Before World War II, many of the Jodo Shinshu Buddhists experienced hardship and discrimination in the early stages of Japanese immigration into Canada. During the war, they were forced to leave their homes on the west coast and move into remote areas, gradually reaching the east coast of Canada. After the war, they reorganized the Buddhist Churches of Canada for the new era and established Buddhist Churches in major cities throughout Canada. The BCC is now moving forward into the future, the twenty-first century.

The book, **One Hundred Year History of Canadian Immigration** describes the lifestyle of Jodo Shinshu Japanese immigrants that "kept a *myogo* (Name of Amida Buddha) or a little pictorial Buddha in their wallets when they left their home country." They were able to overcome their hardships, loneliness, and sorrow by realizing the guiding light of Amida Buddha's compassion and wisdom. We must commemorate this anniversary in appreciating Amida's guiding light for 90 years in Canada.

For the Toronto Buddhist Church, this year marks the 50th Anniversary of its founding. The Toronto Buddhist Church began its Buddhist *sangha* activities in 1945, the year that World War II ended. In commemorating its 50th Anniversary, this history book of Jodo Shinshu Buddhism in Canada was published with the support of the BCC with the title of "Bukkyo Tozen." "Bukkyo Tozen" is a unique and dynamic aspect of the Buddhist movement in Buddhist history.

Buddhism has been moving east from India for the past 2,500 years. This book records the historical movement of Jodo Shinshu Buddhism for the past 90 years in Canada, which is a part of the long and great history of Buddhism. Each Buddhist country has recorded the history of the Buddhist movement in that country, but for Canadian Jodo Shinshu Buddhists, this is the first complete history book available. I am extremely happy to be able to share this publication with many Buddhist friends today and in the future. I wish to thank the writer, Mr. Terry Watada, and Mrs. Dorothy Kagawa, Chairperson of the Toronto Buddhist Church History Committee, and her committee members for their dedication and all those who contributed to the publication of this history book.

Finally, I would like to express my sincere appreciation to the pioneer ministers and members who are no longer with us who dedicated their lives to establishing and carrying on the great *sangha* in Canada.

March 1995

Roy Akune
President
Buddhist Churches of Canada

May I take this opportunity to express my heartfelt joy in the publication of **Bukkyo Tozen**: *A History of Jodo Shinshu Buddhism in Canada* by the Toronto Buddhist Church in the celebration of their 50th Anniversary.

Bukkyo Tozen is a collection of facts, dates and significant events of Jodo Shinshu Buddhism in Canada and gives a detailed account of its development. The information was gathered by the history committee through personal interviews, manuscripts, minutes of meetings, letters and notes. It is, however, more than facts, dates and personal recollections. It is the history of religious people struggling to be accepted in an alien culture and unyielding in their efforts to retain their culture and Buddhist identity despite the pressures and influence of Christianity. They tenaciously held onto the principles of Jodo Shinshu Buddhism. These early immigrants suffered from tremendous economic hardships, personal discrimination and negative societal attitudes, but they still maintained their faith in Amida Buddha and never lost their human dignity and belief in the goodness of mankind. Their indefatigable efforts in the propagation of Buddhism in Canada remain as hallmarks in the history of Buddhism in Canada. I humbly bow my head in deepest gratitude and appreciation to these *issei* pioneers - members and ministers. The *Nembutsu* was their unfathomable source of strength and energy.

Today, from a very humble beginning on the West Coast prior to the Second World War, Jodo Shinshu Buddhism has spread to many parts of Canada and the light of the *Nembutsu* continues to shine brightly from generation to generation. This propagation is a testimony to not only the *issei* but also to the *nisei* and *sansei* who, in the present, through their undying faith and unselfish labours continue to nurture Jodo Shinshu Buddhism in Canada. The situation from fifty years ago has changed considerably - no longer do we have an enclave of Japanese who look towards their church as their community. The church is becoming less and less the fabric of their cultural, educational, social and recreational activities. With these needs having been met through community based resources and without the language barriers, the present generation of young adults and the youth have found the church to be less significant in their lives. Nonetheless, the leaders continue to provide yeoman service to the church and remain undaunted in their optimism. To these *nisei* and *sansei*, I pay my highest tribute and express my deepest gratitude for their untiring efforts. The *Nembutsu* remains to be an indomitable spirit in their lives.

The Buddhist Churches of Canada was one of the major financial contributors to this publication. It is through such support that the Toronto Buddhist Church was able to make the publication a reality. Without a doubt, it was the wholehearted co-operation and generous contribution of the Jodo Shinshu Buddhists across Canada that made this monumental undertaking a success.

Bukkyo Tozen is the culmination of the remarkable dedication, commitment and hard work of the Toronto Buddhist Church and the members of the History Book Committee. This success is also largely due to the leadership of Mrs. Dorothy Kagawa, chairperson of the committee, and the writing of Mr. Terry Watada. To each and every member, I wish to offer my sincerest appreciation for their magnanimous effort and congratulations for a project well done.

It is my earnest desire and fervent hope that this Toronto Buddhist Church 50th Anniversary publication, **Bukkyo Tozen:** *A History of Jodo Shinshu Buddhism in Canada*, will serve as a tribute to the accomplishments of our Jodo Shinshu leaders of yester years and today.

The future of Jodo Shinshu Buddhism in Canada is indeed a challenge to all of us. The challenge remains in our hands. Let us dedicate ourselves to the strengthening of our faith in Amida Buddha, the upholding of Buddhist values in our homes and communities and the propagation of Jodo Shinshu Buddhism.

Namo Amida Butsu

February 5, 1995

Rev. Kenryu Tsuji
Resident Minister
Ekoji Buddhist Temple
Springfield, Virginia

My wife and I wish to extend our sincerest congratulations to the members of the Toronto Buddhist Church on the happy occasion of the 50th Anniversary of its founding.

Half a century ago about thirty-five faithful followers of the Buddha *Dharma*, who had relocated to Toronto during the height of the Pacific War, gathered at the home of Mr. and Mrs. Genjiro Mori to celebrate the first Obon Service. From this humble *sangha* was born the Toronto Buddhist Church.

I wish to extend my heartfelt thanks to all the faithful followers, who followed in the footsteps of these pioneers - the ministers, the volunteer lay ministers, the Temple leaders, the youth and the Sunday School teachers. They laid a strong foundation for the Buddha *Dharma* and the *Nembutsu* to thrive in eastern Canada.

It is my strong conviction that the new creative leaders and the members of the Temple will build on the beautiful foundation constructed by the pioneers and develop a Buddhist Education Program that will meet the spiritual needs of countless Canadians, irrespective of race, color or creed.

Congratulations on this happy occasion!

February 6, 1995

Bukkyo Tozen

Rev. Newton Ishiura
Resident Minister
Sacramento Buddhist Church

May I extend a joyous message of congratulations on your 50th Anniversary.

In contemplation, it is meaningful to quote from the "Praises of the Buddha" (Sanbutsuge), an epilogue queried by the disciple Ananda after seeing the benign mien of the Buddha.

The virtues of the Tathagata are innumerable and broad. His knowledge is deep; His majestic light illuminates the thousand worlds. "I (Dharmara Bodhisattva) after attaining Buddhahood and becoming master of the *Dharma*, may I deliver mankind from birth and death."

Living amidst a calamitous year, with rampaging flood, continuous conflict between racial and political adversaries, raging typhoon and earthquakes, we need stability and assurance. Tathagata's appearance instills in us unending solace and comfort.

May your *sangha* provide this strength and guidance.

January 24, 1995

Rev. Orai Fujikawa
Resident Minister
Vancouver Buddhist Church

I wish to join with my wife, Minako, and my children, Bud and Sari, to congratulate you for your 50th Anniversary celebration and for publishing the history book about the Buddhist churches of Canada.

I recall with fond memories that I was very fortunate to have served the TBC for over 14 years from 1980 to 1994, which was the prime of my life. I remember that the TBC was such a busy and challenging place to work. There were over 500 funerals and 180 weddings during my tenure.

The TBC is presently the only active Shin Buddhist temple in eastern Canada and the majority of members consist of Canadians of Japanese origin. Therefore may all of you be aware of your important role and work hard to maintain your active mission into the 21st Century, so that Shin Buddhism will be truly a living religion for all Canadians in the future.

December 16, 1994

Rev. Yasuo Izumi
Resident Minister
Toronto Buddhist Church

Since the first minister of the Hongwanji of Jodo Shinshu was dispatched from Kyoto, Japan, to Vancouver, Canada, ninety years have elapsed. During these years, weathering wind and storm, the wheel of the *Dharma*, the teaching of the *Nembutsu*, has been kept revolving toward the east. The wheel reached the eastern provinces over fifty years ago after crossing the Rocky Mountains and the vast prairies and continued to spread widely. Our fellow Buddhists worked together for the propagation of the Buddha *Dharma* and established temples in Toronto, Montreal and Hamilton.

Looking forward to the 50th anniversary of the Toronto Buddhist Church in 1995, the history committee was set up in 1988 to compile and relate the history of Buddhism in Canada. From that day on, the committee members, headed by Mrs. Dorothy Kagawa, have gathered historical information from file documents, through numerous interviews and meetings, of past events relating to Jodo Shinshu followers, ministers as well as lay people, in chronological order. I believe it has been a painstaking task, but undertaken with much diligence and effort. Through their careful research, we may now be able not only to learn and reflect on the past of Buddhism in Canada but also to foresee its future.

When I hear talk about the future of Jodo Shinshu, I find there appears to be two extreme conclusions: one is that Jodo Shinshu will die in Canada in fifty years or so; the other is that it will spread and grow for generation upon generation. I do not know which will prove to be true, but I know that mere talk is not enough.

Sakyamuni Buddha said: "Do not dwell in the past, do not dream of the future but concentrate the mind on the present moment." What he meant was that "By acting now, one can live a good life."

With the publication of this history book which is pivotal to the past and future, we may be able to set a sound direction and act now toward the future of Buddhism in Canada.

January 1995

Rev. Grant Ikuta
Resident Minister
Toronto Buddhist Church

On this occasion of the 50th Anniversary of the Toronto Buddhist Church, it is with great honour that I share my thoughts on the History Project. As a commemorative project for the 50th Anniversary, a committee was formed to write a book on the history of the Buddhist churches of Canada. Since its inception, the History Committee, along with author Terry Watada, has spent countless hours in researching, collating and writing a most insightful and interesting book about the Buddhist churches of Canada. As an individual with a keen interest in knowing how the Buddhist churches throughout Canada developed, I would like to express my sincere feelings of gratitude to all of the people involved in this monumental undertaking.

Rennyo Shonin, the 8th Lord Abbot of Jodo Shinshu, has written in one of his Epistles:

> In the Larger Sutra it states, "If there is not the prime condition of related past conditions, it will be most difficult to even hear this Teaching..." Further it states: "In examining the Sutras and commentaries, it is clearly taught that there is nothing without the maturation of the related past conditions. Because of this, I believe that one must always teach the doctrine of our school, and be fully cognizant of the importance of the principle of the culmination of related past conditions."

The History Project has given all of us throughout Canada the opportunity to ponder our present existence and to realize the many causes and conditions that have allowed us to be here today. We are grateful, of course, to all the members who laid the foundations for our present organization, but on a much larger scale, it is to Amida Buddha that we place our hands together in *gassho* of gratitude.

When we realize that the dedication of all of the members throughout the history of Buddhist churches of Canada were expressions of gratitude towards Amida Buddha, then it can be said that our existence today is due to the compassionate working of Amida Buddha. Herein, also lies the secret for the continuous growth of Jodo Shinshu in Canada for the many years to come in the future. We have been and always will be within the light of Amida Buddha's Compassion.

January 1995.

David Azuma
President
Toronto Buddhist Church

Congratulations to all who dedicated time and effort towards the preparation of this fascinating book about the Jodo Shinshu Movement in the past and at present in Canada.

The idea of preserving the old documents and treasures of our church originated many years ago. An ad-hoc committee of the Toronto Buddhist Church History led by Mr. Shinkuro Kozai was formed. However, due to the Chairman's poor health, a meeting was never called.

On August 21, 1988, the President, D. Azuma, called the first meeting. It was attended by Mr. Shinkuro Kozai, Mr. Sumie Watanabe, Mr. Eizo Ebata, Mr. Eddy Yoshida and Mr. Tak Yoshida. Mr. Kozai expressed his wishes to resign from the Chairmanship because of his failing health. After some discussion, the committee accepted his resignation with regret. Some of the priorities established at that time were to compile an official history book of the Toronto Buddhist Church, photograph and catalogue all the treasures, and to complete this project by 1990 (The Toronto Buddhist Church's 45th Anniversary year).

After many months of searching for a new Chairperson, Mrs. Dorothy Kagawa was approached. She graciously accepted the position and the project was under way. She called monthly meetings to try and meet the 1990 deadline. Because of difficulties in gathering old records and translating them into English, time became a limiting factor. Therefore, for the 45th Anniversary, a photo display was created.

In 1990, the committee set up a three stage completion plan with the Toronto Buddhist Church's 50th Anniversary in 1995 as their deadline.

This project expanded into a national history of the Jodo Shinshu Movement across Canada when a grant from the Japanese Canadian Redress Foundation and financial assistance from the Buddhist Churches of Canada were received. As time went by and the need arose, more members were added to the committee.

Now after five years of tireless effort, we have the first Jodo Shinshu History book written in English in Canada.

Congratulations to Mrs. Dorothy Kagawa for her leadership and thank you to all the committee members who supported her fully. Thank you to Mr. Terry Watada for his excellent documentation, the many *issei* who were interviewed, and to all the temples who supplied their records. Finally, thank you to the Toronto Buddhist Church, the Buddhist Churches of Canada, the Japanese Canadian Redress Foundation, the Buddha Dharma Kyokai (BDK) and the Multicultural Programs of the Department of Canadian Heritage who helped this mammoth project financially.

March 1995

ACKNOWLEDGEMENTS

The Toronto Buddhist Church History Committee was formed in October 1988. In 1990, the Toronto Buddhist Church had just celebrated 45 years of service in Toronto, so the History Committee decided that a history of the Toronto Buddhist Church in English might be a suitable 50th Anniversary project.

The financing of any project is always a worry. In September 1990, we applied to the Japanese Canadian Redress Foundation for a grant. They replied that they would consider our application if we would broaden the scope of the project and go from local (Toronto Buddhist Church) to national, that is, to include the history of all Jodo Shinshu Buddhist Churches across Canada. After many meetings and discussions, we decided to go national. Because of the whole-hearted support and financial co-operation of the Buddhist Churches of Canada, we were able to obtain monetary assistance from the Japanese Canadian Redress Foundation. Appreciation is given to the Toronto Buddhist Church for their full support and for giving the committee "free reign" of their facilities and office equipment.

One early concern was how we would be able to gather historical information from all the churches across Canada. A workshop was decided on March 5, 1992 in Lethbridge, Alberta, to take the opportunity of meeting members of the Buddhist Churches of Canada since the AGM was being held there on March 5, 6, 7, 1992. Through this workshop, we were able to make connections with personnel of the Jodo Shinshu Buddhist churches across Canada who were willing to act as co-ordinators for their church.

We wish to extend our thanks to the co-ordinators for taking the time and effort to compile and send the reports, information, photos, books regarding the history of their churches.

Buddhist Churches of Canada Co-ordinators across Canada are as follows:

Calgary Buddhist Church	Mr. Casey Yoneda
Coaldale Buddhist Church	Mr. Tom Tsukishima
Fraser Valley Buddhist Temple	Mrs. Ayako Kagawa
Hamilton Buddhist Church	Mrs. Tomi Suenaga
Kamloops Buddhist Church	Mr. Roy Inouye
Kelowna Buddhist Church	Mr. Yosh Terada
Lethbridge Honpa Buddhist Church	Mr. Robert Hironaka
Lethbridge North Buddhist Church	Mr. Akira Terashima
Manitoba Buddhist Church	Mr. Ken Teramura
Montreal Buddhist Church	Mr. Fred Okimura Mr. George Nakano
Picture Butte Buddhist Church	Mr. Bob Masuda
Raymond Buddhist Church	Mrs. Reyko Nishiyama
Rosemary Buddhist Church	Mrs. Mariko Hironaka
Steveston Buddhist Church	Mr. Roy Akune
Taber Buddhist Church	Mr. Jack Nagai and the late Mr. Stan Kanegawa

Toronto Buddhist Church	Mrs. Dorothy Kagawa
Vancouver Buddhist Church	Mr. Tad Ohori
Vernon Buddhist Church	Ms. Rose Okazaki
FELLOWSHIPS:	
Edmonton Jodo Shinshu Dojo	Rev. F. Ulrich
Thunder Bay Buddhist Fellowship	Mrs. Naoko Hayashi

We also wish to thank the numerous members and organizations of the Buddhist Churches of Canada and the Toronto Buddhist Church who assisted immensely by giving freely of their time with interviews.

Throughout the years, several of the translators diligently assisted with the translations of books and reports from some churches forwarded in Japanese. The translation assistance was provided by Izo Ebata, Yae Ebisuzaki, Masako Hawryluk, Fred Kagawa, Dorothy Kagawa, Fred Kotani, Harry Kondo, Rev. Fukashi Nakatsumi, Gloria Sumiya, Harry Yonekura, Ed Yoshida, Toshiko Yoshikawa.

Had it not been for the effort and co-operation of each member of the History Committee this book would not have been completed. From 1988 to the present, the committee members have followed through with this history book - the unique and interesting history of Jodo Shinshu Buddhism in Canada. Thanks and appreciation are extended to the hard-working committee members. Research Director - Harry Yonekura; Treasurer - Izo Ebata; Recording Scty. - Hedy Yonekura; Yae Ebisuzaki; Fred Kagawa; Misao Nishikawa; Gloria Sumiya; Ed Yoshida. Advisors - Rev. Grant Ikuta, Rev. Yasuo Izumi, Jesse Nishihata and Toyo Takata. Appreciation and thanks are especially extended to Ed Yoshida and to Harry Yonekura for their valuable knowledge; to Jesse Nishihata and Toyo Takata for contributing from their experience toward a project as large as this.

Appreciation is extended to all members who updated and placed in order the Toronto Buddhist Church and Buddhist Churches of Canada files. Assisting were Yae Ebisuzaki, Pat Hirota, Aki Kotani, Fred Kotani, Haruko Nakashima, Misao Nishikawa, Peggy Ohara and Yasuko Tsuchiya.

Thanks go to the talented *sansei*, writer and poet, Terry Watada, an English professor at Seneca College, who contributes a monthly column in the **Nikkei Voice**. Thanks also to the editor, Dr. Irene Uchida, a well-known *nisei* geneticist and to Sandy Usami, the *sansei* graphic artist, and to Kaz Hamasaki, the *nisei* artist, for their contributions towards this history book. If the name of any person or organization has been omitted or misspelled, please accept our sincere apologies.

United with the thought of "Oneness with the Amida Buddha - *Okagesame de* - we have accomplished our goal. *Arigato gozaimashita*".

In *gassho*,

Dorothy N. Kagawa,
Chairperson
Toronto Buddhist Church History Committee
April 1995

Introduction

Labour Day Weekend, 1992. During the ten hour bus ride from Toronto to Chicago to attend the 47th Eastern Buddhist League Convention, the predominantly *nisei* contingent passed the time by floating around various Japanese snacks: *manju*, candy and *hana arare*. On the closed circuit video screen, hours of programs taken from Japanese television pounded the ears with rapid fire Japanese and blaring music. Most of the travellers conversed to one another in Japanese.

The first night of the conference consisted of an impromptu banquet of leftover *bento* from the bus trip. It was held in a delegate's hotel room, the food spread out across the double bed while everyone ate from paper plates on any available chair or on the floor. The Blue Jays exercised on the small t.v. screen.

The next day, Reverend Jay Shinseki, a *sansei*, led an interesting seminar on the changing nature of the Buddhist Church in America. Participants commented on the fact that intrinsically Japanese concepts and terms like *okagesama de* were disappearing. The original meanings have been lost over the years. What was once a wholly Japanese congregation is now multicultural.

Parts of the Buddhist church in Canada too are changing to reflect the diversity of Canada, not so much as a reaction to reality but as a method of survival. Most of the congregations across the country, however, struggle to maintain their Japanese heritage. Unfortunately, there are consequences. Smaller congregations, like Hamilton and Montreal, have simply lost their resident ministers. Others have shut their doors altogether and amalgamated with larger centres. Major temples like Toronto and Vancouver worry about the future in the face of declining numbers. On the whole, the Jodo Shinshu Buddhist church at present is going through the upheaval of change while seeking ways to preserve its Japanese character.

Bukkyo Tozen: *A History of Jodo Shinshu Buddhism in Canada* looks with a somewhat candid eye at the 90 year existence in Canada of a people and a church that faced hostility, suspicion, segregation, legislated racism, disestablishment, destruction, imprisonment and exile. There are scandals, power struggles and petty rivalries. On the other hand, there are stories of great devotion, diligence, piety and sacrifice. Above all else, hard work emerges as the hallmark of the church. It is what sustained the ministers and members as they established the first temple in 1905 Vancouver, as they built roughly hewn temples in the British Columbia interior during World War II, and as they forged eastward in the aftermath of that selfsame war. The Buddhist Church flourished in the face of it all, yet the most demanding challenge is obviously still ahead.

Bukkyo Tozen is a history of perseverance, ordeal and great joy within the light of Amida Buddha. In the end, it is the unswerving faith in the Buddha *Dharma* that carried the various congregations through the years of struggle and will carry them into the 21st century.

Jodo Shinshu Buddhism is a religion for and of the people. Bishop Matsubayashi outlines the essentials of the sect in the afterword to the book. On a personal level, I came to an understanding of Jodo Shinshu after a long journey of self discovery and consideration.

My parents first brought me to the Toronto church when I was too young to know anything. Mostly for special occasions at that. I really didn't develop an interest in religion throughout my childhood.

When I became an adolescent, other forces came into play. Amy Nakamura stopped me in one of the corridors of our high school to invite me to the church because a new youth group was forming. I knew her from the interminable Saturday morning classes at the Japanese Language School.

Not only was I flattered that this rather attractive girl paid attention to me but I thought here was an opportunity to have something to do on a Saturday night. Joining a religion was not part of the equation.

What followed were years of involvement with the church. I formed a rock band with other *sansei* musicians with the encouragement of Mrs. Mary Ishiura. I went to several house parties. I attended Sunday School with others of my age group. Unfortunately, the teachers were not skilled enough in relating the tenets of Buddhism in a comprehensible way. The religion remained a mystery to me throughout my adolescence. It got to the point where I and my friends simply "hung out" on the front steps of the church until service concluded. Then we and "the girls" who always attended service went to have lunch at the local greasy spoon. The Hamburger Deluxe with fries and cole slaw was a favourite.

After university, I began to question the relevance of Buddhism to my life. After all, I had been going to that church for ten years by that point. I first learned to look inward for the answers rather than outward as Christianity preaches: "Accept Jesus Christ and you will be saved." Saved? I always wondered about the Afterlife and Heaven, but I just couldn't see the validity of placing faith in an omnipotent being who walked the earth two thousand years ago. The other concept I took to heart was the fact that "life is suffering". Still I needed guidance.

Two ministers played pivotal roles in my development. Rev. Ron from Hawaii came for a visit and held a seminar for the youth groups. I thought it very refreshing that here was a *sansei* minister who didn't stand on formality. I never did learn his last name. He basically put Buddhism in context. We all suffer when we want something. As soon as desire appears in everyday life, the mind and body struggles to satisfy it. Rev. Ron taught it is better to strive for a goal without ego, using what he called "effortless effort". When a professional basketball player moves toward the basket, he is not thinking how great a player he is or how much money he will make during the next contract rounds. No, he is simply concentrating on scoring two points. He does so without conceit, almost without conscious effort. In fact, effortless effort. Rev. Ron's point was that we should all work toward our goals without the intrusion of vanity.

The second minister, Rev. Unno of California, spent a weekend at Camp Lumbini with the YBA talking about Buddhism. I learned about "Buddha nature" from him. Everyone has the potential to be a Buddha. It is within all of us. We just have to create the right conditions for that nature to emerge. I remember asking if even Adolph Hitler had such potential. Rev. Unno wisely let me figure it out. Yes Hitler did but he chose not to explore such a possibility with disastrous effect.

I therefore have been trying to live my life without desire, free of the encumbrance of ego. I have set goals and worked toward them without worrying about outcome. I have not been entirely successful but I am not a Buddha. On the other hand, I am always mindful of my Buddha nature and how the teachings of Amida Buddha and Shinran Shonin can help in nurturing that nature.

As for the afterlife my Christian friends keep asking me about, I cannot say. I do know entry into The Pure Land is dependent on the working through of *karma* (consequences of action) but where or what Nirvana is I haven't a clue. I have faith I will find out about it at the proper juncture. In the meantime, why worry about it? Why suffer?

No project of such scope and depth could be accomplished without the immense co-operation of many dedicated individuals. The translators, regional reporters and researchers committed dozens of hours to the ferreting of information. What a task it was. Because of the war, records of prewar activity were lost. Much was dependent on diaries, personal histories and interviews with those who could remember. The major source of prewar information was Rev. Shinjo Ikuta's work **The History of Buddhist Churches of Canada** (1980). Unfortunately, the original manuscript was lost in the mail. The editor Shoken Yamasaki and Rev. Ikuta's wife, Mino, worked hard to replicate the lost book.

> For some time, the late Rev. Shinjo Ikuta fully realized the necessity of the compilation of the history. The Vancouver Buddhist Church asked him for the compilation on his retirement from

> ministerial work. He collected the data by all possible means and, in his later years, visited the library of the University of British Columbia and made the manuscript by hard work and by extracting articles from old Japanese newspapers stored in there. However, it was with great regret for us that he passed away before the publication.[1]
>
> Publication Committee

The war history of the church could not have been completed without the scholarship of Akira Ichikawa of Lethbridge, Alberta. His paper **Canadian Treatment of Jodo Shinshu Ministers During World War II** provided the necessary information to complete the sketchy details derived from RCMP reports, newspaper articles and interviews.

Post war material was plentiful, perhaps overwhelming. Again, it was the tenacity of the regional reporters and the Toronto Buddhist Church translators and researchers who trolled the sea of facts to harvest the relevant.

In particular, the tenacious leadership of Committee Chair Dorothy Kagawa, the determination of Gloria Sumiya, the depth of knowledge of Ed Yoshida, the translating skills of Fred Kagawa and Rev. F. Nakatsumi, and the support and wisdom of Harry Yonekura, Jesse Nishihata and Toyo Takata augmented the already considerable efforts of the Toronto Buddhist Church History Committee to advance the writing of the book. Sandy Usami's design work and Kazuo Hamasaki's inspired art gave the book its beauty. Reverends Fujikawa, Murakami, G. Ikuta and Izumi provided religious guidance while Elaine Wyatt gave timely advice about publishing. Dr. Irene Uchida's editing proved to be meticulous, thorough and in the end invaluable in shaping the text.

Bishop Matsubayashi's concise and comprehensive background to Jodo Shinshu Buddhism lends the necessary spiritual underpinning to any history of a religion.

To all these good people I give thanks. Generations hence will appreciate their dedication.

Owing to the times and individuals interpreting the details of the Buddhist Church history, very few women emerge in the telling. I as the author cannot apologize for the omission. In light of the situation however, I do dedicate **Bukkyo Tozen** to the women of the Buddhist Church, especially Mary Ishiura who gave me the confidence to pursue my goals with effortless effort (not altogether successfully I must admit). I further dedicate the book to Rev. Newton Ishiura for the effortless effort he demonstrated throughout his long life.

Terry Watada
October 1995

Part One

Formation and Disestablishment

Beginning in Japan

Chapter 1

Bukkyo Tozen

Bukkyo Tozen: A History of Jodo Shinshu Buddhism in Canada

Jodo Shinshu, "True Pure Land Teaching", is the sect of Buddhism first established in Canada. It was founded in Japan in 1224 AD by Shinran Shonin.

The basic tenet of Jodo Shinshu lies in the phrase Namu Amida Butsu (*I rely upon the Buddha of Infinite Light and Life*). The phrase, called the *Nembutsu*, links the Amida Buddha to the common people and crystallizes "all the practices accomplished and virtues accumulated for the sake of (the) attainment".[1] In other words, the follower who utters the *Nembutsu* is expressing his gratitude for the awakening of Faith that will lead to Enlightenment. Thus Buddhism through Jodo Shinshu is a religion accessible to everyone.

Shinran Shonin

Shinran Shonin was born in 1173, the third year of Shoan. He was a member of the famous Fujiwara clan that ruled Japan for centuries. In the village of Hino, southeast of Kyoto, he began life under turbulent circumstances. The land was plagued with civil war, famine and pestilence. Much despair and suffering visited the people of Japan. Shinran's father, Hino Arinori, left his position as court official to become a recluse. His mother died shortly thereafter. Thus the young boy became an orphan, seemingly destined to lead a lonely life.

When he turned nine, Shinran went with his uncle to the Shoren-in Temple to enrol as a student. There he received his first ordination and given the priest name, Hannen. He was placed under the tutelage of Jichin, a distinguished master of the Tendai[2] sect who took him to the Tendai monastery on Mount Hiei. There he began twenty years of study.

Little is known of his life of scholarly seclusion. Eshinni, Shinran's wife, gives little insight into his life. What she does do is to confirm Shinran's time on Mount Hiei in one of her letters to her youngest daughter, Kakushinni:

> This letter certifies that your father was a *doso* at Mt. Hiei...[3]

Doso is the term for a priest who practises the *Fudan Nembutsu*, a special form of practice developed by Ennin, the third Abbot of the Tendai sect. The priests walk constantly, thinking of Amida Buddha and reciting *Namu Amida Butsu*.[4] The influence of the Mt. Hiei monastery on Shinran was profound.

Shinran realized that knowledge can lead to many questions and perhaps some frustration. He therefore concentrated on knowing the Amida Buddha and came to the conclusion that he could not "remove the illusory self-powered thoughts"[5] that kept him tied to the material world. Consequently, he left Mount Hiei at the age of twenty-nine and "confined himself at Rokkaku-do for one hundred days".[6]

The Rokkaku-do temple was established by Prince Shotoku who was considered by Shinran to be the founder of Buddhism in Japan. As Eshinni recounts, the Prince came to Shinran:

> [Shinran Shonin] left Mt. Hiei, remained in retreat for one hundred days at Rokkaku-do, and prayed for salvation in the afterlife. Then on the dawn of the ninety-fifth day Prince Shotoku appeared in a vision, revealing the path to enlightenment by reciting a verse from Kannon (Avalokiteshvara Bodhisattva):[7]
>
> You (Shinran) shall take a wife as the consequence of past *karmic* life. I [Kannon (Avalokiteshvara Bodhisattva[8])] will be that [reincarnated] wife. I shall guide you, so that you will lead an exemplary life and at death enter the Pure Land.[9]

Shinran immediately left the temple to seek out Honen Shonin, founder of the Nembutsu Order in Yoshimizu. The Order was so called because of its exclusive practice of repeating aloud Amida's name.

Through the teaching of Honen Shonin, Shinran was able to see the path to enlightenment. As Eshinni reports, Shinran was a dedicated follower and he declared so on many occasions:

> Wherever my Master Honen goes, I [Shinran] shall follow him, no matter what others may say - even if he says he would go to hell, I will accompany him. The reason is that I am such a person, floundering in the world of delusion from the beginningless beginning of time, that I would have nothing to lose, even if I did so.[10]

Honen's sermons so moved the young Shinran that he changed his name to Shakku to celebrate his conversion to the true *Nembutsu* life. He later changed it again to Zenshin, the result of a dream in which Avalokiteshvara (Kannon) Bodhisattva of Rokkaku-do called him by that name. Kannon indicated that marriage was no hindrance to enlightenment.

In 12th Century Japan, Buddhist monks and priests were not allowed to get married. Certainly Prince Shotoku's verse affected Shinran; the subsequent dream of Kannon indicates how deeply he considered marriage to be an issue. Honen Shonin advised:

> People should always live by creating the proper condition for being about to say the *Nembutsu*. If you cannot say the *Nembutsu* as a celibate, say it by getting married. If you cannot say it being married, say it as a celibate...If you cannot say it while securing your daily necessities, say it by having others obtain them for you. If you cannot say it by others obtaining the necessities for you, say it by securing them yourself... Food, clothing and shelter are necessary only in so far as they create the proper condition for people to say the *Nembutsu*.[11]

The exact date of Shinran and Eshinni's marriage is not known. Events of Eshinni's early life are mere speculation. According to Yoshiko Ohtani (author and grandmother of the current Lord Abbot,[12] Hompa Hongwanji), the couple married circa 1210 since Eshinni herself reveals that her son, Shinren-bo, was born on the third day of the third month in the year of Kanoto-hitsuji (1211). If the date is correct, Shinran took a bride during his exile.

The popularity of Honen Shonin's approach to Buddhism is well known. His congregation flourished by attracting those left out of the traditional monastic Buddhist life. The sect was therefore open to those of all levels of society. Unfortunately, such popularity raised the ire and jealousy of older Buddhist schools. Responding to continuous protests by these groups, the Imperial Government in 1207 ordered Honen to cease and desist his practices and teachings. The Nembutsu Order was thus banned and persecuted. So thorough was the disestablishment movement that four of Honen's disciples were executed while Honen himself and seven others, including Shinran, were exiled.

Shinran Shonin by order left for Echigo Province (Northern Japan, near Sado Island); there he was given the secular name, Yoshizane Fujii. The usual practice at the time was to reduce monks and priests to layman status. Shinran, considered a common criminal, later took the name Toku (Unshaven One) which signifies a non-priest and non-layman. He went further by eventually calling himself Gu-toku (Foolish Unshaven One).

Little is known of his life in Echigo. Yoshiko Ohtani speculates:

> Shinran arrived by boat on these shores at the end of the third month of the year...but the chilly wind from the northern seas was probably colder than what I felt on the day of my visit. Snow may still have been on the ground...Even though Shinran was accustomed to the severe winters of Mt. Hiei...surely he must have felt apprehension when he first set foot on this beach as an exiled criminal facing the stark and threatening landscape.[13]

In 1211, the first year of Kenryaku, Shinran and Honen were pardoned from exile. Soon thereafter Honen died in Kyoto. Shinran decided to move to the Kanto District far from bustling Kyoto. There he began teaching the *Nembutsu* to the local farmers.

Although he had no ambition to begin a new sect of Buddhism, he wrote his major work, the **Kyo Gyo Shin Sho** (*Teaching, Practice, Faith and Enlightenment*), in 1224 (the first year of Gennin) to instruct his students. Perhaps it was Shinran's lack of ambition that inspired them to come to him and later to form groups to learn from his teachings.

When Shinran turned sixty-three, he and his family returned to Kyoto. There he began to revise the **Kyo Gyo Shin Sho** and to write other great works such as the **Wasan** (*Hymns in Praise of Buddha*) and the **Gutoku Sho** (*Notes of the Ignorant and Sinful*). Shinran wisely composed the hymns using the simple language of *kana*. The teaching too became simplified through constant verbal repetition and easy language. Even today the ritual chanting and the daily worship services are accessible to all who listen. Shinran Shonin remained dedicated to his writing until his death.

One major event, nonetheless, upset his rather tranquil life in Kyoto. Zenran, his son, was alleged to have misled the people of Kanto and caused much disquiet with questionable teaching. Eventually, Shinran had to disown Zenran to protect the faith of the *Nembutsu* followers. Shinran was eighty-four at the time.

The youngest daughter, Kakushinni, was devoted to her father and chose to stay in Kyoto to take care of him. During the second year of Kocho (1262), surrounded by his son Masukata, daughter Kakushinni, and several disciples, Shinran Shonin peacefully passed into Nirvana at the age of ninety. He recited the *Nembutsu* until the moment of death.

Eshinni and most of her children had accompanied Shinran to Kyoto, but after twenty years, she moved back to Echigo. The reason for the separation is unclear. It may have been for financial reasons or to take care of inherited land. In any case, what is clear is her love for and devotion to her husband.

To her daughter, the elderly Eshinni relates an incident that occurred during her life in Kanto many years before:

> I saw the following dream. The scene appeared to be a dedication ceremony for a recently completed temple. The temple faced the east, and it must have been an evening festival, for the light from the candle stands was burning brightly in the front. But to the west of the candle stands and in front of the temple, there was a piece of wood placed horizontally, as if it were a *torii* on which were hung the images of Buddha.
>
> ...all was light and the centre seemed to emanate from the head of the Buddha...There was nothing but rays

> of light. The other image clearly showed the face of Buddha, so I asked, "What is the name of this Buddha?"...there was a reply, "That one which shows only rays of light is Honen Shonin"... "Who then is the other image?" That is Kannon Bosatsu (Avalokiteshvara Bodhisattva). He is none other than Zenshin (Shinran).
>
> ...Although I never told your father about the dream...I never regarded him as just an ordinary person and continued to serve him.[14]

Eshinni died at the age of eighty-nine, ten years after she returned to Echigo.

Shinran Shonin and Eshinni lived lives full of the turbulence of human desire and action. Yet they endured, united in a deep and abiding faith in the Amida Buddha. Their example went a long way in creating a world of mutual respect and tolerance; their example is truly inspirational. Their example is the way of the *Nembutsu*.

The Hongwanji

During the late 19th Century, the Emperor Meiji recognized Shinran Shonin's importance to Japan since Jodo Shinshu Buddhism had become the most popular sect in the country. He therefore granted Shinran the title of *Kenshin Daishi* or *Great Master, Seer of Truth*. The name is proudly exhibited at the Hongwanji in Kyoto.

The Hongwanji is the mother temple (or headquarters) for the Jodo Shinshu Hongwanji-ha denomination; it is also referred to as the Nishi Hongwanji. Originally, the Hongwanji was founded at Ohtani, Higashiyama. Its present location at Horikawa-dori, Shimokyo-ku, Kyoto was established in 1591.

Kakushinni buried her father's ashes in a small temple and had a statue erected in his honour. In 1277, she consented to be responsible for the care of the temple as the *Guardian of the Mausoleum (Rusushiki)*. She donated the site of the mausoleum on condition the office of Rusushiki be passed to her descendants. Thus her son Kakue and then her grandson Kakunyo inherited the honoured position.

Unfortunately, the Jodo Shinshu sect was fractionized by various interpretations of Shinran's teachings. Eventually, Nyoshin emerged as the second Lord Abbot (Gomonshu), an end result somewhat ironic since his father Zenran (Kakushinni's brother) was censured by his grandfather, Shinran Shonin, for suspect teachings. Since Nyoshin was a follower of orthodox Jodo Shinshu, he gained the faith of all of his grandfather's (Shinran) disciples and therefore was able to rise to such heights.

A great-grandson, Kakunyo, followed Shinran's example and studied at Mt. Hiei. At eighteen, he met his uncle Nyoshin and studied the teachings of the Jodo Shinshu sect. After he became the third Lord Abbot, Kakunyo declared that the Ohtani Mausoleum and the mother temple should be one and the same. The Hongwanji therefore should be the headquarters for the entire denomination.

There was much opposition to the proposed unification since so many small groups had formed. For the next one hundred years, the controversy raged.

In 1415, Rennyo, the future eighth Lord Abbot, was born. He was determined to teach Jodo Shinshu so that all people would be able to understand and accept the true doctrine.

He composed plain language versions of Buddhist epistles and encouraged the building of temples throughout the country to unite as many of the faithful as possible. Perhaps the best known is the temple at Yoshizaki in the Hokuriku District. It immediately became a centre for missionary activities, attracting devotees from as many as ten nearby provinces.

Rennyo was an inspiring and tireless teacher of the Jodo Shinshu religion. In his disciples, he inspired loyalty, devotion and self sacrifice as the following anecdote indicates:

> Early in the summer of the third year of Bummei (1471), Rennyo left his place of sojourn in Otsu (a town on Lake Biwa, several miles from Kyoto) for the province of Echizen in order that he might spread Shinran's religion without provoking the priests in Mount Hiei. He was (so well) received by the governor and the people of Echizen that in the autumn of the same year a temple was built for him on the hill at Yoshizaki, which commanded a very fine view and

> was well accessible to people in the area. Many houses were soon put up within and without the precincts of the temple by his leading disciples. They thought that these houses might be placed at the disposal of not only their own but also of their followers, when they should come to listen to Rennyo's preaching. Before long, the summit of the hill...developed into a town crowded with people from far and near.
>
> Three years later, one evening in the sixth year of Bummei (1474), a fire broke out in a house near the south gate of the temple. Because water was not sufficiently available on the hill, and moreover, a strong wind was blowing, the fire raged unchecked and the temple and all other houses in the precincts were consumed by the flames. When the temple was ablaze, Rennyo looked back to his disciples and said, "I am sorry to see the temple destroyed by fire, but it can be set up again. It makes me rather heart-broken to think that I have committed an irreparable blunder. I have left on my desk a precious volume of **Kyo Gyo Shin Sho** autographed by the author, Shinran Shonin. It will be burnt to ashes." Then one of his disciples named Honko-bo thrust himself before Rennyo and with a determined air said: "Master, I will bring the book out of fire; pray, have no fear." Rennyo, by grasping his sleeve, stopped him from rushing into death. But Honko-bo broke away and dashed into the burning temple, never to be seen again. When the fire had burned itself out and search was made, the fellow disciples found, to their great sorrow, Honko-bo lying dead with his face downwards at the spot where his teacher's room had been. When his body was removed, the book which Rennyo had left was found under it perfectly protected from the flames. Rennyo was greatly moved by Honko-bo's self-sacrifice. The master had him buried on the hill with ceremony and attended by mourning crowds.[15]

When Rennyo returned to Kyoto, he built the Yamashina Hongwanji and a retreat known as Ishiyama Gobo (Ishiyama, Osaka). The retreat later became the Ishiyama Hongwanji.

After Rennyo's death in 1499, Japan was hurtled into the era of chaos known as the *Sengoku Jidai*. Much blood was spilled.

In 1532 a feudal lord aided by the soldier monks of Mt. Hiei burned down the Hongwanji at Yamashina. Fortunately, the Lord Abbot Shonyo escaped to Ishiyama Gobo and started the Ishiyama Hongwanji. In 1570, Nobunaga Oda, another powerful feudal lord, attacked the Hongwanji but was repelled by an army of Jodo Shinshu followers.

Oda's concern was to protect his hold over Kyoto. In order to do so he planned to move against the war lords Miyoshi, Matsunaga and Saito who had built forts around Osaka. If he did so, however, he would have to contend with the armed strength of the Ishiyama Hongwanji, perhaps the most dangerous.

> For not only was the Ishiyama Hongwanji the cathedral of the Ikko (Shin) sect, it was a great fortified place. There was a garrison composed of believers from each section of Osaka and from the sect's provincial congregations in Kaga and Echizen and elsewhere. They were always on patrol, and were several hundred in number, easily multiplied by more than ten times over on the ringing of an alarm bell. The Hongwanji was considered as impregnable.[16]

For the next ten years, the feudal lord attacked Ishiyama repeatedly but to no avail. Finally, the Emperor intervened to end the conflict.

Peace ruled with Oda's death in 1582. Hideyoshi Toyotomi came to power and favoured Buddhism. Such was his benevolence that he donated 700 acres of land at Nishi Rokujo, Kyoto, to the Hongwanji. Kennyo, the 12th Abbot, subsequently built a temple on the site. Today, it is the site of the Nishi (Hompa, Hongwanji-ha, or West) Hongwanji. Thus, the mother temple of Jodo Shinshu returned to Kyoto.

Lord Abbot Kennyo knew the question of ascension would arise with his passing. He therefore named his second son Junnyo rather than his first, Kyonyo, who did not agree with the abandonment of the Ishiyama Hongwanji. Kyonyo consequently worked to establish the Higashi (Dai-ha, Ohtani-ha, or East) Hongwanji in 1602 on the land Iyeyasu Tokugawa had granted to the order.

Thus it is that there are two centres of Jodo Shinshu in Kyoto today - the Nishi and Higashi Hongwanji.

Meiji Japan

Chapter 2

Bukkyo Tozen

Meiji Japan

The Meiji Period (1852 - 1912) was arguably the most profound in the history of Japan. It certainly was the most dramatic. Scholars agree that the period is ideal for the study of world cultural history. Its influence was to effect change at every strata of Japanese society. Educational institutions, government and especially religion were changed forever by the societal upheaval brought about by the shock of the new.

Commodore Perry's black ships may have alarmed the Japanese as they saw the black smoke spiralling towards the heavens, but the technology the ships represented fascinated as well. Daikichi Irokawa, professor at the Tokyo University of Economics, recounts an incident during Perry's visit that is prophetic of Japan's coming fate.

> He [Perry] brought the *samurai* of this closed country a small model train as a present and set it in motion before their eyes. At first, the Japanese watched the train fearfully from a safe distance, and when the engine began to move, they uttered cries of astonishment and drew in their breath. Before long, they were inspecting it closely, stroking it, and riding on it, and they kept this up throughout the day. A mere hundred years later, those same Japanese, by themselves, developed and built the high-speed *Hikari* trains that travel along the Tokaido safely at speeds of two hundred kilometres an hour. And now they are exporting that technology to Perry's country.[1]

Sweeping changes immediately took place at the governmental

level. With the restoration of imperial rule, a cadre of a few hundred young men, made up of *samurai* and a few members of the court nobility trained in practical politics, attempted to make Japan a modern nation.

In 1886, the Meiji regime introduced, on behalf of the Emperor, the Charter Oath, a set of five principles that were to be the guiding force of the country.

The Charter Oath

1. Deliberative assemblies shall be widely established and all matters decided by public discussion.
2. All classes, high and low, shall unite in vigorously carrying out the administration of affairs of state.
3. The common people, no less than the civil and military officials, shall each be allowed to pursue his own calling so that there may be no discontent.
4. Evil (or absurd) customs of the past shall be discarded and justice shall be based on the just laws of heaven and earth.
5. Knowledge shall be sought throughout the world in order to strengthen the foundations of imperial rule.[2]

The rush to adopt new things and new ideas became the vogue. Advocates called it the "spirit of civilization".[3] Western languages and Christianity enjoyed a surge in popularity. In 1872, baseball was introduced, and by the end of the century, the sport was part of every high school program. The Japanese began to eat beef.

A children's song at the time listed the ten most desirable objects of the age: gas lamps, steam engines, horse-drawn carriages, cameras, telegrams, lightning conductors, newspapers, schools, postal mail, and steamboats.[4]

Iconoclasts demanded people use the Roman alphabet and adopt English as the official language. Intermarriage with white people was considered necessary to improve the Japanese racial stock.

A low regard for the traditional emerged. Woodblock prints were used as wrapping paper for fish and vegetables. Once cherished buildings were torn down for firewood. Buddhist artifacts were seized and destroyed.

The aristocracy and prominent leaders benefitted the most. Fancy costume balls were held at the government-built social hall, the Rokumeikan. Their lavish cotillions, however, led to criticism of the participants, and soon the new-found glamour subsided. The trend to indiscriminate imitation of the western way of life came to a close by the end of the 19th century.

Hardest hit by this fad to be modern were the fishing and farming classes. It was not easy for people to leave their native village and head out into the world. Traditionally, the home village was considered to be ordained by heaven and could not be changed. They believed that upon death the loved one must receive memorial rites by blood relatives or happiness could not be found in the next world.

The *o-butsudan*, the household altar, was reserved for ancestral spirits.The dead or *hotoke* were considered at rest in the mountains, rivers and forests of the village watching over their families. The Buddhists thought them to be wandering spirits who returned to their homes during Obon and Higan each year. Buddhism then was a haven for those wandering spirits.

The Meiji government brought pressure to bear on farm families to break up and live in different villages, cities and countries. The poem below by the Buddhist monk Gessho reflects the attitude of the times:

A young man sets a goal before himself
And leaves his ancestral home.
Should he fail in his studies
He will never again return, even though he die.
How can the village graveyard be the only resting place?
There are green hills for men everywhere.[5]

The supreme importance of continuing the family line was being supplanted by what Professor Irokawa called a "revolution of consciousness" among the young people. These fit adventurers, armed with the slogan "Go to work wherever it may be: be prepared for any resting place", were willing to move overseas to seek a new life clearly alien to anything in Japan.

> People so motivated burned with enthusiasm to leave their ancestral homes behind and set out for new frontiers, where they became the founding fathers of new houses.[6]

Modernity had invaded the Japanese psyche of the period, but that same movement strengthened the need for an ethnic and national identity. After the infatuation with western culture, the Japanese came to embrace Japanese aesthetics again. Japanese morality, tradition and way of life came under intense scrutiny. Professor Irokawa cites Tenshin Okakura's Japanese Arts Movement, Rohan Koda's movement for native literature, the folklore movement of Kunio Yanagita and the National Essence Movement of Setsurei Miyake and Katsunan Kuga as examples of the search.[7]

Religion during the Meiji Period

The Meiji Period was an era of paradoxes. On the one hand, there was complete rejection of the past and an encouragement to move away to other lands; on the other hand, there was the restoration of imperial rule and the seeking of traditional values. Any move by the government to balance the paradox was to have dire consequences for all facets of society, especially in the area of religion.

Shinto became the religion of choice for the Emperor Meiji and his government. He swore allegiance to the Charter Oath before all the gods of the Shinto pantheon.

For ten centuries, Buddhism and Shinto coexisted, actually incorporating each other's precepts to a certain degree in the interest of harmony. Some members of the Imperial family married into the Buddhist hierarchy. In 1868, the Meiji regime established the Department of Shinto, effectively separating the two religions. The move was largely seen as an effort by the government to remove financial support of Buddhist temples. However, other consequences ensued.

The Department issued a Separation Edict on the grounds that Buddhism was contrary to the "indigenous Japanese" way of life. A year later, the Department of Shinto was elevated to the same status as the Grand Council of State. The government then issued the Proclamation of the Great Doctrine which advocated "the way of the *kami*"[8] as the guiding principle of the nation.

During the previous Tokugawa era, everyone was obligated to register in Buddhist temples. With the Great Doctrine, everyone was enroled by government order at Shinto shrines. People were encouraged to have family funerals performed by Shinto priests. A nationwide education program was instituted. The program's three goals were as follows: reverence for the *kami*, the importance of the Law of Heaven and the Way of Humanity, and loyalty to the throne and obedience to the authorities.[9]

During the bureaucratic purge of Buddhism, priests who had been associated with Shinto shrines returned to secular life or were reinstated as Shinto priests. All temple lands were confiscated by the government in 1871. Buddhist ceremonies in the Imperial Household were forbidden. All ranks and privileges given to Buddhists were revoked. The name of the True Pure Land Sect was changed from Ikko-shu (Single Directed Sect) to Shin (true) sect.

A violent anti-Buddhist movement *(haibutsu-kishaku)*[10] erupted among the people in the sweep of change. In Toyama district, 1730 Buddhist temples were reduced to seven overnight. Most were destroyed; others consolidated.[11] The Pure Land temple of Zojo-ji in Tokyo was designated as a training centre for Shinto priests. The statue of Amida Buddha was replaced by the altar of four Shinto *kami* - Ame-no-Minakanushi, Takamimusubi, Kammusubi and Amaterasu.

The reaction was predictable. Some rejected Buddhism altogether, revelling perhaps in the freedom from their strict upbringing. Others protested against the anti-Buddhist movement, Shinto, Christianity, Western influence and even the Imperial order. They staged insurrections and riots. The most notable incident occurred in Echizen in 1873. Buddhists marched on the prefectural government demanding that Christianity not be allowed into the prefecture and that Western thought (*yogaku*) not be taught in the schools. They carried bamboo spears with banners inscribed proudly with the *Nembutsu*, **Namu Amida Butsu**. Emotions ran so high that the uprising developed into a full scale peasants' revolt only to be quelled by government troops.[12]

On the other hand, the Meiji period provided Buddhism with the opportunity to expand intellectually and spiritually. Buddhist scholars were greatly stimulated by the Western influence. In 1873, Shimaji Mokurai, a priest of the Hompa Hongwanji, visited India and Europe. Meanwhile, Bunyu Nanjo of the Higashi Hongwanji studied Sanskrit at Oxford University.[13] Thus it came to be that Buddhists welcomed the separation of state and their religion. Buddhistic scholars and priests could concentrate on the spirituality of pure religious thought. The Meiji era acted as a stimulus for the spiritual awakening of Buddhism.

From a scholarly Buddhist standpoint, it was unfortunate the religion could not stay divorced from the institutional. During the fervour for change, Christianity led the way for the principle of popular rights or *minken* to take hold amongst the peasant classes.[14] Such a movement was understandably unpopular with the ruling class. Seeing the swing of the leadership to nationalistic sentiments, Buddhists allied themselves with the Shinto, Confucian and Nationalist leaders in an all out anti-Christian campaign (named by Buddhists as *haja kensho*, the refutation of evil religion and the exaltation of righteous religion)[15]. A spokesman for the Jodo Shinshu sect, Tetsujo Ugai, led the protest with an essay entitled **Sho-ya-ron** in 1869. In it, the priest argued that Christianity was ridiculous as a religion. Although an advocate of religious freedom, Mokurai Shimaji also argued against Christianity in his book **Fukkatsu Shinron** (*New Thoughts on the Resurrection*). Finally, Enryo Inouye, a Buddhist scholar, criticized the "irrationality" of Christianity and praised the "rationality" of Buddhism. His objections arose from the inseparability of Christianity from the political structure of Western nations.[16] Other Buddhists argued against monogamy citing that it was somehow "un-Japanese". Although never an advocate of the Russo-Japanese War (1904-5), Buddhists supported the Imperial government by offering spiritual guidance. In fact, Kozui Ohtani, Chief Abbot of the Nishi Hongwanji, was praised by the Emperor for his role in keeping up the morale of the soldier during the campaign. Thus the popularity of Christianity subsided.

The Meiji Era posed many problems for Buddhists. Still, many consider the period a glorious time since government machinations offered, on the one hand, Buddhist scholars access to Western thought and philosophy, and on the other, inspired the Hongwanji to look overseas to spread the Buddha's Teachings eastward.

The Early Buddhists of North America

Chapter 3

Bukkyo Tozen

The Early Buddhists of North America

> Nothing remained for it [Buddhism] but a watery grave in the Pacific.[1]
>
> Christian students at Doshisha University during the height of the *haibutsu-kishaku*.[2]

During the mid 1800s, Japanese Christians regarded Buddhism to be in decline in Japan. They relished the idea of Buddhism being exiled to such obscure enclaves as Hawaii. Some went so far as to declare the religion a "standing corpse".[3]

By the end of the century, however, Buddhism resurfaced as the religion of the people. The Hongwanji and other Buddhist groups, in order to consolidate their position, began philanthropic work in Hokkaido, Taiwan, Korea, South China and Manchuria. As the Imperial government established these spheres of influence, more and more Japanese soldiers and citizens requested the services of Buddhist missionaries.

Little thought was given to the needs of the Japanese who had crossed the Pacific. In 1889, Soryu Kagahi, a native of Oita Prefecture and ordained minister of the Hompa Hongwanji, went to Kyoto seeking an audience with Lord Abbot Myonyo Shonin. He wished to discuss the situation overseas - Hawaii in particular.

Kagahi knew thousands of Japanese lived in Hawaii and beyond. Many had died without the comfort of the Buddha's teachings and its religious rites. Consequently he pleaded with the Lord Abbot to send missionaries right away.

Myonyo was not convinced since he felt the pressing need was in Manchuria, South China and Korea. He did however allow Kagahi to go to Hawaii to survey the situation first hand. So on the 2nd of March 1889, Rev. Kagahi stepped off the Omi Maru into the humid air and lush islands of Hawaii.

Kagahi met much resistance at first but eventually he was able to establish several Buddhist groups. His success and findings must have encouraged Myonyo, for The Lord Abbot began to realize the need for the propagation of Jodo Shinshu Buddhism in other countries.

Today, Myonyo Shonin is considered the father of the Overseas Missionary Program. "His zeal for Buddhist propagation is well known through the many historical documents found at the Honzan (Mother Temple), Kyoto, Japan."[4]

Towards North America

Motoyori mo hito ni
Hedate wa nakari keri
Hitotsu Minori no
Tane ya shikamashi.

Among all men
who are equal,
Let us disseminate
The seeds of Dharma.

Myonyo Shonin

Records are dim and somewhat rare, but it is thought a Chinese Buddhist monk, Hui Shen (or Hoei Shin), returned to China in 499 A.D. after spreading Buddhist teachings throughout Mexico. There is some evidence for this conjecture. Many of the religious beliefs, architecture and arts of Mexico and Central America are similar to those found in Asian countries.

Moreover, the following statement can be found in **The Buddhist Discovery of America**, a book by John Fryer LL.D., Professor of Oriental Languages, University of California, written in 1901:

> The former director of the mission at San Francisco, the Rev. Dr. Shuye Sonoda, before leaving California last year to study in Germany, made a visit to Mexico for the express purpose of examining the ruined temples

> and other antiquities of a Buddhist character which are to be found there. Other persons have spent much time in making investigations on this and similar lines. The result is that, link after link, a chain of evidence of the early arrival of Buddhist missionaries in America has already been found, which is sufficient to satisfy the judgement of all who are not wilfully sceptical.[5]

Several other ministers and interested Buddhists travelled through the United States during the push for Western thought and fashion of the Meiji period. Rev. Renshi Takuyu Umegami after completing studies in Europe returned to Japan via the United States in 1873. These early contacts led to the establishment of Jodo Shinshu missions throughout North America.

In 1897, Reverends Sanju Kanayasu and Shoi Yamada arrived in Hawaii as the first and second assigned ministers to Hawaii. The first missionaries of the Buddhist Faith arrived in San Francisco on September 1, 1899. The first Canadian Buddhist temple opened in Vancouver in 1905 with Rev. Senju Sasaki as the assigned minister.

Towards Canada

In 1833, a fishing boat was caught in the grip of the Kuroshio, the Black Current, off the storm-ravaged shores of Japan and was literally driven across the Pacific. Three survivors staggered on to the beach near Cape Flattery (close to Vancouver Island). The rest of the crew had died of starvation or disease. The men were immediately taken prisoner by Native Canadians only to be "rescued" later by a ship of The Hudson's Bay Company. The ship returned the hapless sailors to Japan. This misadventure was the first recorded visit of the Japanese to Canada.[6]

Some forty years later, the first Japanese immigrant came to stay. Manzo Nagano, an enterprising man, jumped ship at New Westminster B.C. in 1877 and spent the next 46 years in British Columbia. He fished for salmon on the Fraser River with an Italian partner. As a longshoreman on Burrard Inlet, he loaded cargo bound for Australia, Mexico, the Orient and the United States. In 1892, he opened a store selling Japanese novelties and goods in Victoria. Later, he returned to Japan, married and brought his bride to Canada. The couple then "enlarged his novelty store, opened a hotel and organized a Japanese social club."[7] He returned to Nagasaki to retire in 1923.

The first woman to arrive in Canada was Yo Shishido. In about 1887, she came as the bride of immigrant Washiji Oya. Yo Shishido, her sisters Kinu and Ima, and Naka Oya (Washiji's niece) "formed a gritty quartet of pioneer *fujin* in early Vancouver."[8] The first *nisei*, Katsuji Oya (born 1889), was Yo and Washiji's son.

The peasants of Japan had found hardest the economic brunt of the Meiji regime. Greedy landlords taxed the farmers to the point of eviction. Consequently, farm couples worked long into the night tending rice fields. Food for them was scarce since most of the crops went to pay the outlandish rents; thus abortion or *mabiki*[9] was common practice to prevent more mouths to feed. There were even some cases of infanticide.[10]

Such oppression can only lead to rebellion. Some insurrections were protests against Western influence, but most were staged to fight against the brutality of the landowners. As Ken Adachi put it in **The Enemy That Never Was**: "the seeds of emigration lay in the general discontent and malaise of the depressed lower classes, who though they might have realized, no matter how vaguely, the enormity of the task their country had undertaken, could not see that in any way it was lightening their daily burdens."[11]

It is no wonder that an adventurer like Manzo Nagano left his ship for the apparent greener pastures of Canada. Japan held no promise for such a young man with nothing in his pockets and ambition in his heart.

But what of the others? Most Japanese of the Meiji period lived in their villages surrounded by the rituals of time-honoured tradition. The government encouraged them to move, but something more urgent pressed them all the more to overcome their inertia and leave the security of village life to settle abroad in Canada - the lack of money.

Money was the key to education which in turn held the promise of prosperity. A national education program benefitted about 95% of Japanese children by the end of the century. Unfortunately, the lower classes could not afford too many of the benefits because of the prohibitive tax rate. Close to 2000 men armed with bamboo spears and guns destroyed buildings and schools in Tottori prefecture in 1873 because it was rumoured that new elementary schools meant an increase in taxes.[12]

During the early period (1885-1909) of Japanese migration to Canada, the immigrants were young men, the second sons of poor farmers, fishermen and labourers. Eldest sons stayed in Japan with the promise of inheriting everything from their fathers. Other sons received nothing or next to nothing. Daughters had no choice but to obey a father's edict to marry and perhaps go abroad.

Most of these second sons held much hope for success in Canada. The idea was to work in Canada for a few years to earn quick fortunes and return victorious as prodigal sons. If truth be known, Robbie Burns' adage -"the best laid schemes o' mice and men gang aft a-gley"- applied.

> The average immigrant, possessing little money, knowing nothing of the English language and entering a totally strange land, had to rely not only on his hopes and ambitions but also on a great deal of energy. The amount of money per capita owned by Japanese immigrants at the ports of entry in 1900 showed that each possessed an average of $39.59...[13]

Four prefectures in the south of Japan provided most immigrants to Canada: Wakayama, Shiga, Kagoshima and Hiroshima. They continued their former occupations. The fishermen went to Steveston and the farmers to the Okanagan and Fraser Valleys. Some established businesses in Vancouver.

Perhaps it was Mio-*mura*, a village in Wakayama, which best exemplified the hopes and dreams of the Japanese emigrant. The village was very poor; the prefectural government supported it with relief rice rations. Storms ruined crops, destroyed boats and razed houses. With fishing rights lost to a neighbouring prefecture, fishermen with over 70 boats were thrown out of work. Their only hope was to cast their eyes across the ocean.

Gihei Kuno who settled in Steveston sent back word that the salmon was plentiful and the money good. Young men followed in hordes. By 1926, over 1000 Japanese in Canada had roots in Mio-*mura*. The village itself underwent a wholesale change. The support money from Canada inspired those remaining to adopt Western clothing, food and housing. A striking contrast to the surrounding area, but since the village was referred to as either America-*mura* or Canada-*mura*, the idiosyncratic characteristics were not thought to be out of place.

A substantial number of "secondary" immigrants came to British Columbia from the United States and other unlikely places.

> Some trudged across the border from the United States, others trekked into the Yukon from Alaska during the Klondike gold rush (1899-1900), and there was considerable secondary immigration from Hawaii (1906-07). A gang of rail workers sent to Mexico, finding conditions intolerable, wound up with the Canadian Pacific Railway. A few came the other way around, by way of Europe and the Atlantic.[14]

Immigrants too came from Okinawa who, after World War I, settled in Southern Alberta.

Life in Canada

> The motley collection of stunted brown humanity furnished a curious and interesting study of Japs half-converted to Occidental customs. For example, all or nearly all were garbed in what are broadly titled "European" clothes - incongruous examples of misfits suggesting that the emigrant Japs had ere they walked abroad at Kobe fallen into the tender clutches of some Baxter Street outfitter and been thankfully done brown... Each man evidently regarded his make-up as quite the proper thing in swell tailoring - yet what samples of incongruity! There would be one with fancy, cloth-topped, patent-leather shoes, a flannel shirt, and shrunken cutaway coat; another with a barred summer shirt, celluloid collar, Prince Albert and white yachting shoes; a third with tweeds and a seaman's stogas - but almost all with the headgear of the crop of '75.[15]
>
> **Victoria Colonist**
> April 20, 1900

Despite anti-Japanese feelings, the Japanese continued to come to Canada. They landed in Victoria or Vancouver and spread to where the work took them. Besides salmon fishing on the Fraser River, hardy men worked in the coal mines of Cumberland on Vancouver Island. Lumbermen started at Hastings sawmill in Vancouver but soon settled in pulp and paper mills and logging camps all over British Columbia. In the early 20th Century, the Japanese worked for the railroads (Canadian Pacific, Canadian

Northern, and Grand Trunk Railways).

The average age of these men was 22. Most had grade six education, many had higher. They expected hard living conditions and got them. Shacks and bunkhouses, nothing more than a place to sleep. During the off-season, they moved into squalid rooming houses in the "Little Tokyo" area of Vancouver. The money they earned (about $1.00 a day) was sent to Japan to parents and children. They were a lonely lot: women did not come in significant numbers until 1907.

Although 98% were literate in Japanese, a few learned English. Such a state contributed to the cohesiveness of the community. Some attempts were made to venture into the largely white populace, but they preferred to stay together where Japanese was spoken exclusively and where they did not have to deal with a society in which ignorance prevailed and racism was the creed.

Little Tokyo became the haven of the community for these men and eventually for all Japanese in Vancouver. The area was bound approximately by Alexander St. to the north, Hastings St. to the south, Jackson to the east and Main to the west. Powell Street running through the middle was the main drag.

The area included two- and three-storey buildings, some store fronts, wood frame homes, tenements and cabins. Upper floors over stores were divided into cubicles for transients, derelicts and seasonal workers. Single family dwellings were overcrowded and run down. Cabins were mean one-bedroom affairs with none of the amenities.

Still, Little Tokyo was the sanctuary for the Japanese. Restaurants provided familiar meals. Festivals produced homeland sights and sounds. Department stores maintained supplies from Japan. Traditions were maintained and the community evolved naturally.

The expectation for these early men was to return home in the very near future. After all, the Japanese government held a tight rein on its citizens. Each had a passport and a certified copy of the family register. Permission to emigrate was granted by the Japanese Foreign Office but for only a certain number of men from each prefecture. That number was determined by an emigration company. The government also expected them to return after three years. In time, however, emigration became a process on a more permanent basis.

The Early Japanese Canadians and Religion

> Although the immigrants tended to cluster in the southwest corner of the Lower Mainland, they lived wherever they could find work. As the province's natural wealth was scattered over vast areas - in mines, lumber mills, farms, canneries separated one from the other often by hundreds of miles - they soon learned about the vast size of the province. They also discovered the peculiar way in which the terrain, the "sea of mountains", divided and isolated the people in different areas not only in terms of transportation and accessibility but also in terms of climate, soil and natural resources, blocked in by the solid, imposing range of the Rockies in the east and the mass of the Pacific in the west. Their seasonal wanderings took them not only to mines, lumber mills and fisheries in Vancouver Island and the Lower Mainland, to Comox, Nanaimo, Cumberland, Port Alice, Chemainus, New Westminster, and scores of farming towns in the lower Fraser, but also to the dry inland plateau of the Cariboo, the lush valleys of the Kootenays and the Okanagan. And up the coast they went from Steveston to Woodfibre, Britannia Beach, Bella Coola, Rivers Inlet, the Nass and the Skeena until they could almost touch the Yukon from the remote mines of Atlin.[16]

Given the nomadic and scattered nature of the Japanese Canadian pioneers, religion was of little concern. The hard life consisted of heavy labour, poor living quarters and isolation. They had to bear great instability since most jobs were seasonal or temporary. Miners, for example, moved from played-out copper mines to logging rafts along the coast of Vancouver Island. Most labourers found solace in gambling, drinking and prostitutes.

Shinkichi Tamura was one of the first to change this trend. Tamura, from a *samurai* family, came to Canada to seek his fortune. He began as a general office boy sweeping floors, running errands and performing some clerical duties. His exuberance and perspicacity led him to many opportunities. Eventually, he became a major business force in British Columbia. The Tamura Building, still standing today on the corner of Powell and Dunlevy Streets in Vancouver, was the headquarters for the Japan-Canada Trust and Savings Company, a Tamura holding.[17]

As a community leader, Tamura excelled. He established many institutions in order to bind the Japanese Canadians together. He started a night school called the Japanese Kyogeikai for anyone interested in learning English. He had a hand in starting the **Vancouver Shuho**, the first community newspaper. Tamura was also interested in the souls of his compatriots. In 1894, he met Masutaro Okamoto, an *issei* sent by the Japanese Christian Endeavor Society of Seattle to preach Christianity in a small Japanese Canadian settlement in Steveston. The two later enlisted the help of Rev. Goro Kaburagi,[18] a graduate of Northwestern University in Chicago, to establish the Japanese Methodist Church in 1896.[19]

Through the **Vancouver Shuho** (later renamed the **Vancouver Shimpo**), Kaburagi, publisher in addition to being minister, made clear his belief that the Japanese should assimilate as quickly as possible. Immigrants should learn English, adopt English customs and convert to Christianity.

Perhaps Kaburagi was bolstered in his proselytizing by the constant attention of the Christian missionaries to the Japanese. By 1902, missions had been established in Victoria and Vancouver. A Methodist church, in fact, was built at the corner of Jackson and Powell in Vancouver in 1906. A gymnasium and social hall was added after 1918 through the efforts of Reverend Yoshimitsu Akagawa and his congregation. The Methodists finally joined with the Congregationalists and the Presbyterians in 1925 to form the United Church of Canada. Reverend Kosaburo Shimizu was the first pastor of the Powell Street United Church. By the 1930s, the United Church claimed 4789 Japanese members.[20]

Many Japanese immigrants became Christians as the result of a conversion to the faith. However, most were drawn to the religion because it represented Western civilization. To be Canadian was to be God-fearing and white. Of course, it was impossible to be white but to assimilate as a Christian was considered a part of the "Canadianization" or acceptance process.

A second factor was the sense of obligation the missionaries developed in the Japanese. The Christian church was the first Canadian institution to assist the immigrants in establishing a foothold in the new land. Ministers provided interpreters, employment agents and legal aid. The Japanese with their keen sense of obligation could not help but convert.

> The missionary comes to the door and in very polite Japanese invites the *issei* mother to a tea at the church. There she sits around and talks to some of her neighbours. As she is leaving, the missionary politely expresses the wish to see her again. And the *issei* mother, having accepted his hospitality, feels obligated to attend the church.[21]

Despite the success of the Christian missionaries, a good 68% of the Japanese preferred Buddhism. Still, Christianity was seen as a threat to Buddhism and vice versa. In Japan, Reverend Kagahi of the Hompa Hongwanji in a popular article advised Buddhist missionaries in North America to identify the Christian God with the Eternal Buddha.

> Devotion to the Supreme Reality was what really mattered, not the different and culturally contingent names given to Reality.[22]

Buddhists regarded such advice as a perversion of the *Dharma* and adhered to the original precepts of Buddhism. The Japanese in Canada moreover saw Buddhism as their one link to Japan and thus to their roots. Their religion was a tool in teaching the children obedience to the Emperor, the teacher, the parents, and the elder brother or sister.[23]

Many have exaggerated the conflict between the two religions in Canada but there can be no doubt of its existence. Opinions more in the form of a complaint were lodged in the community newspapers on a regular basis.

> Our compatriots do not like to put funerals in the care of the Japanese Methodist Church...as such those who dislike the Japanese Methodist Church are increasing in number by the day and the voices which have been crying for the construction of a Buddhist church for over three years now are finally becoming a reality.
>
> Being influenced for the worse by the English people's way of thinking destroys the order of our society. It is extremely improper and a dangerous way of thinking...[24]
>
> **Vancouver Shimpo**, 1903

The cry for proper Buddhist representation in Canada was loud and palpable. An ancient legend claimed that Buddhist priests knew immediately of the death of one of their parishioners. The *shin-hotoke* (newly dead) came to the family temple and rapped heavily on the doors.

In Canada, *issei* argued that there was no temple for the *shin-hotoke* to come calling. Moreover there was no one to chant the *sutras*, burn incense and send the dead to the Pure Land. Most pitiable were the forgotten dead who had been buried ignominiously in shallow, unsanctified graves.

Thus it was on October 10, 1904 a group of devout Buddhists who had settled in Vancouver gathered at the residence of Tadaichi Nagao to discuss the possibility of establishing a Buddhist temple in Canada.

The First Church

Chapter 4

Bukkyo Tozen

Bukkyo Tozen: The First Church

My sister and I went to public school not knowing a word of English. Since we spoke nothing but Japanese at home, however, somehow we managed. After school, we went to Japanese Language School, catching a street car and barely arriving in time. We studied from text-books sent from Japan. I have heard so many of my friends, especially those who lived in the Japanese community, say that they hated to go to Japanese School. But to me this school was a refuge. Many a time, we were chased by bullies as we walked from the street car, so I think the school was my *Nembutsu* so to speak. My parents were always understanding. Since we did not have any relatives in Canada, I was constantly asking my parents questions about Japan. Their families were both devout Jodo Shinshu Buddhists. I did not realize my mother's house had such a beautiful Buddhist shrine until I saw it with my own eyes when I visited Japan for the first time in 1974. My aunt in Tosu City was surprised and pleased that I knew the *gatha* **Shinshu Shu Ka.**

We had many Buddhist friends as well as Christian friends and many of my parents' Christian friends tried to persuade my dad to convert to Christianity. He would always say very strongly, "No, never! I was brought up a Buddhist and I will never renounce my Buddhist faith."

Dorothy Kagawa
nisei
Toronto Buddhist Church

The *issei* managed to instill in their children a sense of great devotion to Jodo Shinshu Buddhism. The religion was interpreted as the direct link to Japan and the only proper vehicle to teach the children loyalty and obedience to the Emperor, to the teachers and especially to their parents.

Buddhism at first had to be administered and spread through the community by the lay minister or leader; that is, particularly devout men, who lacked formal training but were fortified with good intentions, saw to it that the *Nembutsu* was brought to any who needed the comfort of the familiar and the spirituality of the *Dharma (the Teaching of the Buddha).*

Typical of the practice was Hatsutaro Nishimura, a man originally from Shiga Prefecture, Inu-kami-gun, Kita-Ao-Yagi-mura, Aza-oh-yabu. Around 1901 while living in Sapperton, a small town near Vancouver, Nishimura received a portrait of the Buddha on a scroll from Lord Abbot Myonyo of the Nishi Hongwanji. He promptly mounted it in a large room of a friend's house. Every Sunday thereafter, Buddhist followers gathered in front of the scroll to conduct *Dharma* talks amongst themselves probably with Nishimura leading the discussion. Today the house is near the site of a cemetery just north east of New Westminster.

Courtesy of Kay Shibuta

Sapperton, B.C. Obon, July 1928. Rev. Naito presiding.

With increased immigration came the realization that religious teaching was important. In fact, moral instruction became much more important than doctrinal differences. Thus it was that the *issei* turned to the established churches of the Methodist and

Anglican faiths as the place to send their children. Some saw such a move as a natural method of assimilation. Others fulfilled some kind of perceived obligation to the Christian missionaries. Still others did not see it as an abandonment of Buddhism but rather a pragmatic way of conveying moral values to the children since no Buddhist Church existed at the beginning of the 20th Century.

Such expediency caused much concern amongst the followers of Jodo Shinshu Buddhism. Thus it was that on October 10, 1904, fourteen Buddhist laymen and volunteers gathered at the home of Tadaichi Nagao to discuss the construction of a Buddhist temple in Vancouver. The first task was to call their Buddhist friends together for an assembly aptly called a *Dobo-daikai* or *Fellow Travellers Conference*. Records of the proceedings were not kept or were destroyed during the war, but two decisions of the plenary sessions were clear: they voted unanimously to build the temple and they resolved to request that a minister from the Nishi Hongwanji be sent from Japan.

After nine months of deliberation, the head bishop of the Nishi Hongwanji, Rev. Sonjun Oda, sent word to Canada that the first *kaikyoshi*,[1] Rev. Senju Sasaki, was on his way. Apparently, there had been much discussion in Kyoto about the selection of a suitable minister.

Reverend Senju Sasaki

Reverend Senju Sasaki was born in 1871 at the Kozenji Temple of the Jodo Shinshu Hongwanji in Kozenji, Ima-tachi-machi, Fukui Prefecture. The temple, the most widely known in all of Japan, was founded by Reverend Zesho who had met Shinran Shonin near Echizen. The founder of the Jodo Shinshu sect was on his way from Kyoto to Echigo to spend his exile.

Senju Sasaki's birth was fortuitous since at that time Japan was improving its elementary school system. Slowly more and more of the population were gaining access to education. In Fukui prefecture alone, many students travelled to foreign countries to study. Schools themselves invited teachers from The United States to teach English. Books central to the curricula were Yukichi Fukuzawa's **State of Things in the Western Nations** and the "Mr. Smiles" book called **Self Help**.

The Buddhist Disestablishment Movement by the government discouraged many from seeking an education through the Hongwanji. Senju Sasaki's father Shinku, however, was bound and determined to raise his son as a Buddhist. The government's anti-Buddhist policy and the consequent impoverished conditions remained with Senju as he made his way through to Hongwanji Senior College. Legend has it that he was so poor he used a coarse rope for a belt. His indigent childhood and adolescence were to influence his later life.

While taking literature at the college, Senju was exposed to the influence of teachers and fellow student scholars who embraced Western thought. Among the luminaries were Lafcadio Hearn, famous for translating the collection of ghost stories known as **Kwaidan**; Kotaro Sugimura, later an influential journalist with the Asahi Newspaper; Renjo Akamatsu, a scholar who taught Jodo Shinshu in English; Junjiro Takakusu, a great Buddhist scholar; Sako Egen, at 39 years of age, the first principal of the Buddhist University; and Keimo Imamura who later became Bishop of Hawaii and who influenced Donald Keene a student of Japanese literature at Columbia University.

From within such a cadre of modern thinkers came the "New Buddhist Movement of the Meiji Era". Their students pushed and protested for change and reform. With Senju Sasaki as a prominent member, a temperance movement began. The students started a magazine called **Reflections Upon Oneself**. Today, the magazine still publishes under the name **Chu-Oh Koh-Ron** or *Central Public Opinion*.

Two years after he graduated, Senju married Tomie Egen, sister of his compatriot Sako Egen. They travelled to India and Europe, exposing themselves to the full impact of Western culture and history.

Following the trip, Rev. Sasaki's first appointment was as resident minister of Singapore. He stayed six years. During that time, he experienced first hand the misery that colonialism could bring to a conquered country. Of the 1800 Japanese living in Singapore half were young women known as *karayuki-san* (prostitutes). Tomie Sasaki befriended these women, gathered them at the temple and taught them sewing, manners and the Japanese language.

The Sasakis tragically lost their first son Sengaku shortly

after his birth in Singapore. Oddly, their second son, also born in Singapore, was named before his birth. While his parents travelled through India, the name Senzo[2] came to them because they were surrounded by a country with many elephants.[3]

When the 1904 Vancouver Fellow Travellers Conference took place, Rev. Sasaki was completing his fifth year in Singapore. Nine months later, he was appointed the first Buddhist minister to Canada. The much travelled, weary minister upon returning to Japan was dispatched to Canada without delay. He must have fulfilled the requirements of the Hongwanji admirably.

While the minister was travelling across the Pacific preparations were being made for the construction of the church. The Dobo-daikai formed the Foundation Committee with the following elected representatives:

Tadaichi Nagao	Hanyemon Hayashi
Mohei Sato	Suteya Yamada
Tetsutaro Ikuno	Torakichi Tsuchiyama
Yaichi Horibe	Ikunoshin Murakami
Eiji Morino	Jinshiro Nakayama
Kazuma Hayashi	Shichimatsu Hamakawa
Yasuyuki Sawada	Kanekichi Nakanishi

On October 12, 1905, Rev. and Mrs. Senju Sasaki arrived in Vancouver on the Empress of Japan to a joyful welcome by a contingent who were soon to become his new congregation. The gathering immediately retired to a local Japanese inn to celebrate.

Since there was no temple, the Foundation Committee rented a room at the Ishikawa Ryokan at 330 Powell Street for services to take place. The hotel provided a dining room with a statue of the Amida Buddha enshrined. The neophyte congregation named the room The Japanese Buddhist Temple. December 12, 1905 was declared the foundation date.

In the meantime, Rev. Sasaki wasted no time in bringing the word of the Buddha to the devoted followers. Barely settled in his new home, the reverend delivered a talk on the Buddha at Vancouver City Hall on October 26th. Rev. Shinjo Ikuta reported in his book **Enkakushi** (*History of the Buddhist Churches of Canada*):

The *Dharma* talk, heard for the first time in Canada,

thundered like the lion's roar to the ears of some 500 persons in the audience. The audience was enthralled by the wisdom of the Buddha. Rev. Gendo Nakai of Seattle Buddhist Temple was also in the audience to give moral support...[4]

JCCC archives

Rev. Senju and Tomie Sasaki, circa 1905.

Using simple language so that all who listened understood, Rev. Sasaki emphasized the importance of following the Buddha's teachings.

Rev. Sasaki was a man of great compassion and many talents.

He was multilingual: English, Japanese and even Devanagari (an Indian language). His proficiency with Devanagari, in particular, attracted Hindu people who needed help in writing or deciphering letters.

He composed a special dictionary of English and Japanese called **Simplified English for Hospital Patients** so that the sick and weak could communicate their needs to their doctors and nurses. Moreover, he visited the hospitals every week in order to help Japanese speaking patients. Here was a minister who not only responded to the needs of his congregation but to all those people in need.

His wife, Tomie, was totally committed to giving behind-the-scene support to her husband. She became involved in teaching the Japanese immigrants various skills like sewing, homemaking and etiquette, a compassion she perhaps acquired in Singapore. She generously opened her house and provided food to single men. It is no wonder, she was affectionately called *Okusan, Naishitsu* and *Bomori*.[5]

In Canada, they had three more children, all girls.

Despite Rev. Sasaki's philanthropic activities, his priority was the building of the first Buddhist temple in Canada. The reverend and the Foundation Committee visited every sawmill in the Vancouver area to advertise his arrival and to solicit donations.

With the help of energetic laymen outside Vancouver (Ichitaro Suzuki, Iwakichi Narimura and Tomekichi Homma of Steveston; Sujiro Kato of New Westminster; and Mr. Horita of Courtney, Cumberland area), the Foundation Committee was able to raise $5668 by March 1906. The amount was substantial considering a loaf of bread cost five cents; $5668 is equivalent to over $100,000 today.

On November 9, the congregation approved the purchase of property three lots wide at 32 Alexander St. The existing house on the property was renovated and became the centre of activity for Jodo Shinshu Buddhism. Various church-related organizations were formed. The Young Men's Buddhist Association and an English language night school were established for the education and welfare of the young people.

Together with the main temple in Vancouver, Buddhists in the surrounding area established meeting places in Sapperton, Barnet and Port Moody. Keen effort to spread the doctrine of the Buddha succeeded in raising the number of practising Buddhists to 650 by 1907, the year of the Anti-Asian Riots.

JCCC archives

English language night school. Alexander Street Buddhist Church, circa 1907.

The Riot of 1907

The Russo-Japanese War of 1904-05 had no direct consequences for Japanese Canadians or Canada for that matter, but it did prove the technological superiority of the Japanese. The small country's upstart fleet had defeated one of the mightiest navies in the world. Japan's reputation as a military power reached as far as Europe. Kaiser Wilhelm of Germany coined the phrase "Yellow Peril" in describing "The Oriental".

The Japanese no matter where they resided were seen as a threat to business and property. The Vancouver press railed against the "Yellow Peril" that ate away at "the livelihood and security of the white population" of British Columbia. If something wasn't done "the whites... would die - be ousted absolutely out of existence".[6] Over 7000 new Japanese immigrants had entered Canada and had supposedly taken jobs away from white workers.

The sentiment erupted into a full scale riot on September 7.

> The mob, estimated at about a thousand strong, swept on to "Little Tokyo", and when the plate glass of a large store was shattered on the corner of Powell and

> Westminster a wild series of scenes was set off in the best tradition of frontier lawlessness.[7]

To get a sense of the mood the riot created, Frank Uyehara, one of the first *nisei*, wrote in **The New Canadian**:

> When word came that the crowd was nearing, those along Powell Street got their first taste of a blackout; lights were turned off. All was dark and still. A deadly hush reigned. It was broken by a distant murmur which quickly filled the night air. Soon the tramp, tramp, tramp of many feet and the sound of many voices became audible. Mothers clutched their children closer in the darkened backrooms of their homes. Not a word was spoken. At last, a mass of marching men swung around Main heading up Powell picking up crushed rocks from the semi-paved street and hurling them at the windows... A child's shrill cry split the dark silence of one of the houses. It was followed by another and another. A bedlam of wailing broke loose.[8]
>
> **The New Canadian**
> August 1, 1959

Fortunately the Japanese were ready and pelted the rabble with rocks from the rooftops, followed by a head-on assault using clubs, bottles, iron bars and any other weapon available. The rabid mob was soon dispersed.

Consequences

The riot was successful in two opposing ways. The Asiatic Exclusion League, the organization responsible for inciting the riot, managed to convince the federal government to restrict the number of Japanese labourers immigrating to Canada. No legislation was required, however, since the Japanese government, under a "gentlemen's agreement" with Canada, discouraged emigration. On the other hand, the restriction did not apply to women. Thus large numbers of women began to migrate to Canada under the picture bride system. The birth rate increased at a rapid rate, and the Japanese community expanded and closed its rank to protect itself.

According to Rev. Takahatake in his extensive and controversial biography, Rev. Sasaki himself became outspoken against the influence of Anglo-Canadian assimilation forces within the community.

> Looking at several aspects of Senju's achievements, referring to his responsible position on the Japanese Language School which followed the Imperial Message on Education, Senju was carried along with the anti-Canada group and then helped with write-ups in the **Tairiku Nippo**; the occasion when the young people who attended the night school studying English were forcibly made to join the Canada Assimilation Group; further, the Kyodo Cemetery incident where the graves of the Japanese deceased were not looked after, and when Senju went to the cemetery to look into the matter he was not allowed to enter the cemetery proper. There was also a tragic incident when Senju had to witness the hanging of a Japanese while chanting the Buddhist *sutra*. These are part of the hardships and mistakes in the new land that Senju went through together with his people.[9]

Above all else, Rev. Sasaki abhorred the racism inherent in the 1907 Riot. The experiences of his penurious childhood and of colonialism in Singapore must have reminded him of the devastating effects of oppression in its myriad forms. Rev. Takahatake further offers a revealing speech by Rev. Sasaki.

> In May 1909, two Japanese navy training ships, the "Aso" and the "Soya" docked in Vancouver harbour. In his welcome speech to the navy visitors, Rev. Sasaki stated, "The reason why the Japanese people here find prejudice against them is because the rest of the world does not fully understand the nation of Japan." He concluded by appealing to the candidates for the Navy high office to "uphold the national prestige of Japan."[10]

Although it is not clear that Rev. Sasaki ever offered the same advice directly to his Japanese immigrant congregation, Rev. Takahatake inferred that the passionate minister strongly held the belief: "If Japan and the Japanese people do not possess a strong national consciousness, they will be conquered by the West..."[11]

In any case, the Buddhist Church became the centre of the community since it offered a refuge from the threat of white racists and a haven where a common language existed and tradition was upheld.

1909: Towards Building the First Church

On January 28, 1909 a tragic accident at the railroad construction site near Sapperton caused the deaths of twenty-three Japanese workers from Seattle. Rev. Sasaki tended to the needs of the bereaved families and arranged for the funerals of the deceased. In the end, the Great Northern Railroad paid $1500 in damages to each of the victims' families.

Thirteen days later, the topic of the construction of a new building was discussed in earnest at the Vancouver temple. Rev. Sasaki submitted the following plan of action:

1. Purchase property for the purpose of erecting a building.
2. Sell within one month the present church property together with the building on it.
3. The entire congregation is responsible for financing the construction of the new temple.
4. It is hoped to have all the Japanese carpenters (in the Buddhist community) put forth their best efforts toward construction of this new building, rather than opening the bidding to the public.

Nine men were chosen to act as the Construction Committee:

Saroku Horita	Mohei Sato
Eiji Morino	Tetsutaro Isono
Kanekichi Nakanishi	Kenjiro Isoda
Gentaro Nakagawa	Shichimatsu Hamakawa
Tonakichi Ikeda	

Two events provided Buddhists with the incentive to complete the project. On April 21, 1909, the B.C. government granted official recognition to Buddhism. In May, Reverend and former Abbot Komyo Ohtani (father of the 23rd Abbot Kosho of the Nishi Hongwanji) left Japan and travelled to London via the Siberian Railroad to study the various religions of Europe and the world. He also visited Jerusalem, toured South Africa, visited sacred Buddhist remains in India, and on his way home visited Vancouver on September 12.

An unfortunate misunderstanding sent Mohei Sato and Hanyemon Hayashi to Seattle to meet the well travelled former Abbot who was rumoured to be on his way to Canada by road. In fact, Abbot Komyo Ohtani arrived in Vancouver by train about 3 p.m. With him was the communication head of the Nishi Hongwanji, Tetsushin Watanabe, a former resident of London, England.

Rev. Sasaki; Mr. Yada, the Consul General of Japan; and several hundred Buddhist followers met the Abbot at the train station. From there, the honoured guests were taken to the Hotel Vancouver by horse drawn carriage. Later, the Abbot took the carriage to the temple. He entertained several reports from such organizations as Church Maintenance, the Young Buddhist Men's Association, the English Language Evening School and other area Buddhist meeting groups. He then spoke of his happiness with the situation in Canada and offered words of encouragement to Rev. Sasaki and his followers. Following a gala banquet in his honour, he departed at 11 p.m. by ship for Seattle. The Consul General and many of the faithful stood on the dock bidding him a fond farewell.

In January of 1910, the Construction Committee sold the Buddhist Temple on Alexander Street for $24,512.50. The location of a new property was discussed at length and selected carefully. It was expected that the Japanese population would eventually move out of the Little Tokyo area of Powell Street and settle in the "Heaps" area of Vancouver.

> "Heaps", a motley of more than a hundred residences and rooming houses, was a handy label tagged onto Little Tokyo's eastern annex, collected around Heaps Sawmill, a longtime employer of *nikkei* labour. Like most waterfront settlements, the original shelters of Fairview on the south bank of False Creek, a mud-bank in low tide, were shacks built atop pilings or makeshift huts on millside scows. Later, they built more durable habitations.[12]

The committee agreed to purchase a two lot property for the new building at 1603 Franklin Street[13] just east of Little Tokyo towards the Pacific National Exhibition grounds.

JCCC archives

Franklin Street (Heaps) Buddhist Church, 1910 - 1936.

Opening of the Buddhist Church Hall

The new hall was built quickly. On October 21, 1910, the sod turning ceremony took place. On February 23, 1911, the builders completed the project.

During the dedication service on April 6, Rev. Sasaki announced that the opening service was to be held in the fall of that year. He also thanked Genroku Nakamura, a devoted Buddhist from Toshiki-gun, Fukui-ken, Japan, for his generous donation of furniture and Buddhist adornments for the *naijin* (shrine) of the temple.

The service in celebration of the new edifice took place on September 25, 1911. Church elders invited Supervisor Koyu Uchida from San Francisco and Reverend Hoshin Fujii of Seattle to participate.

Reports say the day was bright and sunny. The front of the hall was draped in red and white bunting. A Union Jack and the Hinomaru of Japan were crossed above the entrance. The place was filled to capacity and the overflow spread outside into the street.

Order of Service

Tokutaro Chikamura rang the temple bell for assembly. *Gagaku* music filtered in as the procession of ministers entered the hall. Rev. Sasaki rose to the podium to lead the gathering in the Aspiration. *Sutra* chanting followed. Once everyone was settled into their seats, Supervisor Uchida and Rev. Fujii delivered their *Dharma* talks.

The service concluded with a treasurer's report. Mr. Sawada reported that the total cost of the building and furnishings totalled $28,445.

Individuals were recognized for their dedication in completing the project. The church did not present plaques or certificates of commendation; instead, Rev. Sasaki read out their names before placing them in the church files. The distinguished men were:

Reverend Sasaki	Hanyemon Hayashi	Ichitaro Suzuki
Eikichi Kagetsu	Torakichi Tsuchiyama	Yaichi Horibe
Suteya Yamada	Otokichi Shiomi	Genroku Nakamura
Gentaro Nakagawa	Jinshiro Nakayama	Mohei Sato
Denji Omatsu	Eiji Morino	

In subsequent meetings, church members decided that this first temple would come under the umbrella of the Buddhist Churches of America (an association of all the Buddhist Churches in North America) since it was the only one in Canada.

Rev. Sasaki expressed a desire to return to Japan and requested the congregation to look for his replacement.

The good reverend had worked hard for six long years to bring the word of the *Dharma* to the followers of Jodo Shinshu Buddhism. He educated the young, he brought comfort to the sick, he translated and looked out for those in need, and he offered compassion to the dying. Many were upset with the prospect of his leaving, but they recognized his long years of hardship and acquiesced reluctantly.

On March 19, 1912, Rev. Sasaki, his wife and his children boarded a ship bound for Japan and sadly left Vancouver. Many people appeared on the dock to wish him and his family well and to thank him and his wife for their dedication.

Rev. Gungai Kato took over the duties of the church until he was ordered to return to Japan in November 1913.

A Church Divided

Chapter 5

The End of the Meiji Era

At 43 minutes past midnight, July 30, 1912, the Emperor Meiji died at the age of 61. The last years of the era were tumultuous ones for Japan; 1904-05 saw Japan emerge as a military power in the Far East and throughout the world with its victory during the Russo-Japanese War. In 1907 six year compulsory education was put into effect. In 1910 the annexation of Korea, that came to a head with the Russo-Japanese War, was completed. In that same year, Kotoku Shusui, an extremist of the socialist movement, plotted to assassinate the Emperor.

The Japanese felt it was the end of an era. The Emperor had won the affection of his subjects by the end of his reign. During his final illness, thousands of people gathered before the gates of the Imperial Palace to pray for his recovery. A central figure in **Kokoro**, a popular novel by Natsume Soseki, comments:

> At the height of the summer, Emperor Meiji passed away. I felt as though the spirit of the Meiji era had begun with the Emperor and ended with him. I was overcome with the feeling that I and the others, who had been brought up in that era, were now left behind to live as anachronisms.[1]

The funeral procession was grand. The Emperor was borne in "a casket drawn by five oxen, and his body was interred near Kyoto with four earthen effigies of warriors in full armour."[2]

At the moment the procession left the palace gates, General Nogi, the victorious commander at Port Arthur during the Russo-Japanese War, and his wife committed suicide to join the emperor in death.[3]

At the Buddhist Church in Vancouver, memorial services were held on the evenings of July 30 and 31. More than 300 gathered to mourn the passing of the Emperor. Reverend Kato, Rev. Sasaki's replacement, presided over the services and gave the *Dharma* talk. Consul Yada gave the eulogy followed by another by Mr. Tashiro, the principal of the Japanese Language School.

From the outset, the Buddhist Church in Canada did not recede into a shell of isolation. The congregation and ministers were keenly aware of world events, especially those pertaining to Japan. On July 8, 1912, for example, the church held a memorial service for those 1500 lost at sea when the ocean liner Titanic struck an iceberg and sank in April.

That same year, Reverend Genei Sato visited Vancouver to announce the forthcoming 650th Memorial Service for Shinran Shonin. He was the first travelling minister or *fukyo-shi* sent by the Nishi Hongwanji to the United States and Canada to propagate the Buddha *Dharma*.

Coincidentally with the death of the Emperor, Canadian politicians began to close the door on the Japanese. The Immigration Act of 1910 gave them the means since the act prohibited "the landing in Canada...of immigrants belonging to any race deemed unsuited to the climate or requirements of Canada, or of any immigrants of any specified class, occupation or character."[4] As a result, anti-Asian sentiment grew in British Columbia and in Saskatchewan, fuelled perhaps by Chinese and Japanese labour strikes and riots on Vancouver Island in 1913 and the Hindu riots on the Komagata Maru in May 1914.

No overt ban or taxation tactic on Japanese immigration took place, as in the case of the Chinese, since the "gentleman's agreement" of 1907 was still in place. The Japanese Imperial government simply discouraged immigration to Canada by limiting the number of labourers leaving the country. Consequently the Japanese community was no longer under the influence of cultural and societal changes in Japan. A Japanese Canadian culture emerged steeped in the Meiji paradox of embracing Western technology while fiercely adhering to Japanese tradition.

Reverend Ryosei Wada

On May 25, 1913, Vancouver women organized themselves

under the banner of Bukkyo Fujinkai. Over 100 women attended the inaugural service to hear Rev. Gungai Kato speak about the women's role in the church. The first elected president was Tomiye Yamamoto. Unfortunately, she returned to Japan after serving only one month. Next year, the following executive members were elected:

President:	Fumi Nakamura
Vice-President:	Matsuyo Sato
Secretary:	Shige Kaminishi
Treasurer:	Riye Nakamura

Soon after the election, the group received a letter from the Hongwanji in Kyoto. The director of the World Women's Federation, Lady Takeko Kujo, wrote to welcome the group in Vancouver into the Federation. On behalf of the world organization, she formally acknowledged Mrs. Fumi Nakamura as President of the Women's Federation of Canada.

During the formation and activity of the Fujinkai, Rev. Junichi Shigeno and Rev. Ryosei Wada arrived from Japan in September. In their first year, it seemed to be business as usual at the church. On April 11, 1914, the widow Empress Shoken died at the age of 64. An Otsuya Service was held on the 15th and a Memorial Service the next day. Less than a year later, Rev. Wada decided to return to Japan.

At about the time of Rev. Wada's departure, Rev. Banyu Yatsubuchi visited Canada as part of his speaking tour. The renown priest of the Hongwanji was scheduled to attend The World Buddhist Conference in San Francisco in August 1915, but his ship was delayed and his plans altered as a consequence. Instead he went on a speaking tour of the North American churches. He landed in Vancouver on September 6 accompanied by Rev. Tetsho Ono of the San Francisco church. The charismatic minister held listeners in the palm of his hand. He utilized poems, amusing anecdotes, quotations from Rennyo Shonin's teachings and jokes to convey his message. However humourous his talks were, his message was clear:

> If a person is sincere and takes refuge in the Buddha wholeheartedly, he comes to feel oneness with the truth of the universe.

During his stay in Canada, the 70 year old minister gave a

two hour lecture to an audience of 400 gathered at the Heaps church. He also addressed crowds in Nanaimo, Cumberland and Steveston. He later visited the Mountainview Cemetery to preside over a memorial service at gravesite. Afterwards, he suggested the Buddhist group erect wooden grave markings to identify the deceased Japanese Canadians. That afternoon, he spoke to the Buddhist Women's group in Vancouver before leaving for Seattle. He then returned to Japan.

World War I

The church's attitude to the war was not clear. During the Russo-Japanese War, the Hongwanji provided solace to the Japanese soldier but did not actively support warfare. Although a popular story of the time claimed a "Buddhist priest wired Japan to report that he sighted part of the Baltic fleet (of Russia) passing through the ocean outside of Singapore",[5] it is highly unlikely the story bears any truth since such action would be a violation of Buddhist precepts.

In any event no support whatsoever was forthcoming from the Hongwanji, let alone the church in Canada, for the new war even though Japan was an ally of Britain. It is curious however that the Buddhist Church in Vancouver said nothing about the war since more than 200 *issei* volunteered to fight in Europe, the majority of whom were members of the church. Perhaps such a stand was considered to be under the purview of the Japanese Association of Canada, the political arm of the Japanese community, which did call for Japanese Canadian involvement to counter the anti-Japanese sentiments with a grand show of loyalty. Fifty-four *issei* died in battle.

Reverend Junichi Shigeno and the Hint of Scandal

From the beginning of his tenure in Vancouver, Rev. Shigeno was headed for trouble. Jinshiro Nakayama in his exhaustive **Kanada-doho-hatten-taikan** (*Encyclopedia of Japanese in Canada*) claims that the Hongwanji considered the presiding minister Rev. Kato incompetent. Apparently, several complaints had come from the members over the financial administration of the church. As a result a rift was created in the membership. Rev. Kato was thus ordered to return to Japan. It was incredulous to all concerned that he did not obey the order and defiantly remained in Canada.

It was at this time that Rev. Shigeno and Rev. Wada had arrived to try to resolve the problems. Rev. Kato did not take kindly to their presence, especially to Rev. Shigeno, and reacted by launching a campaign to discredit and ultimately to oust Rev. Shigeno. He first wrote a damning article in the local Japanese newspapers blaming others rather than himself for the church's problems. He then spread rumours about Rev. Shigeno's moral character to gain supporters.[6] In the final analysis, Rev. Kato was successful. For what purpose is still unfathomable.

Rev. Junichi Shigeno was born in Wakayama-ken in the late 1800s and received his education from the Hongwanji in Kyoto and the Teikoku University (Imperial University) in Tokyo. At 21 years of age, he went to India to study the history of Buddhism. Eventually he returned to Japan to begin his work for the Hongwanji as head of the Missionary Supervisory Department. A well qualified, well read and devout man, his downfall was perhaps his progressive nature and his bachelor status.

After arriving in Vancouver in 1913, he initiated the inclusion of non-Japanese followers of Jodo Shinshu Buddhism much to the consternation of the congregation. The first were Mr. and Mrs. Group (pronounced Gu-leep). Rev. Shigeno gave them their Buddhist names: Shaku Kaku Ryo and Shaku Ni Myo Kaku, respectively.

He also demonstrated his great capacity for compassion. Jinshiro Nakayama tells the story of a man from Hiroshima who was a patient in a New Westminster hospital suffering from mental illness. Rev. Shigeno saw the plight of the man's family and invited the wife and two children to stay in the temple's living quarters.

When the husband left the hospital, he rejoined his family and stayed in the temple as well. He eventually managed to get a job at a local sawmill. After two years, the family's financial situation improved and they moved out.

Unfortunately, the flu epidemic of 1923 caused the situation to turn bad once more. Rev. Shigeno had no choice but to take in the flu stricken family again when they appealed to him for help. Shortly thereafter, the mother died and the father suffered a relapse of mental illness. He reportedly left the temple never to be seen again.

The good reverend out of a genuine commitment to his beliefs took care of the two children, two and six years old. He fed them, sent them to school and raised them as his own.

Normally, a man of such conviction and compassion would have been praised for his actions. Not so, given the enmity of his rival and the vulnerability of his position.

Gossip amongst the women of the Fujinkai soon flared up about Rev. Shigeno's womanizing ways. As the talk escalated, there were stories of excessive drunken behaviour and meetings held at *ryokans*, meals and drink ordered by Rev. Shigeno and paid for by the church.

None of these allegations could be substantiated. It was just that Rev. Shigeno being a single young man was an easy target. Present day speculation implicates Rev. Kato having dropped innuendos in the right ears about the woman and two children living within the temple.

On April 16, 1916, Hanyemon Hayashi reported the church was in debt in the amount of $4312.50. Board members Kannosuke Kaminishi, Masaichi Hayashi and Akezo Oya reviewed the statement to verify the accounting. They acted quickly by canvassing the community for funds. They raised $6185.

Perhaps the debt could have been explained by cost overruns in building and maintaining the new church hall; instead, gossip fanned the fires of scandal brighter and blame came to rest on Rev. Shigeno's shoulders. There were those who supported the minister and believed him to be innocent of all charges; however, Rev. Kato had mustered his supporters as well.

The rumours about Rev. Shigeno's personal behaviour and financial administration of the church became so rampant and the conflict so vicious between the two factions that a conference, *Shinto Taikai*, was called to deal with the status of the reverend. In October 1920, Matsunoshin Abe as chair called the conference to order. The Steveston delegate, Mr. N. Yasuno, called for a vote of confidence for Rev. Shigeno. The group in Steveston held the minister in high regard and supported him. A long and heated debate ensued. Hanyemon Hayashi and Otokichi Shiomi of the Vancouver Buddhist Church opposed the vote; they wanted Rev. Shigeno out. It is unknown where the newly established Fairview Buddhist Temple stood on the issue. What is clear is that the conference ended in acrimony.

The Buddhist Church in Canada was thus divided into two distinct groups.

Later that month the group that opposed the vote of confidence established a church at 326 Jackson St. It actually was the large living room of Saburo Okabe in Little Tokyo. The splinter church called itself the Canada Bukkyo Kai. The Nishi Hongwanji recognized this group and sent Rev. Takunen Nishimoto to begin missionary work with the members.

On February 11, 1921, a new constitution was approved and accepted at the Canada Bukkyo Kai's general meeting. This official Declaration of the Vancouver Buddhist temple was registered under provincial regulations. The three Vancouver Japanese community papers carried the following story:

> Under B.C. legislated proclamation, the Buddhist Churches of Canada [Canada Bukkyo Kai], dated Feb. 12, 1921, is the officially government recognized Jodo Shinshu Buddhist Church. The Executive Board is comprised of President, Genroku Nakamura; Vice-President, Koroku Sato; Secretary, Ritsu Ide; Treasurer, Toru Kunihisa; and auditors, Waichi Satta, Masataro Ebisuzaki, Matsujiro Tsuji.[7]

The board of directors having received the provincial mandate to carry on as the Buddhist Church in British Columbia immediately seized control of the business and administration of the church. The board then declared Rev. Shigeno officially suspended from the ministry. The Hongwanji agreed, cut all ties with Rev. Shigeno and installed Rev. Nishimoto as the head minister of the Canada Bukkyo Kai. Rev. Kato finally left for Japan in 1925 probably satisfied at having escaped blame.

Despite the conflict, Rev. Shigeno continued to operate the Franklin Street Church. The executive consisted of Co-chairmen and Vice-Presidents, Matsunoshin Abe and Ichitaro Suzuki; Secretary, Tatsuki Nakamura; and Treasurer, Junzo Ejima. Other board members were Mohei Sato, Ichitaro Hamazaki, Chugoro Wakabayashi, Mataichi Okimura, Gohei Miyauchi and Tatsuzo Hato.

A Familiar Mediator

The situation proved an embarrassment to the church and

confusion amongst the followers. In February 1922 the Nishi Hongwanji sent Rev. Senju Sasaki, Canada's first minister, to bring the two sides together to mend the split.

Rev. Sasaki arrived with his wife and 17 year old daughter, Fumiye. The reverend wanted his daughter to experience Western civilization in the true spirit of the Meiji Restoration. While in Vancouver, they stayed at the Patricia Hotel on East Hastings.

A young woman came to their door shortly after their arrival. She had been a prostitute, but now was married and had a family. She wished to repay the reverend and his wife's kindness toward her in the past. Evidently, their compassion had saved her from a life of destitution. She offered to look after Fumiye.

Rev. Sasaki presided over extensive and intense negotiations. In the midst of all the activity, the president of the Canada Bukkyo Kai, Genroku Nakamura, died. It was a great loss. Nakamura might have been instrumental in bringing the two sides together since he reputedly possessed a talent for negotiation. Although his successors Gentaro Nakagawa and Kannosuke Kaminishi often proved to be skilful in reaching compromise, they made little headway at this negotiation table.

As a result, Rev. Sasaki could not resolve the differences between the factions. After two months of fruitless negotiation, the Hongwanji assigned the reverend to the Buddhist Churches of America headquarters to manage the affairs of the Bishop. He left for San Francisco with the dispute unresolved.

Canada Bukkyo Kai

While negotiations were taking place, Rev. Nishimoto conducted his business with gusto. He recognized the fact that the Japanese immigrants came as permanent settlers. He organized a Sunday school in 1921. Families were at first reticent since they had never heard of such a thing and it smacked of Christian propagation. However, it soon became very popular and flourished. This first school was the foundation for the Sunday Schools of the later established umbrella organization Buddhist Churches of Canada.

He next decided to organize a Buddhist Young Men's Association. He called on young members not only in the

Vancouver area but in the surrounding vicinity, even as far away as Vancouver Island. With all the activity, the Hongwanji dispatched Rev. Gencho Shibahara as a travelling lecturer to help Rev. Nishimoto. Rev. Doko Minamoto arrived in May 1924 as assistant to the resident minister.

Initially, Rev. Nishimoto convinced twenty young Buddhists to assist as Sunday School teachers and administrators of church affairs. In later years, the Buddhist Young Men's Association grew to a membership of over 800 in the Vancouver area.

World events again shaped the concerns of the congregation. On September 1, 1923, the great earthquake of Tokyo erupted and killed 90,000 people while injuring 100,000 others. Altogether 380,000 homes were destroyed. The Bukkyo Fujinkai spearheaded a massive relief operation and managed to send a significant amount of much needed clothing and food to the thousands of homeless in Tokyo.

Reconciliation

Chapter 6

Reconciliation

The Nishi Hongwanji must have felt it had a vested interest in the Buddhist foothold in Canada, since Rev. Chiyen Matsubara, head of the Hongwanji Document Promotion Department, arrived in November 1923 to mediate the differences of the divided church. Unfortunately, he could not find a way to bring the factions together and soon left Vancouver for San Francisco.

Not until a year later did negotiations open again for a resolution of the problem. In September 1924 former head minister of the Sacramento Buddhist Church Rev. Keitatsu Kudo and Rev. Yuhaku Shimizu of the Seattle Buddhist Church came to Vancouver at the request of the North America Buddhist Federation. With the help of Consul Gomei and Momotaro Honda, an ardent Buddhist, the team made overtures to the two factions to compromise.

On September 19, the negotiators met with the Canada Bukkyo Kai officials (Gentaro Nakagawa, Ritsu Ide, Kannosuke Kaminishi and Shigeo Furukawa) at the residence of the Consul. The following evening, the team met with the executives of the Canada Buddhist Church (The Heaps Church). In attendance were Eikichi Kagetsu, Isamu Tanida, Tatsuki Nakamura and Ichitaro Suzuki. After much heated discussion, both sides agreed to discuss amalgamation.

Two days later, elected representatives from both churches met for a frank outspoken meeting about their differences. A series of five resolutions came about that signalled an air of co-operation had been established.

1. Since this amalgamation is based on the spirit of Buddhism, with the main objective being the prosperity and well being of all Buddhist followers, we, the representatives, will make the utmost effort to bring this about.
2. With regard to the ministers, decisions will be left entirely to the discretion of the Head Temple.
3. Debt or liabilities will be dealt with as soon as possible.
4. The church when amalgamated will be given a new name.
5. The structure of the church will be determined after the amalgamation. However, the present members of the Maintenance Boards of both churches will remain the same following amalgamation.

Some haggling over terms took place, but after two weeks of separate discussions, the two churches gathered at the Alexander Street Japanese Language School on December 22, 1924, to ratify the final agreement.

Rev. Kudo and Consul Gomei started the meeting with rousing speeches of hope and expectancy. Then chairman Eikichi Kagetsu and Matsunoshin Abe presented the following resolution for adoption:

1. The issue regarding the ministers will be left in the care of the Head Temple (in Kyoto).
2. With the amalgamation of the Hongwanji Buddhist Church and the Canada Buddhist Church, the two churches will be united as one under the name: Hompa Canada Buddhist Church.
3. The Canada Bukkyokaido[1] will be renamed the Canada Bukkyokaikan.[2]
4. Until a new minister is appointed, as directed by the Hongwanji in Japan, Rev. Keitatsu Kudo will stay on as head minister.

Twenty-two clauses regulating the church were discussed and passed that evening. Elections followed with the resulting executive: President, Eikichi Kagetsu; Vice-Presidents, Matsunoshin Abe and Gentaro Nakagawa; Secretary, Ritsu Ide; and Treasurer, Momotaro Honda.

Further discussions took place concerning the status of Rev. Shigeno. In 1921 the reverend was suspended by the Hongwanji from all duties related to his ministry. He defiantly carried on at the Franklin Street Church. However, after the 1924 amalgamation, he could not continue as minister. The congregation therefore upheld the decision and asked him to leave. Junichi Shigeno, relieved of his duties and in disgrace, announced his departure for Japan.

With records scarce, testimonies lost and memories dim, it is difficult to confirm or deny the allegations against Rev. Shigeno. It is also impossible to find evidence of Rev. Kato's alleged vindictive character. Nakayama's account certainly portrayed Rev. Shigeno in a favourable light; on the other hand, Rev. Ikuta's history makes no mention of Rev. Kato's diversion from his Buddhist principles.

Even if the behaviour of the two ministers was as bad as rumoured, to believe that the proclivities of one minister and the machinations of another solely divided the church for four years is to over-estimate their influence.

Many today believe Rev. Shigeno was the scapegoat for other scandals hitherto unknown to the public: power struggles or financial improprieties that involved those whose reputation were above reproach. All that remains is mere speculation.

It is a fact however that Rev. Shigeno did not return to Japan. Instead he went to Toronto. He never married although one *nisei* recalls that in a confectionery store in the Kitsilano district of Vancouver there was employed a single mother with two children who were said to be Shigeno's. This too may be the result of gossip surrounding the mother and two children Rev. Shigeno took into his care so many years before.

Rev. Junichi Shigeno died in Toronto rumoured to have left behind a massive collection of rare books. The date of his death and the place of his burial are unknown.

The Hompa Canada Bukkyokai

The February 1925 editions of the three Japanese community newspapers reported that the two Buddhist churches were merged into one, morally, spiritually as well as legally. Moreover, the old Hongwanji Bukkyokaido was henceforth to be known as the Canada Bukkyokai Hall. Funerals and services were to be conducted only at the Hompa Canada Bukkyokai and various meetings were to be held at either the church or the hall.

The Canada Buddhist Young Men's Association was newly established with the members of the former Hongwanji Bukkyokai forming the nucleus of the organization. The executive consisted of Yutaka Yasunaka, President; Gensaburo Nakamura and Seiji Mori, Secretaries; Ichiro Nakatsuka, Treasurer; and Tasaburo Chaki and Heizo Kitagawa, Auditors.

Rev. Nishimoto and Rev. Minamoto were relieved of their duties and Rev. Kudo was ordered by the Mother Temple to act as head minister until a new one could be found. In the meantime, the Hongwanji sent two ministers, Rev. Kanji Goto and Rev. Shujo Okabe, as well as Rev. Senju Sasaki to Vancouver to give lectures in appreciation of the relief effort made by the Buddhists in Canada following the 1923 great earthquake in Tokyo.

The Tragedy of the Izumo

In February 1925 the training ship Izumo docked in Vancouver Harbour for an extended stay. On the 7th the executive crew was invited to a welcome party by the city of Vancouver. All went well until late at night when the craft carrying the sailors back to the ship became entangled in the cables that linked a barge and an anchored ship. The transport boat sank instantly, tragically drowning all on board. Eleven crew members, including First Class Warrant Officer Shokichi Nakano, died.

At first only nine bodies were recovered. Fishermen from Steveston volunteered to dredge Vancouver Harbour for the missing victims. Nothing was found until one of the men suggested they might be under the ship that caused the mishap. Once the ship was moved, the fishermen found the final two.

The Church was asked to conduct an appropriate ceremony the next morning. On the Izumo's stern, a platform was built to display eleven mortuary tablets side by side. At 9 a.m. Consul Gomei and representatives of thirty-three Japanese Canadian organizations gathered.

A light rain began to fall. The ship's flags flew at half mast. Remarkably, all the flags on the rooftops of Vancouver were respectfully lowered to half staff as well.

A melancholy air settled over the ceremony as Reverends Kudo, Nishimoto and Minamoto recited a *sutra*. Captain Shigeoka of the Izumo then stood up and addressed the mourners and the spirits of the departed:

> In retrospect, eight months have elapsed since this warship was assigned to serve as a training vessel, and as such we have cruised in and out of different places, have fought with wind and waves, have endured cold and heat, have gone through many hardships and lately have accomplished an important mission. Thus, we were on the verge of sharing in the joys of our success, when unexpectedly under foreign skies we have been forced to go our separate ways. Our sorrow is almost intolerable. Our country, Japan, is presently in the midst of complexity in both domestic and foreign affairs and was depending greatly on its brave and loyal men, when suddenly this had to happen. Oh how sad it is. In human life, all are destined to die. These men were brave men dedicated to their country, loyal and patriotic, and faithful to their duties. They lived a life of devotion and died in the life of devotion. Such is the duty of military men. Although this ceremony is conducted in a foreign land, the 800 comrades here in attendance do reverently and single-heartedly express their condolences to you. It is our hope that the spirits now residing above descend softly and accept this message of condolence.

The "important mission" the Captain cites is unknown, but the "complexity in both domestic and foreign affairs" in Japan must have been a reference to the ascendancy of the military. Japan was arming itself and beginning to capitalize on the weaknesses of its neighbours like Korea and China. Soon the clashes between the Japanese army and Chiang Kai-shek were exaggerated in the Japanese press in order to sway public opinion toward imperialism in the guise of intervention. In 1928 the Japanese accused Chiang Kai-shek of slaughtering 300 Japanese at Shantung when in reality only thirteen were killed for suspected opium smuggling. As a result, troops were sent and thousands of Chinese residents were injured and killed.[3]

The ceremony continued with incense offered by the officers, men and community and church representatives. At 11 a.m. the funeral entourage left the Izumo led by a torpedo boat and followed by the coffin boat with two men guarding each coffin. Captain Shigeoka and a group of officers travelled in another boat at the rear. Every vessel was decorated with floral wreaths offered in tribute by Admiral Momotake, Consul Gomei, the Kenjinkai and several other organizations.

The coffins were transferred to a hearse at the dock and taken to the Thompson Funeral Home on Homer Avenue for inspection and cremation.

On the 15th of February a memorial service in honour of the lost sailors took place at the church. Nearly 400 people representing various organizations within the community and sympathetic mourners attended. President Eikichi Kagetsu gave the opening address before asking Reverends Kudo, Nishimoto and Minamoto to render the *sutra*. Consul Gomei and representatives of various organizations expressed words of condolence before offering incense. Rev. Kudo presented the memorial service message and Shonoshin Abe delivered the final speech thanking all in attendance.

A wire was sent to the training ship docked in the harbour describing the memorial service. Money raised by a collection was given in Capt. Shigeoka's care for the members of the bereaved families in Japan.

On Feb. 25, Rev. Doko Minamoto and Rev. Takunen Nishimoto and their families left for Japan. In July Rev. Sonjin Takayama came to serve the congregation, but soon developed acute pneumonia. He returned to Japan after a month's stay only to die of complications soon thereafter.

Renshi Sonyu Ohtani's Visit

On October 8, 1925, Rev. Keitatsu Kudo, his work done, returned to Japan eight months after the amalgamation of the churches. Just days before his departure, Rev. Yoshihiro Tokuno arrived as his replacement.

What followed was a series of visiting ministers culminating a year later with a visit by Rev. Shun-un Hanada, Head Minister of the Northern U.S.A. and Rev. Keimo Moriki from the Hongwanji. Both were cordially welcomed and invited to dine at the Yoshino Restaurant in the Little Tokyo area of Vancouver.

During the days that followed, they spoke at the Hompa, Fairview and Second Avenue Buddhist Churches. Their purpose was to announce and make arrangements for the forthcoming trip to North America of the Renshi Sonyu Ohtani of the Nishi Hongwanji.

The Hompa Buddhist Church then began making preparations. An ad hoc committee sought an appropriate hotel for the Renshi to stay in while in Vancouver. Word came from the Hongwanji that the Renshi preferred a Japanese-run hotel for reasons of language and food. Since none existed, the committee decided to renovate part of the church to accommodate their honoured guest. The members of the church then launched a fund raising drive. Kiyomatsu Kobayashi, an *issei* of Raymond, Alberta, recalled the difficulty he encountered in the Vancouver community when he lived there:

> At one home where I stopped to ask for a donation, the person asked, "Is this person named Sonyu a human? If he is a human then I am a human too; therefore, are we not both the same? I will not put forth such expense money." And he did not donate any money toward this cause.
>
> Then I went to a grocery store. The parents were not in, only a daughter was there. At first, the girl had difficulty in replying because she was embarrassed but after awhile she put out one dollar as a donation and said, "Because my parents are not at home, I do not know how much is enough - this is strictly my own feeling" as she made her contribution. I felt very grateful at that time.
>
> At the next house, the party gave me 25 cents, saying, "I am not that interested, but because you have taken the trouble to come I shall give you something."
>
> Some time later, after the service had been performed by the Most Reverend Ohtani, the receipts for donations were sent out from Hongwanji, even for an amount as small as 25 cents. It was said that the person who had donated 25 cents was ashamed of his part.[4]

On October 20, 1926, the Renshi arrived on the ship Gohshugo in Vancouver Harbour. The announced intentions for the visit were as follows:

> Originally, the reason for sending Rev. Koyu Uchida (head of the Buddhist Churches of North America) and Rev. Senju Sasaki was to establish a fellowship or *kyodan* during the tour for spreading the Buddhist religion in America and to encourage *issei* to grasp a deeper knowledge of Buddhism. However, there was also an urgency of acquainting the *nisei* with a westernized version of Buddhism in a thorough manner, dispelling whatever fears they harboured in the way of sentiments and beliefs. In order to achieve this goal, it was felt that the Right Reverend Sonyu should come to America and see first hand the situation as it exists and then formulate positive policies towards improving the environment.

Renshi Sonyu Ohtani gave several sermons and conducted a number of confirmation rights before leaving on October 23.

However vague the results of the visit, there was a clear concern for the *nisei* in the Buddhist community. Thus the 1930s saw the rise of the Bussei, the next generation of Japanese Canadian Buddhists.

The 1930s: Growth and Prosperity

Chapter 7

Bukkyo Tozen

The 1930s: Growth and Prosperity

Despite the 1929 stockmarket crash, the resulting Great Depression and the escalating threat of war, the 1930s were a relatively prosperous time for the Japanese Canadian community. No longer content to be itinerant workers or migrant labourers, *issei* began to purchase farms, fishing boats and small businesses.

This is not to say all Japanese Canadians were so enterprising or even successful. In the New Westminster area, for example, nearly 400 *nikkei* workers at the Canadian Western Lumber Company lost their jobs because of the depression. B.C. politicians as well continued to rail against the Japanese which caused many big operations to weed out their Japanese workers.

As a result fishermen and lumbermen unions, farming co-operatives and business associations formed in order to protect their *nikkei* constituency from the prevailing racism. Still the British Columbia Legislature passed laws in the mid 1920s limiting the number of fishing licences issued to the Japanese. Furthermore, The Camp and Mill Workers Union was never able to gain for their Japanese members equal pay for equal work. Some *nikkei* therefore saw the wisdom of going into business for themselves. A few started lumber camps of their own. By the 1930s, fourteen were operating, collectively producing $1,185,000 worth of timber each year.[1]

With several avenues to financial independence cut off, many *issei* turned to farming mostly in the Fraser and Okanagan Valleys. Through months of back breaking work, the new owners cleared the land exposing some of the richest soil in B.C. Their stubborn will to succeed soon created vast tracts of land that produced bountiful crops.

Farming was a practical and attractive enterprise for good reason: the market for produce was booming with high prices during the '30s, the proficient use of English was not required, and there was little opposition from white farmers at the beginning. By 1927 the Japanese owned 9,238 acres specifically for farming.[2]

Both photographs, TBC archives

Left: New Westminster Buddhist Church, 1932 - 1942.
Above: Fairview Buddhist Church, 1918 - 1942.

The Buddhist Church

The Buddhist Church also prospered during the 1930s. Before the organizational dispute of the 1920s, three churches existed: the Hompa Canada Bukkyokai, established in 1905; the West 2nd Avenue Bukkyokai,[3] 1916; and the Fairview Bukkyokai, 1918.

Following the resolution and owing to the prosperity of the community, the number of *bukkyokai* flourished:

Marpole............................1928
Steveston..........................1928
Royston............................1930
Raymond (Alberta).........1930
New Westminster............1932
Maple Ridge....................1933
Okanagan (Kelowna).....1933
Chemainus......................1933

None of these churches except the Hompa Canada Bukkyokai had its own minister. Instead the Vancouver temple ministers were responsible for tending to the needs of the parishioners for all the churches. This was particularly difficult for the

Raymond Bukkyokai, the only church established outside British Columbia.

After Rev. Nishimoto, there came a rapid succession of ministers from Japan: Rev. Doko Minamoto, 1924; Rev. Keitatsu Kudo, 1925; Rev. Sonjin Takayama, 1925; Rev. Yoshihiro Tokuno, 1925; Rev. Gijin Taga, 1925; Rev. Shozen Naito, 1927; Rev. Kakusai Tada,[4] 1929; Rev. Seisho Ishiguro, 1930; Rev. Zesei Kawasaki, 1934; Rev. Zenyu Aoki, 1936; Rev. Eon Mitsubayashi, 1937; and Rev. Renshin Tachibana, 1938.

There are a few possible explanations for the short tenures in Canada. The Canadian government imposed a strict limitation on Buddhist ministers. They were allowed into Canada through a special work visa which was valid for only five years. The visas were also subject to immediate revocation at the whim of the government. Moreover, the extensive travel and work caused a high burn-out rate. *Nisei* speculate today that the ministers of the time found little in common with the farmers and fishermen of their congregations since the ministers were highly educated and were used to an intellectual class of people. Quite often they were scorned and gossiped about for their superior use of Japanese and lofty concerns. As a result, a few ministers were seen wandering the streets drunk. Many *nisei* in fact recall the sight of these intoxicated men frightening them as children which made going to Sunday school and language school an ordeal.

JCCC archives

Buddhist funeral. Reverends Tada and Ishiguro presiding. Heaps Buddhist Church, May 1932.

By 1937 several of the branches became independent of the Vancouver church and lobbied for their own ministers. Most received their wish in rapid succession.

Steveston..................... Rev. Shojo Mohri and
Rev Katatsu
Royston........................ Rev. Kogo Osuga and
Rev. Sokan Asaka
Raymond...................... Rev. Yutetsu Kawamura and
Rev. Shinjo Nagatomi
New Westminster........ Rev. Ryuzan Hayashi and
Rev. Shinjo Ikuta
Maple Ridge................ Rev. Keikyo Abe
Fairview........................ Rev. Kakusai Tada and
Rev. Ryuchi Hirahara

The Status of the President

An interesting sidelight of the church organization was the position of the president. The office was highly regarded and thus highly coveted. So much so that it was considered the height of society to travel in the same circle as the President of the Church. The status was parallel to the respect accorded the mayor of any Japanese village, town or city during the Meiji Era.

To become and remain president, however, the candidate needed to be wealthy. He had to be very generous especially during election time. After being elected, a president was expected to pay for food and drinks at meetings and key gatherings. As a result, not too many could afford the position and the general impression of Buddhists as drinkers was fostered.

One prominent *issei* who rose to the presidency for several terms was Eikichi Kagetsu. This enterprising man, who was a hero of the Russo-Japanese War, managed to raise $120,000 to start the Deep Bay Logging Company. He purchased 3000 acres of Douglas fir at Fanny Bay on Vancouver Island.

> An ambitious undertaking, a settlement was created to house the workers and their families, with a messhall for the bachelors, a meeting and recreation place, and later, a language school with a paid teacher. To haul logs from the woods to water, a railroad was constructed and a locomotive and flat cars purchased.[5]

Kagetsu as well devoted himself to the betterment of the *nikkei* community. Besides serving as President of the Hompa

Buddhist Church for several terms, he was the President of the Canadian Japanese Association. He was instrumental in forming the Saisei Club (Social Welfare Club) with a grant from Japan in 1936. For such devotion, he received the Certificate of Commendation from the Japan Industrial Association in 1929.

The Formation of the Buddhist Churches of Canada

The Buddhist churches in Canada were originally under the auspices and control of the Buddhist Churches of America (BCA). During November 1930, members from the Hompa, Fairview, West 2nd Avenue, Steveston, Marpole and New Westminster Bukkyokai met to discuss the establishment of a Canadian Buddhist Church headquarters.

The first proposal was put forth by Shintaro Toda of the New Westminster Church but it was tabled for future discussion. On February 21, 1931, the loose association of churches engaged in extensive discussion. In the end, they decided that they wanted the "establishment of the Canada Buddhist Headquarters Kaikyo Hombu and will further discuss the possibility at a meeting when the BCA Socho, Bishop Kenju Masuyama, visits Canada sometime in 1931."

The application was expedited the following year with the help of Bishop Masuyama. He personally presented the request to Chief Executive Rev. Sonyu Ohtani of the Nishi Hongwanji.

The contents of the request were written by a thirteen member establishment committee:

> In October 1905, interested Buddhist followers formed a church. They asked the Canadian government for approval. Leaving the country of their birth over 5000 miles behind, many now living in this new country remembered the Teachings of the Buddha. They gathered to live their lives as Buddhists. There was a need for the community to gather and listen to Amida's Vow and receive His Compassion. As time went on, the building became too small to accommodate the followers; therefore, we built a new hall.
>
> After 28 years of various problems and hardships, we have come to live in harmony by listening to the *Dharma*. Looking back, we see many prosperous fellow Buddhists even after two wars - Japan against China,

> Japan against Russia. Immigration was the natural course to take in order to develop the future. Many families decided to settle in the New Land by becoming farmers and investing in business enterprises forming a solid foundation. The second generation receiving education in this country will become good Canadian citizens.
>
> Naturally, the followers of Buddha's Teachings volunteered to invest their fortunes to build churches in various localities. They invited ministers to preach the *Dharma* and to educate their children as Buddhists. As independent churches, Royston, New Westminster, Raymond and Steveston are waiting for their own ministers. There are two other locations in Vancouver and four outside districts in the planning stages for a church.
>
> We believe these conditions indicate prosperity for Buddhists in Canada. Our Hompa Buddhist Church proposes to establish a headquarters for all the churches so that Amida's Teachings can be spread far and wide and to contribute to the culture of the community. This is what the members wish. We hope you will agree to our request.
>
> Kannosuke Kaminishi
> President
> Hompa Buddhist Church of Canada

On June 20, 1933, permission came from Kyoto to establish the Buddhist Churches of Canada (BCC) headquarters, named the Canadian Kaikyo Kantoku Ku. Almost immediately an office was set up with a room for a supervisor and a recording secretary to ease the transition. Bishop Masuyama met with local ministers and delegates to iron out the details for the establishment of the organization. The functions of the supervisory office were to oversee all ministry affairs including obtaining ministers for the various temples, to co-ordinate educational materials, to train lay leaders, to establish a foundation to raise money for the churches, and to train teachers for Sunday School.

The following temples came under the BCC's jurisdiction: Hompa Canada, Fairview, West 2nd Avenue (Vancouver), Steveston, New Westminster, Royston, Maple Ridge, Raymond (Alberta), Marpole, Chemainus and Kelowna.

The Ascension Celebration

In the early part of 1933, President Kaminishi died and Eikichi Kagetsu took over as his successor. Kagetsu's first task was to prepare the church and its organizations for the Ascension Celebration. Kosho Ohtani was about to become the new *Gomonshu* (Lord Abbot) for the Nishi Hongwanji.

Over 1000 people crowded into the Vancouver temple to attend the service on April 30. A *chigo*[6] procession consisting of the children (catamites), Reverends Ishiguro, Tada, and Hayashi and Pres. Kagetsu moved from the Cordova Street Church to Dunlevy Street. There they boarded cars and drove to the Franklin Street Buddhist Church (Heaps). Before entering the auditorium, they were photographed. As the procession moved inside, musicians led by Kihei Otsuji played to welcome them. Here the *chigo* ended.

During the ensuing service, Ritsu Ide acted as emcee. Pres. Kagetsu offered a congratulatory message and then presented to Tadaichi Nagao, Jinshiro Nakayama and Mohei Sato Certificates of Appreciation for their work in preparing for the ceremony. The festive day closed with a *Dharma* talk and refreshments in the basement.

Young Buddhists Federation: Bussei Renmei

Rev. Nishimoto had founded the Sunday School and Bussei organizations in 1920. A decade later, the adolescent and young adult *nisei* began to organize into a formidable group. In January 1928 the Hompa, Fairview and West 2nd Avenue Bukkyokai joined together to create the Bussei Renmei or Young Buddhists Federation. Other member groups that joined were the New Westminster Young Buddhists Association (YBA), Steveston YBA, Marpole YBA and Maple Ridge YBA. In fact, as each church established its own youth group, that group joined the federation. The size of the membership swelled to over 800 at its peak in 1941.

The following comprised the first executive:

Advisor/Councillor....... Bishop Kenju Masuyama (USA)
Executive Secretary...... Zesei Kawasaki (Hompa)
Honorary Director........ Sumiye Watanabe (Hompa)
Board Chairman........... Kikuzo Morino (Hompa)
Vice-Chairman.............. Masao Edamura (Hompa)

Director	Yoshio Hayami (Hompa)
Treasurer	Yasuzo Kojima (Kitsilano)
Auditors	Shunji Fukunaga (Hompa)
	Yonejiro Tatebe (Fairview)
	Kiichi Yamamoto (Fairview)

Founding members were young *issei*. *Nisei* entering later as members, especially as Directors, were encouraged to learn Japanese in order to converse with senior members. However, as more and more *nisei* members joined, the Board of Directors soon established the office of English Recording Secretary.

Although the function of the association was basically social, the Bussei also delved into religious and societal concerns. It helped to organize other YBAs in new districts and co-ordinated all the groups to study and respond to social issues: dances took place, outings were planned, lectures scheduled, picnics held, baseball games arranged between churches and outside organizations (a Bussei league was formed in April 1933), and conferences staged. Their newsletter, **Kogen**, linked the federation with the American Young Buddhist League to co-ordinate English Buddhist textbooks.

In the English section of the **Tairiku Nippo** of the late 1930s and early '40s, a variety of announcements for activities and opinion pieces appeared. A dance at the Peter Pan Ballroom of the Ambassador Club took place during the winter of 1939. A popular column of the day was "Women Speak for the Men" by Mary Nisei; basically, it was an advice column on grooming and deportment. In "From Day to Day," another popular feature of the paper, *nisei* girls expressed their "opinions of the boys".[7] Again, it offered advice about social interaction between the sexes. The raging controversy of the day, discussed in the July 15, 1941, article titled "Nisei Dancing Habits Aired", seemed to centre on *issei* objections to *nisei* dances. The *issei* parents didn't like their children "dancing so close together". They further complained that the get-togethers should start at eight o'clock instead of nine so that the event could end "at a decent hour". The *nisei* reacted with an article titled "Issei Should Understand Nisei Better."[8] A conference was also planned for the 1941 Thanksgiving weekend in Victoria to discuss the "problems *nisei* face in the world". Obviously those problems included and perhaps centred on *issei* objections. Unfortunately, coverage of the conference did not appear in subsequent issues of the community paper.

Sunday School and Language School students were exclusively *nisei* and so the Bussei Renmei responded to their needs. In April 1927 the Hompa Church started a kindergarten with 60 children and two teachers, Mrs. Kikuchi and Mrs. Fielding. In February 1934 the Hompa Church with the support of the Young Buddhists Federation and the financial aid of Eikichi Kagetsu established the Canada Hompa Chu-Jogakko (Middle School) and formed an accompanying Japanese Language School on April 11.

The administration included:

Principal.................................... Eikichi Kagetsu
Head Instructor.......................... Rev. Seisho Ishiguro
Director....................................... Rev. Zesei Kawasaki
Treasurer..................................... Koichi Takahashi

Instructors:
Moral Philosophy...................... Rev. Seisho Ishiguro
Japanese Language.................... Rev. Kawasaki
Japanese History........................ Bogetsu Suzuki
Japanese Calligraphy................. Ryukichi Miyake
Japanese Composition............... Shigeo Furukawa
Rokuro Nagazawa
Flower Arrangement.................. Kazo Nose
Tea Ceremony Etiquette.............Mrs. Danjo

Thirty students attended the opening ceremony. Henceforth, classes were six days a week, two hours every evening, Sundays excluded. By May of 1934, 65 students had enrolled with eight teachers.

Rev. Zesei Kawasaki who headed the Fairview Showa Gakuen (Japanese Language School) eventually proposed that the Federation of Japanese School Teachers be culled from the ranks of the Young Buddhists Federation. In fact, the teachers organization became part of and solely supported by the Federation.

The first Dharma School (Sunday School) was organized by Rev. Nishimoto in April 1921. The Bussei then started a lay teachers study class in order to provide teachers for the Sunday School. From 1921 to 1929, the staff grew to 27 with a student body of 250. Three years later, the Bussei Renmei formed the Dharma School Teachers Federation because 1260 students had enrolled with 180 teachers on staff in the ten participating churches. The aims of the Federation were to upgrade teaching skills, to acquire teaching materials and to provide English textbooks.

The Bussei Renmei also took on other tasks. In early 1934, they proposed to erect a stone monument to commemorate the pioneer *nikkei* who had died. The original wood marker was put in place when Rev. Banryu Yatsubuchi visited Vancouver in 1915. By the 1930s the monument had deteriorated and thus the Bussei decided to replace it with a ten foot high granite one.

Once the resolution was accepted, the youth organization collected donations from the entire community. The inaugural ceremony was held at Memorial Park Cemetery in Vancouver on August 5, 1934. In attendance were Yasushi Ishii, Consul of Japan, and Eikichi Kagetsu, Church President.

In 1936 to celebrate Vancouver's 50th Anniversary, the Bussei staged a program featuring Japanese Canadian *odori*. Some 80 dancers took part before the Powell Grounds grandstand.

One of the principal activities designed to bring the various YBA groups together was the Oratorical Contest. *Nisei* speakers, representing groups such as the Japanese Canadian Citizens League, the alumni of the Gakuyukai (Japanese Language School) and the Christian Young People, spoke exclusively in Japanese. The audience consisted of *issei*, young and old.

The first two contests were held at the Vancouver Hompa Church but moved to Kitsilano for the third (1927), to Fairview for the fourth, and then to various other churches until 1940.

Most topics centred on the place of the Japanese Canadian in Canadian society. Many spent time outlining the discrimination the Bussei faced and suggesting how to overcome it. Following are highlights of significant speeches from these contests:

> The young *issei* emphasized the pioneer spirit of the older *isseis* and racial consciousness and to strive to build a strong Japanese community. The Canadian born *nisei* voiced the importance of having Japanese character building - a law abiding and unique background.[9]

From the Bussei Magazine **Buddha**:

> We should not be discouraged of this racial discrimination hoping that some day we will be able to gain our rights. In building a strong, conscientious, harmonious

> Buddhist family and community, we are desirous of maintaining high moral standards. Try to gain more Caucasian friends. Make them understand our plight.[10]

Marpole Young People's Society:

> Emphasize strong *nisei* organization comprising of individual *nisei* membership to study employment opportunities. Research higher education despite the present discriminatory situation.[11]

Mission City Junior Bussei - speaker Takashi Tsuji, 17 years old:

> Raised racial discrimination issue pointing to the fact that the only ones given voting rights were the World War I veterans (1915). A long time before the *niseis* can acquire the franchise. Put up a co-ordinated front to combat this issue.[12]

After his speech, the young Takashi Tsuji announced his intention of becoming a Buddhist minister. The Bussei Renmei gathering gave its utmost support and endorsement.

Through its activities and concerns, the Bussei Renmei was clearly a responsible and ambitious group of young people with the stability and growth of the church in mind. Their future as individuals and as an organization was wrapped up in the survival and growth of Buddhism in Canada. They were also acutely aware of their disadvantaged position in society. Fortunately they decided to persevere through the Buddha *Dharma* and hold the faith that in the end they would realize their rightful position with all human rights intact.

Construction of a New Buddhist Church

One of the negative ramifications of the dispute and resolution within the Buddhist Church in Vancouver was the fragmentation of the church administration. In the mid 1930s, Reverend Kawasaki and his family lived in the Heaps Buddhist Church. Services and church activities for the majority of the congregation were held at the Cordova Street house in Little Tokyo. All Buddhists agreed that a church was needed closer to the main body of the Japanese Canadian population.

When the subject of a new building for the secondary school began, talk turned to a new church that would incorporate the school. Plans called for the old Cordova Street Church to be used by the Bussei Renmei and for the minister and his family to live on the second floor. The membership then established a building committee:

Chairman	Ichitaro Suzuki
Vice-Chairman	Toichi Tsuruda
Treasurer	Koichi Takahashi
Secretary	Fukuzo Okano
Members	Eikichi Kagetsu
	Yaichi Horibe
	Ritsu Ide
	Otokichi Shiomi
	Shotaro Fukushima
	Takaji Suyama

Courtesy of S. Watanabe

Cordova Kai Kan, April 1927. Farewell for Rev. Tokuno.

A separate fund raising committee was then struck. Members included Reverends Ishiguro and Kawasaki, Chugoro Wakabayashi, Tsuruichi Oike, Jutaro Nishimura, Kumataro Kotani, Junzo Ejima, Rinhichi Kuramitsu, Kikuzo Morino, Kihei Otsuji and Kiyoji Natsuhara.

Rev. Kawasaki himself travelled to places like Victoria to canvass the Japanese community for donations. The committee concentrated on calling everyone in Vancouver. In all, they collected $10,783.

Two lots at 604 Cordova St. (near Princess Ave.) cost $1500. Construction began almost immediately under the supervision of the carpenter, Takeichi Ono, assisted by Shotaro Fukushima. President Eikichi Kagetsu guaranteed the purchase of all building materials.

Opening ceremonies occurred on November 17 and 18, 1934. On the first day following the 2:00 p.m. service, a *chigo* procession led by the elders and ministers left the old church and walked to the new hall. After entering, Rev. Ishiguro carefully enshrined the *Gohonzon*[13] in the new altar. Chanting and a dedication celebration sermon by the ministers followed. The second day saw another procession consisting of sixty children and all the ministers. It started at 1:00 p.m. and proceeded around Powell Grounds and entered the new temple to a full congregation. After the service, a reception banquet with entertainment was held in the lower hall. Almost $3800 was collected in the offertory which helped to defray the incurred debt of $4419.50 for construction.

Two years later, the Heaps Church was sold to Sanjiro Matsuzaki for a mere $200 plus the back taxes of $1400. Originally the building and land cost in excess of $20,000.

The Steveston Buddhist Church

The village of Steveston, about 30 km south of Vancouver, attracted many of the Japanese immigrant fishermen. It must have seemed like the "wild west" at the turn of the century. One *issei* described it as an "*otoko-mura* (all male village), full of hotheads".[14] Generally, the inhabitants came to Steveston to earn a lot of money quickly and return home. Religion was the farthest thing from their minds.

By the 1920s, however, the Buddhist followers began gathering in each others' homes to hold services. It was a difficult journey for the Vancouver ministers to make so lay ministers stood in their place. Portable *butsudan* (family altar) were carried to homes when ceremonies, such as funerals, required one.

The reaction to such activity was predictable. Japanese Christian ministers advised Japanese Canadians to "do as the Romans do". They preached that to promote Buddhism in Canada is to commit treason and to damage the development of the *nikkei* community.

The Steveston community as well saw Buddhism as a catalyst for more anti-Japanese feelings amongst the white population. In particular, the Japanese Fishermen's Association objected vigorously to Buddhist practices. In the early 1900s, the Association had fought many discriminatory measures. Ottawa in 1923 revoked 40% of the gillnet licences of the *nisei* and 10% each year thereafter until all *nisei* gillnetters were eliminated. Japanese fishermen were permitted to fish only in certain areas. In 1927 the federal government ceased issuing licences to the Japanese at the urging of the Fishermen's Union.

Although it was an uphill battle, the Union became, after a Supreme Court appeal to overturn the partisan legislation worked in 1928, a formidable labour force in Steveston. A Buddhist community with a church at its centre was a threat to that force. The church was seen as a perpetrator of Japanese culture and ethical code.

A graphic example of the division in the Steveston community is described in Rev. Kawasaki's memoirs. In 1928, the Hompa Bussei sponsored one of its well known oratorical contests. The youth organizations from the Fairview, Kitsilano and Hompa churches sent speaker representatives to Steveston. The as yet ordained Zesei Kawasaki presided.

> The Bussei Renmei gathered February 28 in the evening at a hall in Steveston (maybe it was a room used for Japanese language classes) and I still recall noticing the curtains being blown by the wind coming through the partly open windows. In about one-half an hour it could be seen that the numbers of "opponents" who crowded outside the open windows to try and hear what the speakers were saying could be seen in the light of dusk (the numbers outside were greater than those inside). Somehow - it struck me at the time like a Western movie (i.e. the crowding of people outside) with the feeling of hostility emanating from the crowd outside.
>
> The two smaller rooms were converted to one large room by removing the partition in between and a small stage was constructed with drapes as a backdrop. On this backdrop were displayed the names of the ten speakers and the titles of their respective

speeches, with the chairman's name written first.

The speakers that evening were Kikuzo Morino, Yoshio Okano (Hompa Buddhist Church); Genichiro Yada, Bunjiro Tanaka (Fairview); Masukichi Ebata, Yasuzo Kojima (Kitsilano); and Zesei Kawasaki.

...the ones outside the windows were shouting catcalls at the speakers; and the young ones were using extremely crude language in their shouting.

Each speaker brought to the gathering the best subject he could find and the crowd applauded them enthusiastically. As each new speaker took to the stage, the voices from the outside became more fierce!

Just before I was to go up to the stage as the last speaker, one of the Steveston members who gave the appearance of a very strong *issei* character said to me, "Because you are the one who will make the concluding remarks for this occasion, please speak freely on whatever topic you choose, without any hesitation. I shall be here with my shotgun and watching everything, so you do not have to worry." With these words, this gentleman shoved his rifle forward to show it to me. "The outsiders are making a lot of noise but if they even raise a hand, I'll shoot them dead!" he said strongly. I wondered how things would turn out.

I spoke for about thirty minutes, and when I left the stage, an *issei* gentleman and one other (Tokumatsu Atagi) said, "Because the situation looks a bit scary, we don't think we will be able to even have dinner together tonight. Because we don't want anything to happen to you while you are here, we shall take you out the back way and put you in a truck and take you to the streetcar stop so that you may return to Vancouver ahead of the other speakers from Vancouver."

In this manner, we sped to the station and I caught the train back to Vancouver. This kind of dangerous experience still remains as one of my memories after over sixty years have gone by.[15]

The speech contest experience, however, must have been a great source of inspiration for the Steveston *nisei* Buddhists.

One month later, in March, everyone gathered at the rear of the second floor of Tokumatsu Atagi's store. A card bearing the Buddha's name was placed on a card table. Zesei Kawasaki led the congregation in the chanting of the Junirai *sutra*. According to Atagi, this was the first *nisei* Buddhist service in Steveston. The six or seven women in attendance requested Kawasaki's presence every two months in order to conduct a service.

In November there were so many at the Ho-onko service that people had to stand amongst the goods of Atagi's store.

The First Steveston Buddhist Church

Discussions about the possibility of building a church in Steveston took place in 1924 with the first gatherings of Buddhists. However, the objections as manifested in the boisterous opinions and demonstrations by non-Buddhists postponed plans for four years. A Christian spokesman in an interview with historian Ken Adachi expressed the typical fears of the time.

> Almost all the Japanese immigrants who came to Steveston in the early days were Buddhists. When a large number of them...first proposed to erect a Buddhist temple in order to provide a gathering place for lonely Japanese fishermen, I objected to such a proposal for I thought that erecting a temple and spreading out this religion in this community might create unnecessary suspicion and fear on the part of the lower classes of white Canadians. For this reason, the erection of a temple was postponed until 1928 when the Japanese decided that the adoption of Buddhism should not necessarily be inharmonious to the Canadian people.
>
> S. Yoshida
> Steveston B.C.[16]

Building actually started in the spring of 1927. The property was purchased for about $8000. When completed, the church included a temple for worship, a section for youth activities on the main floor and a suite of rooms on the second for the minister. Rev. Gijin Taga of the Vancouver Hompa Church began conducting the services from the opening of the building.

TBC archives

Steveston Buddhist Church, 1928 - 1942.

Late in 1928 almost before the church was built, a women's group was formed. With 160 members, its original name was the Oyori Kai; in 1932 the group became the Fujinkai. Next, a religious school was established with eight teachers and 160 pupils. In 1932 the Young Buddhist Men's Society was formed. Known as the Bussei, they organized lectures, study groups of the *Dharma*, and athletic and cultural activities. Sixty of their membership volunteered with the local Fire Department as a Fire Brigade. They also published a monthly newsletter called the **Gyo Sho**.

The Young Women's group was formed in 1929. The Shojo Kai had 65 members and were aged 14 and up. In 1936, they became known as Bukkyo Joshi Seinen Kai.

These groups staged oratorical contests and held discussions and debates with other youth groups from Vancouver and Seattle. The topics of concern included race relations, discrimination, stress, the generation gap, hereditary and cultural traditions with their problems, and the future of the *nisei* in Canada. Of concern also was the significance of being a Buddhist in a Christian society.

In 1933 the Steveston Buddhist Church became independent of the Vancouver Hompa Buddhist Church. Rev. Shojo Mohri came to serve the more than 250 members. He returned to Japan in 1938 and was replaced by Rev. Toshio Katatsu. Rev. Katatsu stayed until the evacuation in 1942.

Royston Buddhist Church

The temples of the Lower Mainland in British Columbia served the majority of Buddhists prior to the war, but there were other temples outside their sphere of influence worth noting. The Royston Buddhist Church[17] for example was the only church on Vancouver Island. Buddhist groups congregated in other towns like Chemainus but Royston had its own building and resident minister. It served the surrounding communities of Cumberland, Courtenay, Union Bay and Comox.

Many Japanese Canadians worked on Vancouver Island in fishing, mining, logging and farming, yet they had few opportunities to attend a service to hear the words of the *Dharma*. The ministers from the Hompa Bukkyokai visited two or three times a year to conduct Obon, Gotanye or Ho-onko services. Many felt the need for a permanent congregation not only for themselves but for future generations.

On a fortuitous occasion, Kenroku Uchiyama, manager of the Royston Lumber Company, made the long arduous trip to Japan to visit his family. While he was there, he travelled to the Nishi Hongwanji in Kyoto and met with the Supervisor of Educational Affairs, Rev. Shojo Okabe.

Uchiyama described the situation in the Royston area claiming a pressing need for Buddhist guidance. He must have made an impressive case because soon thereafter the Hongwanji dispatched Rev. Kogo Osuga to Royston in June 1930.

Courtesy of Dewey Uchida

Rev. and Mrs. Osuga with pupils and board members, Royston Buddhist Church, 1930.

The Japanese Community Association, called the Royston Aiyukai consisting of about 60 Buddhist families, welcomed the minister and established the Royston Bukkyokai. Rev. Osuga wasted no time and started a Sunday School and Japanese language classes. A year later the members founded the Girl Guide Club. In 1932 Rev. Osuga presided over high school grades in the language classes.

Rev. Osuga's wife held language classes (grades one through six) every day after regular school. The reverend taught senior classes three evenings a week in Royston and three evenings in Cumberland, three miles away.

On Sundays all the children went to Dharma School. Rev. Osuga and his wife conducted these lessons as well. These classes were held in the large Community Hall in Royston. The members also observed certain services and special occasions there. For Hanamatsuri, Obon or Gotanye, for example, Buddhists gathered from the surrounding communities to listen to the minister's *Dharma* talk and to enjoy songs, dances, skits and plays put on by temple members.

Rev. Sokan Asaka and his wife replaced Rev. Osuga and his wife in 1935. They carried on the heavy schedule set in place by Rev. Osuga until the evacuation when Rev. Asaka and family left for New Denver.

Courtesy Hideo Ed Yoshida

Royston butsudan, circa 1940. The altar was sent to Raymond, Alberta, after the war.

In 1946 the remnants of the Royston Buddhist Church congregation donated their shrine to the Raymond Buddhist Church in Alberta as the consequence of an Order-in-Council in 1943 disposing all property held by the Custodian of Alien Property and an ultimatum issued by the Dept. of Labour in 1945 that all Japanese were to resettle east of the Rockies or apply for repatriation to Japan. Rev. Shinjo Ikuta arranged the transfer with Kenroku Uchiyama.

On April 21, 1946, the Raymond Buddhist Church members received the shrine in the presence of four ministers: Rev. Ikuta, Rev. Kawamura, Rev. Hirahara and Rev. Asaka. They held a Consecration Service with a ceremonial *chigo* parade afterward.

Skeena Buddhist Church

Prince Rupert stands at the mouth of the Skeena River. Before the war, fishing cannery towns dotted the river. Places like Port Essington, Haysport, Cunningham Cannery, Point Lambert, Cassiar, Carlisle, Balmoral Cannery, Port Edward and Sunnyside bustled with activity during the fishing season. Port Essington for example swelled with 700 people. During the off-season (fall and winter), its population fell to about 400.

Courtesy of Lillian Ebata

Above: Building the Skeena Buddhist Church, Spring 1934.
Below: The completed Skeena Buddhist Church.

Courtesy of Matsujiro Ohashi

During the spring thaw of 1934, a remarkable occurrence took place near the town of Port Essington. A flotilla of logs came rumbling down from the engorged Upper Skeena River. The logs washed ashore in front of Ohashi's cannery and general store. Matsujiro Ohashi took the incident as a sign. With the help of friends and relatives, he gathered the logs together and hauled them to Brown's Sawmill. The lumber was subsequently used on Ohashi's land to build the Skeena Buddhist Church.

Ohashi as a matter of course became the *hokkyoshi* for the congregation. Before the raising of the church, he had held services in his home. He also had organized regular Sunday services and Obon, Hanamatsuri and New Year's gatherings. He built coffins with materials from his store in order to conduct proper funerals arranged through a Justice of the Peace. His wife, Take Ohashi, and daughters made crepe paper flowers and provided food for the edification of the grieving families.

Another prominent member of the church, Shinkuro Kozai, formed a group known as the Hachisu-kai that oversaw the Japanese Language School in town.

Itinerant ministers from the Vancouver Buddhist Church came for a visit from time to time. Rev. Ishiguro arrived in 1934; Rev. Aoki in 1936. Matsujiro and Seichi (brother) Ohashi, Sasuke Nakagawa and Shinkuro Kozai always greeted these ministers with a boat trip to the Skeena hot springs.

World War II confined all Japanese Canadian residents in the Skeena area to Hastings Park in Vancouver. They left Port Essington on a large scow to Haysport across the river before heading by rail for an unknown fate. Ohashi made arrangements for the Buddhists to "evacuate" to Sandon, B.C. He also carried the Skeena Buddhist Church's *hotoke-sama* to the camp. After the war, he took the image of the Buddha to the Toronto Buddhist Church. Later, the *hotoke-sama* was enshrined in the Hamilton Buddhist Church.

After the war and exile subsided, Ohashi travelled home only to find that a fire had destroyed the entire town of Port Essington except for the cemetery. He sadly returned to Toronto where he and Sasuke Nakagawa erected a monument to the deceased members of the Skeena River community in Mount Pleasant Cemetery. A brother, Tom Ohashi, later arranged for a monument in Vancouver's Mountain View Cemetery.

Our sincere thanks go to our many friends and supporters, *nori no tomo*, who gave their time and effort to the building of the Skeena Buddhist Church, even though it was only for a short while. We thank all those who have gone before us to the Pure Land of Amida Buddha.

Lillian Shizue Ebata (nee Ohashi)
Toronto, 1994

The 1930s: The Spectre of War

Chapter 8

Bukkyo Tozen

The 1930s: The Spectre of War

On April 15, 1934, the Victoria Buddhist Church was inaugurated. On September 22, the Skeena Buddhist Church opened. Later that year on December 6, Renshi Shojo Ohtani arrived by train from Seattle accompanied by his aide Rev. Tetsujo Sasaki and Bishop Masuyama to conduct the 33rd Anniversary Memorial Service of Myonyo Shonin. About a year later, on October 10, 1935, the Ocean Falls Buddhist Church opened. Finally, the Whonnock Buddhist Church opened its doors, October 11, 1939.

The Buddhist Church in Canada was flourishing. At the same time, a "Christianization" of Buddhism seemed to be taking place. The church adopted terms like "Bishop", "minister", "priest", "offertory" and "church". Bazaars and concerts were held to raise money.

> The altar of the Buddhist temple with its lotus flowers, candles and icons of the Amida Buddha came to be housed in an auditorium containing pews, hymn books and organs in the Christian manner. The kindergarten was adopted...Moreover Buddhists adopted Sunday services, Sunday schools and societies paralleling those found in Christian churches. The Buddhist children even sang hymns such as "Buddha loves me, this I know; For the Sutra tells me so."[1]

The church elders probably saw the ranks of the *nisei* generation growing and decided in order to keep these intrinsically "Canadian" youth in the church to adapt to the predominant religion of the land at least at the most superficial level.

Meanwhile the *nisei* continued to become involved in the fabric of Canadian society by joining the war effort. In the late '30s and early '40s, the *nisei* began to feel Canadian.

Lily Ide sang regularly on Mondays and Saturdays at 1:15 p.m. over radio station CJOR. Tamotsu Murayama, San Francisco lecturer, traveller and war correspondent, addressed a largely *nisei* audience at the Hompa Buddhist Church about the war campaign in Manchuria. Later, attorney Clarence T. Arai came from Seattle to speak. He was the first *nisei* to pass the bar examinations in the Northwest. Various churches held picnics for the war effort. In particular, the New Westminster Buddhist Church chose White Rock as its favourite picnic spot. The **Tairiku Nippo** edition of July 5, 1941, proudly displayed the headline: *Buddhist Women Present Contribution to Soldiers.* Fujinkai members and younger *nisei* women raised money for the Red Cross Soldiers Aid Campaign and put together kits of bandages and mementos of home for the boys overseas. Such relief effort actually began in 1939.

Inspired by the patriotism, two *nisei* boys were turned down at a recruiting station for the army. One took a Native name and was accepted. He would have been fighting in Europe if not for his father's attempt to see his son at training camp. The army discovered the recruit's true identity and promptly discharged him.

On the other hand, the paradox of the church's character continued between the generations. The *issei* congregation in Vancouver observed the Abbot Kosho Ohtani's wedding with a celebration service on April 26, 1937. They also held a memorial service February 20, 1938 for the soldiers who died in Manchuria. One hundred dollars were collected and sent to the Japanese army.

The Canada Hompa Buddhist Church 35th Anniversary Service

On October 8, 1939, the Hompa Bukkyokai in Vancouver celebrated its 35th anniversary with a special service. At 1:00 p.m. precisely, the church gong rang loudly. The *chigo* parade started from the front of the Cordova Street temple and travelled west to Dunlevy Ave. It then turned north to Powell St. and east to Princess Ave. From there the children's parade proceeded back to the temple. The group, at the end, gathered together on the front steps for a commemorative photograph.

The gong pealed again as the *chigo* entered the *hondo* (temple sanctuary). Personages presiding included: Rinshichi Kuramitsu, Chairman; Rev. Aoki, Kantoku of Canada Kyodan; Bishop Matsukage (BCA); Reverends Tachibana and Mitsubayashi (Hompa); Rev. Hirahara (Fairview); Rev. Ikuta (New Westminster); Rev. Abe (Maple Ridge); Rev. Asaka (Royston); and Rev. Katatsu (Steveston).

Chanting and offering of incense by representatives then took place, followed by the history of the Hompa church related by Fukuzo Okano.

Of the fourteen original Founding Committee members of the Vancouver church, only three surviving members were present. They were given certificates of commendation by Rev. Tachibana. Numerous other members were then presented with certificates for their devotion and spirit of volunteerism.

The chair then presented congratulatory telegrams and letters from various areas in Canada, the U.S. and Japan. Bishop Matsukage gave the *Dharma* talk, and President Kagetsu expressed the thanks of the church to the Bishop for his warm and inspiring words.

Following the service, the ministers and representatives adjourned to the Maruman Restaurant for dinner. In the meantime, the congregation gathered in the social hall downstairs for food and entertainment with skits, singers and dancers. The festivities lasted until 11:00 that evening.

The Ministry

During the 1930s the ministry changed several times. Rev. Zenyu Aoki arrived from Seattle in April 1936 to take over the directorship of the Buddhist Churches of Canada and to become the head minister of the Hompa Bukkyokai. Unfortunately he had to leave his family in Seattle, the result of immigration red tape. Rev. Seisho Ishiguro returned to Japan that summer.

On October 26, 1936, Rev. Shinjo Ikuta landed in Vancouver to be later assigned to the New Westminster Buddhist Church succeeding the first minister there, Rev. Ryuzan Hayashi.

Rev. Eon Mitsubayashi then came to the Hompa Bukkyokai in early November 1937. Rev. Kawasaki left in May 1938, being transferred to the Denver Buddhist Church in the U.S.A. Rev. Renshin Tachibana came soon thereafter to take over as head minister. Director Aoki resigned his post with the BCC and left with his family from Seattle for reassignment in Hawaii. In 1938 the first *nisei* left for Ryukoku University in Japan to study to become a Buddhist minister.

Rev. Kenryu Tsuji

Takashi Tsuji, future Toronto Buddhist Church head minister and later Bishop of the Buddhist Churches of America, started life on a poor farm in 1920 in the small British Columbia town of Mission City. One of four boys, he was introduced early to Buddhism by the example set by his father, Kamejiro Tsuji.

Mission City featured no temple and no regular minister. Thus the needs of the predominately Jodo Shinshu Buddhists were not adequately met.

> When there was a funeral, it was a very sad situation because there was no temple. Families would have to go to the cemetery, open the casket and have the funeral there. Flies would be flying everywhere. The people, including my father, thought that something had to be done.[2]

Courtesy of Sumiko Fujino

Buddhist funeral, August 29, 1934. Mission City, B.C.

Kamejiro Tsuji approached the problem in a twofold manner. First, he became one of the lay ministers of the town along with Mr. Kudo and Mr. Miyagawa. The three organized and led services on a weekly basis. Moreover, Vancouver ministers on their rounds came periodically to take care of the spiritual and sacramental needs of the congregation. Second, he decided one of his sons should become a minister. The atmosphere of the household must have been conducive to such encouragement since travelling ministers stayed with the family.

> They (the ministers) would stay mostly Saturday night and Sunday. They would go to service then go back to Vancouver Sunday night. I was very impressed with their sermons and the way they brought the teaching of the Buddha to the people. I was very inspired by them. I thought I would like to follow in their footsteps so I'd keep in touch with Kawasaki Sensei.[3]

In 1938 Takashi Tsuji took the first step to become a Jodo Shinshu minister. Unfortunately there was no Institute for Buddhist Studies in North America. A ministerial candidate had to go to Japan. His father with the help of his three other sons raised the necessary money. With one hurdle conquered, Takashi Tsuji faced an even greater challenge.

> I didn't know any Japanese but I was enrolled. In those days, the Nishi Hongwanji was very sympathetic and had a very broad-minded view regarding the students who came from overseas. They knew their background: very little Japanese, maybe a little conversational Japanese. That's about it but when it came to writing and reading, that was absolute zero. I only had a grade four education so they said, "All right, we're going to put you into a class and you have to go through a procedure"...I failed my entrance exam in writing. I couldn't even read the questions because it was in regular Japanese...I was admitted and they stuck me in a class and that was it.
>
> But in two years, if you soaked in this tradition, in two years I was able to take about 75% of the notes. The first year I was just sitting there but I had one good friend, a man by the name of Sumi. He was sitting next to me, saw me and thought there was something

> wrong with this guy because he's not taking any notes. Then he discovered that I had come from overseas. He took me under his wing and said, "All right, I'll help you." He would copy the notes for me. It must have taken hours and hours... he was a great help that way. So the first year, he helped me. The second year, a bunch of other guys helped me. By the third year, I was on my own.[4]

Everything seemed to go well for the bright young foreign student until October 1941. His plan was to study six years, three years in a specialized Buddhist course of study and three in advanced Buddhist study.

About the middle of October the former Bishop of the American Churches called Rev. Tsuji into his office. What followed was a frank discussion about the impending conflict in the Pacific.

> The Bishop said, "Do you know this Pacific situation is getting really bad. Since you have Japanese and Canadian citizenship, I think you should go back to Vancouver." I said I don't want to go back because I intend to study here for six years and then I would be able to understand Buddhism better. But he said, "This is no time to be talking about something like that. I think it is worthwhile that you go back to Vancouver because at least you can be of some service to them when you go back...If you don't have funds to buy a ticket, I'll give you the money. I think there's a boat leaving Yokohama this Friday." And this was Wednesday morning.
>
> I went to the British Legation and Consul in Kobe and the guy said, "Well you're a Canadian citizen so we don't handle that. You've got to go to the Canadian Legation in Tokyo." So I went rushing back and went to Tokyo...And they said, "Well you were born in Canada, why don't you go?" I said, "Wait a minute, I think you'd better sign this because I don't want the secret police to stop me on the boat."[5]

Rev. Tsuji was issued a long document certifying that he was "seen by the Canadian Legation". He then proceeded to the docks with no time to say goodbye to the former U.S. minister with whom he had stayed during his studies or to many friends. Some passengers were told to take whatever possessions they could manage to carry. At the docks, the Maritime Police checked Rev. Tsuji's documents. They allowed him on board on the sole evidence of the signature on the certificate. Little did he know he was on the last ship out of Japan to Canada.

The trip took two weeks. During a short stop before reaching the terminal docks of Vancouver, he telegraphed ahead to tell people of his return. A large contingent of well-wishers met him at the landing. They took him to the church first to greet the congregation.

> Afterwards they took me to a Chinese restaurant to eat and then the rumour started that this minister has come back, that he must be a very brilliant minister because he finished a six year course in three years![6]

Rev. Takashi Tsuji was ordained at the Nishi Hongwanji in Kyoto, receiving his Buddhist name "Kenryu". At about the same time, the Bussei Renmei met in a convention at the Maple Ridge Bukkyokai. For the first time 375 delegates discussed in English and Japanese the situation in the Pacific. They finally resolved to send a telegram to Ottawa to reaffirm the Bussei Renmei's loyalty to Canada.

Bukkyo Tozen

War

Chapter 9

Bukkyo Tozen

Bukkyo Tozen: War

War!

Oahu Bombed by Japanese Planes

Washington, Dec. 7 - Text of a White House announcement detailing the attack on the Hawaiian Islands is:

"The Japanese attacked Pearl Harbor from the air and all naval and military activities on the island of Oahu, principal American base in the Hawaiian Islands."

Oahu was attacked at 7:55 this morning by Japanese planes. The Rising Sun, emblem of Japan, was seen on plane wing tips.

Honolulu Star - Bulletin
Sunday, December 7, 1941
1st Extra

By all accounts this act of war by the Japanese came as a complete surprise in most quarters. No one imagined such violence could have been perpetrated against Americans on American soil. President Roosevelt declared December 7th "a day that will live in infamy". It was inconceivable to citizens of Japanese ancestry in North America that they too were about to be brushed with the blame for that selfsame infamy.

The Canadian government acted quickly. In rapid succession Japanese community newspapers and language schools were closed, public gatherings were forbidden, churches could no longer hold services although funerals were allowed. A curfew came into effect to keep the "enemy alien" off the streets after sunset. Fishing vessels, automobiles, radios and cameras were confiscated, all left in the "care" of the Custodian of Alien Property.

In February 1942 an Order-In-Council from Ottawa at the insistence of the B.C. Liberals dictated that Japanese male nationals 40 years of age and under were to be relocated to areas at least 100 miles away from the Pacific coast to temporary road camps. Soon, older Japanese nationals, naturalized males and *nisei,* joined their counterparts in work camps in the interior of B.C. as well as in Ontario.

Finally, all persons of Japanese ancestry, some 21,000, were forced to move at least 100 miles away from the coast (later known as the Security Zone) to remote ghost towns and small settlements like New Denver, Kaslo, Slocan, Greenwood and Sandon, as well as to crude shacks thrown up in Bay Farm, Tashme and Lemon Creek.

The Buddhist Church

No one knew it but the regular Sunday service held on December 7, 1941, at the Canada Hompa Buddhist Church in Vancouver was to be the last. Soon thereafter public gatherings were forbidden, effectively closing down the Japanese Canadian community churches.

There did not seem to be any direct persecution of the Japanese according to religion. Japanese and white Christians, racist politicians and rabid journalists did preach that Buddhism was an obstacle to assimilation, but the government did not see Buddhists themselves as a threat to Canadian society. Instead, the religion, its leaders and its ministers were accorded the right of freedom of religion.

> The treatment of the ministers was based ostensibly and curiously on religious freedom, curious because even as government demanded the observance of religious liberty it denied the more fundamental one of due process.[1]

Akira Ichikawa of the University of Lethbridge speculates that the leniency of "religious liberty" was more an act of political expediency. To deny or forbid the Buddhists of Canada the rites and practices of their religion was to give the Japanese government the ammunition "to register complaints with the International Red Cross or Spain, which served as intermediary between the warring countries."[2] There was also the fear of reprisal against Canadians in Japan.

Nevertheless, the government and its representative organizations, the British Columbia Security Commission (BCSC) and the Royal Canadian Mounted Police (RCMP), did have their suspicions. A 1942 report issued by British Intelligence cited an article in **The New Canadian** about a meeting of the New Westminster Young Women's Buddhist Association. Apparently the meeting began with a minute of silence, an action interpreted as follows:

> This would probably be included, as is the custom in Japan at such meetings, in order that all might remember Japanese soldiers killed in action.[3]

Ichikawa further explains:

> Jodo Shinshu gatherings typically began with a moment of silence or meditation during which time the mind might be cleared to help hear the "call of the Amida Buddha", in short, a ritual to intensify the religious experience. This is not to deny that there may have been those at the meeting who remembered deceased family members or friends, some of whom very likely may have been killed serving in the Japanese military; but, typical of an intelligence mindset, the operative's singular interpretation runs counter to a more plausible explanation and exaggerates the possibility of a direct link between the meditative act and support for Japanese militarism.[4]

The intelligence report goes on to accuse Rev. Shinjo Ikuta of the New Westminster temple of praising the Axis alliance with Japan during a speech he gave at the Vancouver temple. It further recommended that Rev. Ikuta be arrested if the need arose. Accordingly, he was listed as number 20 among 35 Class A suspects "who were considered the greatest threat to security..."[5] Class B suspects were also recommended for arrest, and Class C suspects were to be considered for arrest if enough evidence could be gathered from the interrogation of Class A suspects. The list was compiled by W.S. Stephenson, director, British Security Co-ordination.

During the first sweep of the Japanese Canadian community to apprehend "security risks" or community leaders, only one minister was taken into custody. Among the first 37 Japanese Canadians arrested by the RCMP was Rev. Eon Mitsubayashi, assistant minister of the Vancouver Hompa Church. The minister apparently had been a reserve officer for the Japanese army.

Rev. Mitsubayashi was detained in the Vancouver Immigration Branch holding centre until mid February 1942. He was taken away from his wife and son for the duration of the war, imprisoned as he was in labour and concentration camps at Seebee (Kananaskis), Alberta, and Petawawa and Angler, Ontario. At the end of the war the Buddhist Foundation of Canada (the post war umbrella organization of the Jodo Shinshu temples) petitioned for a minister for the Coaldale Buddhist Church in Alberta. The government granted the request and Rev. Mitsubayashi was released at first to a hostel in Moose Jaw, Saskatchewan, in July 1946, then to Coaldale. Coincidentally, the Angler *Ganbariya* Group continued their protest against the incarceration of Japanese Canadians and the breakup of the family during "The Evacuation" in Moose Jaw, perhaps the same hostel.

A resistance movement was staged by 280 men in Moose Jaw against the orders to resettle by the government. It wasn't until July of 1948 that the authorities raided the hostel and forced the resistors to leave. Rev. Mitsubayashi did not participate in the protest; like Rev. Ikuta and Rev. Kawamura however, he probably counselled the protestors to give up the cause peacefully. In any case, he was reunited with his family in Coaldale where he served briefly as the minister of the temple. He was ultimately deported to Japan on the ship Marine Falcon, December 24, 1946.

In the meantime, Rev. Ikuta was largely ignored despite RCMP suspicions. In fact, he was allowed to travel and relocate with his wife and five children to Raymond, Alberta. He became minister there with seemingly little trouble.

> British Columbia Security Commission Permit No. 01152, dated May 25, 1942, and signed by Grant MacNeil, secretary for BCSC, was issued to Rev. Shinjo and Mino Ikuta and their five children to travel from New Westminster to Lethbridge, Alberta, "to the Japanese Church there." The destination was Raymond, Lethbridge having no Buddhist temple.

The permit further read, "They must travel by rail, leaving Vancouver by May 30th and must not re-enter the Restricted Area. This commission assumes no responsibility for the cost of education of children of school age." The point regarding education cost was a general problem between local and BCSC jurisdictions for all families with school-age children.

Rev. Ikuta's oldest son, now resident minister of the Calgary Buddhist Temple, recalls getting off the train in Calgary and trying to find a restaurant. From his recollection, security on their movements was lax and hardly consistent with the expectations demanded by Stephenson's characterization of Class A suspects.[6]

TBC archives

Left: Rev. Shinjo Ikuta, Calgary, circa 1965. Right: Rev. Kyojo Ikuta, Calgary, circa 1990.

The Ido

ORDERS FROM THE B.C. SECURITY COMMISSION

Notice to Vancouver Japanese

> Persons of Japanese origin residing in Vancouver should terminate, not later than the 30th April, 1942, all leases or rental arrangements they may be working under. They must also be prepared to move either to Hastings Park or to work camps or to places under the Interior Housing Scheme at twenty-four hours notice. No deferments whatsoever on business grounds may be made to the above orders.
>
> **The New Canadian**
> April 29, 1942

The Japanese community came to call the *Evacuation*[7] the **Ido** or *The Great Movement*. The destinations for the "evacuees" were the internment camps of the British Columbia interior. Most of these were hastily refurbished ghost towns or segregated areas of towns willing to accept the Japanese. At first the British Columbia Security Commission planned to assign the prisoners according to religion; thus, United Church members were to be sent to Kaslo, Anglicans to Slocan, Roman Catholics to Greenwood, and Buddhists to Sandon.[8] The plan was eventually abandoned for two reasons. A common religion in a camp was seen as a catalyst for solidarity amongst the Japanese, and the sheer numbers of Buddhists demanded more than one location.

JCCC archives

Internees arrive in New Denver, B.C., circa 1942.

Still at the beginning of the **Ido**, the government offered the Buddhists a camp of their own. In fact, the church ministers and leaders became actively concerned that the Buddhists have a centre of their own.

> The Roman Catholics had picked out Greenwood and the United Church had picked out Kaslo, and I suppose some of the members were apprehensive about where they were going.[9]

Unfortunately, the government's orders to leave Vancouver caused many short term problems. Rev. Tsuji, being the only minister to speak English, stayed in Vancouver as organizer. Toshio Mori, who lost his job as a presser in his family dry cleaning establishment when the business closed down, volunteered to help the minister.

> ...they told me that Mitsubayashi *sensei* got hauled away and Tachibana *sensei* had to go some place. He went to Tashme as soon as the place opened, and then the treasurer came and said "I have to go too and so I'm going to leave you here with all the books...and here's $300 cash.[10]

$300 is not much money to organize a move of such proportions especially since the church was prevented from operating. Unlike the Christian organizational infrastructure, the Hongwanji could not help its followers in Canada. The geopolitical nature of the war severed all contact with Japanese institutions for the Japanese Canadian Buddhist Church. By June there was very little of the $300 left. Mrs. Fujimoto, a *Fujinkai* member, suggested the church hold an Obon ceremony. Rev. Tsuji seized upon the idea and immediately sent notices to all the inhabitants of Hastings Park.[11] It was also the ideal opportunity to offer his congregation the comfort of the teachings of Amida Buddha during those sad and uncertain times.

The church was full and the donations plentiful. Rev. Tsuji and his volunteers were then able to make the arrangements for the exile.

With Terrie Sugiura acting as office assistant to Rev. Tsuji and sometime interpreter, Rev Tsuji and a devout member, Mr. Tsuruda, arranged a meeting with Col. Mead of the RCMP to discuss a specific place for the Buddhists. Since the church was willing to do all the organizing, the mounties were quite willing to give them the next town under consideration. Rev. Tsuji agreed to go to Sandon to assess the possibility.

Terrie Sugiura was born in 1922 and lived in the 700 block of Pender Street before the war. After finishing grade eight at the Alexander Street Japanese Language School, she attended the Hompa Bukkyokai to learn more Japanese. Her instructor was Rev. E. Mitsubayashi.

> Until then, I never really went there to the Buddhist Church although my family was Buddhist. My mother was a widow. She had to bring up children. She didn't have time for church. We had the *hotokesan* but I went to the United Church because that's where I went to kindergarten...so I didn't have too much involvement with the Buddhist Church until I went to the Japanese

School. Because the ministers wanted us to join the church group, the Junior YBA was the first one where I got a membership and from then on, I really haven't left the church.[12]

Terrie Sugiura was to play a pivotal role in the mass exodus of Buddhists to the ghost town of Sandon.

Courtesy of Terrie Komori

A winter day in Sandon Valley, 1942.

Sandon

About 500 miles from Vancouver, between the Selkirk and Purcell Mountain Ranges, there lies the ghost town of Sandon. In its heyday, the town boasted a population of 7000 prospectors and settlers. Silver and lead were mined with a degree of efficacy until the mines "went bust" in the early 20th Century.

Carpenter Creek ran through the middle of the tight valley where the town was established. With planks laid over the rushing water, the boardwalk became Main Street. The creek was a natural sewage system until the spring when the runoff and/or heavy rain tore away the street. The town itself consisted of 20 hotels and bars, two breweries, an opera house, several brothels, a Methodist Church, houses and one general store.

The surrounding mountains that towered over Sandon caused many problems. The town itself had only one way to grow: straight up the sides of the mountains. Twenty feet of snow fell on Sandon on average and the consequent snow slides posed a constant danger. Similarly, summer land slides were a major concern. Only one narrow road with a 1000 foot drop beside it and a spur line of the CPR serviced the internment town. There were only two to three hours of sunlight a day. In Vancouver, internees were warned that Sandon was "a land of perpetual night, a mere ravine caught between two mountain precipices, where men dared not breathe, lest their very breaths turned to ice."[13]

Rev. Tsuji made little comment of his first impression of Sandon. Terrie Komori (nee Sugiura) remarked simply "they (Rev. Tsuji and Mr. Tsuruda) took a trip and came back and said it was okay...it was acceptable as far as they were concerned."[14]

Word went out to all the ministers and their respective congregations. Names of families then poured into the Vancouver Hompa Church from Marpole, Fairview and other districts requesting a place in Sandon.

In the meantime, a large group of carpenters travelled to Sandon to refurbish the town as best as they could for habitation. What they found was cause for optimism.

> Sandon, in 1942, had a resident population of less than 50. There were many vacant and abandoned buildings which, with minimum repair, were usable as accommodation. At that time, many of the old wild west furnishings and artifacts were cleared away and destroyed to make room for the (Japanese Canadian) internees. Many people had left Sandon during the Depression years thinking they would return one day. Because of this, many homes had been left furnished and intact.[15]

What was lost were long bars, plate-glass mirrors, glorious paintings from the mining days and many other artifacts. One eerie note: workers found in one of the old brothels a perfectly preserved full-length *kagami* or Japanese mirror. Many thought this an omen of an ill-fated future. The more rational concluded the mirror belonged to an itinerant Japanese prostitute who had come through Sandon as part of her circuit (circa 1890).

The industrious work crews managed to repair the serviceable edifices quickly. They also were able to provide electricity to most of the buildings.

> Under the directions of the BCSC, the internees did extensive repair work to the Silversmith mine power house penstock which was becoming quite deteriorated. During WW II, the power from this plant was used throughout the townsite in addition to J.M. Harris' old plant which was taxed to its limit.[16]

The first group of Buddhists left for Sandon in the spring of 1942. Terrie Sugiura went with that group since she could speak English. Her task was to keep in touch with Rev. Tsuji in Vancouver.

> Rev. Tsuji would say that the Commission wanted to send the next group over. Then I would have to check out the houses, because Sandon had no new houses. They were renovating old houses because Sandon was an old mining town. Half the houses were standing up and half were not livable, that's for sure. They had to renovate these houses and make them livable. So I had to phone him and say we're not ready...when we felt there was room for more we'd say okay and make sure they came.[17]

Courtesy of Terrie Komori

Sports Day, Sandon Valley, May 1943.

The BC Security Commission was anxious to clear out the detention centre at Hastings Park. It therefore exerted some pressure to move the largest group of Buddhists out of "The Pool" with the first wave to Sandon. They were from Port Essington. Once relocated, the group's lay minister, Matsujiro Ohashi (from Skeena), became the initial leader of the camp.

Ohashi organized the adults into committees: the *keiro-bucho (a respect-for-age* association), sports, education and welfare committees. Perhaps the most important was the Welfare Committee.[18] Anyone who had trouble with finances would go to the Welfare Chairman who in turn approached the Security Commission. The committee system actually strengthened the community into a solidified whole. No one ever had to approach the authorities alone.

JCCC archives

Obon Odori, Sandon, B.C., circa 1942.

Toshio Mori arrived in Sandon with the second group of internees. His recollections are vivid:

> I helped out in the Sunday School department. There were many young Buddhist members there, both in Sandon and in the Slocan Valley. In Sandon, I remember the first Bon Odori. This was soon after we settled in that town, July of 1942. We had some young girls who could teach and lead the group in Bon Odori. They were, as I recall, the Mori sisters, Hisa Baba, Nishikawa girls, Miyake sisters and many others. Terrie Komori was also in Sandon. The men built a large platform in the centre of the town and the girls came down from

> the top of a hill, dancing to the music blaring from the P.A. system. They danced around the platform and soon everyone joined in the *odori*. It was a time to celebrate, and despite everything terrible happening to us, we could still follow the teachings of Buddha.[19]

By September some 953 internees had embarked on the long journey to Sandon.

As Rev. Tsuji organized the internees in Vancouver for travel, he began considering the fate of the church buildings and artifacts inside. The temples themselves fell under the purview of the Custodian of Alien Properties as did most of the properties owned by Japanese Canadians. Family *butsudan* (altars) were stored in the basements of these buildings. Rev. Tsuji himself took some of the artifacts, like the wooden statue of the Buddha and scrolls, to Sandon with the last group of internees.

> There was one more train that left carrying those people who were sick. I was on that last train.[20]

Rev. Shinjo Ikuta had the foresight to ask his friend, Mr. Harris of New Westminster, to ship approximately 200 urns containing the ashes of church members to the Raymond Buddhist Church for storage. Other churches stored the ashes of the deceased in their temple columbaria. Some were taken by the internees.

> I think they [the urns] were destroyed. You couldn't send them to any camp. We couldn't do anything about that...so there upstairs [at the old Hompa building in Vancouver after the war] I examined... big boxes. There were bones in some of them. They weren't ashes... There were lots we didn't know [their identities], because it was pretty old, old, many, many years. Some bones, the relatives took them. Other than that we don't know.[21]

Unfortunately, most of the temples were vandalized, some even set on fire. The fate of the Steveston Buddhist Church was typical. Barry Broadfoot in his book **Six War Years**: *1939-1945* includes an anonymous testimony about the Steveston temple.

> They moved the Japanese out and Steveston which was like their capital, their city, was like a ghost town

> because most of the stores and houses were Japanese. There was this building, their Buddhist Temple and my husband was a carpenter and he worked around it so he sort of kept his eye on it, you know, but soon people started going in, white people, you know. All around the walls were small shelves and out of curiosity the whites who came out to the temple for a look-see would look in the little jars. The containers around the walls on the shelves and they started to take them. They disappeared pretty fast after that when people started taking things out of the temple. You know, there was something in them but they didn't know what it was, black and powdery, that's what it was like. And then somebody said that the material in them was the ashes of the Japanese ancestry, their fathers and grandparents and that the temple was a holy place. So one by one the white people started to bring them back and before long the word had gotten out all around. And soon all the little urns were back in place and the back doors had real good locks to protect the place from then on.[22]

Alex Johnson, the son of the Steveston Chief of Police in the 1940s, tells an entirely different story of desecration.

> Two days after the Japanese Canadians left Steveston, the beer parlour gang at the Steveston Hotel decided to break into the church because they were looking for gold. They had heard that the Buddhists were rich, sort of like the Catholics. So they decided to break into the church, and when they got in there, they started smashing things because they were all drunk. And they did find these urns but they didn't look carefully inside and touch them or whatever else. What they did was they smashed them, threw them all over the church, desecrating it basically as well as the altar. They ended by starting to fight with each other, fighting over the gold candle holders and of course they were brass.[23]

The drunkards actually thought the remains were gold dust. In an addendum to the story, Harry Yonekura, a prewar fisherman in Steveston and prominent member of the Toronto Buddhist Church, visited Steveston in the 1950s to find not a trace of the original Buddhist Church building.

Rev. Kawamura visited the Maple Ridge Buddhist Church during the war and discovered a similar scenario. The temple was vandalized, the contents upended or stolen, religious symbols destroyed. The only thing salvageable was the *butsudan.*

In the end, the Custodian of Alien Property sold the temples for next to nothing. The Canada Hompa Buddhist Temple went to the Ukrainian community. The contents of all the churches were in all likelihood burned, although some family *butsudan* were moved to a separate storage area; they were even returned to their rightful owners. Surviving temple altars were eventually shipped to Buddhist Churches in Alberta, Manitoba and the interior of British Columbia.

Further Dispersal

As the Japanese Canadian Buddhists left Vancouver, the BCSC already began to see the impossibility of segregating internees by religion. By far the Buddhists outnumbered all other groups, 5000 in total; therefore, those who could not be placed in Sandon went to Tashme, Lemon Creek and Kaslo.

Rev. Sokan Asaka of the Royston Buddhist Church on Vancouver Island initially went to a labour camp at Sander River, B.C. After six months and some negotiating with the BCSC on his behalf by the Vancouver church members, he was reunited in Sandon with his wife and two children who had been detained in Hastings Park. Rev. Toshio Katatsu (Steveston), Rev. Ryuchi Hirahara (Fairview) and Rev. Tsuji joined Rev. Asaka. Because of the overflow of Buddhists, Rev. Katatsu eventually took care of the Lemon Creek Church; Rev. Asaka at New Denver;[24] Rev. Hirahara at Bay Farm; and Rev. Tsuji at Sandon and Bay Farm. Rev. Renshin Tachibana of the Vancouver Church went to Tashme. Rev. Yutetsu Kawamura of the Maple Ridge Church worked as a labourer on a sugar beet farm in Raymond, Alberta. From there, he and his family moved to Picture Butte (near Lethbridge) where he set up a church serving 250 members.[25]

In effect, Buddhism was expunged from the west coast and survived in a handful of makeshift churches led by itinerant ministers. The only permanent temple with a resident minister in the country was in Raymond, Alberta. Given the racist tenor of the times, the city council initially tried to close it down. Fortunately, the federal government interceded and overruled that decision. It was truly in the best interests of the Canadian government to keep Buddhism alive, however faint.

Life in the Camps

> In Bay Farm, there were many young Buddhists such as Bonnie Kubota, Fumi Maeda, Dewey Uchida and Charlie Nekoda to name a few...I remember Rev. Asaka saying how grateful and humble he felt that the congregation came to listen to him week after week even though some of his *Dharma* talks were repeats and the *sutra* books were so old and were falling apart. During the camp years, there was understandably no communication with the Honzan [Mother Temple in Kyoto] and the ministers and members had to cope with what little materials that were on hand.
>
> I remember our funerals. Due to the uncertainty of our future in the ghost towns, the deceased were cremated. There was an undertaker in New Denver whose services we often used. His name was Draper.[26]

Rev. Tsuji decided to be based in Bay Farm which allowed him to travel the Slocan Valley with some ease. Having the largest house, he held meetings there until a church was built. Other difficulties soon presented themselves.

> Some of the old people were dying and we didn't know who to contact. Finally we got this funeral man from New Denver and he would work in the garage. When there was no one to help him I would help him prepare the bodies...In Slocan many didn't have relatives when they died...pile of dried wood, and they would put the casket on it...the oldest son used to light the fire...They tended the fire all night to keep it going.[27]

Everyone had to improvise. The ministers, cut off from Japan and the regular donations that a service generated, faced the prospect of having to work at manual labour. Unfortunately many of them were not suited for such work. Hence the BCSC decided to provide welfare based on provincial relief rates with certain conditions. Buddhist ministers were restricted in their activities. Commissioner Collins of the BCSC made it clear that he would not authorize travel to the various camps and communities for missionary work.[28] They were, however, allowed to travel between camps to perform marriages and funerals, but it fell to the Japanese and white Christian ministers, who had the spiritual and financial support of a fully entrenched national organization, to care for the Japanese Canadians no matter what their religious affiliation.

In Sandon, the old Methodist Church became the Buddhist Temple. Three Catholic nuns from the Sisters of Christ the King started a high school for 45 students upstairs in the CPR station. They also taught music to 20 students. In other camps, the United Church set up kindergartens, high schools and Christian fellowships which Buddhists joined.

JCCC archives

Slocan Buddhist Temple, circa 1943.

> In Slocan as well as in Lemon Creek, there were many people of the Christian faith. Catholic sisters taught in almost every ghost town...at the secondary level. The Anglican churches were very helpful too in the educating of kindergarten groups. They all had their own church services and meetings for their congregation.[29]

The Buddhist Education Committee in Sandon, chaired by Kohei Usui of Port Essington, did not stand idle. The members were concerned about the grade school children who had nothing to do. During the latter part of the summer of 1942, Terrie Sugiura approached Lois Lind, a teacher who held a class for six children (four of them her own) in the local school house, to allow the Buddhist internees to use the school. She agreed. All high school graduates in camp volunteered to teach and a rudimentary school system was born.

Subsequently the BCSC paid eight of the volunteers to be Commission school teachers. Terrie Sugiura became the principal. The established provincial education system came to the aid of the fledgling school.

> ...the local system was very good. They let us have good books...everything was sort of just trying to get the kids back...because they had been out of school for so long...(we taught) just reading and writing, whatever math we could pick up. Girls were very good, and we carried on after we got into the BC Commission school.[30]

In the Commission school, students were allowed access from grades one to eight. Lois Lind was taken on as a grade six teacher. All of this activity was housed in the original school house until a work crew partitioned a warehouse for more classrooms.

> [Students] got along so well that the city kids never laughed at the ones who didn't know much. I remember my sister teaching. As an example, she said, "We learned *molasses* in spelling. Now write a sentence with *molasses*. And this boy wrote, *Molasses* was walking down the street. He came from a community where molasses is unknown. This is in grade seven." However by the same token, she had the brightest kids from Fairview District. They were really bright students. You could tell by their report cards, but you see, none of them made fun of each other...therefore as far as discipline [problems] was concerned we never had any. I don't ever recall having a discipline break except once when they all ran out of the classroom to watch a train come up. Boy I told them that I would throw them out of school if I ever caught them doing that again...the leaders took the leadership, the others followed...that kid from the country, I'm sure they were helping their father make a living. In that sense, they were way superior to the city kids. They knew how to fish and they knew how to farm. Their education was way advanced in that sense, so it was very interesting.[31]

Despite all the hardships, quite a large and organized Buddhist community grew in the middle of the Rocky Mountains.

> I was concerned with filling their needs. There were a large number of Buddhists in Bay Farm and Popoff and even in Slocan. So I thought we'd better hold something to bring these people together. That's why we rented the hall in downtown Slocan City. We were holding services for quite some time and Sunday School and *issei* service. We sure had a big congregation in those days. Then they decided to build a temple. They applied for permission to do that and of course they said go ahead and do it. When they said they wanted some lumber they said go ahead and use it. But there were certain restrictions on the lumber they could use. They certainly used more than they were supposed to use. I think the supervisor had his eyes closed. He was pretty good. They cut down the logs...the first log temple in Canada. Most of it was log. They used government lumber where it was necessary and designed their own shrine, *issei* did, and that's how they got that built. Lemon Creek and our place and Sandon, we had a very thriving Buddhist community. There were conferences once in a while.[32]

Building the Slocan Buddhist Temple, circa 1943.

Courtesy of K.S. Yoneda

The Dispersal

By the spring of 1943, a few *nisei* began leaving the camps to find work on farms in other provinces, predominately Alberta and Ontario. Most however stayed with their aging parents perhaps suffering from guilt or a fear of the outside world. As time went by, the realization that the outside world was their destiny became apparent.

> I knew I would have to leave Lillooet sometime in the future; Lillooet was too small and isolated. In preparation for future relocation, I took correspondence courses from Victoria B.C. Our settlement (the Japanese village) in East Lillooet was four miles away from Lillooet, a small town of approximately 2000 people scattered within a wide area, 100 miles from Squamish and very inconvenient to travel to. Most Buddhist ministers were interned or sent back to Japan - Japanese language school was also condemned when war broke out. Buddhism in our community and the Japanese language were literally erased. It was a bleak period for us indeed. This period must have been the most depressing in my life - culture was gone, our language school and religion were also gone.
>
> Dorothy Kagawa
> *nisei*
> Toronto Buddhist Church

Ottawa and the BC Security Commission decided the security issue of the coast became a dispersal issue for the Japanese. By Order-in-Council, the Custodian of Alien Property was ordered to dispose of all property under its purview. All single men lost their pay from the Commission. Next the small ghost town internment camps like Sandon and Kaslo were closed by the summer of 1943. Sandon seemed a logical first choice to close since the weather conditions were so severe. Finally in 1945, the Department of Labour ordered the remaining 10,000 internees to make a choice: resettle east of the Rockies or apply for repatriation to Japan. The Japanese Canadians could not go back to the coast. Their hard won properties and holdings no longer existed. They could not stay in their mountain homes no matter how meagre. No matter what choice they made, Japan or east of the Rockies, they moved out of the camps to an uncertain future. One practical option seemed available. The Christian Church instituted resettlement and employment programs to eastern Canada to help internees. Many Buddhists took advantage of the opportunity.

In the spring of 1946, I was teaching in the Bay Farm Pine Crescent School but one cold and drizzly day in April, I took the bus to Rosebery to bid farewell to a good friend. We had taken summer courses together and taught at the same school. Now she was living in Rosebery, teaching classes there and helping her family prepare for "repatriation". Through her letters, I knew that going to Japan was not her choice but a necessity. The family relied heavily upon her to help take care of an invalid father.

I found her house early in the afternoon. We chatted for a while and then, although it was damp and chilly, we decided to go for a walk. We walked to the edge of the camp, then along the railroad track that ran alongside the lake. We walked and we talked and we sang. We sang songs from the latest Hit Parade and some of our favourite Japanese songs. Then she started to sing **Besame Mucho**. I did not join in. This was her song. It was one she often sang on stage at ghost town concerts. It was her encore piece.

Suddenly, she stopped singing and put her hands to her face. Her shoulders shook with sobs. Alarmed, I led her to a large boulder beside the track and asked her what happened. Slowly and between sobs, she told me that she had met a fellow in Rosebery and that they had been seeing each other, but last week they decided to call it off. He will be going east in a few weeks and she was headed for Japan. As things stood, there was no future for them together. She had accepted all this but she was crushed, and there was nothing she could do either. All I could say was "I'm sorry. I'm sorry." And there we sat, my friend and I, on the cold unrelenting rock on the side of the railroad track, and cried.

a *nisei*[33]
Toronto Buddhist Church

Ministers of the Canada Hompa Buddhist

Church - Vancouver B.C.

Rev. Senju Sasaki	1905 - 1912
Rev. Gungai Kato	1912 - 1913
Rev. Junichi Shigeno	1913 - 1924
Rev. Ryosei Wada	1913 - 1915
Rev. Takunen Nishimoto	1920 - 1925
Rev. Doko Minamoto	1924 - 1925
Rev. Keitatsu Kudo	1924 - 1925
Rev. Sonjin Takayama	1925
Rev. Yoshihiro Tokuno	1925 - 1927
Rev. Gijin Taga	1925 - 1930
Rev. Shozen Naito	1927 - 1930
Rev. Kakusai Tada	1929 - 1934
Rev. Seisho Ishiguro	1930 - 1936
Rev. Zesei Kawasaki	1934 - 1938
Rev. Zenyu Aoki	1936 - 1939
Rev. Eon Mitsubayashi	1937 - 1941
Rev. Renshin Tachibana	1938 - 1942
Rev. Kenryu Tsuji	1941 - 1942

Ministers of the War Era

Rev. Renshin Tachibana	Tashme
Rev. Toshio Katatsu	Lemon Creek
Rev. Ryuchi Hirahara	Slocan
Rev. Kenryu Tsuji	Sandon/Bay Farm
Rev. Sokan Asaka	New Denver
Rev. Shinjo Ikuta	Raymond, Alberta
	Rev. Yutetsu Kawamura
Rev. Eon Mitsubayashi	Angler

Part Two

Restoration and the Movement East

Southern Alberta:
The Struggle to Survive

Chapter 10

Southern Alberta: The Struggle to Survive

When my wife [Yoneko] and I arrived in Raymond, Alberta, as minister and partner, to serve at the Buddhist Temple there, it was July 5, 1934 some 48 years ago. I was 26 and my wife was 22 at the time.

Before leaving Japan, I spoke to a former minister in Canada Rev. Gijin Taga, who was leader with the Tokyo Railway Express Association, and who had mentioned that a minister in Canada must have a morning coat, so before departure I had one tailored at Uyesaka-ya in Hikone.

When we reached the train station of the town to which I was assigned, I wore my morning coat and my wife wore her evening dress as we got off the train at the CPR Station in Lethbridge. There were about ten people at the station to meet us, from Raymond and Hardieville, but being harvest time, the faces of the people were tanned dark; some appeared to have come in their work clothes, and some men were dressed in overalls.

When we saw the town of Lethbridge, we thought a town of that size shouldn't be too bad; however, we drove through twenty miles of gravel road through the country to finally reach Raymond. We entered the Buddhist temple, paid respect to Amida Buddha with *gassho*; then we were informed that we were to be quartered in a single room downstairs.

> The temple building was of fair size, a two storey building. I thought it was a fine structure.
>
> That day, in the evening, in South Raymond (about four miles distant), at the rented farm home of Toshio Matoba, there was a welcome reception sponsored by the Raymond Bukkyokai. Being summer time, the sun took a long time to set. After having a bath there, as I gazed at the western sky, I could see over vast distances of crops and the horizon of the great prairies, and as I viewed the golden colour of the setting sun I thought, "Here is the heaven on earth which I had dreamt of."[1]
>
> Rev. Y. Kawamura

While Rev. Kawamura's recollections may have been idealized, the Buddhist community in Southern Alberta is cohesive and sincere in its devotion. The members certainly had to call on these strengths in order to withstand the racism and paranoia of post war Alberta.

Buddhist Beginnings in Southern Alberta

Since 1904, the Japanese had traversed the formidable Rocky Mountains to seek employment on the prairies. Many worked for short periods on farms, in mines and railway hotels. In 1907, the CPR proposed to bring 1000 Japanese to southwestern Alberta to build an irrigation project, but the hostility expressed by local farmers dissuaded the railway from implementing the plan.

One group that was consistently attracted to the area was the Okinawans. In Japan, they had experienced much prejudice and persecution. Ken Adachi explains, "...Okinawans, the very name often carrying a derisive or contemptuous overtone, in memory of the time when Okinawans used pork as a main staple of diet as part of their Chinese cultural heritage and when they had established themselves in Japan as proprietors of piggeries, an occupation which placed them almost on a level with the despised *eta*, the butchers and tanners and shoemakers of the old days."[2] Ostracized and discriminated against by the Japanese even in Canada, they migrated away from the concentrated areas of Japanese settlements in B.C. in order to organize amongst themselves.

Most Okinawans who came to Canada settled in Southern

Alberta. In the early 1900s, they worked as part of the section gangs of the railroads. Eventually, a coal mine in Hardieville (a small mining town north of Lethbridge) opened, providing many jobs. Later the sugar beet processing plants offered employment, and finally many came to start their own farms.

> One early arrival, Tomosada Ohkutake, was sent to Canada to study, but later decided to settle in Alberta when he first saw the area after arriving as a bookkeeper for a group of 70 labourers that he had gathered together. When in Vancouver, he had scouted the boarding houses to look for Okinawans who would go to Alberta with him. Except when he enlisted in the Canadian Japanese regiment during World War I, he remained, like the other Okinawans, a resident of Alberta, working in the mines and later buying a potato farm.[3]

Although many moved to Coaldale, Raymond received the majority of settlers. Some of these men formed the "Japanese Society" which carried on social and community activities. The Society in fact took on an active role in propagating Buddhism which continued through the war. Women eventually came when the men saved enough money either to travel to Japan to bring back a wife or to bring a "picture bride" to Alberta. In order to help the devoted, Rev. Kawamura sought permission of local authorities to conduct a "cemetery day" or Obon service in Raymond. Rev. Mitsubayashi led the observance in 1941.[4]

The Buddhist movement itself was started by Kyojun Iwaasa, Yoshio Hatanaka, Yoichi Hironaka, Tanesaburo Kosaka, Eita Sonomura, Takejiro Koyata, Buhachi Nishimura and Kisaburo Sugimoto. The congregation then grew to a significant number. Considering that there were only 578 Okinawan Japanese in the entire province by 1941, the congregation of 125 in Raymond was substantial. Families sprouted and, as a result, members felt the need for religious education and a community centre.

The First Church

The members decided to establish a temple in Raymond affiliated with the Nishi Hongwanji. In 1929 newly elected President Yoichi Hironaka and Yoshio Hatanaka approached the Morman Church to negotiate the purchase of their building.

The price was $5000, a daunting amount for the time and area. Nevertheless, a hundred year plan was devised and the members of Raymond and the other localities of Hardieville and Coalhurst pledged support. In fact 124 people were committed to $7383.16. The effort was commemorated with a plaque designed by Toshiko Moriyama that still hangs over the entrance to the church.

On July 1, 1929, the first *Obon* service took place at the home of Mr. and Mrs. Kyojun Iwaasa. Rev. Taga from Vancouver presided. There was much anticipation for a bright future.

Still there were persistent expenses of remodelling the building and supporting a resident minister. In order to cover the monthly outlay, some members donated a share of the profits from grain. Others decided to start a co-operative store. The Kobai Kumiai, started in 1932, sold staple food to local farmers and settlers. The profit gained from bulk food buying went to support the church. Later, a second store opened, selling gasoline, oil and twine. These same stores were in operation throughout the 1980s, managed by Mrs. Tak Sugimoto.

First Ministers and the Dirty Thirties

Rev. Shinjo Nagatomi arrived in Raymond on June 4, 1930 to a special dedication service (*Nyu Butsu Shiki*) when the scroll of the Amida Buddha was placed in a home-made shrine built by the carpenter S. Motoyama.

The reverend was promised a salary of $30.00 a month, but the Dirty Thirties had taken their toll on Alberta, and most months the wage could not be met. Instead the church members supplied the minister with flour, chickens, eggs and vegetables. The community also came together to dig coal from the bed of the St. Mary River for the church and themselves to keep warm. Such sacrifices were made despite everyone's own plight with poverty.

> One lady told with tears in her eyes that during the Depression for almost a year, she was not able to have rice for dinner.
>
> ...Mrs. N., two or three years after arriving in Canada, her parents in Japan wrote and asked for photos of the children so they could see how they looked. But she reminisced they did not own a camera; they

> would have had to travel to Lethbridge to get photos taken. Who had money to do that?
>
> As a result, they never had photos taken to send to Japan.[5]

To escape the poverty, some members actually proposed to move to Manchuria to utilize their skill at mechanized wheat farming on virtually virgin land. They even contacted the Japanese Consulate in Vancouver to explore the possibility. Unfortunately, they discovered the cost to ship such machinery across the Pacific prohibitive. The plan was soon forgotten.

There were good times as well. The community frequently came together for such social activities as *haiku-kai* (poetry club), *karuta* (card) parties and picnics.

Rev. Nagatomi returned to Japan in 1934. Replacing him came a dynamic, young minister, Rev. Yutetsu Kawamura, and his wife, Yoneko. Conditions were not ideal and despite the minister's initial optimism, he had moments of doubt.

> I observed Mrs. Matoba cleaning the chimneys of the kerosene lamps. At the time, there was no place in Japan which used such lamps, so I was concerned and asked whether there was a power cutoff tonight in the city. Mrs. Matoba replied however, "In this area, there is not a single home with electricity." I was surprised at first, then depressed. "What a real rural area I have come to," I thought. At the same time, to see the truly Japanese woman who had come to Canada who has to clean kerosene lamp chimneys brought tears to my eyes.[6]

Undaunted, Rev. and Mrs. Kawamura brought new *gathas*, *odori* and teaching skills. They started a Sunday School and a Japanese Language School.

> During the long summer holidays, we taught Japanese to the children of Monmouth County, renting a local public school for the purpose. Some girls in the higher grades of high school came to pick us up early in the morning, with single and two horse carriages over 9 miles of road; then following the classes, they took us back to the temple. It was indeed quite an undertaking.
>
> For the Japanese language classes, I wore a black

> summer suit. Because I did not possess many changes of clothes, I always wore the same suit. By the time we arrived at Monmouth School, my suit was white from the road dust. Also, the children who came to school to study, they had to travel 2 to 3 miles, and they were brought there on horseback by their older brothers and sisters.
>
> They were all bareback horses. One horse carried maybe 2 or 3 children. The front child would hold the reins, and the ones after him/her carried lard tins with lunch in them and also carried the books at the same time.[7]

The church also had a problem in meeting the promised salary for Rev. Kawamura every month. Consequently, the community devised ways to keep the good reverend and his wife well fed and healthy.

> In the area about ten miles south, Shozo Kosaka, who was growing wheat, stated he would supply us with eggs and meat. [He suggested] that my wife and I should serve as sales staff at the co-op store [in the temple] and therefore we could avail ourselves of the rice, *shoyu, miso* and dried Japanese *dashi-iriko* for our meals.[8]

Sunday services were always a trial for the congregation to attend. In Raymond itself, there was only one family at first: Mr. and Mrs. Yasukazu Oshiro operated a restaurant. Everyone else lived in the surrounding area engaged in wheat, sugar beet or potato farming. The times were especially hard for the dry wheat farmer who had to cultivate wheat without irrigation. Many became impoverished by the lack of rain.

> When clouds were seen in the sky, the dry farmer gazed up with gladness but by the time the clouds passed overhead, they had disappeared somewhere and were completely gone, so all the farmers looked dejected and could only gaze at the blue sky. With the hot summer breezes, the wheat sheaves were drooping and were being dried up. We heard the words "dry-dry" for the first time, and we found out how disastrous it could be for the farmers if there was excessive dryness.[9]

On the other hand, there were times of joy which inspired acts of great generosity.

> In the month of July the year after we arrived in Raymond, our first son Sumio was born. Unlike today, when babies are brought into this world in a hospital, a Mrs. Oshiro who lived in the town centre came to the house and delivered the infant. Later, Mrs. Kawamura had occasion to be examined by a Dr. Leach in the city, but his fee was $25.00. Some days later, I went to his office with $5.00 in my hands. I said, "At this time, this is all I can pay. The balance I shall pay later." Dr. Leach knowing that we were in a poorly situation stated he would not worry about the balance.[10]

The Debt

Perhaps the single greatest worry during the prewar years of the Raymond Bukkyokai was the construction and mortgage debt. The members simply felt the money had to be repaid at all costs. With bemused spirit, President Hironaka vowed to give up smoke and drink while donating the money saved from such abstinence. Rev. Kawamura gave $3.00 of every $30.00 paycheque he received. Potato farmers donated one to two tons of their crops. In this manner the debt was actually redeemed by the spring of 1940.

Life was hard for the Japanese settlers of Southern Alberta, especially for Rev. Kawamura and his family. Despite a flourishing church with a Japanese language school, Sunday School, Young Women's Buddhist Association, Fujinkai and strong administration, Rev. Kawamura decided to leave for Japan in January 1940.

In Vancouver however, Rev. Zen-yu Aoki, Supervisor of Ministers, BCC, requested he temporarily fill a vacancy created with the death of Rev. Abe, the resident minister at the Maple Ridge temple. Rev. Kawamura never reached Japan. With the war, he found himself back in Southern Alberta caring for the needs not only of those Buddhists who had fled ethnic persecution two decades earlier but also those newly displaced Buddhists suffering that selfsame persecution.

The War

The Japanese Okinawan settlers of Southern Alberta were keenly aware of Japan's aggressive machinations in the South

Pacific. As Japan's international relations deteriorated, they became more and more concerned for their safety. However, they felt they could do nothing except to live as quietly and as cautiously as possible among the white population of the area.

During November of 1941, Japanese Consul Kawasaki of Vancouver paid a visit to Raymond. Since there were so many Japanese in the temple congregation, he felt the need to assuage any fears they may have had. The church administration decided to take advantage of Consul Kawasaki's visit by arranging a meeting with city officials.

The Consul advised all who attended if there was an eruption of war to observe Canadian regulations; the Canadian government would protect them and their properties from coming to any harm.

When war did break out on December 7, 1941, the members devised a course of action set down on paper to assure their religious freedom.

1. Destroy some important documents by incineration; for example, the application list and papers for temporary exemption from conscription.
2. Remove any display inside the church with Japanese orientation.
3. Move anything related to the Imperial Family to a safe place to avoid suspicion.
4. Abolish all official meetings. Make Sunday School the main activity and use it for communication among the community.
5. The church should stay open until it receives the order from the officials to close. Keep as low a profile as possible.

Such tactics seemed warranted since the temple, its subsequent ministers, Reverends Ikuta and Kawamura, and the hundreds of exiled Japanese Canadians came under the close scrutiny of the RCMP. Two men, for example, claiming to be a doctor and a priest, came to the Raymond temple to inspect the building on some vague pretence. They searched the premises in great detail, ferreting in such sacred areas as the *naijin* with such disrespect as to cause concern.

Southern Alberta was ideal for many west coast Japanese Canadians since they could come as a family. However, not many of them could have been prepared for what awaited them.

> As the uprooted west coast inhabitants tried to re-establish themselves in a landscape which must have been forbidding to those more familiar with temperate winters and maritime conditions, old religious ties helped to knit the dispersed in southern Alberta towns. Lethbridge was open - and grudgingly at that - to the newcomers only for employment, the city council of that largest of area towns having voted to prohibit the Japanese from dwelling within its limits.[11]

Ironically, it was the prohibiting of Japanese Canadians in the major towns that propagated Jodo Shinshu Buddhism in the area. Temples, as a result, were established in Picture Butte, Coaldale, Taber and Rosemary and finally Lethbridge which lifted its restriction soon after the war.

By March of 1942, the Raymond church administrators decided to petition the RCMP for a new resident minister in order to survive and to help the burgeoning population of Buddhists. A group of exiles from Haney-Hammond B.C. arrived in Raymond at the beginning of May. Among them were Rev. Yutetsu Kawamura and family.

> Japanese farmers were hired to work on the sugar beet farms in Alberta and Manitoba and the government endeavoured to gather people for this venture. Because this allowed family units to move together, I travelled around the area explaining the setup and persuaded the families to take this up. I had not been asked by the government to do this. I did this of my own volition. There was considerable response in numbers, especially from the Maple Ridge and Mission areas where I lived. It was gratifying that there were so many who responded positively to the idea.
>
> At that time, from the area near Lethbridge, a Mr. Andrew went to Vancouver representing the local farmers to present their case. Before that, Hironaka-*san* wired us stating, "Why don't you come back to Alberta?" He advised us to meet with and talk to

> Mr. Andrew. Already by then, the *nikkei* were forbidden to venture outside after dark. Just at that time, I had business in the Mission area so my wife Yoneko, with Mrs. Nobue Teramura as interpreter, went by taxi to Vancouver and met with Mr. Andrew at the Hotel Vancouver and discussed moving to Alberta, and because he knew Hironaka-*san* quite well, he spoke favourably of the move.
>
> Those of us from Maple Ridge boarded a special train carrying our small amounts of baggage and left the CPR station in Haney on April 28. Next day around noon, we were picked up by *hakujin* people who came to meet us; then we were taken separate ways.[12]

According to an RCMP report dated July 4, 1946, the total number of Japanese Canadians in Alberta was 4000. Over 3000 were displaced *nikkei* from the west coast.

A month after Rev. Kawamura's arrival, Rev. Shinjo Ikuta came with his family. At first, the two ministers were employed as labourers on the sugar beet farms surrounding Raymond. On Sundays they conducted services. In October of 1942, Rev. Kawamura and his family left for Picture Butte, a town 25 miles northwest of Lethbridge. About 250 *nikkei* families had settled in the area and they expressed a need for a food distribution centre. Rev. and Yoneko Kawamura set up a co-op store which sold rice, *miso, shoyu* and a variety of other Japanese staples. Yoichi Hironaka was a great help in organizing the move and establishing the store.

> Because Hironaka-*san* said for us to consult him regarding business finances, we were able to start and operate the co-op food store, and for the duration of the war, we were able to exist without undue hardship.[13]

In the meantime, Rev. Ikuta became the centre of the Raymond Church activity. He suggested in 1943 that a part of the children's education should be training in *kendo* and *judo*. Yuichi Akune, a fifth *dan* black belt in *kendo*, became the instructor of 37 students. Subsequently, Yoshio Katsuda, a fifth *dan* black belt in *judo*, was appointed as instructor of 30 students. Juzo Saruwatari was chosen as president of the two new departments in the church.

The basement of the church became the *dojo* for the once-a-week instruction. Surprisingly, the activity was so popular that the students trained hard until midnight some nights and soon *hakujin* students began to join the club.

In 1944 Rev. Ikuta suggested forming a daycare centre during the busy planting and harvesting seasons. Mrs. Ikuta undertook the role of supervisor, a wholly volunteer position.

As if a premonition of things to come, a Japanese Christian began spreading ill will amongst the Raymond population about the subversive nature of *kendo* and *judo*. Rumour had it that the martial arts were propagating Japanese nationalism. If not careful, the proponents may lead an insurrection of some kind.

To counter such ridiculous accusations, the club invited several representatives of the city, including the mayor and teachers, to observe a practice. It was agreed afterwards that the martial arts were some of the best sports to train the mind and the body.

Postwar Conflict

With the end of the war, the Japanese Canadians began their exodus to Japan or east of the Rockies. Raymond remained the centre of Buddhist activity for all of Canada. Rev. Toshio Katatsu paid Rev. Ikuta a visit in February 1946 and left the statue of the Buddha from the Steveston temple in his care. Rev. Katatsu stayed a few days before leaving for Japan.

Rev. Ikuta then contacted the custodian of the Royston Church, Kenroku Uchiyama, to make arrangements to transfer the altar from that church to the Raymond Bukkyokai. The altar arrived in April 1946.

To mark the occasion and to elevate the spirits of the congregation, a special ceremony was held. The *chigo* procession, led by a band, started at the townhall with Reverends Ryuchi Hirahara, Sokan Asaka, Yutetsu Kawamura and Shinjo Ikuta following. After a photo session at the temple garden, everyone entered the church to view the new candle-lit altar. Reverends Hirahara and Asaka spoke of the Buddhist revival with great optimism. They both felt Canada would accept Buddhism as part of its social fabric.

Unfortunately, such optimism was short lived. The end of the war seemed to signal some malcontents within the Japanese

Christian community to begin a campaign of persecution against the Buddhists. RCMP reports of the time made it clear the Japanese Christians felt that, while they had no objection to the Buddhist religion *per se*, Japanese of "marginal Canadian status" should stop practising "Japanese nationalistic ways" (speaking the language and indulging in the martial arts) and assimilate as quickly as possible.

> ...through the acceptance of Christianity, the Japanese will find themselves accepted as an integral part of Canadian society.[14]

Since Buddhist ministers were in Canada under a five year permit system, most were given deportation orders in 1946. Specifically, Rev. Ikuta received his order to leave the country on June 6 and Rev. Kawamura shortly thereafter. The RCMP cites the support of the Japanese Christian community which may have been integral in the government's decision to act.

> Sources state that this development has given the Buddhists quite a scare as all of their six Buddhist priests in Canada are only here under the permit system. In the meantime, this development was generally welcomed by the Christian Japanese and several have voiced the hope that the Immigration authorities would not be swayed by political pressure which the Buddhists are trying to foster.[15]

In the same report, a "leading Japanese Christian" states emphatically:

> I and others are pleased to hear that it is planned to send one, and we hope the rest, of the Buddhist priests, back to Japan. The sooner they do, it will be better for all the Japanese. As the spiritual leaders of the Buddhists, these priests hold the Japanese to the Japanese modes and ways of living. In their services, they always speak of the soul and spirit of Japan. They promote the continued use of the Japanese language and when they have spare time they teach the Japanese language to Canadian born Japanese. They promote Japanese culture at every opportunity, they form groups, clubs and societies to keep the Japanese together. By so doing, they build up small

> Tokyos which only bring the displeasure of the white residents upon us as a whole...In my opinion, the Buddhist priests are about the only personal ties the Japanese in Canada have with the old Japanese Nationalism and customs. When they go and the Japanese accept Christianity as a lot of us have done, we will be able to live on almost normal grounds with the Canadians... The Buddhists often state that Christian Japanese are traitors to the Japanese way of living... That is certainly Nationalism as preached or taught in the Buddhist Churches. In saying this I am thinking of the future welfare of the Japanese in Canada. We can be assimilated, as far as that is possible, and live in harmony here, as soon as the old Japanese customs are dropped and that will not take place as long as Buddhist priests, of the Japanese variety, remain here.[16]

For their part, the Buddhists reacted quickly.

> This communication [Rev. Ikuta's deportation order] threw the Buddhist executive of Raymond into a flurry of activity and a party under J. Sawada of Raymond went to Lethbridge on the 5th of June where they engaged the services of a lawyer...as a result of which telegrams were sent to Ottawa to stop the deportation...[17]

Furthermore, they enlisted the help of Mr. W. Baker, the Chairman of the Sugar Beet Growers Association, and Senator William A. Buchanan to petition Ottawa. As a result, Reverends Ikuta and Kawamura were granted a year's extension of their permits. (Extensions were then renewed on a year to year basis.) Eventually, Rev. Mitsubayashi and four other ministers (Reverends Katatsu, Hirahara, Asaka and Tachibana) were deported. Rev. Tsuji, the only Canadian born minister, relocated to Toronto to start the Buddhist Church there.

The Buddhist Foundation of Canada

Despite the deportation threat to the ministers, the remnants of the Jodo Shinshu movement that had started before the war in British Columbia and Raymond, Alberta, met to discuss the re-establishment of Buddhism in post-war Canada. About thirty representatives, led by Rev. Hirahara and including representatives of the Alberta churches and former directors of B.C. temples, assembled in the Raymond Church on April 22, 1946. They decided to form the Buddhist Foundation of Canada (BFC), an organization similar to the BCC formed in 1931 and disbanded because of the war. The foundation's purpose was to raise money and to oversee the administration of all Buddhist churches in Canada. Headquarters for the BFC was situated at the Raymond Church. The first Executive Committee consisted of:

Director	Rev. Shinjo Ikuta
Chairman	Kichizo Takaguchi
Deputy Chairman	Takashi Karaki
Treasurer	Juzo Saruwatari
Secretary	Masao Matsuki

Their main concern initially was to establish a communication network between the churches. Thus they drew up a list of priorities.

1. To publish a monthly newsletter to continue the missionary work,
2. To establish the financial means to continue the publication,
3. To compile a list of names of the congregation.

Rev. Ikuta became the editor of **Hojo**, a monthly publication consisting of four mimeographed pages of foolscap. Twenty-five hundred copies were printed and distributed, all in Japanese. Later English pages were added.

Activities

In 1946 the BFC responded to a request for a minister by the Coaldale Church. It petitioned the government for the release of Rev. Mitsubayashi, detained at the Angler Internment Camp. The minister arrived in Coaldale via Moose Jaw in January and stayed for six months before he was ordered to leave Canada. Reverends Hirahara, Katatsu, Asaka and Tachibana were also deported.

The deportation of virtually all ministers left Canadian Buddhism at loose ends. By 1947 the foundation designed four administrative and electoral districts in Canada. They were Eastern Canada (Toronto, Hamilton and Montreal); Manitoba

(Winnipeg); Alberta (Raymond, Coaldale and others); and British Columbia (Kelowna and New Denver). In order to alleviate the heavy burden for the remaining three ministers, Reverends Ikuta, Kawamura and Tsuji, the foundation devised a *hokkyoshi* (lay minister) system. Bishop Enryo Shigefuji of the BCA agreed to the idea on a trial basis.

The candidates for lay leadership were chosen by the BFC's board of directors. The Bishop provided a course of study to be administered by one of the ministers in Canada. When completed, the candidate would become an assistant to the minister.

The initial training group consisted of six members. Of the group, Charles Nekoda of Toronto and Hideo Nishimura of Winnipeg continued their studies in Kyoto, Japan. They later returned to Canada as *kaikyoshi* (ordained missionary ministers). Richard Robinson of Toronto eventually left for London, England, to study. He later became an ordained minister of the non-Jodo Shinshu Western Buddhist Order of England.

In the 1950s the organization cemented its structure and assigned Rev. S. Ikuta to Raymond, Rev. Kawamura and Rev. Nekoda to Alberta as district ministers, Rev. Nishimura to Winnipeg; and Rev. Tsuji to Toronto and Eastern Canada.

All remained secure until 1951 when the Kelowna Buddhist Church requested a district minister to serve British Columbia. The Foundation sought the advice of Bishop Shigefuji who approved the proposal. He further suggested that one of the Alberta ministers be assigned.

Unfortunately, an over-zealous reporter for **The New Canadian** announced in the paper that Rev. Ikuta was going to Kelowna as the new minister. The Raymond Church members became extremely upset since they valued Rev. Ikuta and honoured his accomplishments for their temple. Bishop Shigefuji again interceded and after much consultation with all involved announced in April 1951 Rev. Shinjo Ikuta's appointment to British Columbia. Rev. Kawamura took over as editor of the newsletter, **Hojo**.

The Foundation carried on until 1967 when the Buddhist Churches of Canada (BCC) was formed with its own Bishop. During this period the Buddhist Foundation of Canada launched several worthwhile projects. The Raymond Church YBA with the BFC's help built a *Nokotsudo* (repository) to store the many urns brought by the evacuees. The assets of the Slocan Buddhist Church were donated to the Raymond YBA for this purpose. The Foundation also provided accident insurance for the ministers, bought English textbooks for the Sunday School and supported the Montreal Buddhist Church in its struggle to be recognized in Quebec. The BFC established a scholarship to help aspiring ministers. Kakuei Tada, Rev. Kakusai Tada's son, graduated from Ryukoku University and expressed a desire to return to Toronto to become a *kaikyoshi*. The Foundation sponsored his return with the approval of the Toronto Buddhist Church.

In 1952 the BFC made arrangements for the Abbot Kosho and Lady Ohtani's tour of Canada. During their visit, the couple visited every temple and the Gomonshu held sessions with students and young members everywhere possible.

Southern Alberta:
Expansion and Prosperity

Chapter 11

Southern Alberta: Expansion and Prosperity

When I travelled here to wed,
Crossing the ocean from far, far away,
The port we reached was the western end of Canada.
Farther inland, farther - some several hundred miles
After a trying journey, I made it to the province on the prairies.

With my husband as my sole support and guide,
Looking at the grain fields swaying like waves,
Watching the colour of the setting sun in the western horizon,
I called to my mother and father.

Last year, the crop was poor, and again this year,
The winds that blew were dry, so dry,
Not having money for an ocean fare,
Wearing the same clothes all the time, their colours faded,
I ended up a poor mother.

In the winter, the mercury showed -30 degrees F.
With the condensation freezing on the windows
And the snow piling up outside,
The only sound in the silence of the night
Is the cry of the coyote searching for his supper.

"The Bride of Alberta"
Rev. Yutetsu Kawamura

The isolation of the 1920s, the desolation of the '30s and the persecution of the '40s combined to test the mettle of the Japanese Canadian Buddhists of Southern Alberta. By the mid to late 1940s, times were definitely getting better and signs of their prosperity flourished in several communities. The end of the war allowed Buddhists to regroup and re-establish the movement of Jodo Shinshu Buddhism. In order to do so, they had to improvise and compromise in order to continue as a church. Many of the churches, for example, did not have resident ministers. They simply had to rely on the itinerant minister. The history of individual temples demonstrates the tenacity of the congregations to overcome tremendous adversity in the wake of World War II.

Picture Butte Buddhist Church

About twenty miles northeast of Lethbridge stands the small farming hamlet of Picture Butte. During the war, 250 Japanese Canadian families were designated to the surrounding area in such settlements as Diamond City, Shaughnessy, Coalhurst, Kipp, Nobleford, Iron Springs and Turin.

Buddhist gatherings took place in Picture Butte only after the arrival of Rev. Kawamura and his family on October 13, 1942. They were provided with a house which belonged to the Snider family. Later, the front of the place was converted into a *kobai-bu* (a co-op store) and the back became the church as well as the minister's residence.

Shortly after the minister's arrival, a committee came together to establish a church with the following members:

S. Tanaka, K. Ichino, H. Miyagawa, K. Shikaze,
K. Kitagawa, D. Ito, M. Tateyama, S. Miyashita and K. Nishii.

The committee rented Koepke Hall and celebrated the official opening of the Picture Butte Bukkyokai January 9, 1943. The Executive Committee of the church was formed at the first general meeting on March 7, 1943. The President was S. Tanaka; Chairman - K. Ichino; Secretary - H. Miyagawa; Treasurer - D. Okabe; *Kobai-bu* Director - S. Tanaka.

Bukkyo Seinen Kai (Young Buddhist Association) Executive included President - S. Nakatsuru; Vice-President - Y. Shikaze; Chairman - K. Toyota; Secretary - George Nakatsuru; and Treasurer - M. Tateyama.

The membership of the temple stood at 189 in 1943. In 1945 the name of the church was changed to the Picture Butte Buddhist Church.

Highlights of the church's history included participation by guest ministers Rev. Hirahara and Asaka from B.C.'s interior in the 1946 (April 28) Hanamatsuri service. A month later, the members were able to purchase Snider's building that housed the minister, his family and the co-op store.

In 1961 Rev. Kawamura moved his family to Lethbridge. Various ministers from then on came to serve Picture Butte. In succession they were Reverends Nekoda, Kosaka, Fujikawa, Izumi, Miyaji, Okada, Terasaki, Miyakawa, Aoki and Watanabe. In 1971 a second building, the old Morman Hall next to the existing church, was purchased in order to accommodate funerals.

After the war and to the present day, the number of members declined at a slow but steady rate. By January 1992 only 40 people remained. At the annual general meeting the members decided to amalgamate with the Lethbridge Church.

Bishop Murakami presided over the combined 50th Anniversary and closing service on March 29, 1992. He recognized the dedication of the membership represented by the current Executive Committee: President - T. Masuda; Vice-President - N. Taguchi; Secretary - Mary and Hugh Osaka; Treasurer - T. Oga; Bldg. Fund Treasurer - F. Osaka; Advisor - M. Tokuda; and Auditors - J. Tanaka and Y. Oga.

On April 19, 1992, the Picture Butte Church officially amalgamated with the Lethbridge Buddhist Church during the Hanamatsuri Service in Lethbridge.

Courtesy of Bob Masuda

Picture Butte Buddhist Church, March 1992.

Taber Buddhist Church

Like Picture Butte, Taber experienced an influx of Japanese Canadians after the war. About 150 families settled into an area from Cranford to Fincastle. None of the Japanese Canadians was allowed to seek employment or residence in any town. They were also restricted to travel within a forty mile limit. Therefore the evacuees worked on sugar beet farms and settled in makeshift buildings some of which were no more than chicken shacks.

Although 90 families were professed Buddhists, it wasn't until 1945 that a committee was formed to study the possibility of a Buddhist Church organization for Taber. Until then and for the next two years, most Buddhists gathered at various homes with the visiting Rev. Kawamura or Rev. Ikuta presiding.

In 1947 the Buddhist Church was founded and a Ladies Auxiliary organized. President Kojiro Sakamoto and Tsurukichi Mishima arranged for services to be held at the rented South Hungarian Hall. Two years later, the members bought the place and planned for an extension to be added. A fund drive, consisting of donations, voluntary work and shares, was initiated in the spring of 1950. It was so successful that by that very summer a 30 X 80 ft. extension was added to the existing Hungarian Hall. The construction foreman was T. Maikawa.

To complete the new church, the *Gohonzon* image of the Buddha was donated by the New York Buddhist Church in March of 1951. Akisaburo Sato, secretary of the church, often travelled to New York. Later the American church was only too happy to help the obscure enclave of Jodo Shinshu

Courtesy of Jack Nagai

Taber Buddhist Church, 1992. Church members prepare for the chow mein fund raising event, Taber, Alberta.

Buddhism. Sato accepted the gift on behalf of the Taber Buddhist Church. Reverends Nekoda, Ikuta and Kawamura conducted the installation ceremony.

The Taber Church grew and prospered such that the Executive Committee was able to purchase a new shrine from Japan in March of 1964. To mark the event, a concert was held.

On December 3, 1972, the members celebrated the church's 25th Anniversary. The ceremony started with a *chigo* parade followed by a service and concert. During the service, scrolls were presented to all past presidents. They were K. Sakamoto, T. Mishima, K. Shimozawa, Y. Setoguchi, K. Ohno, Ted Tsuji, Ken Sakamoto, Yas Kaga, George Nakatsuru and Yoshiharo Miyada. The 1992 Executive Committee is indicative of the extent of the Taber Church's activities:

Stan Kanegawa	President
George Nakatsuru	Vice-President
Tom Kaga	Vice-President
Jack Shigeo Nagai	Secretary
Slim Shimozawa	Treasurer
Saburo Nishi	Chairman
Sonny Nakashima	Vice-Chairman
Roy Sassa	Vice-Chairman
Tad Sakaguchi	Social Convenor
Joe Miyada	Stage Custodian
Joe Nishi and Nori Higa	Asst. Stage Custodian
Audrey Kanegawa	Newsletter Editor

Through the years the church has enjoyed the services of several ministers: Reverends Shinjo Ikuta, Yutetsu Kawamura, Ensei Nekoda, Orai Fujikawa, Seimoku Kosaka, Yasuo Izumi, Leslie Kawamura, Fumio Miyaji, Yasuhiro Miyakawa, Shinji Okada and Itsuo Terasaki. The present ministers are Rev. Eisho Aoki and Rev. Shigenobu Watanabe.

There is a monthly Sunday School attended by twenty children and taught by Rev. Aoki who was assisted by Pat Sassa, Sally Kanegawa and Audrey Kanegawa. Perhaps the church is proudest of its contributions to the Taber community. As part of the Japanese community, it contributed $5000 to the Taber Swimming Pool Fund; it sponsors a scholarship for the most deserving Buddhist high school student; the Taber Buddhist Ladies Auxiliary assists at the Senior Citizens' Annual Tea. The spring and fall bazaars that feature *chow mein* dinners are eagerly anticipated annual social events.

Rosemary Buddhist Church

In 1947 a group of ten Japanese Canadian families in Rosemary met in private homes to conduct Sunday School services. Thus began Buddhist activity in this area. The next year Rev. Shinjo Ikuta came from Raymond to organize the first Buddhist Association. Sunday School was initially held in the home of Mr. and Mrs. N. Takeda. Later that year, the association rented the Clemeanceau School to accommodate the growing congregation.

The school proved to be adequate until 1952 when the members bought the first church - the modest basement of Pete Peters on his farm located three miles northwest of Rosemary.

Seventeen families from Rosemary, Brooks, Rainier, Bassano and Patricia were incorporated under the name Rosemary Buddhist Church. The Executive Committee consisted of Toshio Matoba, President; Gunzo Nishida, Director; and Kaisuke Hironaka, Treasurer. The ministers were Rev. Y. Kawamura and Rev. Nekoda.

In 1958 the congregation purchased a former Latter Day Saints church for $3000. An additional five acres of land adjacent to the building were obtained free. In 1964 Rev Tsuji from Toronto came as guest speaker for the 15th Anniversary. When he heard of the purchase of the building and land, he remarked, "You didn't buy a church, you were given a great gift!"

With the larger building the members felt the need for a larger *butsudan*. The original was donated by Tsuruyo

Courtesy of Mariko Hironaka

Rosemary Buddhist Church, 1990.

Kajiwara of Picture Butte in 1953. The congregation turned their attention to fund raising, primarily through the sale of *chow mein* dinners.

During a visit to the church for the 1965 Obon service, a Mr. Kondo from Japan offered to contact his friend who made *butsudan*. The church agreed. Mr. Shimizu of Japan quickly informed the church he would make the shrine. The church immediately sent a $1500 down payment. After a few years of hearing nothing from Mr. Shimizu, some members became quite worried. Fortunately, word came in March of 1968 that the shrine had arrived. It was waiting in Calgary.

The *butsudan*, a carefully fashioned piece of art, eventually was installed in the Rosemary Church. In February 1969, the receipt of the shrine and the 20th Anniversary of the Church were celebrated with the Nyu Butsu Shiki ceremony.

In the 1990s the congregation dwindled to about 26 people. Rev. Susumu Kyojo Ikuta still comes from Calgary twice a month to conduct services to as few as ten people. On the other hand, memorable moments are still being created. In November 1990 the church hosted the Alberta Buddhist Conference. Reverends McDonald and Ogui from the United States came as guest speakers.

Coaldale Buddhist Church

As with other small centres of Buddhism, Coaldale thrived with the arrival of Japanese Canadians during the spring of 1942. The Matsumiya, Okahashi, Hoyano, Furuse, Teramura, Tsujiura and Yamamoto families were among the first to arrive as sugar beet labourers.

Later that same year the community formed a Buddhist Church organizing committee. The members were Toshitaro Tanaka, Fukuzo Okano, Gengo Nishimura, Yoshio Okano, Tomekichi Takayama and Kikugoro Otani. They established the Coaldale Hoju Bukkyo-kai, and the first service was held on January 31, 1943 in the Teramura home, a converted general store. Rev. Yutetsu Kawamura presided with the help of representatives from Raymond and Picture Butte, K. Takaguchi and S. Tanaka respectively. Throughout the war, services had been held twice a month with the permission of the BC Security Commission and the RCMP.

In early 1943, the membership was able to construct a new church located on the present site of the Coaldale Centennial Library. The New Westminster Church had provided its shrine shortly after the evacuation and the carpenters installed it during construction. After completion, a dedication service took place March 20 with a newly elected Executive Committee:

F. Okano	President
T. Tanaka	Vice-President
R. Tsuji	Vice-President
G. Nishimura	Treasurer
T. Takayama	Altar Attendants
K. Otani	

The Coaldale Church commemorated its first Obon on August 8, 1943; the first Hanamatsuri on April 9, 1944.

By the late '40s, the church became the centre for social activity in the area. An association, called the Bukkyo Doshi Kai, was formed between the Okinawan Japanese and the west coast evacuees. Together they put on concerts, shows, plays and *odori*. Annual attractions included a *shibai* (Japanese play) directed by T. Kimura and a *chow mein* dinner. Through these events, funds were raised for various expenses and projects. In 1952, for example, Lord Abbott Ohtani from the Hongwanji in Kyoto paid a visit to the church.

The congregation grew to the point where a new building was needed. In 1959 the members purchased the Gem Theatre. After renovations were completed by the next year, an inaugural service opened the church.

Courtesy of Tom Tsukishima

Coaldale Buddhist Church, 1982.

During the 1960s, the Coaldale Church congregation split into two during the "Alberta Problem".[1] The majority joined the Lethbridge Honpa Buddhist Church while the few remaining struggled to keep the Coaldale temple alive. In the end they were successful.

Today the same Gem theatre building serves as the Coaldale Buddhist Church. After Rev. Kawamura, the ministers were Reverends S. Ikuta, E. H. Nekoda, S. Kosaka, O. Fujikawa, Y. Izumi, E. Mitsubayashi, Y. Miyakawa, S. Okada, I. Terasaki, and F. Miyaji. The present ministers are Rev. Eisho Aoki and Rev. Shigenobu Watanabe.

Calgary Buddhist Church

By the early 1950s the Japanese Canadians of Southern Alberta began moving from their assigned locations to areas where better employment opportunities existed. Some tried British Columbia again, others moved eastward. Still others moved to the major city of Calgary.

A committee soon formed and invited Rev. Y. Kawamura to discuss the possibility of creating a Buddhist Society. Members of that committee were Mr. and Mrs. Sataro Kuwahara, Mr. and Mrs. S. Odagaki (Sr.), Mr. and Mrs. Yuhei Nawata, George Nishimoto, Mr. and Mrs. George Matsuoka, Mr. and Mrs. Casey Yoneda, Mr. and Mrs. M. Hashimoto, Mr. and Mrs. Kunihei Mura, and Mr. and Mrs. S. Nagai. At Rev. Kawamura's suggestion the group was named the Calgary Hoyu Kai (Friends of Dharma). They commemorated the event and Obon in the Labour Temple Hall on August 17, 1951.

George Nishimoto became the first president and Mr. Wada the first treasurer. For the next several years, services were held in the homes of several members.

A Sunday School was established in 1958. Mick Saruwatari and Hunk Takaguchi volunteered as the first Sunday School teachers to a small group of six children. Shortly thereafter Mrs. Mich Takaguchi took on the responsibility of Chair of the Sunday School Committee and developed the program extensively. Other teachers included Mrs. Tazuko Sawada, Miss Mich Hatanaka and Richard Takahara.

The controversy of the mid '60s in Southern Alberta[2] fragmented the group in Calgary. Despite the dissent, the

Buddhist Society under the leadership of Jits Oishi held a 10th Anniversary Service and Concert at the Golden Age Club Hall in April 1965.

In 1970 the committee conducted a survey to see if a significant number of Buddhist families were willing to support a Jodo Shinshu minister. Shortly thereafter Bruce Kimura, representing the Hoyu Kai, wrote to the BCC requesting "a fluent English speaking minister". Bishop N. Ishiura responded with a few concerns.

> In order to import a minister, the National Office of the Buddhist Churches of Canada must submit a statement of basic salary and other benefits before the Dept. of Immigration will even consider granting a visa.
>
> Your statistics show that there are 10 families plus who will actively support a minister. Your estimated population is at 1000 individuals of which roughly one half might be Buddhists.
>
> Your immediate concern is in organizing yourself into a church oriented organization; with the aid of possibly Rev. Fujikawa, you might do the following: 1. hold regular services; 2. publication (preferably monthly); 3. membership campaign (set goal); 4. fund raising; 5. obtain government charter as a church organization.
>
> In studying church administrative structure, it is possible to maintain a $7500 budget with 40-60 active members. Breakdown the budget into per head (forget per family custom) proration. Supplement with fund raising.[3]

Fund Raising

In order to raise funds to support the church and to finance various projects including the first church building, the association sponsored an annual *teriyaki* dinner. The first was a *chow mein* dinner held in the fall of 1971 at the Stanley Park Community Hall. The members also participated in the Chinook Centre Charity Bazaar every year.

With a subsequent offer from The Buddhist Churches of Canada to support part of the wages for a minister in early 1972, Rev. Susumu Kyojo Ikuta and family came to Calgary to lead a newly formed Calgary Buddhist Church group.

The Board of Directors also took Bishop Ishiura's advice and implemented the Pledge System for membership. Individuals rather than families started in June 1972 to contribute money to operate the church. The old system was a holdover from the Meiji Period and seen as outmoded.

By 1974 the BCC could no longer support the wages of the minister. Rev. Ikuta and the membership decided to start a semi-permanent fund raising project. With investment money from members and friends across the country, Rev. Ikuta opened a *teppan-yaki* restaurant called Omi of Japan.

> The Board of Directors fully support Rev. Ikuta in establishing a church here. Nevertheless, the Board also feels that it would be too much to ask each member to contribute a sum of money towards the construction of a building at the present time since our congregation is small.
>
> For this reason, the Board has decided to form the above named holding company [Calgary Buddhists Equities Ltd.] which will in all probability enter into an association with other organizations to operate a Japanese style restaurant.
>
> We sincerely believe that the only method by which our church will become self-supporting is by entering into an investment project which will be of benefit to the church and be of service to the Calgary community.[4]

The Board then collected $80,000 in cash and promissory notes from members across the country before selecting the site at 2nd Street and 10th Avenue S.W. They raised an extra $40,000 for operating costs. The objectives for the business were as follows:

1. To operate a Japanese type restaurant so that a portion of the profit will be an income to the Calgary Buddhist Church.
2. To return the profit to the members who have loaned monies to the Church in a form of apportion to the loan.
3. To offer working opportunities to the people of Japanese origin.[5]

The restaurant opened in May 1973 and operated until 1982 when it was thought wise to close the business. Until then the business did provide money to run the church and pay for part of the minister's salary. Unfortunately, many investors lost their investment. However, those investors have been promised eventual compensation.

The church building fund began in earnest in 1977. Mitts Ikeda and committee ran a casino and raised about $24,000. In 1980, the President, Mike Kitagawa, approached the Croatian Catholic Society to purchase their building. Soon thereafter, 700 requests for donations went out all across Canada. The response was tremendous; the down payment was soon realized.

On February 1, 1981, the church bought the Croatian Catholic Church at 207 6th Street N.E. The inaugural service for the first Calgary Buddhist Church took place October 18, 1981.

Courtesy of K.C. Yoneda

Calgary Buddhist Church, 1990.

Activities

The Fujinkai of the Calgary Church began informally in 1955 with a group of twenty women known as the Hoyukai. They looked after organizing special services and welcoming new members. In 1972 the Fujinkai became formally organized with elected officers. With approximately thirty members, the club today is the driving force behind such important fund raising activities as the Chicken Teriyaki Dinner and the Chinook Charity Bazaar. In 1978 the Fujinkai joined the Canada Buddhist Women's Federation.

Other activities included the Japanese Language School, founded by Rev. and Mrs. Ikuta in the spring of 1974. Thirty students enrolled initially. A youth camp was begun in 1978 with 60 students under the leadership of Mrs. Mich Takaguchi and Dr. G. Campbell. In 1983 a Lay Leader's Seminar took place. That same year, Rev. Ikuta conducted a tour of the Hongwanji (*Nembutsu Hoshi Dan*) for nine students from across Canada.

In 1984 the present statue of the Amida Buddha arrived after having been on display in Tokyo and Europe. It was carved by the famous sculptor Koei Eri. The church held a dedication service on October 21 with Mr. and Mrs. Eri as honoured guests.

On November 2, the Gomonshu and Lady Ohtani visited the church. During a special service, the Monshu ordained Rev. Fred Ulrich as a minister of the BCC.

Since the early '50s, the Calgary Church has enjoyed a steady growth in its membership, starting with 40 families to a burgeoning 70 families. In the 1990s there is much optimism for the continuance of the church with a number of young families as well as several non-Japanese Canadians joining the congregation.

The temple continues its charitable work within the Calgary community. It collects for the local food bank, sponsors foster children through the United Nations, and raises funds for disaster relief around the world. Rev. Ikuta serves as an advisor to the Calgary Chaplaincy Committee. He also gives talks on Buddhism at colleges, high schools as well as correctional institutions in Calgary and Drumheller.

Lethbridge Buddhist Church

In 1946 after the war ended, the city of Lethbridge lifted the restriction that prevented Japanese Canadians from living within the city limits. The Ichiroh Hisaoka family settled first in Lethbridge early in '46 followed by the Moichi Kosaka and Toyosaburo Nakamura families. The next two years saw a great many Japanese families taking advantage of the relaxation of the restriction. Most of the new settlers came from Picture Butte.

On a Sunday afternoon in December 1948, thirty people attended a service held by Rev. Y. Kawamura of Picture Butte in the lunchroom of the Broder Canning Company. The place was ideal since many of the evacuees worked for the vegetable canning plant.

A year later the community staged its first Obon service at the Rainbow Hall in the north end of Lethbridge. The first Ho-onko service was held at the Labour Temple Hall in January 1950. Afterwards, the congregation called a meeting to form a Buddhist organization in order to consolidate the activities of the congregation. Moichi Kosaka and Yaozo Nomura became Chairman and Treasurer respectively of the Lethbridge Shinto Kai.

A month later the first Sunday School class was conducted in the basement of Yosokichi Kitagawa's house on 16th Street North. Later the school moved to the Miner's Hall with Moichi Kosaka appointed as the *hokkyoshi* by the Hongwanji.

At the first general meeting held in room 14 of the Civic Centre, September 1950, the name of the organization was changed to the Lethbridge Bukkyo-kai. There were 20 members. The Executive Committee consisted of:

President	Moichi Kosaka
Vice-President	Kosaburo Ichino
Chairman	Yosokichi Kitagawa
Secretary	Toyosaburo Nakamura
Treasurer	Kiyoshi Kinoshita

A meeting took place a month later in the chapel hall of the Christensen Funeral Home to establish the Lethbridge Bukkyo Fujinkai. Ten women joined and elected Suma Uyemura president. To mark the two events, Rev. Kawamura and the newly appointed *nisei* minister Rev. Ensei Nekoda led a service at the Rainbow Hall. Afterwards a variety show and concert entertained a packed audience comprised of people from all over southern Alberta.

The First Church

With a growing congregation and established organizations, the members decided to raise funds for a building. The fund drive commenced immediately, presided over by the Building

Fund Committee. A *Tanomoshi-ko* or Credit Union also came together at about the same time. While each member invested a certain amount every month, an interested member borrowed the collected amount and paid interest to the others. One portion of the profits went to the building fund.

Money also came from a grand carnival held at the Lethbridge Civic Centre during May 1952. Over $1000 was earned; $400 came from the Custodian sale of the Buddhist Church in Mission B.C. where most Lethbridge Buddhists originally lived.

Finally in 1952 the church petitioned city hall to purchase land to construct a building. Initially, the city rejected the proposal since the Bukkyo-kai was not a registered organization. The church officials negotiated with the city and finally a building permit was issued with three individuals acting as trustees - Yosokichi Kitagawa, Toyosaburo Nakamura and Kihei Kobayashi. The permit however specified that the building was to be built within one year of the date of issue which was impossible since the money simply was not there. Further negotiation through a lawyer resulted in a five year extension to complete construction. A Building Construction Committee was then formed with Yosokichi Kitagawa as Chairman and Hiroji Takeda, Treasurer.

Construction began September 5, 1952. Lord Abbot Kosho Ohtani performed the sod-turning ceremony on Nov. 9, 1952, during his visit to Lethbridge while on a North American tour. The first service in the new building was the Ho-onko Service held in January 1955. The place was still under construction; there were cracks in the rough sub-floor, the walls and ceiling were unpainted. A *butsudan* was painted on a large piece of cardboard and hung on the front wall. This crude representation remained until a formal shrine was installed in 1957.

On April 1, 1956, the members held a special commemoration service for the completion of the building. A variety show followed. Remarkably, the congregation did not borrow a large sum of money to build the church. Instead, volunteers were used as much as possible. The debt free building was a tribute to the tenacity and volunteer spirit of the congregation.

A temple shrine was then ordered from a Kyoto *butsudan* maker. It arrived in the fall of 1957. In the meantime, volunteers again built a 10' by 50' extension to accommodate the shrine. On April 5 and 6, 1958, Rev. Kawamura presided over an enshrining ceremony (Nyu Butsu Keisan Hoyo). Rev. R. Nishimura of Manitoba participated as guest speaker. The Memorial Service took place on the 5th. The next day featured a *chigo* parade, Rev. Nishimura's speech and a variety show which altogether took all day to midnight.

Activities

The church prospered in its new quarters. In 1959 the 10th Anniversary Service featured sermons given by Rev. Kawamura and Rev. Nekoda. A *horin* (Buddhist emblem) badge was presented that day to 54 people, 65 years and older. In November of that year, Bishop Hanayama of the Buddhist Churches of America paid a visit. Rev. Gishu Kudo, a governor of the Nishi Hongwanji, spoke at a service in 1960.

In 1961 the church decided to add another extension to house the Sunday School. The construction of the 1300 square foot addition was awarded to a local contractor who completed the task by March 1962. Rev. Tetsunen Yamada of Hamilton came as guest speaker for the opening service.

In order to pay for the extension, the church held benefit *chow mein* dinners, exhibition food booths, sugar beet thinning bees and bazaars. Their efforts were successful.

During the summer of 1962, thirty church members went on a tour of Japan specifically to visit the Hongwanji and to participate in the celebration of Shinran Shonin's 700th Memorial Service. They brought back a statue of Saint Shinran and donated it to the church. The church held an installation service in 1965 with Rev. Kenryo Kumata of the Seattle Betsuin Church as guest speaker. Almost as a reciprocal move, Lord and Lady Ohtani visited Lethbridge on their way home from the World's Fair in Seattle and Banff. The members threw a reception in their honour at the Lotus Inn.

With the 15th Anniversary of the Lethbridge Buddhist Church and Fujinkai, the administration purchased an old duplex across the street from the church to house the minister. The Japanese Language School then became affiliated with the church. Teachers in succession for the school were Rev. S. Kosaka, Rev. Y. Izumi, Rev. F. Miyaji and his son Koji, Rev. I. Terasaki, and Rev. and Mrs. E. Aoki. In 1991 the school separated from the church and was incorporated in order to receive grants from the Alberta government. It still uses the church facilities.

In 1964 as well, the youth of the church organized the Young Buddhists Association. Under this department came the Junior YBA, Sunday School classes, Sunday School teachers and the League of Sunday School Teachers. All progressed very nicely until the controversy over the ministers affected all the churches in Southern Alberta.

The Lethbridge Church in particular suffered diminished numbers - so much so, the YBA and Jr. YBA had to fold. Things really didn't begin to turn around until 1968 when Rev. Orai Fujikawa arrived to help Rev. Seimoku Kosaka. The "Alberta Problem" however was not resolved for several years hence.

During the 1971 Ho-onko Service tragedy struck. Rev. Ryokan Nishimura of Winnipeg gave an inspiring speech. The next day at a reception, he became very ill and was taken to Lethbridge Municipal Hospital. He died there on February 7. The Otsuya Service was held in Lethbridge and the funeral in Winnipeg on the 11th of February.

In the spring of 1976, the members began construction of a new church duplex. By the beginning of December, Rev. Fumio Miyaji and his family moved into the residence side of the building.

Courtesy of Akira Terashima

Lethbridge Buddhist Church, 1990.

The seminal year for reorganization of the Lethbridge Buddhist Church is considered to be 1978. The Japanese speaking *issei* members asked the English speaking *nisei* to take over the operational management of the church. Thus Nobby Nakahama served as President and struck a committee to write a new constitution and by-laws. Minutes of meetings and records were then kept in English rather than Japanese. In fact, meetings were conducted in English with Japanese interpretation upon request only.

To recognize the devotion of the *issei* members, a resolution was passed to designate members aged 75 and over a "life member". During the AGM, members reaching the age of 88 received commemorative certificates and canes of longevity.

The Buddhist Federation of Alberta

In order to celebrate the 75th Anniversary of Jodo Shinshu Buddhism in Canada, the executive of the Lethbridge Buddhist Church decided to support the idea of an all Alberta Conference to be held in Banff on November 2, 3 and 4, 1980. The conference was very important since it was to be the first occasion that all the churches on both sides of the "Alberta Problem" came together to work on a co-operative project.

The All-Alberta Buddhist Conference was very successful. Its theme was "In Compassion of Amida Buddha - 75th Anniversary", appropriate considering it served to remind everyone who attended the true intentions of the *Dharma*. Rev. Toshio Murakami and Rev. Seigen Yamaoka were the guest speakers. One hopeful resolution to come from the conference was the formation of the Alberta Buddhist Churches, a loose association of all the churches that continued to sponsor an annual conference. The second all Alberta conference was held during November 1981 in Lethbridge. Rev. Tetsuo Unno of Pasadena and Rev. Zesei Kawasaki of Oxnard, California, were the guest speakers.

Finally in August 1982, Lethbridge and all the churches in Alberta agreed to join together under one umbrella organization. Calgary remained an affiliate member. On June 23, representatives from every church met and constructed a provisional board of directors. Thus the Buddhist Federation of Alberta came into existence "to co-ordinate those activities of the member churches in furthering Jodo Shinshu Teaching".[6] Nobby Nakahama, President of the Lethbridge Church, was elected Chairman of the Board. Rev. Hoshin Okada was appointed head minister of the Buddhist Federation of Alberta with Rev. Yasuhiro Miyakawa as second minister. Rev. Yutetsu Kawamura retired on July 31, 1982. Two years later he was appointed a Member of the Order of Canada for his pioneering work for Jodo Shinshu Buddhism in Canada.

The organization became registered under the Alberta Societies Act as the "BFA - Buddhist Jodo Shinshu Federation of Alberta" in April 1987. The main responsibility of the BFA was to look after the welfare and requirements of each minister, everything from his salary and expenses to his accommodations and transportation. The federation also handled the scheduling of ministers for the various church visits in Alberta.

In 1992, the BFA faced the problem of diminishing congregations. It therefore adopted the following resolution:

> Whereas our 6 churches are experiencing a decline in membership it will be increasingly difficult (financially) to maintain proper service to the membership. Therefore, be it resolved that the federation form a committee immediately, a committee comprised of one representative from each church for the purpose of discussing centralization or other alternatives.[7]

After several meetings, the committee turned the problem over to the Future Development Committee composed of members from the Young Buddhist Association.

The Present Lethbridge Buddhist Church

Throughout the 1980s and '90s, the Lethbridge Buddhist Church enjoyed a period of stability and continuous growth. The Alberta Buddhist Conferences continued on an annual basis with the host city designated on a rotational basis. The Lord Abbot Koshin Ohtani and Lady Ohtani visited Lethbridge in late 1984. The church ran a donation drive for the Lethbridge Soup Kitchen. Furthermore, the church donated significant amounts to the Lethbridge Food Bank and the Lethbridge Interfaith Food Bank.

In 1990 the church decided to discontinue the Exhibition Food Booth during the city's Whoop-Up Days celebration because of dwindling profits. It continues its fund drives through the annual Spring Chow Mein Supper and Bazaar, the annual Fall Chow Mein Supper and Bake Sale, and Mochi-Tsuki Sale.

The Lethbridge Church and Fujinkai hosted in 1992 the Annual General Meeting of the Buddhist Churches of Canada and the 10th Annual Buddhist Churches of Canada Women's Conference.

Although there have been many significant anniversaries, the 1993 45th Anniversary Service of the Lethbridge Church and Fujinkai must have been the most satisfying. With Rev.

S. K. Ikuta of Calgary as guest speaker, the members were secure in the knowledge that despite all the strife and tribulations the church was strong enough to survive and even prosper.

The following is a list of itinerant ministers who served the Alberta Buddhist Churches from 1948 to the present.

Rev. Yutetsu Kawamura	1948 - 1965
Rev. Shinjo Ikuta	1950 - 1951
Rev. Ensei Nekoda	1951 - 1960
Rev. Seimoku Kosaka	1966 - 1972
Rev. Orai Fujikawa	1968 - 1970
Rev. Yasuo Izumi	1970 - 1975
Rev. Fumio Miyaji	1975 - 1982
Rev. Hoshin Shinji Okada	1982 - 1987
Rev. Yasuhiro Miyakawa	1982 - 1985
Rev. Itsuo Terasaki	1985 - 1988
Rev. Eisho Aoki	1988 - present
Rev. Shigenobu Watanabe	1991 - 1994
Rev. Masanobu Nishiaki	1994 - present

Lethbridge Ministerial Aides

Ryoei Yoshio Okano	1948 - 1952
Moichi Kosaka	1950 - 1965
Hikojiro Miyagawa	195? - 1961
Gonpei Fukunaga	196? - 1978

The dates represent the time served at the Lethbridge Buddhist Church.

The revival of Jodo Shinshu Buddhism from near eradication is attributable to the exile of Japanese Canadians from the West Coast to Southern Alberta. As demonstrated in the histories above, there are distinct similarities in the struggles and triumphs of all the churches. It is clear, however, that the Japanese Canadians who had already settled in Southern Alberta by the start of the war joined the evacuees in their devotion to the teachings of the Amida Buddha to overcome all adversity to allow the movement to survive. Such dedication was necessary in light of the dissension that erupted during the 1960s.

The Alberta Problem

Chapter 12

The Alberta Problem

Similar to the controversy surrounding Rev. Shigeno in the 1920s in Vancouver, "The Alberta Problem", a euphemism coined by the Nishi Hongwanji, served to fragment the Jodo Shinshu churches in Southern Alberta in the 1960s.

Japanese Canadian historians and *nisei* church leaders agree, the church was ripe for dissension after the war. There had always been some resentment by the Southern Alberta Buddhists toward the B.C. Buddhists. Albertans were seemingly ignored by their West Coast counterparts in most church matters. The Bussei Renmei for example was 800 members strong but did not include any young Buddhists east of the Rockies. In all probability, the oversight was unintentional owing much to distance and the natural barrier called the Rocky Mountains. Still, the Raymond Buddhist Church was established in 1929 and was an important part of the Buddhist Churches of Canada since it represented Buddhism outside the confines of British Columbia. To be ignored was to be insulted.

When the war began, hundreds of West Coast evacuees inundated Southern Alberta, causing much friction between the newcomers and pioneers. The evacuees were considered presumptuous for trying to take over the church after settling in the area. To complicate matters, they were probably seen as having done something wrong for their exile. The pioneers, on the other hand, had paid their dues with back breaking work and much sacrifice in order to be considered model citizens by the local dominant white population. The dissension also cut across generational lines. The *issei* leaders simply refused to relinquish responsibility to the younger, upstart *nisei*.

The Buddhist Foundation of Canada (BFC) was established in Raymond in 1946 but had no administrative power over the ministers. Instead, all Buddhist Churches in Canada came under the jurisdiction of the Buddhist Churches of America. The situation proved to be yet another source of frustration for Canadian Buddhists. They began to voice their opinion that a Bishop who knew nothing of the area and its problems could not provide the proper leadership to make informed judgments.

On March 8, 1965, the Alberta Buddhist Churches or Kyoku met in Coaldale with Bishop Hanayama of the Buddhist Churches of America and Buddhist Foundation of Canada to discuss ministerial matters. Several issues were at hand, but one in particular rose to the surface. Recalling that meeting, Rev. Y. Kawamura told of a proposal that set off a chain of events of profound proportions.

> Carl Steiner, who was in the tourist business and was not doing well in this business, discussed with me how he could get more business on tourism for Lethbridge. The Japanese Garden was created to attract more tourists to Lethbridge. At that time, some people thought that I would be coming around to ask for money for the Japanese Garden. Emotions were so high that some people threatened to kill me.[1]

Bishop Hanayama became so upset at the threats that he immediately requested Rev. Kawamura be transferred to the small town of Waimea on the island of Kauai, Hawaii.

The stormy debates came to an abrupt end when Rev. Kawamura and his son, Rev. Leslie Kawamura, resigned as ministers of the BFC. He then promised he and his son would continue as ministers based in Raymond. After the declaration, the Alberta churches split into factions: the Raymond and Coaldale Churches and the Southern Alberta Sunday School Teachers League supported Rev. Kawamura while the Lethbridge, Taber and Picture Butte Churches remained in opposition. Attempts were made at the Coaldale meeting to reconcile the two sides but only confusion and a widening gap ensued. In the meantime, Rev. Kawamura and his supporters formed their own organization.

> I was at the Alberta Kyoku meeting as a Sunday School

> Teachers League delegate when the present Lethbridge Buddhist Church and the present Picture Butte Buddhist Church delegate walked out of the "then" Kyoku meeting saying that the Kyoku was finished. If the Sunday School Teachers League had not come up with some solution to retain the ministers, Buddhism in Alberta would have been in a very sad state. Following the break up of the Alberta Kyoku "at that time" the remaining delegates elected eight members plus the minister to formulate something to replace the defunct Kyoku. This was started with the full approval of Bishop Hanayama and Rev. Nishimura of the then head office Winnipeg. From this the Hompa [or Honpa] Buddhist Church came into being. Now you must understand that this was basically *nisei* and there were points not quite in accord with the *issei* thinking.[2]

The next day in Raymond at the Kyodan (Ministers) Conference of the BFC, the members passed a resolution recognizing Rev. Kawamura's supporters as members of the Buddhist Foundation of Canada while ousting those that opposed Rev. Kawamura. In other words, the Raymond and Coaldale Churches were still considered Foundation[3] churches while the Lethbridge, Taber and Picture Butte Churches were not.

On March 21, the Lethbridge Buddhist Church members held an emergency meeting to deal with the implications of the events. After lengthy and much heated discussion, they decided to acquire their own minister and not join Rev. Kawamura's new organization. A protest of the decision was lodged by several Sunday School teachers who promptly resigned.

One month later, the Lethbridge Church led the way in organizing a new association, the Alberta Kyoku or Alberta Buddhist Church Association, with the Taber and Picture Butte Buddhist Churches. In 1969, the Coaldale Buddhist Church joined them, resulting in half the congregation joining the Lethbridge Honpa Church of Alberta with Rev. Leslie Kawamura presiding while the other half stayed with the Alberta Kyoku in Coaldale. Eventually Buddhist groups identified as either Honpa or Buddhist Association appeared in Lethbridge, Raymond and Coaldale. In some cases, the split was acrimonious. In Coaldale, for example, members were described as unceremoniously "taking out money, 100 chairs, two scrolls".[4] Some even said the Honpa members left the church practically empty. On the other hand, a member of the Honpa Church recalled, "The Coaldale Buddhist Church was an incorporated organization and the two parties, with lawyers present, made the division of the properties legal..."[5] In fact, a letter from the law firm of Davidson, Davidson & Williams of Lethbridge, Alberta (May 27, 1969) indicates what their clients, the Honpa faction of the Coaldale Church, felt entitled to:

a) all monies other than...$1000
b) a movie projector and screen, a tape recorder and a complete P.A. system
c) 100 stack-up chairs and cushions
d) 2 scrolls that were recently purchased for the Shrine
e) general utensils such as plates, cups, spoons, etc.
- one-half of those presently held by the Church.

The accusation that the church had been ransacked was dismissed as propaganda.

Nevertheless, a major problem facing the new association of remaining BCC churches was the lack of a minister. They decided to make a direct appeal to the Nishi Hongwanji.

Before hearing the plea from the new Kyoku, however, the Hongwanji decided to do something about the "Alberta Problem". They keenly felt that Alberta could not support two Buddhist organizations. Their fears were soon confirmed. Attendance fell immediately and rapidly. During one of its monthly services shortly after the break, the Taber Buddhist Association had only three members in the congregation. The Lethbridge Buddhist Association lost 45 families out of 160 to the new Honpa Church. Bishop Hanayama and the BCC's administrative director, Rev. R. Nishimura, were therefore instructed to mediate the situation and find a solution.

The reaction was swift. Rev. Kawamura's supporters claimed any mediation would be inappropriate since it was contrary to the resolution passed in Raymond on March 9. Rev. Nishimura countered by stating that he and the Bishop were acting on a directive from the Hongwanji, not on behalf of the BCC.

The first stumbling block the two mediators faced was the resolution to expel the three members of the Alberta Buddhist Church Association: Lethbridge, Taber and Picture Butte. A repeal of the resolution had to take place.

From June 16 to 18, 1965, Bishop Hanayama, Rev. Nishimura

and two Directors of the BCC met with representatives from both sides in a series of meetings. After much negotiation, several decisions were declared.

1. Rev. Yutetsu Kawamura and Rev. Leslie Kawamura will be transferred to posts in the U.S.A.
2. A new minister will be appointed immediately to replace Rev. Y. Kawamura.
3. Rev. Leslie Kawamura will stay in Alberta until a replacement can be found.
4. The Lethbridge, Taber and Picture Butte Buddhist Churches will be reinstated as Buddhist Church of Canada members.

Both sides seemed satisfied with the announcement of the resolutions. What transpired next however ruined all the efforts of the BCC. Both Rev. Kawamuras and their supporters inexplicably broke away from the BCC to form a counter organization known as the Honpa Buddhist Church of Alberta with headquarters in Raymond and affiliate churches in Lethbridge and Rosemary.

Rev. Leslie Kawamura must have known recognition of the new organization by the Alberta government would take some time. The church in fact finally received registration under The Marriage Act from the Dept. of Health Feb. 4, 1969. The Honpa Buddhist Church of Alberta needed registered ministers in order to perform weddings and other ceremonies. Since his father was leaving shortly, Rev. Leslie Kawamura was caught in a bind. As speculation would have it, he took it upon himself to appoint his wife Toyo as a minister and to request a Certificate of Registration for her and himself.

In a letter dated November 9, 1965, Rev. L. Kawamura stated his intentions to J. Colville, Director - Division of Vital Statistics, Dept. of Public Health, Edmonton Alberta.

> Since my father, Rev. Yutetsu Kawamura, will be transferred to Hawaii, I have become the Secretary for the Buddhist Churches in Alberta...
>
> The persons who will require Certificates of Registration will be as follows:
>
> Rev. Leslie Kawamura   Raymond, Alberta
> Rev. Toyo Kawamura   Raymond, Alberta
>
> As to the present, these are the only two ministers in

Alberta for the Buddhist denomination. If anyone else should be officially designated by the Head Temple in Kyoto, Japan, in the future, I shall inform you of the addition.

Yours truly,
Rev. Leslie Kawamura[6]

However, the split to form the Honpa Buddhist Church of Alberta automatically invalidated Rev. Leslie Kawamura's claim as "Secretary for the Buddhist Churches in Alberta" according to the Alberta Kyoku and the BCC. The letter may have been true, albeit misleading, if he considered himself the Secretary of the Honpa organization, although the ordination of his wife was suspect in any event. The Department of Health, as a result, recognized Rev. L. Kawamura as the only authority sanctioned to request ministerial certificates in Alberta and consequently issued Certificates of Registration to Rev. Leslie Kawamura and Toyo Kawamura.

Subsequent letters to the Dept. of Health from the Alberta Buddhist Churches (Alberta Kyoku), Rev. Seimoku Kosaka and the Nishi Hongwanji only served to confuse the authorities for years to come.

On March 29, 1966, several dignitaries met in Calgary to discuss the new developments of "The Alberta Problem". Bishop Hanayama and Rev. Ejitsu Hojo of the BCA; Reverends Shinjo Ikuta, S. K. Ikuta, Newton Ishiura, S. Okada, R. Nishimura and Yutetsu Kawamura; H. Kuwata and Y. Abe, Directors of the BFC; ten members of the Honpa churches; and ten members of the Alberta Kyoku churches attended. Ostensibly, they met to ascertain why the stipulations of agreement reached at the June 18, 1965 meeting were not upheld. Why was there a need to establish the Honpa Buddhist Church of Alberta?

Central to the impasse was Rev. Leslie Kawamura's refusal to be transferred to the United States. He in fact emphatically claimed he never agreed to leave Alberta in the first place. Bishop Hanayama explained the transfer was not written in stone; it was contingent on Rev. Kawamura's co-operation. Still, heated debate ensued without any agreement achieved at the conclusion of the meeting. The day stretched from 1:00 p.m. to 2:00 a.m. the next morning.

The Kyoku Churches still had no minister. Rev. Nishimura

was called upon to travel from Manitoba to conduct funeral services and Hanamatsuri services. The lay minister Gonbei Fukunaga looked after the family services and the Lethbridge Buddhist Church Sunday School. Finally Rev. Seimoku Kosaka arrived on May 21, 1966.

Having received a copy of the Nov. 9, 1965 letter from Rev. L. Kawamura to J. Colville, Director, Dept. of Public Health, the Nishi Hongwanji was anxious to clear the ambiguity of authority in Southern Alberta. The following is an excerpt from a letter from Rev. Banho Kawatsuki, Head, Dept. of Foreign Missions, Nishi Hongwanji to Rev. Nishimura, Secretary General, BCC:

> As to the problems in Alberta, we are as concerned as those who are directly involved. Although we have hoped and tried to open a way to settle the problem as soon as possible, it seems to be getting worse and worse. It is rather painful for those who profess Buddhist faith.
>
> Since there seems to be some misunderstanding about the items listed below, I would like to have you explain them directly to those who are concerned:

1. Rev. Seimoku Kosaka has succeeded Rev. Yutetsu Kawamura. That is, he is ordered to assume the position of the Head Minister of the Buddhist Church of Alberta.
2. Rev. Yoshiaki (Leslie) Kawamura is ordered to assume the position of the minister at Raymond Buddhist Church. (His wife, Toyo Kawamura, has not been ordained as Buddhist minister.)
3. The Buddhist Church of Alberta, Jodo Shinshu, Hongwanji sect, encompasses: Raymond Buddhist Association, Lethbridge Buddhist Association, Coaldale Buddhist Association, Taber Buddhist Association, Rosemary Buddhist Association, Picture Butte Buddhist Association and the Calgary Hoyu Association.
4. We do not recognize the Alberta Honpa Buddhist Association and its branches. We consider them as private groups.
5. Rev. Hanayama is the Bishop of the Buddhist Church of Canada.

6. We do not approve the idea of excluding Alberta from the Buddhist Church of Canada.[7]

On March 14, 1968, Rev. Orai Fujikawa arrived in Lethbridge to serve the English speaking members. A letter with a copy of the aforementioned letter from the Nishi Hongwanji was then sent to J. Colville again to refute Rev. L. Kawamura's claims.

> Rev. S. Kosaka and Rev. O. Fujikawa who arrived in Alberta March 1968 are the appointed ministers for the whole of Alberta. Rev. L. Kawamura is designated as minister for Raymond church only and has no right nor authority over any other Buddhist minister in Alberta. Therefore he has no authority to request a Certificate of Registration for anyone except perhaps for himself.
>
> Also please be advised that Rev. L. Kawamura is not, neither has he ever been, the Secretary of Buddhist Churches in Alberta. Furthermore, as stated in the official correspondence mentioned above, Toyo Kawamura (Mrs. Leslie Kawamura) to whom you have issued a Certificate of Registration has never been ordained to be a Buddhist minister.[8]

Along with this letter was a request for Certificates of Registration for Reverends Kosaka and Fujikawa. Unfortunately, the Division of Vital Statistics was confused by the situation since it had already sent certificates for the same two reverends via Rev. L. Kawamura. The certificates were sent back immediately, but J. Colville only recognized Rev. Kawamura as the clergyman authorized to apply for registration certificates. The situation sank into the mire of bureaucracy and frustration.

Finally, on January 7, 1969, the Division of Vital Statistics, Dept. of Health, Alberta government, decided at least to allow the Alberta Kyoku to apply for status as a religious organization. Unfortunately the department also decided to place the file in abeyance until the status of Buddhism in Alberta became clear.

After much correspondence, Rev. Kosaka was deemed responsible for requesting certification of BCC ministers as of January 27, 1969. The Honpa Buddhist Church of Alberta was then considered to be an autonomous body registered under the Societies' Act of Alberta. Honpa ministers were also allowed Certificates of Registration to perform marriage ceremonies. Effectively then, no one was allowed to marry in a Buddhist ceremony from June 15, 1966, when the Hongwanji requested the Dept. of Health to certify Rev. Kosaka, to January 27, 1969, a period of 31 months. Such controversy must have caused many to suffer heartbreak and dissolution.

The Movement Toward Resolution

On November 1, 1967, the Buddhist Churches of Canada met in conference in Winnipeg, Manitoba. Discussion centred on the need for independence from the Buddhist Churches of America. With its own bishop, the BCC could then deal with Canadian ministerial issues without the need to consult outside authority. The following proposal was made:

> **Establishment of an independent Bishopric in Canada**
>
> Reasons prompting this decision were: 1) the conditions prevailing during the immediate post-war period and today are very different, especially in the apparent increase in membership and the number of ministers serving the organization; 2) there are extraordinary problems which warrant independent solution; 3) in past years, business transactions were carried indirectly through the BCA office and this has created undue difficulties. It was therefore requested that the BCC deal directly with Kyoto headquarters...[9]
>
> Duties, rights and privileges of the Bishopric included:
>
> 1. The Bishop shall be given the power of discretion to attend conferences, meetings, seminars and other social and educational as well as governmental meetings held locally or abroad. The treasury of the Buddhist Churches of Canada should be authorized to finance such trips and incurred expense.
> 2. The Bishop should be vested with the power to place or remove any minister to improve the missionary frontier and structure of the BCC.
> 3. From time to time, the office of the Bishop is expected to issue ecclesiastical proclamation to be read from the pulpit of the Buddhist Churches; these proclamations are interpretation and clarification of the basic tenets of the faith.
> 4. The term of office will be four years. There will be no stipulation to prevent the re-election of the retiring Bishop.[10]

The request was soon granted by the Nishi Hongwanji. At the 1968 Winnipeg Conference, the BCC officially became independent and made a motion to appoint a Bishop. Rev. Newton Ishiura of the Toronto Buddhist Church was the principal candidate. He in turn said he would only become Bishop if "The Alberta Problem" was fully resolved. The conference as a whole then agreed to abide by the Feb. 24, 1967 directive from the Hongwanji to settle all differences and act as a unified organization again. A Mr. Fukushima (representative of the Alberta Buddhist Church Association) and Rev. L. Kawamura were further asked to give their word to support the agreement.

Rev. L. Kawamura in a magnanimous gesture requested to be reappointed as a minister of the Alberta Kyoku. Since he was still considered a minister for the Raymond Buddhist Church, his request was granted wholeheartedly.

At the May 10, 1970 ministerial meetings at the Lethbridge Buddhist Church, Bishop Ishiura discovered that "The Alberta Problem" still persisted, frustrating and confounding all those involved. During the afternoon meeting, Rev. L. Kawamura confronted Bishop Ishiura.

> My last encounter with your minister [Rev. L. Kawamura] was in May, 1970 at Lethbridge. Your minister was very arrogant towards the Abbot Kosho Ohtani, the Hongwanji and the Buddhist Churches of Canada. His choice of words was complete rejection and abusive.
>
> There have been other occasions during a more friendly period when I approached your minister about favours affecting the whole movement of Buddhism in Canada. His answer was "I cannot answer for myself, for I am governed by the directors of the Honpa Buddhist Churches of Alberta." This statement has become a favourite scapegoat for him in almost any encounter.
>
> I have been placed in the position of the Bishop by the members of the Buddhist Churches of Canada, and I am responsible to the National organization. Your minister and other representatives were at the meeting, and they embraced each other in coming together, in fact, the meeting room was just an outburst of emotion and tears. Your minister "cried" his heart out at the "amicability and unity." He made a solemn vow that he will give me his

> fullest support. How a man or a group of men can change overnight. One cannot rely on just feelings and emotions, unless there is a deeper understanding and appreciation of the *Nembutsu*, which a "Honpa" church should be emphasizing...
>
> ...As your minister said to my face in Lethbridge last May: "I'm not one of your ministers, we are independent, I shouldn't be here today talking to you, that goes for the BCC, the Hongwanji and the whole lot"...[11]

At the Lethbridge meeting, it came to light that Rev. L. Kawamura was ignoring any and all requests from the Alberta Kyoku Churches to lead services. Mr. Matsumiya of the Coaldale Buddhist Association explained to the Bishop that the Honpa Church finally told him if Coaldale wanted the minister's services, their organization would have to join the Honpa Buddhist Churches of Alberta. Unfortunately, neither Rev. L. Kawamura nor Mr. Muneo Takeda, Chairman of the Honpa organization, attended the evening meeting to confirm or deny the charges.

The rather contradictory attitudes of and positions taken by the Honpa Churches and its minister seem to be predicated on the attitudes and viewpoints taken by members of the Alberta Kyoku.

> The main reason for this group [Honpa Buddhist Churches] not returning is the dictatorial actions of the leaders of the present Alberta Kyoku. Would you remain in a church where the President would say "If you don't agree with me get out". This was directed at Sunday School Teachers. Or a President that would put a notice on their bulletin board that this person is expelled from the church for his actions. This also was directed at a Sunday School Teacher of long standing. Not one of these actions was taken with justifiable reasons. In fact regardless of any wrong doings no rightfully thinking Buddhist would expel or tell a member to get out. These were done by Buddhist leaders in their respective community and neither one has softened their attitude as yet.[12]

Perhaps finding himself in an untenable situation, Rev. L. Kawamura tendered his resignation from the BCC on March 1, 1969. It was announced at the 1969 Toronto conference. The Hongwanji in reply insisted that he should do his duty and work with the

Alberta Kyoku.

During April 1971, the Nishi Hongwanji decided to take steps finally to resolve "The Alberta Problem". In a letter to Bishop Ishiura, Rev. Chitoku Takeda, Head, Dept. of Overseas Mission, outlined the resolutions agreed upon by the Monshu, Bishop Ohta (chief administrator) and Bishop Kosho Abe.

1. Within the Alberta Buddhist Church, one group is condemned by the other *Nembutsu* followers. However, in as much as basically both groups live with *Nembutsu*, one must not disparage the other but must flow right into the stream to bring a matter to a satisfactory solution.
2. In order to bring this about, Hongwanji shall send Rev. Bunpo Kuwatsuki presently Rinban at Toyama Betsuin, and formerly the Head of the Foreign Dept. of Hongwanji, to the Canadian National Headquarters in September.
3 Through consultation with the Canadian National organization, Rev. Kuwatsuki shall expound the teachings of *Nembutsu* in Alberta and shall hold discussions with representatives of both groups. These may strive for the union of Alberta.
4. Through Canadian National Headquarters, the Hongwanji plans to send another minister who will take over the post of Rev. Kawamura in October.
5. The title "Honpa" must be cancelled from the government registration and members of this group must be recognized as belonging to the Alberta Buddhist Church. With this step, they'll become acquainted with the National movement. Their co-operation and responsibility will bring about a harmonious settlement in Canada.
6. Hongwanji will aid as much as possible in the expenses of the two ministers.[13]

On Sept. 1, 1971, Bishop Ishiura and Rev. Bunpo Kuwatsuki met with representatives of both the Kyoku and Honpa Churches. In the end, the Kyoku Churches asked the Bishop to recommend to the Hongwanji that Rev. Leslie Kawamura's resignation as BCC resident minister of Alberta be accepted. Later, the Hongwanji announced the suspension of Rev. L. Kawamura from the ministry.

At an Executive Meeting of the Lethbridge Buddhist Church in October 1981, Rev. Fumio Miyaji served notice of his resignation as of June 1982. At the same time, the Honpa Churches were having difficulties finding a new minster. They requested Rev. Yutetsu Kawamura to come out of retirement to fill the gap until someone could be found. Both organizations asked Bishop Tsunoda to help them. The Bishop saw an excellent opportunity to bring the two sides together. He sent his representative to make an overture to the Honpa Churches of Alberta to join the BCC. They responded with an application to join which was approved at the BCC AGM in Montreal, March 27, 1982. The action paved the way for the formation of the Buddhist Federation of Alberta in 1982.[14]

Although the factions appeared as one, the members still held quite strong feelings about the controversy stirred up in the 1960s. Roy Akune, Chairman of the BCC, and Bishop Murakami at the 1986 Alberta Buddhist Conference announced a future visit to Alberta in order to assess the "Alberta Problem" through a series of meetings with the Southern Alberta churches. According to Akune, one of the agenda items was to discuss the possibility of reinstating Rev. L. Kawamura, who was teaching at the University of Calgary, but "was not voiced to the members of the churches as such", presumably owing to the sensitivity of the subject. However, the proposal did come to light later according to the November 1986 newsletter of the Lethbridge Buddhist Church.

> Sometime in January 1987, Bishop Murakami and Roy Akune, Chairman of the Buddhist Churches of Canada, will be visiting all Alberta temples...to air and discuss fully the question of whether Rev. Leslie Kawamura should be reinstated as a BCC minister...To do this, BCC wants to meet to hear the views and thinking of its many Alberta members.[15]

They also wished to explore amalgamating the churches because of declining membership and to encourage all churches to continue to co-exist as amicably as possible in the light of Amida Buddha.

In the end, many misunderstood their intentions. Roy Akune and Bishop Murakami felt a trip to see Southern Alberta first hand was essential to understand the situation as a whole. Unfortunately members speculated that their visit would stir up the old accusations and recriminations especially over Rev. Kawamura and fracture the fragile peace. Therefore the objections from many quarters caused the Bishop and the Chairman to rethink this course of action and to decide to "let the sleeping dog lie" as advised by the Lethbridge Buddhist Church.[16]

> Being a Jodo Shinshu follower the one teaching that has remained foremost in my mind is the teaching of St. Shinran and how he had converted Bennen into a follower by forgiving him for his envious actions against him...
>
> It takes two to have a division and both parties are at fault to different degrees for the division to exist because the one not at fault will understand and will not allow the break.[17]

Post War British Columbia

Chapter 13

Bukkyo Tozen

Post War British Columbia

Although temples had been established during the war or shortly thereafter in Kamloops and Vernon and in internment camps like New Denver and Sandon, no church stood in the Lower Mainland until a few years after 1949. Only with the formal lifting of the War Measures Act could Japanese Canadians return to the West Coast and re-establish their institutions without hindrance.

Unfortunately the dispersal of Japanese Canadians meant that all prewar congregations could not be reassembled. Since many Japanese Canadians moved east of the Rocky Mountains to Alberta, Manitoba and Ontario, most of the communities that had temples could not muster the numbers needed after the war to start again. Moreover, there were not enough ministers, so many of the churches that did reform improvised with lay leaders until the mid 1950s.

Vancouver Buddhist Church

By the spring of 1951, some 600 Japanese Canadians had resettled in Vancouver. During the first meeting of Buddhists in June 1951, 25 individuals were nominated to organize a new Buddhist Association. Their nomination didn't pass until after the first post war Obon service, held that August, when a general meeting took place. The service and meeting were co-sponsored by the Japanese Canadian Citizens Association and held at the old Japanese Language School building on Alexander Street. Rev. Shinjo Ikuta acted as advisor. The first

Board of Directors included Eizo Kitagawa, President, and Genzaburo Nakamura, Vice-President. Kitagawa declined and so Genzaburo Nakamura stepped in as President. They decided to call the new group the Vancouver Bukkyokai.

At the time, Rev. Shinjo Ikuta was resident minister of the Kelowna Buddhist Church. He then became district minister in order to accommodate all the centres including Vancouver.

Vancouver's First Church

The search for a new location began in earnest shortly after the Board of Directors was formed. The first thought was to purchase the old temple sold to the Ukrainian group by the Custodian of Alien Properties. Meanwhile, they inquired about the old Cordova Bussei building but the owner did not want to sell. At the same time, the Buddhist Association looked for a minister's residence for Rev. Ikuta. He would need it for his half month visits to Vancouver. In the meantime, the Hastings Auditorium and the Japanese Language School served as temporary gathering halls.

The fund raising drive coincided with a membership drive in Vancouver, North and West Vancouver, Surrey and Aldergrove. The membership fee was $3.00 per person. The members then organized Japanese movie nights, a raffle and a *tanomoshi* (Japanese credit union).

An encouraging number of 60 people attended the January 1952 Ho-onko Service. Another sign of recovery was contained in a notice from the Custodian of Alien Properties. The officials had discovered family *butsudan* in their warehouse. The church with the help of the Japanese Canadian Citizens Association took possession of the surviving altars and placed them in storage with the Kawashima Japanese store.

By 1953 the Cordova Church was still under negotiation but a service was held every third Saturday with significant observances added (Hanamatsuri, Ho-onko and Obon). The Gomonshu's visit in November 1952 was a particularly special event. A banquet in his honour at the Kiwanis Club was attended by 250 members. Another service and banquet was held the next day with an audience of 200 people.

Zenno Tanaka who was elected President that year faced several decisions. He and his Board revived the Sunday

School with Yoshio Okano as Chairman. The church also applied to the B.C. Government for a charter of registration. Buddhism was officially recognized on May 31, 1953.

At the beginning of 1954, discussion had turned to buying the hall on the corner of Alexander and Jackson Streets. Still, the debate continued. The United Church building at Powell and Jackson then became available and seemed the most feasible. A fund raising committee eventually purchased the building for $44,500 in April 1954. Renovations were completed within the year.

Courtesy of Ritsu Saimoto

Vancouver Buddhist Church, 1952 - 1978.

Growth and Prosperity

Soon the church was abuzz with activity. The Young Adult Buddhist Association was formed and the newsletter **Hojo** came into being. In September 1954 Susumu Ikuta (Rev. Shinjo Ikuta's son) went to Japan to begin his studies in religion at Ryukoku University. The Vancouver Bukkyokai decided to join the BC Buddhist League with Kelowna, Kamloops, Aldergrove and Steveston. Initially, the League's main concerns centred on strengthening the Dharma School, improving correspondence and propagation of Buddhism to outlying members.

The 50th anniversary celebration of Buddhism in Canada took place in November 1955. At the commemorative service held in the Japanese Language School auditorium, Rev. Nekoda of Raymond, Alberta, Rev. Sensho Sasaki of Stockton, California, Rev. Nishimura of Winnipeg, Manitoba, and Rev. Shinjo Ikuta presided. That evening members celebrated with a play and entertainment.

At about the same time, the members ordered a shrine from Kyoto, Japan. It was installed soon after it arrived in March. A dedication service took place during the seventh annual general meeting on January 20, 1957. Another such service was held in March presided over by Reverends Ikuta, Ichikawa of Seattle and Kawamura. The Lord Abbot Ohtani, North American Bishop Shigefuji and Kenju Masuyama of the Kyoto Women's College sent messages of congratulations.

The Bussei held a three day convention during November 1956. Rev. Tsuji was the guest speaker.

During the latter part of 1957, Rev. S. Kyojo Ikuta returned from his studies in Japan. The Vancouver Church immediately petitioned the BCC for the new Rev. Ikuta's services. At the eighth general meeting in January 1958, it was announced that Rev. Kyojo Ikuta was to be Vancouver's resident minister and assume ministerial duties for the congregations in Steveston and Aldergrove as well.

When Rev. Shinjo Ikuta retired in 1966, Rev. S.K. Ikuta took on the responsibility for the entire province, serving not only the Lower Mainland temples but Kamloops, Kelowna and Vernon as well. He also visited Greenwood, Midway, Slocan and New Denver twice a year. In Vancouver and Steveston, he presided over the Sunday School with 100 students. Such was his dedication that he picked up ten students in his car every Sunday so that they could attend.

In 1971 the Bukkyokai purchased a second building. The Argyle property was expected to be the site of a new Buddhist temple. Instead, the congregation decided as a Japanese Canadian Centennial project in 1977 to replace the old building at 220 Jackson Avenue with a new temple and auditorium complex. Construction was begun a year later and completed in 1979 which coincided with the 75th Anniversary for Jodo Shinshu Buddhism in Canada.

The Buddhist community pulled together and collected over $1,000,000 rendering the building debt free. Since then, many additions and improvements to the temple have made the church a warm and inviting place to partake in the *Nembutsu*.

Rev. Seimoku Kosaka

In May 1972 what began as a simple resignation of a minister turned into a controversy which proved to expand the church's role in the propagation of Jodo Shinshu Buddhism in Canada. Rev. Shoji Matsumoto decided to return to Japan to continue his religious studies. Genji Yada, President of the Vancouver Church, immediately petitioned Bishop Ishiura for a replacement. The Bishop promptly suggested Rev. Seimoku Kosaka. After much discussion, the Vancouver membership accepted the appointment. All went well until the Buddhist Churches of Canada became incorporated as the recognized administrative body for the Canadian Buddhist ministry in November 1974. Rev. Newton Ishiura's successor was Rev. Kosaka who accepted the office in 1976.

The Bishopric is within the purview of the Buddhist Churches of Canada; whereas in 1976 the Vancouver Church was a member of the BC Buddhist Churches Federation and not of the BCC.[1] In fact, the only B.C. temple which was affiliated with the BCC was in Kelowna. Rev. Kosaka's appointment was interpreted as a ploy to induce the Vancouver Church, and eventually all the B.C. churches, to join the BCC. The issue then broke down into two areas: the Bishopric and membership in the BCC.[2]

> With reference to the subject matter, the Vancouver Buddhist Church (hereafter VBC), at its current joint meeting, reiterated our previously made position, i.e., VBC will not tolerate the dual office-holding by Rev. Kosaka under the existing circumstances.
>
> The main reason...the geographic separation of the BCC's Administration Office and the Bishop's office has virtually prevented Rev. Kosaka to effectively perform his duties.
>
> In fact, Rev. Kosaka has recently had almost no time to serve as the chief resident minister. To fulfil the role of the Bishop of the BCC, he has already been away from our church for a little over two weeks in total in the past nine weeks. Furthermore, we were suddenly

> informed by him that he will be going to Japan for about ten weeks starting June 22, 1976...Needless to say, such a situation does create inconveniences in our church's important summer events, such as Ohaka Mairi, Obon Hoyo, Obon Odori, etc.
>
> Although the Bishopric issue is technically a matter between the BCC and Rev. Kosaka himself, it also concerns our church.[3]

In September 1976 Chairman George Nakashiba and Rev. Moriki, director of the BCC, met with officials of the Vancouver Buddhist Church to discuss the two issues.

> The meeting was conducted under a friendly atmosphere and was adjourned with the following agreements:
>
> 1. Rev. Kosaka, because of his recent election to the Office of the Bishop, will be stationed in eastern Canada.
> 2. Bishop Kosaka will move to the East within six months.
> 3. Moving expenses incurred will be borne by the VBC.
> 4. Bishop Kosaka will receive renumeration [sic] from and his rent paid by VBC until the date of his departure.
> 5. The BCC will do their utmost to find a replacement minister as soon as possible, and,
> 6. With respect to the resolution made by the BC Buddhist Churches Federation, efforts to promote the VBC's earlier joining to the BCC should be kept intact.[4]

In April 1976 the members of the BCBCF resolved to negotiate with the BCC collectively. Not one church then could negotiate independently, although the final decision to join rested with each individual church.

The membership issue was resolved in 1977 with all churches joining the BCC. In a demonstration of co-operation, Bishop Seimoku Kosaka, Rev. Yasuo Izumi and Rev. Shinji Okada presided over the 75th Anniversary Dedication Service on November 24, 1979.

Throughout the 1980s and '90s, the Vancouver Church prospered despite the decline in membership as evident in its staging of public celebrations of Hanamatsuri and Obon and in its participation in the Powell Street Festival, the largest Japanese Canadian and possibly largest ethnic festival of its kind in Canada.

Today the church is organized in a simple manner. Everyone is considered a member of the Vancouver Bukkyokai. There is no distinct men's group. All adult women are in the Fujinkai. There are 25 to 30 members in each of the YBA and Jr. YBA organizations. The Young Adult Buddhist Association no longer exists. The Dharma School thrives. Arguably the most influential organization within the church is the Fujinkai. Through their diligence and determined fund raising, the women's group has prospered to the point where it can influence policy and bring about change.

Rev. Orai Fujikawa of Toronto exchanged places with Rev. Izumi in September 1994 to become the 23rd resident minister of the Vancouver Bukkyokai since Rev. Senju Sasaki in 1905. Although the temple is enjoying renewed vigour in its number of youth, it seeks ways to nurture the interest of the young to encourage sustained growth.

Steveston Buddhist Church

Unlike Vancouver with its vestiges of Little Tokyo buildings and landmarks, there was little trace of the prewar Japanese Canadian community of Steveston in 1949. The old Buddhist Church had literally disappeared. The Custodian had sold the building during the war and the new owners must have demolished it.

Only a few Japanese Canadians trickled into Steveston to resettle. Most had decided to live in Alberta or out east in Manitoba and Ontario. Despite the paucity of Buddhists, Rev. Shinjo Ikuta urged a small core of devotees to form a Bukkyokai. In March 1952 a committee was struck to investigate the possibility.

Soon after the first Ho-onko Service was held in the Red Cross Hall, the 50 member congregation elected an executive board. Coincidentally, the Gomonshu Kosho Ohtani and Lady Yoshiko Ohtani paid a visit to the Lower Mainland area. They officiated the installation service of the new Buddhist Association in November 1952. Lady Ohtani asked that a Steveston Bukkyo Fujinkai be organized; consequently, Koito Okano became the first President of the newly formed women's group.

At the first general meeting in January 1953, the congregation wrote and adopted the constitution for the church. The new Executive Board received $8500 that was held in trust by the executives of the church before the war. The money had come from the sale of the old church building. It was to be used to purchase a new property.

In the meantime, the YBA and Sunday School were formed and met at the old Red Cross Hall. The first Sunday School Service, chaired by Roy Akune, was held in September 1952.

The church bought, in March 1954, the former Japanese Kindergarten School building (Hide Hyodo Shimizu taught in this building before the war) near the corner of Chatham and No. 1 Road. The members renovated it and used it as a temporary church.

Once the church became registered with the B.C. government in 1956, the Executive Board began to look in earnest for a new church site. Finally in 1960 they decided on a five acre lot at 4360 Garry Street. The sod turning ceremony took place in 1963. Under the leadership of President Yuichi Akune, the building was completed and the initial opening service was held in 1964. Rev. Koyo Okuda of the Seattle Betsuin led the ceremony with over 400 in attendance.

Rev. Kyojo Ikuta, resident minister, performed the official inaugural service in February 1965. Bishop Hanayama and Rev. Kubota of the BCA were invited to participate. Professor Ryosetsu Fujihara from Ryukoku University came as guest speaker.

Courtesy of Roy Akune

Steveston Buddhist Church, 1964 - present.

The membership had grown to 178, with 47 honourary members who were over 70 years old. Three temples plus the Steveston Temple came under the purview of Rev. Kyojo Ikuta. The load was too much for one minister and so the BCC asked the Hongwanji to send another minister as soon as possible. Word came back that the request would be difficult to fulfil. The Canadian government was slow to grant work visas. As well, overseas ministers were a scarce commodity at that moment. To alleviate the situation, the BCC in 1959 persuaded Rev. Ikuta's father, Rev. Shinjo Ikuta, to lead the Steveston congregation. After leaving his post in the Okanagan in '61, he did so until Rev. Nagatani arrived in 1966. Rev. Shinjo Ikuta then retired.

Later ministers included: Rev. Takamichi Takahatake, 1970; Rev. Hoshin Okada, 1971-82; Rev. Gyosho Abe, 1983-1987; and Rev. Sammi Kiribayashi, 1988-present.

On October 27, 1984, the Gomonshu and Lady Koshin Ohtani presided over the installation and Dedication Service of a new statue of the Buddha.

Rev. Sammi Kiribayashi

Rev. Kiribayashi came to the Steveston Church from Kyoto in 1988 on a regular visitor's visa as did most ministers. He spent many fruitful and rewarding years in Steveston. He was, for example, instrumental in organizing the 1990 World Buddhist Women's Convention in Vancouver. In late 1993 he, along with his wife Yumiko and three children, applied for permanent resident status, bolstered by the encouragement of church members. Unfortunately, Immigration Canada rejected his application on the insensitive grounds that one of his children was handicapped and therefore inadmissible according to the Immigration Act. The provision was meant to prevent a drain on the social welfare system. Rev. Kiribayashi was ordered to leave the country by June 30, 1994.

The BCC immediately launched a quiet appeal to Immigration Canada. Inquiries made, negotiations offered. Rev. Kiribayashi himself wrote to the Prime Minister and Richmond MP Raymond Chan argued against the discriminatory attitude. The petition, however, fell upon deaf ears.

Then as reported in the **Vancouver Sun**, the **Vancouver Province** and **The New Canadian**, the family found support among the general public.

> Diane Woodman, the Kiribayashi's neighbour, has rallied support from other neighbours and friends to keep the Japanese family in Canada. She is furious at the Canadian immigration policy which she says has "double standards" and is demanding that her elected representatives intervene on the family's behalf.[5]

The Japanese Canadian community also responded with a petition of 1500 signatures initiated by the BCC and a letter of appeal to Sergio Marchi, Minister of Citizenship and Immigration, from Tatsuo Kage, Director of the Greater Vancouver Japanese Canadian Citizens Association. The letter was printed in Japanese Canadian community newspapers and journals.

> As a prominent Buddhist minister serving the spiritual needs of the Japanese Canadian community, Rev. Kiribayashi fills a special role in Canada as a highly trained priest and teacher of a major world religion with a significant following in British Columbia. There is no training available in Canada for Buddhist priests. The members of the community urged him and his family to stay here permanently as he is an exceptional and irreplaceable person...
>
> We would like to question the judgment of your officials in failing to find sufficient humanitarian and compassionate grounds.[6]

More help came from MP Raymond Chan, who succeeded in getting the case reviewed although the original ruling was upheld, and Roy Inouye, President of the National Association of Japanese Canadians and prominent leader of the Kamloops Buddhist Church. Jim Taylor, sports writer of the **Vancouver Province** "contrasted Immigration Canada's attitude toward foreign professional athletes such as the Stastny brothers recruited by the Quebec Nordiques who were given top priority on the immigration list and others like Mari Kiribayashi who are made to wait and wonder and then rejected."[7]

In June 1994 Immigration Canada informed Rev. Kiribayashi that he and his family were granted a one year visa extension with the possibility of permanent resident status in the offing.

Vernon Buddhist Church

Situated by Lake Okanagan, the town of Vernon offers breath-taking vistas, clean fresh air and a peace that is hard to come by in major populated areas. The tranquillity is conducive to meditative thinking and quiet living.

In January 1948 fourteen Buddhists living in Vernon along with invited guest Rev. Yutetsu Kawamura of Alberta gathered at the home of Sansuke Kawamoto to discuss the formation of the Vernon Nori-no-kai, a Buddhist Association. A year later, the group was renamed the Vernon Buddhist Church.

In December 1951 Rev. Shinjo Ikuta of the Kelowna Church arrived in Vernon to lead the Ho-onko Service. The Obon Service during August 1952 was headed by Bishop Shigefuji, Bishop of the Buddhist Churches of North America. A few months later in November the Gomonshu and Lady Ohtani paid a visit to the small congregation. A grand welcoming party was held in their honour.

Courtesy of Mari Cameron

Vernon Buddhist Church, November 1952.

In the following years, the Vernon Church donated to significant charities. In '53, they sent money to the flood victims of Northern Kyushu, Japan. In '58, they contributed to the typhoon victims of Izu Peninsula, Japan. In '59, they donated to the Japanese Canadian Community Centre Building Fund.

Rev. Shinjo Ikuta in 1961 negotiated the deal to bring an old altar from the Steveston Church to Vernon. Six months later, Rev. Koyo Okuda became the resident minister of the Kelowna Church. He also continued Rev. Ikuta's duties for the Vernon temple. A few years later in 1967 the Vernon Church celebrated Rev. Ikuta's 30th year of service in Canada. The much respected minister was the guest of honour.

In 1970 Rev. Orai Fujikawa replaced Rev. Okuda who decided to return to Japan. The Vernon congregation welcomed the new minister with a party in October.

In 1975 the Okanagan Buddhist District decided to hold a joint picnic at the Coldstream Park in Vernon. The members of the Vernon, Kamloops and Kelowna Churches attended. A second picnic was held in the same park two years later.

On the occasion of Rev. Kosaka's appointment as Bishop of the BCC, three Vernon Buddhists were honoured during the "Sarana Affirmation Ceremony". The Buddhist names were bestowed by Bishop Kosaka himself.

On April 16, 1978, the Vernon Buddhist Church celebrated its 30th Anniversary. Rev. Kawamura, guest minister, conducted the Commemorative Service combined with a Memorial Service. He presented mementoes with a Certificate of Appreciation to seventeen members and Commemorative gifts to seven others.

By the late '70s, the Obon Odori was an annual event with enthusiastic participation by members from Kelowna and Kamloops. The local Chidori-kai dancers performed every year with dedication and skill. The Okanagan Buddhist District picnic followed a month later. In 1979, the picnic was held at Canoe Park near Salmon Arm.

In November Vernon members Mr. and Mrs. Y. Yakura, Mr. and Mrs. Natsuhara and Mrs. Hosaki went as representatives to the Dedication Service of the Vancouver Buddhist Church Complex. They presented the church a donation of $50 on behalf of the Vernon Church.

With the 1980s came prosperity and change. Rev. Fujikawa left for Toronto and was replaced by Rev. Norimaru Taniyama. In 1980 Susumu Yamamoto of Winnipeg, Manitoba, donated a new *butsudan* which he had made. Volunteers worked quickly to house the altar. Mr. and Mrs. Y. Yakura donated the lumber and Saburo Yamamoto installed the electricity. Mr. and Mrs. Hosaki donated a plaque. Later, the church made arrangements with Rev. Taniyama of Kelowna to buy the Butsu-gu or altar accessories. They arrived by the end of the year and the church observed the Nyu Butsu Shiki on November 27. The Hongwanji contributed the Go-San-Tai (scroll of Shinran Shonin, a statue of the Buddha and a scroll bearing the words Namu Amida Butsu). That evening, Mrs. Hayako Hosaki supervised and organized a banquet and entertainment.

Throughout the 1980s further developments in the church took place. Services were held once a month. The Gomonshu visited again in November 1984. Rev. Daijun Yakumo became the new district minister in 1987. A year later, the Vernon Buddhist Church celebrated its 40th Anniversary. *Karaoke* singers and the Chidori-kai dancers put on a marvellous celebration.

During the 1990s the church events of Obon, Hanamatsuri and Ho-onko as well as the Okanagan Kyoku Picnic have become annual events anticipated fondly by the members of the Vernon Church. The Japanese Cultural Society's Christmas Party raises money annually for the church. Each year as well, the church recognizes long standing service by presenting appreciation medals. In 1990 Rev. Yakumo presented awards to Yukitoshi Yakura, Sadao Yamamoto and Kizo Natsuhara.

On May 23, 1992, the members held a farewell party for Rev. Yakumo. He had decided to return to Japan. Seventy members from the Vernon and Kelowna Churches attended to partake of a wonderful meal served by the Vernon Fujinbu. A *karaoke* concert followed. Rev. Yakumo was presented with a *sagarifuji* from the Okanagan Sunkiyoku.

The Vernon Buddhist Church has enjoyed many years of growth and prosperity. In fact, the Dharma School today has twenty students taught by Mari Cameron. The temple's greatest joy, however, is expressed in the devotion to the teaching of the Buddha and how it is reflected in their way of life.

Kelowna Buddhist Church

Like Vernon, Kelowna thrives on the shores of Lake Okanagan. The Buddhists with their beautiful temple have been there since 1932 when the first Ho-onko Service took place in December. Shortly thereafter, The Okanagan Buddhist Fellowship was initiated in February 1933. Rev. Kakusai Tada conducted the inaugural service of the fellowship. The opening service for the Kelowna Bukkyokai was held on November 21, 1933, officiated by Rev. Seisho Ishiguro.

In 1938 the members bought some property to house a church. That same year they built, to commemorate the 5th Anniversary, a monument in memory of those buried in the Kelowna Cemetery without families to remember them.

The Kelowna Fujinkai was formed in April 1936. Three years later the Okanagan Buddhist Society was registered with the provincial government, the first Young Buddhist Association was formed and the altar to Amida Buddha was handmade by the members. In 1940 the government began registering all Japanese Canadians including those in Kelowna. When the Pacific War broke out, there was an immediate injunction to prohibit Japanese Canadians from gathering together. The townspeople also made sure no Buddhist temple was built.

The church carried on albeit in a restricted manner. Special services such as funerals and memorial services were allowed but not much else. Rev. Renshin Tachibana travelled from camp to camp in order to preside over the services.

After the war the YBA was dissolved. The young probably saw very little future in Kelowna and so sought their fortunes east of the Rockies as dictated by the Order-in-Council restricting movement.

By 1948 the Kelowna Church began to recover from the setback of the war and the first Sunday School Service was held. The *butsudan* from the prewar Fairview Church arrived. An installation service for the new shrine was conducted by Rev. Shinjo Ikuta in November 1948.

In the 1950s the church sent a delegation to Raymond, Alberta, to attend the first meeting of the new Buddhist Foundation of Canada. Having joined the organization, the Kelowna membership sent $104 as dues.

Rev. Shinjo Ikuta and his family arrived in 1951 to become the resident minister and itinerant minister for the other churches of the Okanagan. A few months later the reverend initiated the Sunday Dharma School. Furthermore, he helped to reconstitute the Young Buddhist Association in March 1952. Later, in August, the BC Buddhist Church Federation met in Kelowna to organize their activities. That same year the Gomonshu and Lady Kosho Ohtani paid a visit.

In December 1953 the Kelowna Bukkyokai celebrated its 20th Anniversary with a commemorative service officiated by Rev. Shinjo Ikuta, Bishop Shigefuji and Rev. E. Nekoda. The Seattle Buddhist Church soon became the Seattle Betsuin or District Church. Kelowna fell under its purview.

Church activities gained momentum by the mid '50s when the Fujinkai celebrated its 20th Anniversary. The Kelowna Church's Boy Scout Troupe was formed. The first picnic occurred. The BC Young Buddhist Association Federation Convention took place in Kelowna in November 1956.

In the late '50s, the Gomonshu and Lady Ohtani visited for a second time. Rev. Ikuta moved to Steveston in 1961 and was replaced by Rev. Koyo Okuda from the Seattle Betsuin.

The BC Buddhist Churches Federation's headquarters moved to

Kelowna in 1964. At this point, the members felt a need for change. The Young Adult Buddhist Association came into being, and a committee to investigate the building of a new temple was formed.

The official opening service for the new temple was conducted in November 1967. Rev. Okuda and Rev. Shinjo Ikuta, guest minister, presided. The inauguration service took place in March 1968 with Rev. Okuda leading. The guest ministers included Rev. Seimoku Kosaka, Rev. Daijun Yakumo, Rev. Kosho Nagatani, Rev. Juyou Terao (from Spokane, Washington) and Rev. Kenryo Kumata (Seattle Betsuin Rinban). As if to mark the occasion, the first volume of the church newsletter, **The Dharma Express**, went to press.

JCCC archives

Kelowna Buddhist Church, circa 1985.

In August 1970 Rev. Okuda and his family returned to Japan. His replacement was Rev. Orai Fujikawa. During his tenure, Rev. Fujikawa helped the Bukkyokai celebrate many milestones. These included the 35th and 40th Anniversaries of the Fujinkai ('71 and '76), the 40th and 45th Anniversaries of the Church ('73 and '78), and the opening of Hinode Home for seniors built by the Kelowna Japanese Canadian Community Senior Citizens Society in 1971. In 1980 Rev. Fujikawa and family left for Toronto and were replaced by Rev. Norimaru Taniyama.

The 50th Anniversary of the Kelowna Church came in May 1983. The service was conducted by Rev. Taniyama with guest ministers Bishop Shodo Tsunoda, Rev. Hoshin Okada and Rev. Yasuo Izumi.

The 50th Anniversary of the Fujinkai and the 35th Anniversary of the Sunday School fell within a year of each other (1986 and '87). Rev. Fred Ulrich of Edmonton came as guest minister for the Sunday School celebrations and Hanamatsuri Service. Rev. Taniyama and his family left in

1986. Rev. Daijun Yakumo arrived with his family to take over as resident minister.

Now the Kelowna Buddhist Church enjoys a healthy congregation which observes the traditions and values of Jodo Shinshu Buddhism. The members give wholeheartedly to charities such as a donation of $5000 to the local hospital during the "Together We Care" campaign in 1991. They also continue to renovate their temple. They receive many guests, like the Chiyoda High School students (a Buddhist school for girls), with warm hospitality.

On April 7, 1990, the Young Adult Buddhist Association celebrated its 25th Anniversary with Rev. Yoshihide Matsubayashi, Ed.D. from the South Alameda County Buddhist Church of California as guest minister.

In 1992 the church enjoyed two more milestones. Rev. Carol Himaka of San Francisco attended the Hanamatsuri on April 12 and the 40th Anniversary of the Dharma School as guest minister. A month later Rev. K. S. Ikuta was the guest minister for the 60th Anniversary of the temple itself.

Kamloops Buddhist Church

On February 8, 1948, 80 devout Buddhists met at the home of Mr. S. Saito to discuss establishing a Buddhist church in Kamloops. The Starting Committee, consisting of H. Tanabe, S. Yamada, and U. Hirowatari, met thereafter at the residence of Rinzo Tahara. In due course, they decided to name the organization the Kamloops Bukkyokai. They set the membership fee at $1.00. A donation of $100 came from the former Kitsilano Church via former members in Chatham, Ontario.

In a subsequent meeting the members decided December 19 to be the date of the Annual General Meeting (AGM) with participation from churches in Vernon and Kelowna as well (represented by one member each). Thus began the Okanagan Federation.

By the following AGM (January 1949) much had taken place. Another $100 came from the former New Westminster Church while $200 arrived from the former Fairview Church via the Toronto Church. In February, Rev. Tsuji visited as guest speaker. S. Yamada brought a *butsudan* and accessories from the Kelowna Church the following month. The Fujinkai formed on April 6, 1949.

The Kamloops Church had no building well into the 1950s. The members met for events like the AGM, Keirokai, New Year's Social, concerts and Buddhist Observances at various locations: the Italian Hall (Jan. 1950), the Ukrainian Hall (March 1951), the Caledonia Hall (Jan. 1952), the Elk's Hall (Feb. 1951) and Legion Hall respectively. Ministers visited to conduct various duties and services: Bishop Shigefuji, Rev. Shinjo Ikuta, Rev. Z. Kawasaki and Rev. Onuma in the early days. The church also opened a Credit Union in 1952.

In the spring of that year, preparations commenced for the visit of the Gomonshu. Rev. Ikuta undertook the task of raising funds. He travelled as far as Lillooet to raise donations. Every member became involved with some aspect of the memorable occasion, everything from the program to the decorations. By all accounts, the Gomonshu's visit was a success.

The First Church

At the 1953 AGM held at the Caledonia Hall, the membership learned of the purchase of property for the express purpose of establishing a church. They agreed to begin payment in February of that year.

By the next year, the Kamloops Buddhist Church Building Fund Committee formed. The individuals involved were T. Uyeyama, T. Sakaki, S. Yamada, M. Kanna, C. Ichii, Y. Nishimura, U. Hirowatari, C. Yoshida, G. Kato, H. Kodama, H. Hamaguchi, T. Nishikawa, T. Uyeda, K. Kaminishi and F. Makihara. The committee then sent a letter of appeal for donations to all the Buddhist members in the area.

On March 14, 1954, the Kamloops Church hosted an organizing meeting for the BC Kyoku (Buddhist Church Federation). Representatives came from Kelowna, Vancouver, Vernon and Steveston. In order to support the association, each church or group was assessed a donation schedule: Kelowna (headquarters), $1200; Vancouver, $360; Steveston, $300; Kamloops, $276; Vernon, $120; Fraser Valley, $80; and New Denver, $60.

Rev. Ikuta's own agenda for the meeting included a pitch for the formation of a Young Buddhists Society. The Bukkyo Seinen Kai was formed in March 1955. The Dharma School also commenced that year.[8]

On March 31, 1956, the members gathered for the Dedication

Service of the new Church building. Everyone was grateful to the volunteer workmen who took care of the construction: G. Kato (Building Captain), T. Uyeyama (Chairman), T. Sakaki (Vice-Chairman), T. Nishikawa (carpenter), C. Yoshida (carpenter), S. Yamada (Treasurer), U. Hirowatari (committee), C. Ichii (committee).

The congregation almost immediately opened a Japanese Language School with classes on Monday, Wednesday and Friday evenings. From then on all meetings, including the AGM, and events like the Bazaar, services and commemorations, were held at the Bukkyokai Kaikan (Hall).

Courtesy of Roy Inouye

Kamloops Buddhist Church, 1990.

Activities

The Kamloops Church participated in the celebrations for the 100th Anniversary of British Columbia in 1958. The church donated a float to the Kamloops City Parade. For its own 10th Anniversary, the church held a *chigo* parade (15 pupils 5 to 8 yrs. participated) beginning in McDonald Park and ending at the Bukkyokai. Later that year the young people formed the Jr. YBA.

In 1959 Rev. S. Ikuta handed in his resignation so that he could move to the Steveston Church. Joint committee meetings were held amongst the Kamloops, Vernon and Kelowna Churches about a replacement minister.

In 1960 the three area churches held the Okanagan Representative Conference in Kelowna. They decided to initiate a search which eventually covered the United States and Japan. The need for a minister became acute in 1961. At an Okanagan Federation Conference, the delegates resolved to hire a resident minister. To support the minister the churches determined the financial assessments needed: Vernon 10%; Kamloops 42% and Kelowna 48%. Since few attended a subsequent congregational meeting in Kamloops, the executives had to conduct a door-to-door survey of the membership to pass the resolution. Most were in favour. The churches managed to arrive at terms with Rev. Ikuta's help: Kelowna will provide the residence; all three temples will provide funds for insurance, a car, house expenses and a salary of $300 a month. Rev. Koyo Okuda from Seattle finally agreed to serve the three area temples in 1961.

As negotiations were underway with Rev. Okuda, the Kamloops temple prepared for the 700th Memorial Anniversary of Shinran Shonin's passing. A budget of $500 was set and eventually the membership raised $691.

In March 1963 Rev. Okuda consented to be guest speaker to celebrate the 15th Anniversary of the temple. Five representatives from Kamloops went to Penticton to greet the arriving Rev. Okuda. The group then returned to Kamloops to attend the welcoming party.

The 1960s were years of stability for the Kamloops Church. Regular events like picnics, *chow mein* suppers and AGMs in addition to the Buddhist Observances kept the minister and congregation busy. In 1965 a seniors group was formed. In '66, the AGM changed the constitution to reflect a more *nisei* organization. In '67, the Gomonshu visited once again.

With the new decade, Rev. Okuda decided to return to Japan. Rev. Orai Fujikawa took his place in 1970. The congregation felt it was a good time to expand the church building. In total, $9450 was raised to cover the $4246 cost of renovations.

By the mid 1970s, the Kamloops Church found itself part of a complex system of associations: the Okanagan Kyoku, the BCBCF, the BCC and the Ministerial Association. Each was paid an assessment fee or membership fee. Fund raising therefore became a priority.

English also was the language of choice by 1978. The Keirokai was stopped after 1977 since the number of *issei* was too small to justify its continuance.

In the meantime the Fujinkai celebrated its 30th Anniversary in April 1978. The church donated toward the $20,000 BCC allotment for the Ascension Ceremony in Japan for the new Gomonshu. The Kamloops Church held a memorial service at the request of the Consul General in Vancouver for three Japanese victims of an accident in the area. In '79, Rev. Fujikawa accepted a position at the Toronto Church. Rev. Norimaru Taniyama came as his replacement in February 1980.

Throughout the 1980s and '90s, the Kamloops Buddhist Church continued to hold regular activities and services. In '81, the Buddhist Women's Federation had its AGM in Kamloops. The BCBCF headquarters moved to Kamloops in 1982. The YBA formed in the same year. Every five years, an anniversary service and concert are staged for the enjoyment of the membership.

Since the first minister, Rev. Taniyama, Rev. Daijun Yakumo and then Rev. Shigenobu Watanabe served the Okanagan temples to great effect.

Fraser Valley Buddhist Temple

The Fraser Valley Buddhist Temple is located in the heart of the Fraser Valley, a forty minute drive east of Vancouver and a one hour drive west of Hope B.C. The church itself was built in 1955 on land donated by Kazuo Imamura at 28941 Haverman Rd., Bradner.

The Bukkyokai was initiated in October 1954 with 20 dedicated Buddhists at its core. The Fujinkai was also formed then. In December the small congregation met at Aberdeen Hall on the Fraser Highway. Rev. Shinjo Ikuta conducted the opening service which continued once a month thereafter.

With the building of the church, the members started the Young Buddhist Association and the Dharma School. A commemorative service for the new church was held in May 1956. Early the following year the enshrinement of the altar was celebrated.

Bishop Daijun Toyohara of the Nishi Hongwanji visited in November 1979. A year later the 25th Anniversary celebrations took place. The Gomonshu Koshin Ohtani and Lady Ohtani paid a visit to the church in October 1984 as part of their B.C. itinerary.

The name Fraser Valley Buddhist Church was changed to Fraser Valley Buddhist Temple in September 1985. In the ensuing years, the temple celebrated its 30th and 35th Anniversaries with special services and concerts at Bradner Hall.

Today, the Fraser Valley Temple has 60 members in the Bukkyokai and Fujinkai.

The Buddhist Churches of British Columbia are a tightly knit group of organizations. There are network alliances that draw the congregations closer together. The Okanagan Kyoku includes the Kelowna, Vernon and Kamloops Buddhist Temples. Rev. Shigenobu Watanabe is the senior minister. He transferred from the Buddhist Federation of Alberta in 1994. The British Columbia Buddhist Churches Federation incorporates all the temples under one umbrella organization. However, the ministers really are the ones who unite the disparate congregations.

The resident ministers are based in the temples in Vancouver, Steveston and Kelowna. They travel to the Fraser Valley, Kamloops and Vernon according to the needs of the respective churches. There are temples in New Denver and Greenwood but the members are so few that regular services are thought to be unnecessary. Fortunately, the historic internment camp Buddhist Church building on its original site in New Denver is the centrepiece of the Nikkei Internment Memorial Centre.

Courtesy of F. Honkawa

Fraser Valley Buddhist Temple, 1990.

The Movement East: Alberta

Chapter 14

Bukkyo Tozen

The Movement East: Alberta

Raymond Buddhist Church

The Raymond Buddhist Church was born during the great eastward movement of Jodo Shinshu Buddhism. The events of World War II brought the church to prominence but at a price. The struggle to survive was difficult and painful in the face of local resentment and postwar prejudices, ministerial deportation, and the tensions created with the Japanese Canadian dispersal. Yet the church has managed to thrive throughout the years to become a valued, contributing member of the Raymond community.

The church building, purchased in 1929, is a two storey wooden structure with a seating capacity of 300. The shrine came from the Royston Church after the war. The *hondo* occupies the second floor while the Kobai or Co-operative Store takes up the first along with a kitchen, parlour, baby room and a reception room used for the Sunday School, a *judo dojo* and other gatherings. In front of the building a pine tree grows to remind the members of the first visit by the Gomonshu Kosho Ohtani in November 1952.

By the late 1940s, the modest two storey building became the focal point for the Buddhist and Japanese Canadian communities. Functions like weddings, funerals and memorial services gave the Fujinkai much to do in catering the many meals required. Special services such as Hanamatsuri, Ho-onko and Obon annually called upon all the resources the church could offer to welcome the capacity crowds that attended.

During the Oshogatsu season, the Kobai handled all the seafood needs and specialty items.

For the youth of the church, New Year's Eve was the social highlight of the year. The YMBA and the YWBA became the Young Buddhists Association in the mid '40s, and a dance was held to celebrate the new year. At the stroke of midnight, young men rang the temple bell 108 times. The celebration was concluded with bowls of *soba* for everyone. The YBA also conducted the Miss Sunny Alberta contest later in the year. In fact, the Miss Sunny Alberta Dance attracted hundreds of people from all over Southern Alberta. Other activities of the youth organization included picnics, *keirokai* concerts and baseball. The Ray Bussei team played in the Southern Alberta Baseball League.

In 1950 Rev. E. Nekoda, a vibrant bilingual minister, arrived in Raymond to assist Rev. Shinjo Ikuta with his duties. Rev. Nekoda wasted no time in organizing the Sunday School with lessons and activities. A year later, Rev. Ikuta left for the Kelowna Church. At the same time, the Raymond Temple joined the Alberta Kyoku, with Rev. Y. Kawamura and Rev. Nekoda responsible for all the member churches. Rev. Nekoda left Alberta in 1959 to work for the Buddhist Churches of America, and it was not unti 1964 that Rev. Leslie Kawamura came to act as minister for the Raymond Church.

After the formation of the Honpa Buddhist Churches of Alberta in 1965, the Raymond Temple became the headquarters. One area the administration concentrated on developing was the youth group. In 1966 the YBA was reorganized and named the Raymond Young Buddhist Association (RYBA). Rev. L. Kawamura was instrumental in connecting the club with the Intermountain Young Buddhist League from Salt Lake City and Ogden, Utah, and the Tri-State Buddhist Church in Denver, Colorado. They held biannual retreats in places like Yellowstone National Park.

The older RYBA members decided to form a group of their own. Thus, they organized the Young Adults Buddhist Association (YABA) at about the same time. During the 1970s, they were the driving force behind the church administration. YABA members in fact held every position on the Board of Directors by the 45th Anniversary of the church.

Perhaps the most important part of the church was the Sunday School. Many activities took place throughout the year with parents and children alike taking part. There were snowmobile, skating and bowling parties, and sports nights which encouraged non-denominational participation. A summer Sunday School program included *sushi* demonstrations, flower arranging classes, and *kimono* dressing. The teachers hoped to integrate religious and cultural heritage throughout all these activities.

The Raymond Temple was deemed a provincial historic site by the Province of Alberta in 1980. As a result the church was automatically eligible for grants toward the restoration of the building. Some work had been done to replace the heating system in 1948 which led to the discovery of a smouldering fire under the shrine floor. However, the building in 1980 was much the same since it was built in 1903 as Raymond's first school house. The renovation fell on the shoulders of a building committee headed by Hisashi Matsuno and Mits Tsuji. Work crews replaced all windows, siding and roofing, and refinished all the hardwood floors. Participants in the 60th Anniversary celebrations (1989) entered the church through a new facade into a freshly painted interior.

Terry Bland Photography, Ltd.

Raymond Buddhist Church Ochigo, March 1972.

With the 1990s the Raymond Buddhist Church faces an uncertain future. Membership has dwindled. The Sunday School was discontinued because of a lack of students. Many in the area simply left to further their education or to find better opportunities in other parts of the country. Still the congregation holds strong to the 100 year commitment the *issei* founding members made in the 1920s.

Whether our church membership is measured in terms of

numbers or whether our church membership should be measured in terms of our spiritual commitment to the teachings of St. Shinran, each of us needs to reaffirm our faith in the great plan that our fathers envisioned when they planned for a 100 year commitment. Let us carry on with this great legacy and not fail in doing our part for the continuation of this great teaching.[1]

Ministers of the Raymond Buddhist Church

Rev. Shinjo Nagatomi	1930 - 1933
Rev. Yutetsu Kawamura	1934 - 1940
Rev. Shinjo Ikuta	1942 - 1951
Rev. Ensei Nekoda	1950 - 1959
Rev. Leslie Kawamura	1964 - 1965

Ministers of the Honpa Buddhist Church of Alberta

Rev. Leslie Kawamura	1965 - 1972
Rev. James Burkey	1972 - 1976
Rev. Nobuyuki Kasagi	1972 - 1976
Rev. Yutetsu Kawamura	1975 - 1982
Rev. June King	1976 - 1981
Rev. Fumio Miyaji	1976 - 1982

Beginning in 1982, the Raymond Buddhist Church became part of the new organization - The Buddhist Federation of Alberta. The ministers who served the temple were:

Rev. Hoshin Okada	1982 - 1988
Rev. Yasuhiro Miyakawa	1982 - 1985
Rev. Itsuo Terasaki	1985 - 1987
Rev. Eisho Aoki	1988 - present
Rev. Shigenobu Watanabe	1991 - present
Rev. Masanobu Nishiaki	1994 - present

Lethbridge Honpa Buddhist Church

In 1966 a group of Buddhists came together to form the Lethbridge Honpa Buddhist Church.[2] They set about making plans to meet the very pragmatic needs of a new church. The neophyte organization started with nothing in the treasury. The following year the building committee decided that despite a membership of only 50 they would build a church with a capacity of 250.

Consequently, they established a building fund to which members committed an annual contribution. The committee soon found property and purchased it even though their money was insufficient. Fortunately the membership increased with the influx of Buddhists from Coaldale, Alberta. The extra funds kicked off the construction of the building. Mel Murakami and Joe Mori were essential to the planning since they had experience in the construction industry. Although the capacity had increased to 375, the plan was approved by the members. Rev. Leslie Kawamura turned the sod to begin construction in October 1970.

As the building went up, there was a great air of excitement and co-operation. Many of the members joined the crew to reduce costs. The women provided lunches and coffee. By the end of the year, the completed work was sufficient to hold the first service on New Year's Day, 1971.

The Dedication Service for the new building took place on August 1, 1971. Rev. Kubose of the Buddhist Temple of Chicago was the guest minister.

> It was a hot and sunny August day. The church was filled to overflowing as members, friends who had helped in the construction and well wishers assembled for this momentous occasion. Reverend Leslie Kawamura was called on by Robert Hironaka, chairman of the building committee, to open the doors and lead his congregation into the building. At the end of the service, Yaichi Kitagawa, who had served as chairman of the board from the beginning, was recognized for his contribution to the church, a contribution that was made even though his employment took him some 100 km away through the week. He made many trips back to Lethbridge over icy and snow covered roads. Such was his dedication.[3]

In addition to the regular church functions, the building served as a seniors centre, a kindergarten until the local school could accommodate one, and a space for *odori* practices and tea ceremony lessons.

In order to raise funds for the church to keep operating, the members engaged in several enterprises. A local wholesaler offered them the job of packing 17,000 roses at a nickel a package. The job became an annual event for ten years. People looked forward to getting together to raise money for the temple and to renew acquaintances.

Another project was to thin beets. The young and old went to farms in Coaldale, Picture Butte and Sunnyside to engage in the back straining work of thinning sugar beets, but the funds earned from the work for the building fund made it worthwhile.

Perhaps the most memorable fund raiser was acting as extras in the film **Pure Escape** starring James Garner and Billie Dee Williams. Not an enduring movie to be sure, but the experience of dressing in period costumes, driving antique cars and meeting the celebrities was worth remembering.

The annual *chow mein* supper was the most successful fund raiser of all. The organizers rented a hall which seated about 200 and provided a kitchen.

> The hall was small and not well equipped to prepare *chow mein* and rice. Members were determined to make it successful. Vegetables were washed and cut up at home and brought to the hall for cooking. Rice was cooked partially in the hall and part in a home with a running shuttle to deliver the rice as it was cooked...We prepared about 800 servings between those who ate in the hall and "take-outs".[4]

Since then, this annual event draws about 1600 patrons to the new church and its modern facilities.

The Lethbridge Honpa Church enjoys many youth activities that occur in tandem with the Raymond youth groups. The Fujinkai is also an active group within the church. The women prepare all the meals, *manju* and noodles for a variety of events that occur throughout the year - most notably on New Year's Eve, concerts and special services. In the beginning, all utensils and most of the food were provided by the Fujinkai. The women also teach *odori*. Mrs. Kimura, assisted by Mrs. Teramura, leads the Sakura Dancers. Every year the dance group is featured at the Obon Odori, a communal dance held in the Nikka Yuko Centennial Japanese Garden. Church members and non-denominational visitors are given passes, compliments of the church. The most popular dance is *Tanko Bushi* or the *Coal Miner's Dance*, an especially appropriate dance since Lethbridge's first industry was coal mining.

Toyo Kawamura teaches flower arranging (Saga-Misho-Ryu) to interested Fujinkai members. Mrs. Inaba teaches doll making

(Mikazu club); and Mrs. Matsushita teaches the torn paper art of Chigiri-e. These and other projects like the annual Alberta Buddhist Conference allow the Lethbridge Honpa Church not only to maintain itself but to thrive.

Courtesy of Robert Hironaka

Lethbridge Honpa Buddhist Church, July 1992.

The 1979 Alberta Buddhist Conference served to bring all the Buddhist Churches in Alberta together. This first convention utilized both Lethbridge temples and a local hotel. The objectives of the gathering were 1) to hold a seminar to increase an awareness of how the Teachings of the Buddha can help in daily life and 2) to honour the pioneers of Buddhism in Alberta. Initially, the conference was organized by representatives from the two Lethbridge churches, Raymond and Calgary. The committee today includes these four as well as members from Taber, Rosemary and Coaldale.

Every year the Alberta Buddhist Conference features two renowned speakers on Buddhism: ministers, professors and teachers from all over North America. One is always English speaking and the other Japanese. The first Conference had 225 attendees; it still maintains about 200 delegates.

> When the closing service [of the conference] was held at Honpa, the lights were turned out and a spectacular candle light ceremony was held with the light passed from the altar to the co-chairmen to each member. We then sang "Farewell" and looked forward to the next year conference.[5]

Jodo Shinshu Buddhism in Edmonton, Alberta

In the mid 1960s, a small population of Japanese Canadian Buddhists in Edmonton requested the help of Reverends Yutetsu and Leslie Kawamura in order to maintain their faith. In response the ministers extended their activities to the northern city. At first these occasional visits included weddings, memorial services and cultural evenings involving slide shows, *Dharma* talks, and get-togethers. About 40 to 50 people attended.

Soon it was evident that the needs of the Japanese Canadian students at the University of Alberta were not being met. These students had attended Sunday Schools in the Southern Alberta temples, but once in university, they became isolated. To meet the demand, Rev. L. Kawamura visited Edmonton once a month to teach the *Dharma* to 20 - 40 students in the Marshall Tory Building. Eventually, the crowd became mixed with several European Canadians joining the seminar. Interest was high as several car loads of people even made the long journey to Lethbridge to attend temple on special occasions. Joan van Loon and her husband Alex were instrumental in organizing the activities.

In 1966 the future Jodo Shinshu minister Fredrich Ulrich arrived in Canada from Germany. He had been teaching school there after studying at the Illif School of Theology in Denver, Colorado. Coincidentally, he and his first wife had heard their first *Dharma* talk from a young minister named Rev. Tsunoda (a future Bishop of the BCC) at the Denver Buddhist Temple.

Soon the group met twice a month, once with Rev. L. Kawamura who drove all the way from Lethbridge and once with the members of the church to deal with organizational and business matters. A newsletter and a logo (a dandelion with leaves representing the Five Precepts and the yellow representing the monk's robe) were adopted in conjunction with the development of the group.

Once a year, the Buddhist group invited the general public to a *sutra* workshop. The first studied was the Heart Sutra (Hannya Shingyo) because it was short, easy to chant and Rev. Kawamura could lend scholarly insight into the Zen Buddhist chant. He had been studying Buddhist psychology at the time. The Edmonton group had decided to inform the general public first with the basics of classical Buddhism to gain acceptance. The Five Precepts were also promoted as the foundation of Buddhist ethics and morality. In this way, Jodo Shinshu Buddhism became accepted as part of the religious makeup of Edmonton.

Edmonton Dharma Sangha

The Edmonton Dharma Sangha (EDS) was formalized with tax exempt status through the efforts of Joan and Alex van Loon. The Sangha, the first Buddhist group to be recognized in Edmonton, was originally made up of various styles of Buddhism. Eventually, many splinter groups were formed and split from the EDS to create their own formal organizations. For example, original member Dr. David Young of the University of Alberta went on to found the Zen Buddhist group in Edmonton. In total, 20 Buddhist organizations were formed by the 1990s with about 25% of them having roots in the EDS.

The Buddhist group maintained a core of volunteers with a highly changeable membership. The Japanese Canadian students were loyal but most returned to their homes upon graduation. Still, the EDS held several workshops and festivals every year. The Bodhi Day commemoration in December consisted of a potluck dinner after the service and *Dharma* talk. With the arrival of Kaldan Rimpoche from Tibet, the EDS enjoyed many lively evenings while he imparted his knowledge of Tibetan Buddhism. In turn, the members taught him English and how to drive, a thoroughly interesting experience since Kaldan Rimpoche had never been in an automobile before and had difficulty knowing which door to open in order to drive. The Schweger family and Harry and Thelma Hapgood offered their homes and hospitality in order for these and many other events to take place.

In the early 1970s, the members wanted the second meeting of the month (reserved for business matters) to be held for teaching purposes. Fredrich Ulrich was asked to act as a lay leader so as not to burden Rev. L. Kawamura with a second trip from Lethbridge. About the same time, a famous German scholar of Buddhism, H.V. Guenther, came to teach at the University of Saskatchewan. Rev. Kawamura saw a great opportunity in furthering his studies with this renowned scholar and decided to request a leave of absence to study for his PhD. Unfortunately, that left the EDS without a teacher. Fredrich Ulrich then decided to attend the California Institute of Buddhist Studies in the summers in order to bring new knowledge to the Edmonton group during the rest of the year. Reverends Tsunoda and Kyojo Ikuta offered much help to the fledging lay leader.

Other activities of the EDS included the teaching of flower arrangement and brush painting by David and Michiko Young. Various schools of meditation were encouraged and taught.

In the early 1980s, the fragmentation of the Buddhist groups in Edmonton demonstrated to the membership of the EDS that the current umbrella organization was no longer necessary. They decided to disband.

> The last Bodhi Day feast...was in fact at the Schweger home. The EDS incorporated a Tibetan meditation into this farewell meal. Dr. Schweger brought some skeletons of untouchables from India bought by the University of Alberta for study in various fields. The children were very interested in the various anatomical functions of the bones. After a late night of fellowship some 15 people spent all night with the bones, liberating them from their untouchability. This was done at a time when the Buddhist movement in India among the untouchables was making headlines. Thus we bade farewell to the old Dharma Sangha as an umbrella organization for many types of Buddhism.[6]

The bank account was closed and the funds donated to the struggling Vietnamese congregation. The money had gone a long way in helping to complete the first Buddhist temple in Edmonton.

Buddhist activity is far from extinct. Every spring, for example, the Buddhist community holds a celebration of the Buddha's birth. The event has been staged for the past ten years under the guidance of Dr. Aung, a prominent Edmonton doctor. The Vietnamese and Chinese temples, hosts of the celebration, initially drew some 500 people. However, over the years, the numbers have been scaled down to about 200 because many of the ethnic Buddhists withdrew to celebrate their own festivals.

Dr. Aung was also key to establishing the International Buddhist Friends Association. It seeks to be an umbrella organization for Edmonton Buddhists.

Edmonton Shin Buddhist Dojo

Rev. F. Ulrich was ordained on Nov. 2, 1984 in Calgary by

the Gomonshu which marked the beginning of the Edmonton Shin Buddhist Dojo. The Dojo is a branch of the Calgary outreach program and all donations are made through the Calgary Buddhist Church. Rev. Ulrich works under the guidance of Rev. Kyojo Ikuta and is self supporting: he keeps his teaching day-job.

The membership consists of a core of ex-EDS members. **The Buddha's Smile** is a newsletter of general interest and reaches 120 readers, Buddhist and non-Buddhist alike. They meet twice on the second and fourth Tuesday of every month in the Japanese Community Centre. Activities include services, chanting, *Dharma* talk, recitation of the *Nembutsu, seiza*, fellowship and general support in living the *Dharma*. One of the meetings for the first three years was reserved for lay education. The Dharma Leaders' Training program was designed to produce lay leaders to complement Rev. Ulrich who worked 50 hours a week outside to support himself.

The program for lay leadership requires three years of study in bi-monthly sessions. Study centres on Jodo Shinshu scriptures, Shin scholar work, Joseph Campbell (eminent myth scholar) in writing and on videotape, Native spirituality, meditations, Buddhism in general and the life of Shinran Shonin. Among the first to graduate were Don MacDonald and Sara McKibben. After a hiatus, the program was initiated again in 1993.

At present, the Dojo has no formal structure or membership. Instead, it seeks propagation of the *Dharma* through monthly meetings, hospital visitations and outreach to isolated Buddhists. The programs are initiated by individuals rather than through central planning schemes. This method is based on the efforts of Shinran some 800 years ago when he emphasized learning the *Dharma* for everyday life instead of constructing complex structures.

Many members are dedicated to social action within the *Dharma*. Alice Baker fights for prisoner and tenants rights. Others are helping recovering alcoholics and are a part of the prison network for *Dharma* teaching. In 1992 the Dojo and the International Buddhist Friends Association arranged for Tibetan monks who were ill to come to Edmonton and be taken care of by the membership. In gratitude, they performed for the *Dharma* community (250 people attended), the public (400 attended) and the Native community at Hobbema, the Indian reserve. The last concert began the mutually agreeable connection between the Natives and the Buddhists that continues today.

Through the leadership of the United Church of Canada, an interfaith movement was started and has made much progress. Anne Paludan, from Denmark and many years in Africa, was engaged by the UCC to explore the possibilities of interfaith structures and dialogue. In 1992 the Dojo participated in an interfaith funeral for the deceased son of one of the Dojo members. The dual service was held at the boy's home surrounded by his immediate family who were Buddhists and Christian relatives. The Edmonton Dojo with Anne Paludan's help is now developing an interfaith marriage, and the UCC is preparing a book of interfaith prayers that will include several Buddhist meditations. The mixing of the faiths in Edmonton has become so accepted that Rev. Ulrich was asked to open city council with a Buddhist prayer.

Although the Edmonton Shin Buddhist Dojo is small in membership with a small cash flow, the members feel a vital part of society. In recent years the group has commemorated Obon with a public celebration. In 1992 it coincided with the annual Ministerial Conference. The ceremonies included an evening meal with the ministers, a tour of the Jodo Shinshu Exhibit at the Provincial Museum guided by curator David Goa, and gravesite services by Reverends Ikuta and Ulrich. The Obon service was held in the Japanese Community Centre.

> Everything that evolves out of a deep commitment to the *Dharma* and out of personal experience will have an impact, no matter what the size of the group.[7]

The Movement East:
Saskatchewan and Manitoba

Chapter 15

The Movement East: Saskatchewan and Manitoba

Jodo Shinshu Buddhism in Saskatchewan

By the 1990s, Japanese Canadian Buddhists settled in Saskatchewan but not so many in number that they felt compelled to start a Buddhist Association. Before the war, only two Japanese Canadians lived in Regina operating a silk goods store. After the war, a small number relocated there. Because they knew the older people, Rev. Yutetsu and Yoneko Kawamura visited them during the summer to discuss Buddhism and to hold Obon services. They stayed in the homes of Buddhists and enjoyed warm hospitality

On the way home, they usually dropped by the town of Moose Jaw where several *nikkei* had settled after the war. Many were the remnants of the Ganbariya Group from the Angler concentration camp. Rev. Kawamura was called upon for gravesite services and the Obon commemoration.

> When I came to Moose Jaw, the gate that people had to pass through (to the cemetery) closed after one person had passed, and the next person had to push the gate open again to proceed along the path. Thus - it appeared the gate was designed to let individuals pass one by one. There I spoke to people visiting the cemetery - they said the gate in the Moose Jaw cemetery is made to permit people to go through one by one.
>
> This is in fact the story of mankind being told. Even

> though we may live in the same house, eat the same food, and enjoy similar lives, when we die, we do so separately...We once discussed how this gate in the cemetery had taught us a lesson.[1]

The Manitoba Buddhist Church

In the spring of 1942, several evacuees came to Manitoba attracted by the prospect of fair wages, free housing, public school education for the children and welfare and medical services. Perhaps the pre-eminent inducement was The Security Commission's promise that families would remain intact.

> When the sugar beet programme was first announced on March 28, 1942, it was stated that 1000 families would be moved to Alberta and Manitoba, each to be given "individual cottages and small plots of land for its own use and cultivation" and assured of at least $1000 for the season.[2]

Altogether 1053 people came to Manitoba. They encountered few of the problems the Japanese faced in Alberta, but they did endure the humiliation of "stockyard inspection" by local farmers who were looking for families with plenty of sons. Once settled they also suffered terrible living conditions. Still, Premier John Bracken saw the evacuees as an economic asset and willingly co-operated with the federal government. It was understood that if Manitoba wanted to rid themselves of the Japanese after the war, Ottawa would do so with alacrity. On the other hand, the **Winnipeg Free Press** "took a vigorous stand against racism, sought to establish the principles of Canadian citizenship in law and to protest against the federal government's *repatriation* scheme."[3]

By 1946 the Japanese community felt comfortable enough to consider establishing a Buddhist Church for social gatherings and spiritual solace. The committee, set up to make enquiries, included Unosuke Hamade, Mataichiro Doi, Terukichi Okabe and Kyusuke Oike. They approached Rev. Shinjo Ikuta for advice. He recommended they ask Hideo Nishimura, an evacuee working on a farm in Emerson, Manitoba, to act as a lay minister.

During August 1947 an announcement appeared in the **Free Press** concerning the first Obon service at the old CP Hall at Higgins and Main Streets. After the service conducted by

Hideo Nishimura, Mataichiro Doi explained the need for a Buddhist Church in Winnipeg. Following some discussion 11 men were elected to the Preparatory Committee for the Founding of the Buddhist Church:

Mataichiro Doi	Unosuke Hamade	Shinkichi Sakai
Terukichi Okabe	Juhachi Matsuo	Mosaburo Okano
Katsutaro Ito	Seiji Ibuki	Taichi Kato
Ritsuma Tachibana	Kyusuke Oike	

At a subsequent meeting, the committee decided to send invitations to people living in the rural areas to join the church. Taichi Kato was appointed to write the constitution. Annual membership dues of $6.00 per family were set. Plans were made for the formation of the Fujinkai and the Seinen Kai. Finally, it was decided to hold an inaugural celebration in mid-April 1948.

Initially, the Buddhist gatherings were held in family homes. Weddings, funerals and special services continued to take place at the CP Hall.

In 1948 the Preparatory Committee became the first Executive Committee. The officers were Mataichiro Doi, Founding President; Unosuke Hamade, Vice-President; Shinkichi Sakai, Chairman; Kyusuke Oike, Deputy Chairman; Taichi Kato, Secretary; Shoji Minamide, Assistant Secretary; Terukichi Okabe, Treasurer; and Seiji Ibuki, Treasurer. Committee meetings were held at the home of Ritsuma Tachibana, 330 Edmonton Street.

The inauguration of the Buddhist Women's Society (Fujinkai) took place in August of the same year. Teru Inouye became the first President; Imae Terakita, Vice-President; Kanae Matsuo, Secretary; Kiku Hisanaga, Correspondence Secretary; and Hatsune Sakamoto and Mrs. Nakata, Treasurer. A month later the Young Men's Association (Seinen Kai) was formed. Its founding President was Ty Minamide.

In April as planned, the celebration of the new organization was conducted at the Hebrew Sick Benefit Temple. Approximately 800 people attended an auspicious beginning.

The First Church

The Executive Committee in 1948 then turned its attention to the building of a church. Several donations came from various West Coast temples which were in the process of closing their affairs since the resettlement restrictions were still in place. The Kitsilano Church sent $300, the New Westminster Church gave $200, and the Mission Church $200. At the same time, negotiations were underway to bring the shrine from the former Maple Ridge Buddhist Church to Winnipeg.

In the meantime, Lay Minister Nishimura left for Japan in April 1948 to study for the ministry. A mere five months later, he returned as a fully ordained minister.

On February 1, 1950, the Manitoba Buddhist Church bought a three lot parcel of land at the corner of Winnipeg and Tecumseh Streets for $1980 from the City of Winnipeg. Fortunately, there were more than sufficient donations ($8000) to purchase the land and to begin construction.

Construction supervisor Hisao Kuwada set a budget of $10,000 for the outer structure. He and his crew, however, encountered many difficulties. The first structure collapsed under the onslaught of strong winds. During August the building fell again, this time for unknown reasons. Much discussion ensued with accusations made. The supervisor resigned in the face of the controversy, but the construction continued despite the escalating costs. Mataichiro Doi, Terukichi Okabe, Isamu Katsura, Shinkichi Sakai, Rokusaburo Taniguchi and Chutaro Teranishi guaranteed a $5000 loan.

The building was completed by the end of the year and in February 1951 the church held an inaugural celebration. One minute of silence was observed for the passing of Unosuke Hamade, a founding member. Letters of appreciation were presented to Hisao Kuwada, Terukichi Okabe, Mataichiro Doi, Isamu Katsura and Kazuuemon Sawada for meritorious service.

Soon thereafter, a building construction fund was started in order to repay the loan. The church, through the efforts of Rev. Nishimura, secured a three year labour contract with local sugar beet farmers. Volunteers worked on the farms every weekend during the summer months. They even paid their own way to get to the farms. Unfortunately, the work carried out between 1951 and 1954 earned only $3000.

By September 1951 the Maple Ridge *butsudan* arrived and was enshrined in the new building. Rev. Y. Kawamura, Rev. Nekoda, Rev. Tsuji, Rev. Nishimura and Acting Minister Miyazaki conducted the ceremony. Thirty-five children participated in the *chigo* parade through the city.

Courtesy of Ken Teramura

Manitoba Buddhist Church, circa 1965.

Events and Activities

Sunday School was opened in 1952 with the following administration and staff:

Supervisors	Rev. and Mrs. Nishimura	
Staff	Yoshimaru Abe	Isamu Katsura
	Hisao Kondo	Kiyoshi Sakai
	Shoji Minamide	Tamiko Miyanishi
	Kanae Matsuo	Yaeko Yamashita

There were no classes as such in the beginning; instead, the staff gave religious talks.

In late 1952 Gomonshu Kosho Ohtani and Lady Yoshiko Ohtani accompanied by Bishop Miyazaki and Bishop Shigefuji, Director General of the BCA, visited Winnipeg while on a tour. Their itinerary included a courtesy call on the Mayor and visits to the Legislative Building and the Memorial Cenotaph. The Gomonshu, Bishops Miyazaki and Shigefuji delivered discourses to the congregation during the evening of October 31. They also delivered *Dharma* talks the next day at the Sarana Affirmation Service (Kie-Shiki).

The Japanese Language School started summer classes with 95 students in the church led by Mrs. Nishimura and Tamiko Miyanishi until 1955 when classes were held all year round. With the conversion, Kikuko Nishikihama and Mrs. Sato became instructors and Taichi Kato assumed the position of Supervisor. Classes were held Fridays and Sundays.

Courtesy of Terrie Komori

Ochigo parade as part of Inaugural Service. Rev. Nishimura leads. Manitoba Buddhist Church, 1951.

The school officially became an affiliate of the church and was known simply as the Japanese Language School. The Supervisor was designated the Principal. With Kono Kawasaki as the first President, a Parents Association was formed to promote close relations between the school and the parents.

On November 10, 1956, the temple celebrated its 10th Anniversary. During the festivities, the congregation attended the Presentation Ceremony for the altar fittings. Rev. Nishimura gave the address and Bishop Gyodo Kono delivered a sermon of felicitation.

Late in November 1958 the Gomonshu and his entourage arrived in Winnipeg again. At the memorial service on the evening of the 27th, Lady Ohtani gave a discourse.

The Buddhist Young Womens' Club was formed in 1959. Mrs. Nishimura acted as advisor. One of their activities was the Fall Tea held at Eaton's Assembly Hall. Flower arrangements were displayed and prizes given. The Manitoba Young Buddhist Association was organized in 1960. In 1961 the Young Womens' Club officially changed its name to the Maya Club. Within a year, the Hoyu Kai, Lotus Girls Club and the Boys Club were formed. The Hoyu Kai met once a month for *sutra* chanting and sermons. The members, open to anyone over the age of 55, enjoyed many pleasant days of companionship and spiritual contentment.

By 1963 the congregation felt the church needed an extension to house all the activities and to provide living space for the minister and his family. Estimated cost for the construction was $250,000. To raise the money, the Executive Committee decided to ask each family to donate $250. After much discussion the membership rejected the proposal. Instead, they tried to establish a building extension reserve fund, the money to come from donations and fund raising ideas. Accordingly, $3550 was collected. A raffle raised an additional $5000. Later, a *sukiyaki* dinner for the public brought in $500 for the fund.

The Maya Club held a concert at the Playhouse Theatre for the building fund in May 1965. They realized a profit of $1248. For that concert, the members formed a choir that was so warmly received that there was much interest in continuing the choir. Thus the Chidori Kai came into being. Rehearsals were held at the church every week. They became proficient enough to perform at a number of events. Richard Seaborn, MLA and former Concert Master of the Winnipeg Symphony Orchestra, conducted and arranged the music. Mary Steeds performed as piano accompanist. Eventually, the choir was honoured with the patronage of His Honour Lieutenant-Governor Errick F. Willis and Hon. Duff Roblin, the Premier of Manitoba.

In November 1967 the planned construction of the building extension was cancelled. Instead, a proposal was adopted to extend the rear of the building and to buy the house next door as a residence for the minister. The cost was $12,600. A committee of three (Yoshimaru Abe, Hisao Kondo and Hiroshi Morishita) investigated the possibility. The construction committee consisted of Akira Tamoto (Chairman), Kenzo Teramura, Tazo Nose and Shigeru Shimoji.

Later that same year the church lawyer Bruce Forrester advised the organization to incorporate. Up to this point, the church property was held by three trustees. Incorporation, it was thought, would put the responsibility into many more hands. A Board of Directors was appointed shortly thereafter.

President	Hisao Kuwada
Vice-President	Yoshimaru Abe
	Ty Minamide
Secretary	Kenzo Teramura
Treasurer	Hiroshi Morishita
Building Manager	Harold Shimane

The official name of the church became the Manitoba Buddhist Association, Inc.

Rev. Nishimura resigned following incorporation in order to retire to Vancouver. At the next annual general meeting in April 1968, his resignation was accepted. The membership decided to buy a car for the good minister for his many years of dedicated service.

Bishop Ishiura of the BCC responded to the request for a new minister by recommending Rev. Takamasa Moriki, a successful 22 year old ministerial aspirant in Japan. The Board accepted him after some discussion. Rev. Moriki arrived in December 1969. Rev. Nishimura stayed on to help the young minister become acclimatized to his new environs. A welcome dinner was held in Rev. Moriki's honour in conjunction with a New Year party.

In September 1969 an addition to the rear of the church was begun with a budget of approximately $10,000. The use of volunteer workers brought the costs down to a minimum. Yoshinori Tsutsumi supervised the construction. Richard Seaborn obtained permission from city officials to allow volunteers to work on the addition on Sundays. The extension was completed by October and the Fujinkai prepared a *sukiyaki* dinner for about 37 volunteers to celebrate. The Maya Club served and the Chidori Kai Choir entertained. Upon their arrival in December, Bishop Ishiura and Rev. Moriki led an Installation Service. Everyone continued the celebrations at the Shanghai Restaurant after the service.

The 1970s saw many developments in the Manitoba Buddhist Church. Rev. and Mrs. Nishimura said farewell to 240 well-wishers on March 22, 1970. Executive meetings were held in both English and Japanese, an indication of the changing times. Rev. Moriki married his bride Namiko Sasaki in a grand wedding ceremony on October 23, 1970, presided over by Bishop Ishiura.

In early 1971 Rev. Nishimura suddenly fell ill during an official visit to Lethbridge. He succumbed after an operation. Rev. Moriki and President Yoshinori Tsutsumi rushed to Lethbridge to offer spiritual guidance and condolences. With Mrs. Nishimura's consent, they made arrangements for a funeral at the Lethbridge Buddhist Church. Subsequently a farewell service and wake were held in Winnipeg.

The YBA was reorganized for the 16-20 age group. The Lotus and Boys Clubs were amalgamated as the result of falling membership. Rev. and Mrs. Moriki's first child, a son named Kodo Takamichi, was born on Sept. 20, 1972. A new basement for the addition plus renovations for the kitchen and front entrance were completed by November 1972.

In 1975 Rev. Moriki was transferred to Toronto. As a replacement, Bishop Ishiura recommended Rev. Yoshiharu Hayashi who sent a taped message in English and Japanese to Winnipeg from Japan. The Executive felt his English was adequate and hired him. The arrival of Rev. Hayashi and family coincided with Rev. Moriki's departure in September.

The church celebrated its 30th Anniversary in 1976 with a banquet, a concert and guest speaker Bishop Tsuji from the Buddhist Churches of America.

By the late 1970s and early 1980s, the activities of the Manitoba Church were numerous and varied. The BCC held their 1979 AGM in Winnipeg. A bust of Rev. Nishimura was unveiled at the church with Mrs. Nishimura in attendance. Annual fund raising Walkathons and Bowlathons were held to include as many members as possible. Through a generous donation from Rokusaburo Taniguchi, a scholarship named after its benefactor was established. The award was open to the children of all paid up members. Allan Teramura received $300 as the first recipient. In 1981 the Bukkyokai celebrated its 35th Anniversary with a service (Rev. Miyakawa of Calgary was the guest minister) and a dinner at the Shanghai Restaurant with Consul General Kitamura and Art Miki of the National Association of Japanese Canadian (NAJC) as guests. In 1982 the Sunday School celebrated its 30th Anniversary during the Hanamatsuri Service. Rev. Kyojo Ikuta of Calgary presided as guest minister.

In November 1984 the Gomonshu Koshin and Lady Noriko Ohtani visited Winnipeg. Upon their arrival, Nozomi Hayashi presented flowers to Lady Ohtani. They stayed at the Fort Garry Hotel. The church was modified for a service led by the Gomonshu. Nine members received confirmation during the service.

Rev. Hayashi tendered his resignation and left Winnipeg in early 1985. Rev. Itsuo Terasaki arrived as an interim minister until Rev. Yasuhiro Miyakawa and his family arrived from Lethbridge four months later on April 1, 1985.

The 40th Anniversary of the Bukkyokai Service was held on November 16, 1986 with Bishop Toshio Murakami as special guest speaker. Consul General Masuda, Mrs. Nishimura and Mrs. Kono Kawasaki formally congratulated the church. Awards bestowed by the Hongwanji were presented to Yoshimaru Abe, Hisao Kuwada and Rokusaburo Taniguchi for outstanding service. Taniguchi was also recognized with a gift for his 99th birthday.

Throughout the 1980s there was a disturbing trend in the membership of the church. The Japanese School could not sustain classes for lack of students. Rev. Hayashi took over the lessons which were held only on Saturdays. Rev. Miyakawa discontinued the classes in 1987. The Sunday School too curtailed its activities because of the lack of children. In April 1987, there was no concert for the first time during the Hanamatsuri Service. Classes were stopped for one year until more children became available.

The Manitoba Buddhist Church however did not give up the propagation of Buddhism in Canada. Instead, the members reassessed and reorganized into the 1990s. The Maya Club and the Fujinkai amalgamated in 1988 to become simply the Fujinkai. The minister's house was sold to allow a more affordable residence. The membership fee was raised to $75 a year. The Sunday School was reactivated in September 1988 with Naomi Miyai, Barbara Takeuchi and Lana Vanderpont teaching 12 students.

In 1991 a special general meeting was called to find ways to encourage more participation in the church, especially in executive positions. Unfortunately only 21 people attended. Despite the lack of interest, the church and its members continued building on the good work of the past. A minister's residence was bought at 75 Essar Avenue in the summer of 1991. In November the Bukkyokai celebrated its 45th Anniversary with Rev. Kyojo Ikuta as guest minister. Mrs. Nishimura flew from Vancouver to address the congregation and Bishop Murakami presented gifts and Certificates of Appreciation to Mas Miyai, Fred Nishikawa, Ken Teramura and posthumously to Shig Kato. The anniversary dinner was held at the Radisson Hotel.

The Manitoba Church continues today as a vital member of the Buddhist Churches of Canada and as a cornerstone of the Winnipeg community.

Ministers of the Manitoba Buddhist Church

Rev. Ryokan Nishimura 1946 - 1971

Rev. Nishimura was the prime organizer of the Manitoba church. He started his activities in Emerson, Manitoba, in 1946 as a Lay Minister. He was ordained in 1950. During his years as minister, he worked full time at the Martin Paper Company. In

1970 he retired to live in Vancouver. Shortly thereafter, he died suddenly while on ministerial business in Lethbridge.

Rev. Takamasa Moriki 1969 - 1975

Rev. Moriki's first church was in Winnipeg. Soon after he began his tenure in Manitoba, he married Namiko Sasaki in October 1970. They had a son, Kodo Takamichi, and a daughter, Mayako. Rev. Moriki transferred to Toronto in 1975. His wife died tragically in Japan in 1979.

Rev. Yoshiharu Hayashi 1975 - 1985

Rev. Hayashi came from Japan with his wife Satoko and daughter Nozomi in 1975. His second daughter Mayura and son Shugo were born in Winnipeg. After his resignation in 1985, Rev. Hayashi and family returned to Japan.

Rev. Itsuo Terasaki 1985

Rev. Terasaki served as an interim minister for 4 months.

Rev. Yasuhiro Miyakawa 1985 - present

After serving in Lethbridge and Calgary, Rev. Miyakawa arrived in Winnipeg in 1985, bringing with him his wife Noriko and son Muga. His wife died in 1987; he and his son continue to live in Winnipeg.

Bukkyo Tozen

The Movement East:
Thunder Bay, Hamilton and Montreal

Chapter 16

The Movement East: Thunder Bay, Hamilton and Montreal

Thunder Bay Buddhist Church

Most members of the Thunder Bay Buddhist Church were originally from various west coast temples who migrated to Thunder Bay and Fort William during the dispersal. After the war, remaining funds were distributed to settlements of Japanese Canadian Buddhists across the country. Thunder Bay was no exception.

With a small amount of money, Buddhists began gathering in Fort William led by the lay minister Shinzo Miyazaki. The meetings were held in an old Japanese food store, nicknamed "The Chickencoop", in the east end of town. A shrine was donated by the Kitagawa family after the mother returned to Japan.

In August 1949, the first Obon was held. Rev. Kenryu Tsuji came from Toronto to preside. For Shinran's Memorial Service two years later, Rev. Nishimura of the Manitoba Church arrived as guest minister.

Unfortunately Shinzo Miyazaki soon retired leaving the church confused as to what to do. Eventually Chu Hayashi stepped forward to take his place. Because of his work and his family obligations, he was not able to attend as many Sunday services as he would have liked, but the Bukkyokai carried on as best as possible.

In early 1952, Chu Hayashi received word from Rev. Tsuji that the Gomonshu was coming to Toronto. The reverend suggested

Hayashi go to Toronto to be confirmed as a lay minister, but with great humility he declined, saying he was not worthy. He finally accepted after much persuasion. Transportation was not a problem since he worked for the railroad. In Toronto, he and six others were confirmed. He was the only one under 50 years of age. From then on, Chu Hayashi attended service regularly.

In 1958, meetings were held in Jimmy Saisho's store. Twenty people gathered to listen to the teachings of the Amida Buddha. In 1961 Chu Hayashi purchased an altar while attending a Shinran Commemorative Service in Japan.

During the Japanese Canadian Centennial Year (1977), the Thunder Bay Church invited the Manitoba Church to celebrate Obon. Rev. Yoshiharu Hayashi with several members arrived by bus and stayed at the Airlane Hotel.

In 1988 the Thunder Bay Museum ran an exhibit entitled "Reflections of Glory" which included the church's shrine and other Buddhist artifacts lent by Chu Hayashi.

The church held its first confirmation in November 1990. Confirmed were Bonnie Blake, Mr. and Mrs. Horiuchi, Alice Hayashi, Chiyeko Dulude and Roy Masuda.

In 1971 when Jimmy Saisho's store became a rooming house, services took place at Chu Hayashi's country home. In 1992 the church decided to meet every third Sunday.

In the 1990s the Thunder Bay Church experienced dwindling numbers since the members were aging and the children and grandchildren of the members were not joining. Lay minister Chu Hayashi was well into his eighties. Recent members in fact were not Japanese. The church reacted by reaching out to the community inviting any who were interested in Buddhism. They developed close ties with the Arrow River Theravedan group and Dharam Doije and held joint celebrations in the summer.

> I found some information (about Buddhism) in Thunder Bay libraries and bookstores. Most of this was Zen. I reached the point where I needed to talk to someone who practised Buddhism. Through the Multicultural Society, I found Mr. Chu Hayashi who became **my** *sensei,* or teacher. Mr. Hayashi practised Jodo Shinshu Buddhism. I was confused by the cultural trappings and symbolism. But it didn't matter. Mr. Hayashi was a patient man. He never pushed, never told me what I

should or should not do. He simply said, "This is what I know. I am willing to share with you."

For three years, I travelled out Rosslyn Road to ask and listen, borrow books, attend services and watch. The people I met at Mr. Hayashi's home were kind, welcoming, humble, and good-natured. We seldom spoke of the theology of Buddhism, but actions do speak louder than words and I saw for myself Buddha's compassion in them.[1]

Hamilton Buddhist Church

Japanese Canadians started to arrive in Hamilton in 1946. Their immediate concern was shelter and employment. Still, Buddhists gathered to practise their faith. The first gatherings were in private homes. In the home of Sukegoro Mori, Tsuneto Yamashita, Toichi Nakamura, Tomekichi Yoshida, Kikuzo Morino, Tomekichi Hikida, Shinichi Sato, Kiyozo Kawai, Tokujiro Takeshita, Shinjiro Nishikawa, Naojiro Hashimoto, S. Funamoto, Lionel Tanizawa and Mantoku Sakata (*hokkyoshi*) formed the core group for a new Bukkyokai.

In 1948 two members, Tomekichi Yoshida and Tsuneto Yamashita, bought a family house at 44 Strachan Street East for $5000. The building became the first Hamilton Buddhist Church. The first Board of Directors included:

Tomekichi Yoshida	President
(Kanji) Kikuzo Morino	Chairman
Kiyozo Kawai	Treasurer
Shinichi Sato	Advisors
Tsuneto Yamashita	
Naojiro Hashimoto	
Shinjiro Nishikawa	

The Dedication Service for the church took place in May 1952 with Rev. Tsuji presiding. Thereafter, Rev. Tsuji became responsible for establishing the church and the Hamilton Young Buddhist Society. His dynamic personality and enthusiastic leadership proved to be an inspiration to the Sangha members at the time. Activities teemed at the church throughout this period with picnics, bus trips, bazaars, Obon Odori and various fund raising events.

In October 1952 the Gomonshu (Abbot Kosho Ohtani) with many dignitaries came to Hamilton. He presided over the Confirmation Service held at Cannon Hall since the church itself was not large enough to accommodate the numbers. Naojiro Hashimoto, Lionel Tanizawa, and Sam and Tomi Suenaga were confirmed during his visit

After Rev. Tsuji went to the United States to become Bishop, Rev. Tetsunen Yamada took up his duties as resident minister in Hamilton from 1963 to 1966. When the city decided to expropriate the land in and around the church, the members began looking for another property. They finally purchased the building at 671 Tate Avenue in the spring of 1967. Reverends Ishiura, Okada, Watanabe and Nishimura attended the Dedication Service.

Courtesy of Tomi Suenaga

Hamilton Buddhist Church, March 1990.

For the next several years, lay ministers Tanematsu Okubo and Kozaburo Horibe conducted Sunday services. For major services, Toronto ministers Watanabe, Miyaji and Moriki and Bishop Ishiura presided. Fifteen children attended Sunday School taught by Oscar Kawai and Sam and Tomi Suenaga. Eventually the school was closed, the result of falling enrolment.

In 1971 when the church celebrated its 25th Anniversary, 150 people attended to hear guest speakers Rev. Seki of New York and Rev. Fumio Miyaji of Toronto. The Hamilton Church enjoyed a resident minister, Rev. Seimoku Kosaka, who held regular services throughout his tenure from 1976 to 1980.

During the 1980s services were held once a month by one of the Toronto ministers. Still, the membership was active. In 1982 Mrs. Nui Horibe and Mrs. Tomi Suenaga attended the World

Buddhist Women's Federation Convention in Hawaii. In that year the Women's Buddhist Federation of Canada joined the world organization.

The congregation hosted the AGM of the Buddhist Churches of Canada in 1986. Rev. Toshio Murakami was elected Bishop at that meeting. During that same year, the church celebrated its 40th Anniversary with Rev. Tsuji as guest speaker. Mrs. Horibe and Mrs. Suenaga again attended the World Buddhist Women's Federation Convention held in Kyoto. They took the opportunity to visit their former minister Rev. Yamada.

On November 9, 1984, the Gomonshu Koshin Ohtani arrived in Hamilton for a visit. After a dinner reception at the Royal Connaught Hotel, the Abbot confirmed 11 people at a church service.

The 1990 World Buddhist Women's Federation Convention took place in Vancouver. Several attendees came from Hamilton. Susie Kondo, Teresa Kawai, Kazuko Koshiba, Nui Horibe, Masaye Sakata, Joan Nakano, Yumiko Takeda and Tomi Suenaga joined the Toronto Buddhist Choir for the event and sang in the Vancouver Convention Centre.

In June 1993 the Hamilton Church and Hachisu Kai (a group of eight Fujinkai women formed to perform *odori* and *shibai)* held a Tsuito Hoyo and a Keirokai to honour seniors over 75 years old. Rev. Tsuji flew in from Washington D.C. to attend.

Presently, the activities of the church have subsided, again the result of declining membership. Fund raising, for example, is limited to the year end Mochi Tsuki. In 1967 the number of Buddhists at the church was 80. Today, there are about 46. Ministers from the Toronto Church on a rotational basis travel to Hamilton once a month to conduct services.

Montreal Buddhist Church

Buddhists in the Montreal area first gathered at the home of J. Hori on February 2, 1947. The modest gathering of six soon led to a larger general meeting a month later at St. Raphael's House. The new Nori no Kai elected K. Hashimoto Executive Secretary, Sataro Tanaka Secretary and J. Hori Treasurer. Later K. Hashimoto was elected President.

The organization held its first service on April 6 to commemorate Hanamatsuri. Rev. Tsuji presided. Things moved swiftly after that event. The Bussei formed and the Sunday School opened in quick succession.

On February 1, 1948, the name was changed to The Montreal Buddhist Church. That same month about twenty women gathered to elect the founding committee of the Fujinkai. The following comprised that committee:

Moto Hashimoto	Hatsue Hori	Kiku Yamada
Waki Hashizume	Tami Hayashi	Tome Sawada
Kiyo Tsuchida	Hatsue Hasegawa	Kiku Tanaka
Mitsue Inamoto	Tsune Imai	Yasue Iwasaki
Toshie Hoshiko	Yasu Matsubara	Ume Tatebe
Yao Ebata	Yoshi Sugie	--- Shimizu

By the spring the club was named the Montreal Buddhist Church Fujinkai and formed an executive committee including:

Hatsue Hori	Director-General
Kiku Yamada	Assistant Director-General
Moto Hashimoto	Treasurer
Tane Yasui	Auditors
Toshie Hoshiko	
Yoshi Sugie	

Several highlights characterized life at the church during the 1950s. The 5th Anniversary service was conducted by Rev. Tsuji with lay minister Sataro Tanaka assisting. Afterwards the 300 people attending enjoyed entertainment. In late 1952 the Gomonshu and Lady Ohtani accompanied by Bishop Shigefuji of the BCA visited the temple. A combined Memorial and Affirmation Service took place. The first bazaar was held at the Jewish Hall. The church took in about $800 in profit. Again at the Jewish Hall, the members celebrated their 10th Anniversary with Reverends Tsuji and Tada.

The members said farewell to Rev. Tsuji and welcomed Rev. Ishiura at the same time in 1959.

In 1961 Bishop Hanayama of the BCA, Rev. Ishiura and Rev. Yamada received the newly built altar with a service followed by food and entertainment at the Jewish Hall.

The Montreal temple welcomed Rev. Shinji Okada during its Obon Service in 1964. He served the congregation well until 1971 when he was transferred to the Steveston Church. In his place, Rev. Takamichi Takahatake came from Steveston.

Rev. Takahatake saw the church through growth and slow decline until the early 1990s. Today the church is served by ministers of the Toronto Church. Highlights of Rev. Takahatake's tenure include the Memorial Service during the Japanese Canadian Centennial Year (1977) and the 35th, 40th and 45th Anniversaries of the Montreal Buddhist Church.

The Montreal Sangha Society

Sataro Tanaka called a meeting in late February 1955 to discuss the possible formation of a *nisei* club within the church. Out of the discussion, an organizing committee emerged: Kiyoshi Suga, Hideo Yamada, Toby Shinohara, Steve Ebata, Mas Ishihara, Yo Hayashi and Mary Asazuma. Rev. Tsuji was contacted for a copy of the Toronto Sangha's constitution. The first general meeting took place on March 20, 1955. Fifteen members discussed and adopted the constitution. The organization became The Montreal Sangha Society.

The Executive Board included:

Toby Shinohara	President
Mas Ishihara	Vice-President
Kiyoshi Suga	Executive Secretary (English)
S. Ito	Executive Secretary (Japanese)
J Shepherd	Recording Secretary
Ty Suga	Treasurer
Mary Asazuma	Social Chairman
George Nakano	Membership
Dick Okuda	Welfare
Steve Ebata	Education
C. Wakabayashi	Councillors
Hideo Yamada	
G. Asazuma	
G. Hayashi	
Y. Hayashi	

The initial priority, as expressed by Rev. Tsuji for the Sangha, was the purchase of a church building. A Building Study Committee was formed in 1950 but any prospect of purchasing a building was thought to be a few years off. In the meantime the *nisei* group organized bowling tournaments, movies, dances and picnics. For the 10th Anniversary, they presented the first church concert. By the 1960s the Sangha had organized an annual bazaar, held a spring family social and staged several Variety Concerts.

On September 23, 1961, Bishop Hanayama, assisted by Rev. Ishiura and Rev. Yamada, officiated the Dedication Service for a newly purchased building costing $12,500 in the St. Urbain area of the city.

Courtesy of Fred Okimura

Montreal Buddhist Church, 1990.

Throughout the 1960s, the church prospered and the activities increased. The Sangha formed a ten pin bowling league that sponsored a Family Bowling Night with participants from the United, Catholic and Presbyterian Churches. In August 1964 Rev. S. Okada, the first resident minister, was greeted with a welcoming dinner

In 1966 the church held weekly Athletic Nights at St. Laurent College Gymnasium. A variety of guest speakers, such as Earl Schwartz, a Notary; John Bishop, Corporate Lawyer; and Professor Shunsuke Tsurumi, to name a few, spoke to the congregation during evening services.

By 1968 the Issei-bu became inactive and their Tanomoshi (credit union) was taken over by the Sangha. J. Shikatani, G. Nakano and Y. Hayashi took over the reins with T. Tatebe of the Issei-bu as advisor. The organization was discontinued in 1990.

During the 1970s and '80s, the church held annual events that the congregation and in some cases the entire city of Montreal enjoyed: the annual picnic, the Obon Odori, the Food-a-rama Bazaar and Mochitsuki. The Montreal Sangha Karaoke Club was formed in 1985 with Butch Hayashi as the first chairman.

Today the church still holds the same but no less popular events: the Annual Dinner/General Meeting, the Valentine Dance, the Eastern Sangha Dana League Conference, the Seafood Dinner Get-Together and the Year-End Social.

The Montreal Dana-Fujinkai

Since its inception in 1961, the Dana Club's activities have been numerous. The first meeting of the organizing committee was held at the church on January 22, 1961. Founders included Mary Asazuma, Amy Nakano, Josie Okimura, Annie Shinohara, Yae Yamada and Marge Hayashi. The name "Montreal Dana Club" seemed appropriate since *dana* means "to give to others". The purpose was to promote fellowship among its members, the church and affiliated bodies. It exists today to give of itself spiritually, culturally and financially to the community.

The initial general meeting started with 27 members which elected the following executive:

Mary Asazuma	President
Yumi Nose	Vice-President
Marge Hayashi	Executive Secretary
Besse Ishii	Recording Secretary
Amy Nakano	Treasurer
Toki Ishihara	Social Convenor
T. Yokota	Welfare Convenor
Annie Shinohara	Membership Convenor
Mika Takahashi	Education Convenor

An annual membership fee of $3.00 was set. Immediate projects included forming classes for Japanese cooking, *ikebana*, ballroom and Japanese dancing, and interior decorating. Rev.

Ishiura conducted a candlelight service in April to install the executive.

The first major event for the fledgling club was a Mother's Day Luncheon with Mrs. Ikawa, wife of the Japanese Consul General, as the special guest. The annual event became the Parents Day Luncheon, held after the Gotanye Service, up to 1979.

During the summer, the Dana joined the Sangha in organizing the church picnic. Initially, the Dana sponsored the Valentine Dance in 1962. A decade later, the dance became co-sponsored by the Dana, Sangha and the Montreal Buddhist Youth. At the first dance, Miss Jean Orida was crowned the Valentine Queen and received a bouquet of roses and a pearl pendant.

Activities remained consistent throughout the ensuing years: cooking demonstrations, handicraft lessons, a May rummage sale, a Pre-vacation Windup Social in June, Bon Odori, a year end Holiday Social, lectures on various topics (Mrs. Corobow of the Family Council Bureau talked about family relations in 1963), catering, and participation in various concerts including the Sangha Concert.

Fund raising included the staging of Spring Fiesterama, a Japanese festival held for the first time in 1964. It netted for the newly formed Montreal Dana Scholarship Fund $745. In 1968 the Dana ran the Fooderama, an annual event until 1974, with the proceeds again going to the scholarship fund. The women produced more than 600 assorted *manju* for the festive occasion at the height of its popularity.

By 1970 the Montreal Dana had a membership of 45. Their activities continued as they had in previous years. The first scholarship was given to Julie Takeuchi in 1972. In the following years, Rodney Ikeda, Brenda Sakauye and Carolyn Kato received the award. Also in 1972 the Dana started its Lay Away Plan - members put away at least $5.00 per month for three years. The money was then used towards travelling expenses for the Buddhist Women's Federation Convention. The practice still continues.

For its 20th Anniversary, the Dana donated a huge restaurant refrigerator to the church. That same year the church celebrated its 35th Anniversary with a service and variety concert. The Dana participated as entertainers and caterers for the concert.

In 1983 the Dana and the Fujinkai were amalgamated as the result of the diminishing numbers of Fujinkai members. The name of the club was officially changed to the Montreal Dana-Fujinkai.

Up to the present day, the women's organization has been contributing to the life of the church with many projects. In 1988 the presidency was replaced by an administration divided into three groups, each serving on a rotational basis. The secretary and treasurer, however, are still elected at the AGM.

For the church's 45th Anniversary in 1991, the Dana-Fujinkai donated a handmade set of *zabuton* (comforters) plus $500. Later that year, the organization held a luncheon at the Ming Yeng Restaurant to celebrate 30 years of participation in the Montreal Buddhist Church.

The Quebec Situation

> Lastly, a charter for the Buddhist Church in Quebec must be obtained. Space is limited for a full explanation of this case but a few years ago the Eastern Canada Young Buddhist League spearheaded a movement for the registration of the church in the province of Quebec. After expending close to $2000 the project failed. As a result, the church in Quebec is still not authorized to keep a civil register, which means that official records or confirmation will not be recognized under provincial laws, no weddings under the Buddhist rite can be performed and the Buddhist Church cannot hold land. Though it may require a great deal more of our time and money, Buddhists throughout Canada must not forget this case. Once again in the near future, we must put our heads together and work for the success of this project.[2]

By the early 1960s, the Montreal Church became interested in incorporation to administer the affairs and property of the church and to exercise all the normal functions of established churches in the province. Without such status the temple could not, as Rev. Tsuji explained, own land and perform or keep records of marriages, births and funerals legally.

As early as 1949 the membership had asked Paul Massey, a lawyer, to estimate the cost of incorporation. He said approximately $2000. The Executive Board thought this too expensive and delayed the effort. The Montreal Church enlisted the aid of the Eastern Canada Young Buddhist League to raise the money. The campaign was successful, but the League and the

Montreal Church were not successful in gaining the charter.

In 1965, F.Y. Okimura requested a legal opinion on the possibility of incorporation. The firm of Howard, Cate, Ogilvy, Bishop, Cope, Porteus and Hansard responded with very few alternatives for the church.

> The Freedom of Worship Act 1964 R.S.Q. c301 grants: The free exercise and enjoyment of religious profession and worship, without discrimination or preference, provided the same be not made an excuse for acts of licentiousness or a justification of practices inconsistent with the peace and safety of the Province, are by the constitution and laws of this Province allowed to all Her Majesty's subjects living within the same.[3]

The Buddhist temple has the right of "free exercise and enjoyment of religious profession and worship" as long as civil ceremonies do not take place. The Quebec Civil Code provides that marriages and funerals must be solemnized by "a competent officer recognized by law".[4] "Competent officers" is defined as priests, rectors, ministers and other officers of the Catholic, Protestant and Jewish faiths only. In other words, if a couple wishes to celebrate their marriage in a Buddhist ceremony, a "competent officer" of another faith must be present to register the marriage. Births and deaths can only be registered with the clerk of the municipality or city or a Justice of the Peace within four months of the event.

The Civil Liberties Union suggested the MBC be incorporated under Part III of the Quebec Companies Act. Such action, however, would only give the church the power to perform marriages and funerals without the power to keep registers.

The only other alternative was for the church to seek a private act of the Quebec Legislature for incorporation. The precedent had been set in 1965 when a private act was passed in the legislature on behalf of the Islamic Centre of Quebec. Henceforth the Centre and any of its individual congregations were allowed to be incorporated and keep registers of civil status. The Montreal Church saw these suggestions as impractical because of the expense and expertise needed.

In order to seek a solution to the situation, Bishop Ishiura sought the help of several prominent individuals who felt there was a breach within the freedom of worship represented by the Buddhists of Quebec.

> The Lieutenant Governor (I forget his name) was also open for suggestion...In fact, for the Montreal problem, he wanted to step in, but the Montreal Buddhist Church said no...In Chicago I met Martin Luther King's (man), one of the big shots [Dr. Ralph Abernathy]. I mentioned [the Montreal situation] to him and he went to see King. He says, "My boss is willing to come up and march." But the Montreal Church didn't want to rock the boat...Another [Canadian] Senator, a lady, was willing to come in and help and the Lieutenant Governor too. But the Montreal Church members didn't want to rock the boat any more.[5]

Although Bishop Ishiura tried to persuade the Montreal congregation to act, the church in every case turned down the offer. They all felt that "rocking the boat" would jeopardize their position within the Montreal community. Bishop Ishiura had no choice but to respect their wishes.

In 1981 George Imai, Chairman of the Committee on the Constitution for the National Ethno-cultural Organizations of Canada, raised the issue again in his remarks made to the Inter-Parliamentary Committee on the Constitution.

> As in the past, our faith in our legislators is suspect even today. During the first Ministers conference we heard some of the Premiers state that we do not need an entrenched Bill of Rights in our Constitution because the provinces protect all of its citizens. I wonder if those citizens of Alberta where the crosses were burnt on their front lawn feel that way or the East Indian that is brutally beaten in Toronto or the Filipino that is stabbed in Winnipeg or the members of the Buddhist Church of Quebec which is not recognized by that province.[6]

To this day the Montreal Buddhist Church remains unincorporated.

The Eastern Canada Young Buddhist League

In early 1948 the Toronto Young Buddhist Society led discussions about the organization of the YBAs of the three eastern Canada temples (Toronto, Hamilton and Montreal). By March, Toyo Takata and his committee had drafted a constitution to be presented at the April ECYBL conference, the first of its kind.

The association's initial main function was the exchange of resources, news and ideas for each temple's youth group to keep functioning. Eventually, co-ordinated social events were planned to include all association members. During a meeting in September, 1950, the organization embraced a cause.

> An ECYBL board of directors meeting was held on the Sept. 9th weekend. The purpose was to discuss means of raising $2000 for a Quebec charter. Three ways to raise money were:
>
> 1) ECYBL production to be held in May 1951. Montreal and Hamilton will sponsor a *shibai* (play). Shig Kawasaki is to be the production chairman. Masters of Ceremonies will be Alice Kuwabara and Kameo Kawaguchi.
>
> 2) ECYBL raffle to be looked after by Hamilton. Draw will coincide with ECYBL conference on the Easter weekend in Hamilton. Three prizes will be worth $50 each.
>
> 3) A movie of the conference in Montreal will be shown all over Canada. All collection realized will be put into the Quebec Charter fund.[7]

After the successful raising of the funds, Kiyoshi Suga of the Montreal Young Buddhist Association led the fight for the Quebec Charter through legal means and spent the $2000 from the ECYBL, but all efforts failed.

In the 1950s, the ECYBL wanted to stage an all Canada conference of youth group members to discuss such issues as the Quebec situation. The enormous logistics involved, however, discouraged further pursuit. Instead, the annual conferences with locations on a rotational basis continued.

By 1960 the TYBS membership had dwindled to rather low numbers as did the other member temples. Many had moved to the older Sangha group. The TYBS then folded operations in 1962. With it went the Eastern Canada Young Buddhist League.

In its wake, Kiyoshi Suga, frustrated and alone in his fight for religious recognition in Quebec, dropped the issue and left the church.

The Eastern Canada Sangha Dana League and the Eastern Canada Buddhist League

The first Valentine's Dance of the Montreal Buddhist Church was co-sponsored by the Sangha, Dana and the Montreal Buddhist Youth in 1962. The profits from the successful event went towards defraying the costs of travellers going to the proposed conference of Sangha/Dana members.

In April 1965, Sangha members from Toronto, Hamilton and Montreal met in Montreal to discuss a tri-city league. Toronto and Montreal Dana members attended as observers only. Two years later in March 1967, the first Tri-City Sangha/Dana Conference took place in Toronto. The organization that emerged became known as the Eastern Canada Sangha Dana League (ECSDL) inspired no doubt by the earlier Eastern Canada Young Buddhist League. In order to raise funds, each member was to pay an annual fee of $1.00.

From that point on, the three cities took turns in hosting the conference, each offering a social outlet for the members and workshops in Japanese culture, Buddhist Teaching and the needs of each church. An alternative site in Kingston was used from time to time for convenient travel. In the early '70s, the annual conference included a youth component. The Jr. YBA groups from the three churches met to discuss common issues and the relevance of Buddhism in their lives. Ties became cemented through social activities.

> One of the objectives of the ECSD League was to encourage *sansei* members to take interest in and participate in Buddhist activities. Toward this end the Conference leaders planned their weekend program focused on the youth.
>
> In the decade or so of the League's operation, the contribution made by one *sansei* member is noteworthy. At countless concerts, seminars and workshops, Terry Watada, singer/songwriter, came to our aid to enhance these programs. As a youth he had joined the Tarunas, a TBC youth group, and throughout his high school and university years, he and his band of musicians, all Buddhists, would liven up the hall with songs he wrote and set to music. Many of his songs spoke movingly about the struggles the Japanese Canadian people faced in

> finding their place in Canada. In later years, as a professor of English, Terry would find time to help the Dharma School Department by being a judge at the public speaking contests or give pointers in their essays and poetry writing. Without hesitation, he would sit on a panel where such topics as "Being a *Sansei* and Buddhist" and "What are My Career Choices?" were hotly discussed.[8]

By the early 1980s, the League took on joint projects among the three churches so that all Buddhists in Eastern Canada could benefit; for example, the Education Fund was established to assist with financial grants to individuals or groups and institutions (Buddhist Churches) whose motivation is directed towards:

> a) religious studies (individual)
> b) seminars (religious or organizational, i.e. seminars related to Church Group Leadership)
> c) ministerial training
> d) church library (purchase of Buddhist books and texts)[9]

One such activity was to help applicants defray travelling costs to the Lay Ministers' Leadership Training Course sponsored by the BCC and held at various locations across Canada.

The League also began to take a serious look at the future of Buddhism in Eastern Canada.

> Discussions took place on the survival of the Church. Comments were made that unless something was done soon, the Buddhist Church would soon disappear. In Montreal, there are so few young people and they are not as Church-minded as the *nisei*. Toronto felt it was too "Japanesy" - Junirai etc. only in Japanese - Chinese characters etc. Maybe a change is in order. There was a comment that these are some of the few continuing heritages so we should go slowly and not change things - be cautious.
>
> Some felt we should let go of the reins and let the young ones take over. Transitions must be made pretty soon or there will be no one to carry on since there is such a big gap between groups. Some felt that unless the older ones move up and make space for the younger ones, there will always be a gap so it should be more or less compulsory for older ones to move up. Older Danas would not like to move to Fujinkai as

> they're much too older - generation gap is too great - meetings are held in Japanese - there'll be no compatibility so they do not want to make the move. There definitely is a need for more research and action.[10]

In order to get young people involved in the church, the Executive of the ECSDL proposed in 1983 to merge with the Eastern Canada Buddhist Church League (ECBCL). The ECSDL was largely seen as a *nisei* organization. The ECBCL was part of the district or *kyoku* system set up by the BCC after its separation from the BCA in 1967. Its basic purpose was to allow the three temples in Eastern Canada to discuss activities and problems. Each church contributed funds for travelling and meeting costs.

Since there seemed to be two organizations at crossed purposes and a new organization seen to be involved with the future activities of the three temples would attract younger people, Tak Yoshida of the Toronto Church put forward the following motion in 1984:

> The Eastern Canada Sangha Dana League has formed a feasibility committee on the amalgamation of ECBC League and the ECSD League. The foremost aims and objectives of the merger is to concert their full energy towards all members of the Montreal, Hamilton and Toronto Buddhist Churches to benefit jointly and promote fellowship, religious dissemination, Buddhist educational programs, Social and Welfare activities to each and every member of Montreal, Hamilton and Toronto. A joint meeting of the ECSD League and ECBC League held on March 10, 1984 has recommended the amalgamation.
>
> "Therefore, be it resolved that the ECSD League and the ECBC League amalgamate to promote the above aims and objects."[11]

The steering committee assigned to draft the constitution and aid the transition consisted of Toronto members Tosh Hori, Tak Yoshida, Dave Azuma, Harry Yonekura, Jeanne Akaye and Hedy Yonekura.

At the May 1985 joint ECSDL and ECBCL conference, the general membership voted on and passed the motion to amalgamate. The new organization adopted the name Eastern

Canada Buddhist League (ECBL).

To the present day, the ECBL has conducted annual conferences among the three temples on a rotating basis to discuss and resolve ministerial requirements, church organization issues and religious direction. The League has also promoted good fellowship among its membership as exemplified by Bishop Shodo Tsunoda's farewell message to the league:

Too soon has the day ended!
As strangers we came,
As friends we part
Forged by faith in Amida Buddha.
Farewell, farewell, may the *Nembutsu*
Be our everlasting guardian
And keep us on the Path,
For the mundane steps may vary,
And when again we meet may be uncertain.
Yet, where Amida Buddha resides
In hearts east and west,
There shall be communion close and warm,
The Sangha has been strengthened.

Namu Amida Butsu.[12]

The Buddhist Churches of Canada

Chapter 17

The Buddhist Churches of Canada

The umbrella organization known as the Buddhist Churches of Canada (BCC) began as the Canada Kaikyo Kantoku Ku in 1933. Its basic function was to administer ministerial affairs, co-ordinate educational material, train lay leaders and Sunday School teachers, and act as a foundation to raise money for the existing temples. World War II had closed down all operations. In 1946 the Buddhist Churches of Canada (a.k.a. the Buddhist Foundation of Canada - BFC) was revived to facilitate communication between the churches and to act as the catalyst for Jodo Shinshu propagation. Its headquarters was located in Raymond, Alberta.[1] Shortly thereafter, the mandate expanded to oversee the administration of ministers and related matters within the circle of affiliated temples. The BFC came under the purview of the Buddhist Churches of America (BCA). In 1967, Bishop Hanayama suspended the operations of the BFC, the result of internal squabbles among various churches and the BFC. Rev. Ishiura began revitalizing the organization later in 1967 and proposed the organization become an independent entity. The Buddhist Churches of Canada did so in 1968 with Rev. Ishiura as its first Bishop.

The present BCC is divided into four districts or *kyoku*. The divisions are geographically set and include the following temples or associations:

District of British Columbia:

Kelowna	Steveston
Fraser Valley	Vernon
Kamloops	Vancouver

District of Alberta:
Calgary
Rosemary
Raymond
Taber
Coaldale
Lethbridge Honpa
Lethbridge Buddhist Association
Picture Butte (amalgamated with the Lethbridge Association)

District of Manitoba:
Manitoba Buddhist Association

Eastern District:
Toronto
Hamilton
Montreal

The divisions demarcate the areas so that many of the churches with small congregations can easily share the services of a few district ministers. Representatives from each *kyoku* meet regularly to discuss ministerial assignments, monetary support for ministers if necessary and administrative disputes if any.

The Turbulent Years: 1950 - 1967

In the early 1950s, the members of the BFC began asking pertinent questions about the future. For example, at the 1954 BFC Conference held in Toronto, the topics for discussion included:

How can we strengthen the Buddhist Movement in Canada organizationally and economically?

How can we make Buddhist education more effective for our children in the Public School age?

How can we take Buddhism to young people more effectively?

How can we get the Canadian public to have a better understanding in Buddhism?

How can we recruit *nisei* ministers?

How can we introduce the finest of Buddhist culture into Canada?

The suggestions came from members across the country. Certainly complete resolutions could not be formulated at one conference, but the stage was set for further discussion and future action.

Unfortunately, for nearly two decades the BFC and later the BCC (under the Buddhist Churches of America) experienced growing pains. Besides the well documented "Alberta Problem" (1965 - 1982), the BCC contended with discontented member churches. In a set of minutes of the Toronto Buddhist Church Directors Meeting dated April 22, 1959, the following complaints were lodged:

> A letter from Mr. Tanaka of the Alberta Buddhist Churches League was read. Text of the letter was a complaint that the present Board of the BCC was not carrying out the business as passed at the last meeting of the BCC. Also the Alberta League was seriously considering withdrawing completely any affiliations with the BCC but because of the strong stand of the Eastern Division of the BCC for the support of the Buddhist Churches of Canada, they were delaying their final decision until hearing the present policy of the Eastern Division.
>
> The Toronto Buddhist Church (TBC) as a member of the Eastern Division could not support the present policy of the Buddhist Churches of Canada.

The dispute for the Toronto church centred on BCC policy regarding reimbursement of monies spent for educational materials and travelling costs of the TBC. Questions were asked but no answers came from the headquarters in the United States. As a result, the Toronto church did not distribute the *konshi* or donation envelopes for the BCC to its members.

During a Board of Trustee's meeting for the TBC on Dec. 16, 1959, the following proposal was put forward for the 1960 BCC Conference.

> The Toronto Buddhist Church recommends that all churches study the feasibility of each church individually joining the Buddhist Churches of America and that the Buddhist Churches of Canada be partly dissolved but retain the status of a League to handle any problems that may be caused by international difficulties, that is, problems that may arise which would not affect the BCA but would concern only the Canadian Buddhists.

Such protests were voiced not only in Toronto and Alberta but in British Columbia as well. The Vancouver Temple in particular felt the $4000 assessment levied against the church by the BCC was too high for the services provided.

The friction continued between the districts and the BCC when the latter froze the treasury in 1963 following a unilateral decision by the Vancouver Church to petition the Hongwanji directly for a minister. Two items from the minutes of a "Special Riji Kai Meeting" held at the TBC on Feb. 27, 1965 reveal some of the sentiments about and fallout from the action.

> The minutes of the ministers' conference held in Winnipeg on February 6 and 7 and notice of a forthcoming meeting of the Buddhist Churches of Canada were read by the President, Mr. Mitsuo Amemori.
>
> Ministers Conference: Minutes submitted by the Rev. Okuda of Kelowna...
>
> Six ministers were present: the Reverends Ikuta of Vancouver and Steveston, Okuda of Kelowna, Kawamuras of Alberta and Nishimura of Winnipeg. Absentees were the Revs. Ishiura, Watanabe of Toronto and Okada of Montreal... Noteworthy aspects of the meeting were: the ministers will ask for reimbursement of travelling expenses from the BCC treasury which is currently "frozen", no ministers to be "called" to Canada unless approval is given by the ministers' conference and a meeting of the Buddhist Churches of Canada is to be held in Raymond on Tuesday, the 9th of March.
>
> BCC meeting: Notice of the BCC meeting was received by the Rev. Ishiura and also the Tobu Kyokucho (eastern headquarters). The TBC did not receive a notice or an invitation. Although the BCC assets are "frozen", following the resolution at the last general meeting... held in Toronto in 1963, the Board of Directors at that time had not been ousted by the meeting nor had they resigned...but none of them had been contacted or informed regarding this forthcoming meeting.
>
> The Tobu Kyokucho will send a copy of the notice of the meeting to the Hamilton and Montreal Churches. As the notice was received only this morning, there being less than 10 days to go before the meeting, it is impossible

> to call a meeting of the three eastern centres.
>
> The Toronto Buddhist Church's stand regarding this meeting is to ask for a postponement of the meeting. If the postponement is refused and the meeting is to be held as scheduled, two representatives will be sent to express the views of the Toronto Church. There were many irregularities exercised in calling a meeting of such great importance to the Buddhists of Canada.

Disagreements continued until 1967 when Bishop Hanayama placed the affairs of the BCC in "abeyance", effectively suspending all operations of the umbrella organization.

The Seminal Year

The seminal year for the Buddhist Churches of Canada was 1968. As discussed in Chapter 12 (**The Alberta Problem**), plans and negotiations began in November 1967 to revitalize the BCC by becoming independent of the BCA. Rev. Newton Ishiura of the Toronto Buddhist Church was the primary instigator. The member churches decided the only way to accomplish the break was to establish the organization's own Bishopric.

> **Establishment of an independent Bishopric in Canada**
>
> It was moved that the recommendation, "Establishment of an independent Bishopric in Canada", although acceptable in principle, be a matter of further study by a committee, with an appropriate budget, set-up at the BCC Conference (Winnipeg 1968) which is to report its study of this recommendation at the next regular BCC meeting. Also, re-examine the entire BCC structure to date and prepare a report on this matter. The motion was made by Mr. Shinohara, seconded by Rev. Ishiura. Carried unanimously.[2]

During the Winnipeg Conference (February 24 - 25, 1968), three resolutions were adopted:

1. The BCC headquarters is to be permanently established in Toronto.
2. The BCC will establish its own Bishopric independent of BCA.
3. The BCC conference elected the Rev. N. Ishiura of Toronto as the Bishop of Canada.[3]

There followed extensive discussion about the involvement of the Bishop-elect with the BCC. The concern centred on his continued commitment to the Toronto organization. Will the church suffer as a result? Will the added burden of headquarter status affect the congregation in Toronto?

All doubt was dissipated by May 1968: "In accordance with the resolution passed by the TBC at the meeting of April 17, 1968...TBC will unanimously support the BCC and the resolutions passed at the Winnipeg Conference..."[4]

Shortly thereafter, Bishop Ishiura received an invitation from the Hongwanji to go to Japan for a short period of orientation.

A Period of Stability

From the outset of the newly established BCC, there seemed to be a period of meaningful progress despite the machinations in Alberta. The members wrote and adopted a constitution and charter on November 6, 1974. A Ministerial Association, organized in 1975, became responsible along with the Bishop for the religious affairs of the organization. The National Board, set up in the same year, took on the task of managing the BCC's property and business. One resolution it immediately accepted was the One Church, One Vote system. Various temples argued that the allotment of votes should be based on either the number of members in each church or by the amount of assessment each was required to pay the BCC as a supporting member. The new system effectively reduced the need for the district system except for local concerns and ministerial duties. The One Church, One Vote system also allowed in 1975 each minister of the Ministerial Association one vote. In 1977, **The Canadian Buddhist** resumed publication in Japanese and English once every three months (once every two months starting in 1979). The BCC bulletin came under the supervision of the Ministerial Association.

The first annual meeting of the BCC was held at the Toronto Church during the weekend of March 26 - 27, 1976. Present were the following:

Churches and their Representatives

Kelowna	Roy Tanemura
Toronto	Sumiye Watanabe
Manitoba	Ty S. Minamide

Lethbridge (Buddhist Association)	Mas Terakita
Montreal	Toby Shinohara
Hamilton	Mas Kuwabara
	Sam Suenaga
Coaldale and Taber	Mas Terakita (by proxy)
Calgary	Rev. Kyojo Ikuta

Ministerial Association

Bishop N. Ishiura
Rev. Seimoku Kosaka
Rev. Takamasa Moriki
Rev. Yoshiharu Hayashi
Rev. Kyojo Ikuta
Rev. Fumio Miyaji
Rev. James Burkey
Rev. Orai Fujikawa
Rev. Takamichi Takahatake

National Board

Joe Ebata
George Nakashiba
Oscar Kawai
Roy Sato
Miyo Nakamura
Glenn Nishimura
Bishop N. Ishiura
Roy Kusano

Absent were representatives from the majority of temples in British Columbia. Only the Kelowna Church was a member of the BCC by the first conference. The issue of membership then became a priority during the proceedings.

> Our prime aim from the beginning has been to unite all sixteen churches in the true spirit of harmony in the *Nembutsu*, by requesting your applications for Church Membership. To date, we have received signed forms from ten churches. Of the seven churches in British Columbia, Kelowna Buddhist Church has so far submitted its application and we are awaiting the return of applications from the other six. Nevertheless, the National Board has treated all sixteen churches in the same manner...[5]

In the end, the conference voted to "withhold further action with respect to British Columbia church memberships until further advice is received from Bishop Kosaka and the BC District."[6]

The BCBCF

Central to the disagreement with the BCC was the status of Rev. Seimoku Kosaka as outlined in Chapter 13, **Postwar British Columbia**. Initially, the Vancouver Church supported Rev. Kosaka's nomination.

> The Chairman then advised the meeting that the next item of business was the election of the Bishop of the BCC...Rev. Seimoku Kosaka was duly nominated, and no further nominations being received, it was moved, seconded and unanimously carried that nominations be closed. The meeting further advised that the Vancouver Buddhist Church had consented by telephone to the nomination of Rev. S. Kosaka as Bishop.
>
> Rev. Kosaka then requested the meeting to consider carefully his nomination as Bishop, having regard to his age, language difficulties, his place of residence, and the fact of his church not being a member of the BCC. Upon consideration of the foregoing, Reverend Seimoku Kosaka was acclaimed as the Bishop of the BCC.[7]

Shortly thereafter, complaints about an absentee minister began in Vancouver which evolved into an examination of the relation of the B.C. Buddhist Churches with the rest of Canada. The introspection became "The Membership Issue". Should the BCBCF churches join the BCC?

After the September 1976 conference between the two parties (see Chapter 13), negotiations began for the BCBCF joining the BCC. All matters were settled on February 20, 1977.

> The BCBCF's Representative/Executive Meeting was held on February 20, 1977 at the Vancouver Buddhist Church.
>
> We are pleased to advise that the membership issue to the BCC was finalized at this meeting and all of the churches in B.C. have decided to become members of the BCC. The applications from each church will be forwarded to the BCC shortly through the BCBCF,

possibly together with the payment of the assessment ($5.00/member) for the year 1977...

For the forthcoming Annual Meeting of the BCC, it was also decided that the following churches will send a delegate to that meeting:

Vancouver Buddhist Church	Mr. Cy H. Saimoto
Steveston Buddhist Church	Mr. Ray N. Inouye
Kelowna Buddhist Church	Mr. Roy Tanemura
Kamloops Buddhist Church Society	Mr. Roy Inouye

The Fraser Valley Buddhist Church and Vernon Buddhist Church will participate in the meeting through proxies.[8]

Reorganization

With the expanded number of churches, the National Board in 1977 decided to reassess its priorities. The duties of the directors appeared in a BCC directive issued in early 1977.

The Chairman is responsible for the overall operation of the Board...

The Vice-Chairman will be responsible for...all secretarial and financial operations...The Secretary and the Treasurer will serve under the Vice-Chairman...

One Director should be the Public Relations officer of the Board. This Director will represent the Board at Member Church functions, when required; prepare a quarterly summary of the Board's work; organize for the next Annual Meeting.

A Director will be required to administer the Sustaining Members Fund and Drive and, perhaps, the annual assessment of Church Members.

A lady Director will be required to initiate and coordinate the efforts required in the formation of Women's Federation.

A Director should be responsible for all educational activities which include such items as publications, Sunday School Seminars, English Language improvement for our ministers, distribution of religious materials.

A Director of Japanese Translation will be required to satisfy those Member Churches requiring translation,

> and to help the Board whenever written matter in Japanese is received.
>
> Two Board seats will be left open temporarily for there is the possibility that the Western Canada churches may have members who are businessmen and who come quite often to Toronto on business...
>
> It would be good to start to bring *sansei* as assistants to Directors so that they will have some involvement and participation in the Board's work, and in a few years the *sansei* will have some experience to eventually take over from their elders the Board's operations. Even now, it is soon enough to have a mature *sansei* on the Board.[9]

On the one hand, the provisions made for women, western members and *sansei* reflect the rather paternalistic and regional bias of the BCC. On the other hand, many of the core activities of the BCC were established: the Sustaining Members Fund, Sunday School and religious administration, and the Women's Federation.

The BCC Women's Federation

The Buddhist Churches of Canada Women's Federation (BCCWF) did not come into effect until Bishop Kosaka proposed its formation in 1976. He and a few individuals who attended conferences as observers realized the advantages of a world organization, especially in sharing viewpoints and gaining perspectives with and from so many others. Thus Terrie Komori, BCC Director, campaigned and rallied the Buddhist women's groups across the country to unite under one organization.

> H. Yonekura reported that there was much evidence in the Los Angeles conference that, particularly in Jodo Shinshu, the very backbone and success of the Buddhist Church was the local women's organizations. Although some negative feelings have been heard from some people in Canada, a nation-wide Buddhist Women's organization would be able to achieve a great deal...
>
> T. Komori will be working on a letter to be sent to all women's groups of all Buddhist Churches in Canada, as the first step in organizing the WWBF (World Women's Buddhist Federation) in Canada.[10]

At the first national conference, held in Calgary in March 1978, the discussion proved a revelation of common goals and aspirations.

> [Terrie Komori] reported that Thursday night [of the conference] the ladies had unanimously agreed to forget the proposed agenda and had spent the evening discussing problems and getting to know each other. She noted that it had indeed been a wonderful evening, an evening of enlightenment for all. She stated that she personally had gone into the meeting room proudly representing Toronto with its 200+ Dana and 200+ Fujinkai members, but awoke Friday morning feeling humble, having heard the previous night of the trials and efforts of fewer and younger women in the congregations of other areas struggling to maintain or build a small church in their communities. She reported a universal sentiment among the women attending, not of "What can I do for myself?", but of "What can I do to help?"[11]

The conference resolved that "Those present approve and support a Buddhist Women's Federation in Canada, and will seek final approval from our various executives for the establishment of this organization, to be sent to the acting Chairwoman, T. Komori, immediately."[12]

Not all centres immediately joined. The Vancouver Temple, for example, sent word that their Fujinkai will not join until the B.C. Fujinkai Federation was first established and the BCC was also on firm ground.[13] At the 1982 Annual General Meeting in Montreal, Bishop Tsunoda moved to recognize the women's group officially known as the Buddhist Churches of Canada Women's Federation (BCCWF). Terrie Komori through dogged determination had convinced most of the chapters' Dana and Fujinkai members to come on board except Alberta (with Raymond as the exception). In 1983 the BCCWF sent out an appeal to all Albertans but few responded. Rev. Y. Kawamura, however, encouraged the Board of Directors to continue to send correspondence to Alberta. Finally in 1990 Rits Saimoto managed to convince all 20 chapters to join the federation.

Activities

In 1982, Canada sent its first official delegation of 98 women to the 7th World Buddhist Women's Convention[14] in Hawaii. Lady Yoshiko Ohtani was so taken with Canada's efforts that she donated a generous gift to assure the continuance of the Women's Federation.

The objectives of the Federation and the world organization are:

1. To encourage all members to strive to live within the Jodo Shinshu teachings,
2. To share the belief with Buddhists in other countries,
3. To create interest and build enthusiasm in Buddhist activities around the world,
4. To promote growth in membership,
5. To have children grow up surrounded in an atmosphere of Buddhism,
6. To find warm family togetherness, united in *Onembutsu*.

In 1982 the Women's Federation entered a sister-relationship with the Hawaii Island United Buddhist Women's Association, the result of a resolution conceived at the 7th World Hompa Hongwanji Buddhist Women's Convention (July 1982). The Hawaiian Federation donated a generous $5000 to help the fledging Canadian organization. The BCCWF subsequently launched a commemorative table cloth campaign to supplement the contribution. The relationship was formalized with the visit of Fujinkai members from the Honokaa, Kamuela and Paaulilo churches to the Kelowna Fujinkai's 50th Anniversary Celebrations (May 1985).

The common concern for the Women's Federation was the decline in the enrolment of the Sunday School. In order to raise funds, the group printed Buddhist sympathy cards and *Itadakimasu* serviette holders to sell. The organization then actively supported the Dharma Schools and the various YBAs across the country.

In 1990, The Canadian Women's Buddhist Federation,[15] under the leadership of Rits Saimoto and Bishop Murakami, successfully sponsored the 9th World Buddhist Women's Convention in Vancouver.

The Question of the Bishop

In 1980 with the BCBCF controversy still fresh in the minds

of the BCC and with the imminent retirement of Bishop Kosaka, the BCC decided to address the practicality of a full-time Bishop. At the Kamloops AGM, the membership rejected the 1980 budget proposal to fund one, even though the Vancouver Church insisted the Bishop be independent and under the purview of the BCC only.[16] Cy Saimoto, Vancouver Temple representative, explained that even a large church like his could not and would not sustain a Bishop as the second minister. He further suggested to proceed without a Bishop until such time when the BCC could afford one full-time.[17]

In the end, the position of Bishop was seen as only part-time. With only 2500 or so members spread across a vast country, there didn't seem to be enough work. The Bishop was expected to set his priorities according to the needs of his home church. Resolutions were thus adopted to ensure that no church would be deprived of ministerial services.

1. The Bishop of Canada should not be posted to a small church. This should be obvious from the standpoint of "status". Also, the Bishop needs the resources of a large church.
2. This can only be done if the Bishop is the "head minister" of a large church employing two or more ministers.[18]

The BCC agreed to be responsible for hiring and maintaining the Bishop of Canada, but in order to fund the office adequately, member churches had to agree to accept the Bishop and to share in a cost-sharing plan. It was also decided that the Office of the Bishop should be located in the same city as the administrative head office. In 1980, that office moved from Toronto to Vancouver. Vancouver, again, raised the question of the necessity of a Bishop. The BCC membership decided after a lengthy discussion upon the following resolutions:

1. The Buddhist Churches of Canada should have a Bishop.
2. He shall be the spiritual leader of all Buddhists in Canada, and, in accordance with the "Foreign Missions Regulations" of the Honpa Hongwanji, "supervise" the administration of Churches in Canada that will follow the Teachings of Shinran Shonin as taught by the Nishi Hongwanji.

3. We Buddhists in Canada have steadfastly followed the way taught by the Nishi Hongwanji for over seventy-five years, and the Hongwanji in turn have sent their missionaries throughout those years to guide and comfort us through many difficult times.

   If at all possible, we should continue to hold and nurture this relationship, for the benefit of Canadian Buddhists.[19]

By 1985 the BCC, however, decided to look into the possibility of a full-time Bishop. Apparently the National Board took its cue from the Buddhist Churches of America which found it could not attract ministers let alone Bishop candidates because:

1. Ministers are hard to come by from Japan because of the low economic standard of the minister's life in the BCA and the fact that the financial situation of the Temples of Japan has tremendously improved.
2. Ministerial aspirants have openly [complained about the ministry] and parents of potential ministerial aspirants have objected to the ministry as a profession because the Ministry does not offer financial potential or possibilities. The result is fewer aspirants.
3. Ministerial aspirants, concerned about retirement, openly state that the present BCA Retirement Program is in need of up-grading comparable to the education and personal investment made to become a minister.[20]

Since Bishop Tsunoda had announced his intention to retire in 1986, the BCC formed the Bishop Search Committee.[21] The committee's report advocated the appointment of an individual to the Bishopric who spoke English, was active as a Jodo Shinshu Hongwanji-ha minister and was able to serve two terms (eight years). The Bishopric was to begin as a part-time position in 1986 and to become full-time by 1988. The office of the Bishop was to be located in either Toronto or Vancouver.[22] Finally, the Ministerial Association would handle the nomination of appropriate candidates.

All proposals were accepted at the March 1985 Annual General Meeting conducted in Kelowna.

Various Projects

Since 1980, the BCC has enjoyed steady growth and prosperity punctuated by particular milestones and controversies. During that year the BCC instituted the Dento Hokokue Project (Ascension Commemorative Assessment) in celebration of the Gomonshu Koshin Ohtani's Ascension. Accordingly, the BCC pledged $20,000 to the Hongwanji. The money was raised through donations during special services held between 1978 and 1981. The National Board proposed designating a National Buddhist Week (third week of October) so that special services could be co-ordinated. Moreover, in accordance with the celebrations, the BCC organized and arranged a pilgrimage tour (Sanpai Dan) to Kyoto. About 100 devotees from Eastern Canada and 40 from the West made the journey.

When Rev. Nakatsumi of Toronto in 1979 inquired about taking courses in Kyoto, it came to light that any Canadian wishing to enter Nishi Hongwanji ministerial courses had first to become a member of the San Francisco Buddhist Church. Bishop Kosaka objected and contacted the Head of the International Department, Rev. Okuda, at the Nishi Hongwanji. At the April 1980 National Board of Directors Meeting in Toronto, the Chairman, Harry Yonekura, announced that the Toronto Buddhist Church had been designated a Gai Chi Jiin or District Temple for the Buddhist Churches of Canada. Potential students could thereafter register for enrolment in Japan through the BCC.

With the new status of Gai Chi Jiin, the Toronto Buddhist Church instituted the program known as Financial Aid to Ministerial Aspirants in Canada (FAMAC).[23] Its primary purpose was to encourage Canadian Buddhists to pursue Buddhist studies and to become ministers of the BCC.

> Since the end of World War II, our churches have experienced a shortage not only of ministers generally, but of ministers able to communicate effectively with congregations which comprised increasing numbers of English-speaking members. Meanwhile, fewer and fewer ministers in Japan were available to come to Canada.[24]

The FAMAC program offers five consecutive annual grants of up to $10,000 for a student to complete an MA at the Institute for Buddhist Studies in Berkeley, California, and to study at Chuo Bukkyo Gakuin (Central Buddhist Institute) in Kyoto for another two and one-half years. The only obligation on the part of the recipient was a three year commitment to the BCC after graduation and ordination.[25] Two candidates have so far taken advantage of the generous funding: Rev. Grant Ikuta and Doreen Hamilton.

Inaugurated on July 1, 1991, the Canadian Young Buddhist Association attempted to organize all the Buddhist youth groups across the country. The membership is open to Buddhists 13 years and older. The first meeting to elect the first executive was held in Winnipeg 1991 in conjunction with the BCC's AGM. The Executive Committee consisted of:

National Chair	Grant Miyai	Winnipeg
Vice-Chair	Marilyn Mori	Toronto
Secretary	Thomas Kishibe	Toronto
Western District Representative	Linda Wakahara	Vancouver
Central District Representative	Wes Miyai	Winnipeg
Eastern District Representative	Barry Nishikawa	Toronto

The Bishopric of the BCC

Bishop Newton Ishiura	1968 - 1976
Bishop Seimoku Kosaka	1976 - 1980
Bishop Shodo Tsunoda	1981 - 1986
Bishop Toshio Murakami	1986 - 1993
Bishop Yoshihide Matsubayashi	1993 - present

Part Three

The Toronto Buddhist Church: *50th Anniversary Celebration*

The Toronto Buddhist Church

Chapter 18

Bukkyo Tozen: The Toronto Buddhist Church

The Toronto Japanese Canadian Community

Metropolitan Toronto in the 1940s was about as homogeneous as it is cosmopolitan in the 1990s. A few Japanese Canadians had settled in the area before the war to live or to study at the University of Toronto but it certainly boasted no "Little Tokyo" as did Vancouver. During the war the BC Security Commission allowed some to go to Toronto but only if a job and a sponsor with lodgings were in hand. With the dispersal of the internees after the war and the assimilationist policies of the federal government, Toronto and environs seemed a viable destination. So much so that by the end of the 1940s, Japanese Canadians comprised the largest visible minority in the city, surpassing even the Chinese. The number grew to 5326 according to the 1951 Census, 11,690 in 1971, and 13,665 in 1981, at this point, roughly one third of the entire Japanese Canadian population.

> Japanese Canadians emerged as the largest "visible minority" in both the 1951 Census and the 1961 Census. They were indeed among the "pioneers" of people of colour before Toronto emerged as a city of the world's immigrants... Certainly no American city in the eastern half of North America could claim that, for more than a decade, the largest minority group within its boundaries was of Japanese descent.[1]

Still their presence was not noticed much by the majority white population since most Japanese Canadians lived in the heart of the downtown garment district loosely bordered by Spadina Avenue, Gerrard, Huron, and Queen Streets with Dundas Street as the main drag. The quiet enclave, "the faintest whisper of a Japanese quarter"[2] as described by Ken Adachi, provided social interaction, a common language and a shared culture. The *nisei* in particular saw Toronto as an opportunity, a place where jobs were plentiful.

> Many (male *nisei*) were hired through recommendations by others, usually friends. Some eventually started up small-scale artisan-type businesses like product fabricating which proved easy and profitable due to the postwar shortage of consumer goods and services. While one *nisei* male reported that "you'd quit a job in the morning and you could land yourself off about two, three jobs in the afternoon," another strongly disagreed noting that before the 1960s, discrimination in hiring was commonplace.[3]

Despite the relative anonymity and the wealth of employment, Japanese Canadians once again encountered the racism that had dogged them throughout the internment period. A member of a prominent Buddhist family recalled applying for a job in a garment factory in person. The boss immediately called for a stick so that he could "hit the Jap".[4]

The employment situation was much more difficult for women. Even if they had had university education, they were relegated to factory and domestic work.

Despite the trials by fire, the Japanese Canadian community, hidden as it was, managed to become established in Toronto. Two twice weekly newspapers kept the people informed. **The New Canadian** and **The Continental Times** (the original **Tairiku Nippo**) gave everyone a sense of continuance since both newspapers started in Vancouver before the war.

The New Canadian, a wholly *nisei* paper, began as a voice for that generation in 1938. With its close ties to the Japanese Canadian Citizens League, it was allowed to continue publishing throughout the war years despite a ban on all other media. In fact, the paper literally followed the community. In 1942 Thomas Shoyama continued to edit it from Kaslo, an internment town 500 miles inland from Vancouver. Kasey Oyama took over as editor when the paper moved to

Winnipeg in 1945. **The New Canadian** then moved to Toronto in 1948 where most of its readers resided.

> It continued publishing in conservative North Toronto at 2498 Yonge Street. On May 1, 1949 the paper moved west of downtown to a more permanent location at 479 Queen St. West soon after Toyo Takata became the new editor. In September 1951 Ken Adachi replaced him as the editor, while Takaichi Umezuki eventually became the publisher.[5]

After 50 years of operation, **The New Canadian** in the 1990s is published once a week by Japan Communications, Inc. with Sakura Torizuka as English Editor (replacing K.C. Tsumura) and Shin Kawai, Japanese Editor.

The Continental Times started as the **Tairiku Nippo** (one of three dailies) in 1907. It was closed down the day after Pearl Harbor. Once revived in Toronto by publisher Yoriki Iwasaki in late 1948, the paper began reaching its readership (mostly *issei*) by publishing twice a week from 205 Dundas St. W. Shortly thereafter in February 1949, it featured a one page English section edited at first by Hugo Yamamoto and then Vic Kitagawa. **The Continental Times** continues today as **The Canada Times**, located at 312 Dundas St. West. Harry Taba edits the paper for its once a week run.

Both papers reflected the conservative attitudes of the Japanese Canadian community in the late '40s and '50s. The contents concentrated on social events and Japanese news items. Gone was the need to stand up for human rights; political activism was all but stamped out with World War II, the demise of the Nisei Mass Evacuation Group and the ousting of the Ganbariya Group from their Moose Jaw hostel. The general call was for assimilation through the breakup of a visible community, individual movement to the suburbs and avoidance of controversy ("don't rock the boat").

Although there were many who wished to maintain their faith, some preferred to choose a religion as an act of cooperation or assimilation.

> In 1941, approximately 64% of all Japanese Canadians considered themselves as Buddhists while 21% counted themselves as United Church and 7% identified as

> Anglican, with another 8% as "Other". As a result of Christian involvement with Japanese Canadians during the war, these corresponding percentages rose (sic) in 1951 to 41%, 39%, 14% and 6% "Other" respectively.[6]

Many Japanese Canadians first joined a United Church given the missionary connection the church had established before the war in Vancouver. Constance Chappell, Emma Kaufman, Florence Bird and Rev. James Findley worked as "*nikkei* sympathizers in the Carlton Street United Church at Carlton and Yonge Streets and Metropolitan United Church at Queen and Church Streets"[7] during the war. Rev. Findley was an outspoken supporter of the Japanese Canadian community.[8]

In August 1942, Rev. Kosaburo Shimizu began travelling from Kaslo "to investigate conditions as far east as Montreal and lay foundations for jobs and social acceptance."[9]

> Shimizu held his first Sunday service with Japanese Canadians in Toronto on a crowded third floor room in the Church of All Nations at 423 Queen Street West. While Shimizu met with interested *issei* to plan a congregation for Japanese speakers, he urged the *nisei* to mix in with established white churches. In addition to his duties in Toronto, he travelled throughout Ontario and even into Montreal to give encouragement to those who had ventured east.[10]

Despite Rev. Shimizu's desire for the *nisei* to mix in with established white churches", the United Church *nikkei* congregation closed ranks and created its own church.

> Most *nisei* felt increasingly insecure as they failed to receive invitations to even the most informal parties. One *nisei* noted at the time that "there's a church member where I work who looks at me every day as if my father had shot her son in Burma." [11]

In 1958, the Japanese United Church opened its new accommodations at 701 Dovercourt Rd.

The Toronto Japanese Canadian community also supported an Anglican Church. During the war, *nikkei* Anglicans met at St. George the Martyr Church and the Church of the Redeemer. After the war, the Holy Trinity Church in downtown Toronto was a favourite place for Japanese Canadian Anglicans to gather and worship. By the late 1950s, they held bazaars, activity nights, public meetings and youth dances at St. Anne's Parish Hall. In 1961 the Japanese Anglican group established itself at the Church of St. Alban the Martyr in the Annex area and grew to about 200 families by the end of the decade.

In recent years, the Japanese Canadian congregation has dwindled and the church moved to smaller quarters in Toronto's east end.

Whether a reaction to the prevailing racism toward the Japanese in Toronto or the need to propagate their religion for spiritual or secular reasons, Japanese Canadians established churches to allow themselves the opportunity to congregate together. Japanese Canadians decided to establish some semblance of that community that had existed before the war. However, it was no easy task. For many Buddhists, for example, the pressure to conform often inhibited even admitting allegiance to Buddhism.

> While we were in Huron [Street], we were looked upon with scepticism from both the *nisei* (outside of Buddhists) and the Caucasians. Naturally the *hakujin* people were ignorant of the Buddhistic religion, the Buddhistic ways. The Japanese part of it, I can't say whether they understand Buddhism or not, but as soon as Buddhism is mentioned, the immediate thought that comes to everybody is Japanese. In those days, around the '50s, there was a tremendous move here in the city that we are Canadian. We are not Japanese Canadian, we are Canadian. And they somehow wanted to eliminate this word "Japanese" even though they missed their *tsukemono*. Consequently, when we first started... Rev. Yoshida of some Christian sect wrote a three page version of Buddhism in **The New Canadian** and in the following issue there was a rebuttal from Rev. Tsuji which straightened out quite a few points as to his thinking... Now through the guidance and leadership of Rev. Tsuji, we (Young Buddhist Society) were very fortunate that we were able to grasp quite a few of the fundamental teachings of the Buddha and we were able to slowly bring our heads above water and confidently say "I'm a Buddhist."[12]

For their part too, over-zealous Christians themselves simply could not understand why Japanese Canadians would even want to be anything but Christian; some equated being Christian with being Canadian.

> You think very seriously, if we had thought of really assimilating and becoming Christians then perhaps we wouldn't have been thrown out. You think of these things. I was here alone. I was pretty homesick. And I know I recall having those thoughts very strongly. And this woman took me to these Christian rallies at Maple Leaf Gardens. It was quite impressive, about a thousand young people...[but] I knew that I was a Buddhist.
>
> Well she cried. She says that she cried to think that I wasn't going to be saved by Jesus. But I was telling them the other day that the part that really made me think one day as she was sitting there at the Children's Aid talking to me about seeing Jesus, and I believed that she was a really good woman, what you'd call a good Christian...and it all came to me, I was all alone, somebody came to sell me insurance that in case I died, that I would [be saved]. So right away, when you're alone, you think well certainly, I don't want to put a burden on anyone. When you think of death, you think, what's going to happen to me, and then I knew that I was a Buddhist. That I would never want a Christian burial.[13]

Through their faith in the Buddha *Dharma*, Japanese Canadians with the Toronto Buddhist Church overcame many adversities, societal and internal, to become the cornerstone of the Japanese Canadian community in Toronto.

Rev. Kenryu Tsuji

1945 - 1958

Chapter 19

The Toronto Buddhist Church: Rev. Kenryu Tsuji 1945 - 1958

> I knew that there was going to be quite a congregation of Japanese Canadians in this area [Toronto] because it was a big city, the possibility of employment was very great. At that time [1944] however, there was a restriction on the number of Japanese who could come into the city. So I went to Port Credit. After a couple of months, I applied as a student. I registered at the University of Toronto, and naturally as a student, I could live in Toronto. I checked to find a place where I could hold meetings...the Ukrainian Hall and various halls where ethnic groups would meet. But we weren't organized to be able to rent a hall.[1]

Reverend Kenryu Tsuji ventured out of the Bayfarm area near the Slocan internment camp where he was teaching and leading a Buddhist congregation to go to the Toronto area in 1944. He carried with him the wooden statue of the Buddha he had managed to salvage from the Vancouver Church and a fervent desire to take the *Dharma* to the disaffected Japanese Canadians in the east. He had correctly predicted the largest concentration of Japanese in Canada was to be in Toronto.

The first problem he faced was that he didn't know any Buddhists in the city. He had only been in Vancouver a short time before the war and thus did not know the leaders who had gone to Toronto. He managed to contact Sanro Kobayashi, one of the first to move east.

Kobayashi and his wife, both devout Buddhists, agreed to help to organize a meeting. They advised the reverend to contact Hikobe Mori, a former youth leader of the Fairview Church, who in turn advised him to talk to the RCMP. Mori was afraid the authorities would not allow Japanese Canadians to assemble. Such were the times.

Rev. Tsuji thought it unnecessary but he complied. At the RCMP office, he later recalled, the Mounties asked him if he had a guilty conscious to ask such a question. The minister explained some of the members thought they needed permission. The Mounties assured him he needed no such thing for a religious gathering.

TBC archives

Rev. Kenryu Tsuji
Toronto Buddhist Church,
1945 - 1958.

In the meantime, the ad hoc committee of *issei* (now identified as the Bukkyo Kai[2]) approached Genjiro Mori who had a house at 52 Leonard St. in the Jewish Section of town; he was one of the few Japanese Canadians who owned their own homes. As a devout Buddhist he readily agreed to hold the first gathering in his house.

> So we sent out notices by asking people about other Buddhists in this area...they gave us names and addresses, and we used ditto pads, jelly pads...we sent out about a hundred notices. We had about seventy-five people there at Mr. Mori's place.[3]

Names were also obtained from the city telephone book as well as by word of mouth.

The committee decided to hold the first gathering to coincide with Obon, the Festival of Lanterns (a commemoration of ancestors), on August 15, 1945. The celebration became an auspicious beginning because Buddhist activity steadily increased from that day. Word quickly got around of the minister's presence in town.

While studying at the university, Rev. Tsuji lived at 13 Division St. People sought him out to perform memorial services. He complied but could only offer as a meeting place his room which contained a double bed and a huge *butsudan*, donated to him by the internees of Tashme. Rev. Tsuji looks upon those times with great fondness.

> They [Tashme people] sent this *butsudan*. I had it in my bedroom and we'd hold services there. Everybody'd be sitting on the floor and on my bed, everywhere, but we still had to do it. It was a great time, those days.[4]

He soon quit his studies and found a full time job to make ends meet. His weekends, however, were taken up totally with organizing Buddhist gatherings since interest was mounting.

> ...after that we went to Mr. Onishi's house, and to other people who had homes where we started meetings. When the restrictions into the city became loose or lifted, a lot of people started coming in from places like London...by that time, we rented a room in a Ukrainian Hall. That's where we started holding our meetings. This was small for bigger meetings so we went to another Ukrainian Hall down on Bathurst Street. It's no longer there, but that's when, a few years later, we really had that place full.[5]

So full in fact that the organizing committee by the late 1940s rented the Legion Hall on College Street near Yonge.

> Over 50 *niseis*, equally represented by men and women, gathered at 245 College Street on September 8 for the first English Service and meeting sponsored by the Toronto Buddhist Temple.
>
> Reverend T. Tsuji, who spoke at the gathering, explained the difficulties which the Church has had to face since the evacuation and asked for the whole-hearted co-operation of the young people to realize a vast and complete re-organization of the Church and its activities.

> "To see this task through to a successful end is a responsibility that rests upon your shoulders and mine", he said.[6]

It was about that time that Rev. Tsuji met a man who was to become a great supporter of Buddhism in Toronto and North America.

> I met Mr. Numata who came to visit about 1952. I think he came to visit Canada to introduce his products [micrometers for MTI Corporation]. He was all alone and stayed in cheap hotels by the railroad station. When I was holding Sunday School, here was this man whom I had never seen before sitting in Sunday School [Legion Hall]. And so when it was over, I went and talked to him. He said, "I'm from Japan. My name is Yehan Numata and I have come to do some business...I wanted to make sure that there was a Buddhist group here." He phoned somebody...and this fellow evidently knew where we were meeting...So we got to talking and he said, "You know, we've really got to spread the teaching of the Buddha because it is a teaching of peace." We had a really good discussion. He didn't have any spending money because the Japanese government wouldn't let him take any money out so we fed him and gave him beer. That's how I met Mr. Numata.[7]

The Reverend Yehan Numata, an industrialist turned philanthropist, is considered to be one of the great patrons of Buddhism in modern times. He was born in the late 1800s into a temple family. As a businessman, he established manufacturing plants for his micrometers in Chicago, New York, Los Angeles and San Francisco. He eventually created more in Singapore and Brazil. He then committed a large proportion of his profits to the propagation of Buddhism.

> Throughout my life, I have sincerely believed that Buddhism is a religion of peace and compassion, a teaching which will bring spiritual tranquillity to the individual, and contribute to the promotion of harmony and peace in society.
>
> Yehan Numata
> Founder, Mitsutoyo Corporation
> Summer 1990

He eventually established in 1965 the Bukkyo Dendo Kyokai (Buddhist Promoting Foundation or BDK). Under his guidance, BDK sponsored many activities to spread the teachings of the Buddha. Rev. Tsuji estimates that the foundation published and distributed a million copies of **The Teaching of the Buddha**, a small book containing the essence of the Buddha *Dharma*. He also initiated through the foundation in 1982 the translation and publication of the voluminous **Taisho Chinese Tripitaka** in English. The first phase is targeted to be completed by the year 2000 (10% of the work will be translated). Furthermore, BDK has endowed Buddhist Chairs at leading universities. The Numata Chairs in Buddhist Studies can be found today at UC Berkeley, Harvard, University of Chicago, University of Hawaii, Smith College and the University of Calgary to name a few. Numata personally helped Rev. Tsuji to raise the money to build the Buddhist temple in Washington, D.C.

For his dedication and devotion to Buddhism, Yehan Numata received an honorary Doctor of Humanities degree from the University of Hawaii in 1988 and became a Buddhist priest as well.

He passed into Nirvana on May 5, 1994. The Canadian arm of the BDK donated $50,000 to support the University of Toronto's chair in the studies of Buddhism and East Asian philosophies in commemoration of Yehan Numata's first year memorial observance.

Rev. Tsuji also found opportunities to activate Buddhism in other areas of Eastern Canada.

> When I talked to Mori Hikobe-*san*...he said there's a man in Hamilton, Sukegoro Mori, a very devout Buddhist. Somehow we contacted him. He said we will have Obon and so in 1946 we had Obon over there. Then they said there is Tanaka Sataro in Montreal. Fairview people lived there. So we contacted him and started Obon service there. Obon service has been a very interesting way to start a group because they all congregate there.[8]

Thus the foundation was laid for the Eastern Dana-Sangha League to be formed in the 1960s.[9]

The Toronto Young Buddhist Society

To form a *nisei* group was felt at best to be risky in Toronto in the late '40s but to organize a religious group that was Japanese in nature was considered foolhardy (certainly not courageous).

> Anything remotely connected with things "JAPANESE" was looked upon with great suspicion even by the *niseis*. The following comments appeared in a Japanese Canadian Newspaper [**The New Canadian**, 1946]:
>
> ...in prewar days, the Buddhist Church did militate against effective Canadianization in segregated Japanese communities. It was an unavoidable situation since the culture patterns which accompanied religious worship in the first generation church were naturally distinctively Japanese. We say this frankly, and to any who would dispute the statement, we would reply that the response of Young Buddhists to call for volunteer servicemen early last year admits of no other construction.
>
> The new second generation church, however, can be markedly different and can exist as a far more progressive influence. American experience and, in fact, tentative beginnings in Vancouver itself before the war have shown that around the central core of Buddhist teaching can be built an organizational framework that does not in the least emphasize the importance of Japanese culture. So long as this is true of the new *Nisei* Church in Toronto - and we believe it will be - we wish it every success.[10]

Still, the first organization to form within the ad hoc Buddhist Church was the Toronto Young Buddhist Society (TYBS). The desire to establish such a club stemmed from the large Bussei movement before the war in British Columbia. The *nisei* now in their twenties and early thirties were establishing themselves in Toronto and wanted to resume practising their religion. They moreover wanted to socialize within a common and familiar environment. In order to do so, they met in the Legion Hall on College Street on a fairly regular basis. The *issei* continued to meet separately in private homes. In the fall of 1946, Rev. Tsuji held the first meeting to organize the fledging *nisei* group.

September 15, 1946

The first meeting of the temporary committee was held at Reverend Tsuji's home on 13 Division Street from 2:30 p.m. The people present were Fumi Maeda, Peggy Harada, Tsuruye Koyanagi, Nancy Kido, Harry Kondo, Hitoshi Nekoda, Mamoru Nishi and Toyoaki Takata.[11]

Out of that meeting, the young *nisei* group resolved to start a club. Harry Kondo and his committee[12] began drafting a constitution based on the Hompa Young Buddhist's Constitution in Kyoto. He subsequently presented a draft during a meeting in October 1946. With a few amendments and additions, it was adopted in January 1947. Harry Kondo sat as interim President; Toshio Nishijima, Vice-President; and Fumi Maeda, Secretary-Treasurer. Word then began to spread.

Within a year, 25 sat on the executive board and 100 comprised the membership. The first TYBS Board of Directors included Harry Kondo, President; Mamoru Nishi, Vice-President; Nancy Kido, Fumi Maeda, Charles Nekoda, Peggy Harada, Tosh Nishijima and Gloria Sato, Executive Officers.

First Year Projects

The first year was certainly a busy one for the TYBS filled with social and religious activity. The priority for the group as well as for Rev. Tsuji was to form the Dharma School. Charles Nekoda with Rev. Tsuji as advisor took on the task of organizing it. With the added assistance of Sakaye Tsuji (the minister's wife), classes were held at a succession of locations: Belvin Hall, the Legion Hall, the Huron Street church and finally the Bathurst Street temple.

In 1947 20 pupils were taught by Sakaye Tsuji, Ed Tsuji, Susumu Ikuta, Mak Ikuta, Misao Nishikawa, Louise Motomura, Haruko Nakashima, Mariko Kawaguchi and John Amemori. The growing number of students (32 in '48, 36 in '49) forced the school to move to the Legion Hall in 1950. The teachers then were Sakaye Tsuji, Kaz Tatebe, Jean Amemori, Kay Goto, Sakaye Ogaki, Ed Tsuji, Louise Mototsune and Yosh Tanaka.

The most popular activity for the students was camping during the summer. Kazuko Shimizu and Kakuei Tada supervised. The children first went to Greenwood Conservation Park, slept in tents and cooked in the open. Another site was the Uchibori property at Jackson's Point. It was so hot one summer, the owner provided blocks of ice in a galvanized basin. Everyone chipped off pieces to melt in their mouths. Unfortunately, most became very sick.

> They would chip the ice and I was yelling, "Don't do it. You're going to get sick." They wouldn't listen. I said, "You're going to get sick if you keep chewing that cold ice." Sure enough, I don't know how many people got sick. And we had no out-house.[13]

From 1955 to '57, a good friend of Rev. Tsuji's, Rev. T. Gibson lent his campsite (Beaverton Camp) at Lake Simcoe to the Dharma School. Here the students slept in barns and enjoyed horseback riding and swimming.

The TYBS began a monthly bulletin called the **Guiding Light**. The first edition appeared in the spring of 1947 with Toyo Takata as its editor. **The Busshin**, a Japanese language newsletter put together by Rev. Tsuji, started shortly after. The **Guiding Light** began as an English only newsletter for the TYBS membership but soon carried church news in both English and Japanese, once the **Busshin** stopped publishing.

Social activities flourished with the formation of the TYBS. Most *nisei* were young and single with money to burn but very few owned a car so the church with its central location became a focal point for social interaction.

> The Social Committee was swamped with all kinds of suggestions...Midnight Cruise on Lake Ontario, picnics, a visit to border states to see how their young people were coping. The feeling of being able to do all the normal things without the authorities breathing down one's neck was an intoxicating feeling.[14]

Early in 1947, the TYBS held its first social at the Jewish Synagogue on Henry Street near Cecil thanks to the help of Sukegoro Mori, caretaker of the synagogue. Later two quite successful endeavors, the Japanese Canadian community concert and the Valentine Dance, brought the organization into its own.

The first concert was held in the fall of 1947. **The Nisei Variety Parade** featured singers, musicians and actors during a two day extravaganza. The organizers opened the talent review to all members of the Japanese Canadian communities of Toronto, Hamilton and Montreal. Consequently, the concert drew huge crowds.

> Some of the participants in the concert were George Masuda and his ensemble, an *odori* group including Katsuyo Usami, Miyoko Nozuye, Suyeko Ohashi, Sachiko Usami and Teruko Ura, and a couple of other *odori* artists, Matsuye Ohashi and Tomiko Terakita. Vocalists were Hiroye Nakamura, Misao Furuya, Kazuo Hamasaki, Sam Furuya, Hisaye Baba, Hisako Inamoto and Tamio Fujiwara. Sus and Mak Ikuta, sons of Rev. Shinjo Ikuta, also took part in staging the concert. Piano accompaniment was provided by Mitsuko Ikeda, Tsutomu Hakkaku and Tatsuye Mori. Harry Kondo was master of ceremonies.[15]

Concerts followed annually until the early '60s when the Japanese Canadian Cultural Centre presented within better facilities its own community concerts.

The initial Valentine Dance was held on February 15, 1947. Sometime during the proceedings, the men were asked to write their choice for Miss Valentine on a card and deposit it in a ballot box. The winner received a box of chocolates. The dance then evolved into the Miss Valentine Dance where Miss Valentine was formally chosen by judges who were usually community celebrities. Substantial prizes attracted contestants from every *nisei* and *sansei* group in the city. The dance, the social event of the year for the TYBS and the Junior YBS, continued until the early 1970s.

In June 1947, the City of Toronto held an International Folk Festival at the Art Gallery. Communities representing 42 different nationalities took part in the week long festival featuring displays of their culture and traditions. The Central Committee for Nisei Organizations of Toronto asked the TYBS to participate. Terrie Sugiura, Merle Nozuye and Ginger Terakita took charge to organize *ikebana* displays and children's *odori* performances. It was the first time Japanese culture was presented to the Toronto public.

The First Church

Although the TYBS was very active and growing in numbers

during the late '40s, Toronto Jodo Shinshu Buddhists were divided into two distinct and separate groups: the Bukkyo Kai (*issei*) and the TYBS (*nisei*).

The Bukkyo Kai, made up of first generation Japanese Canadian men in their 40s and 50s, saw the TYBS as a young group motivated only by social activity rather than being interested in the sober responsibility of establishing a church. The TYBS on the other hand was serious in building for the future.

The split became even more obvious when the TYBS in 1947 set out to purchase a house to be used as a church and as a residence for Rev. Tsuji and his new bride, Sakaye. The *issei* objected since they felt the congregation could not afford the purchase. The TYBS in the meantime engaged the services of lawyers Reid, Allen and Campbell. On September 8, 1947, the Toronto Young Buddhists' Society was incorporated. They subsequently ignored the Bukkyo Kai's complaints and began the project.

The first task was to raise enough capital for a downpayment. Several supporters offered loans of $100.00 each in return for promissory notes guaranteeing the return of the money within five years. The guarantors were members of the new executive of the TYBS: Tom K. Shimizu, President; Fumi Maeda, Secretary; and Peggy F. Harada, Treasurer.

With such financial backing, a committee comprised of Harry Kondo, Toshio Nishijima and Mamoru Nishi purchased a house at 134 Huron Street (a block east of Spadina Avenue and a block south of College Street) in October 1947. Thus the first Buddhist Church was established in Toronto.

> The upper two floors were allocated to the minister and his wife; the main floor was used as a hall to hold religious services. The kitchen facilities on the second floor were also used by members who frequented the church.[16]

Three others including Susumu Ikuta (University of Toronto student) and his brother Mak lived upstairs on the third floor.

With the opening of the Huron Street church, there became an obvious need for co-operation between the TYBS and the Bukkyo Kai in order to co-ordinate programs and services. A *nisei* contingent including Harry Kondo, Mamoru Nishi, Hideo Yoshida, Tom Shimizu, Terrie Sugiura, Haruko Ito and Fumi

Maeda met with the *issei* members on a continual basis to dispel the difference of opinion between the two and to open the lines of communication. These meetings paved the way for the founding of the TBC Central Board in 1952. The TYBS offered as a concession to maintain an *issei* as President of the church. Otokichi Onishi was the first.[17]

The Huron Street Church became the focal point of Buddhist activity in Toronto. Soon through the efforts of Rev. Tsuji, *nisei* Buddhist groups were formed in Hamilton and Montreal. All three groups worked together to provide moral and financial assistance for Buddhism to flourish in Eastern Canada. None of this could have happened without the mutual co-operation of the Bukkyo Kai and the TYBS to maintain the Toronto church.

TBC archives

Toronto Buddhist Church, circa 1947. 134 Huron Street.

Organizational Growth

Rev. Tsuji felt the church needed to organize the women into a cohesive whole from the beginning. He therefore suggested the formation of the Toronto Buddhist Women's League or Fujinkai. Nineteen women began the club in 1948. It expanded quickly. The first executive consisted of 32 officers representing 75 members.

From the outset, the Fujinkai shunned administrative power within the church. The members were content to play a "background role" at church services, commemorations, social and fund raising events and church organizations such as the Sunday School. They did, however, insist on control of their own treasury built up by donations from members celebrating the arrival of grandchildren or memorializing loved ones. In such manner the Fujinkai as an organization could support whatever church project it chose and be recognized for it.

One valuable association of the church, initiated and developed by the Fujinkai, was the Mutual Financial Organization or Credit Union. Each member of the union contributed a specified amount per month and each month the total was borrowed with interest by one of the members. The interest then went to the Fujinkai treasury. The union was a good way to raise funds for a mortgage or business without having to go through the bureaucratic scrutiny of a bank or other financial institution. The organization evolved into the Toronto Buddhist Church Credit Union which was incorporated under an Ontario Government Charter in July 1956. The Union held the mortgage for the Bathurst Street temple.

In the meantime, the Issei-bu (Bukkyo Kai) members felt the need for a middle group composed of older *nisei* to "bridge the gap" between the *issei* and the young *nise*i. The problems of language and cultural differences had served to create friction within the new church.

In 1949 some older members of the TYBS formed the Sonen Kai, a middle group aged 30 to 40, that acted as liaison between the Issei-bu and the TYBS because of their fluency in both English and Japanese.

The first joint committee meeting consisted of:

Issei-bu: Rev. Tsuji, Zentaro Shin, Iwazo Sugiman, Sukegoro Mori, and Sakuhei Izukawa

> Sonen Kai: Shota Kondo, Hideo Yoshida, Mamoru Nishi, Heishiro Matsuyama, Yoshio Terada, Minoru Ohara and Kazuo Shimizu

The discussion centred on the practical purpose of this middle organization. It was decided the organization must assist in setting church policy if it was to retain the interest of its members who were mature adults.

In June 1950 the Sonen Kai became known as the Sangha and elected Hideo Yoshida President, Shota Kondo Vice-President, and executive members: Mamoru Nishi, Harry Kumano, Kazuo Shimizu, Toshimi Yamamoto, Minoru Ohara, Yoshio Terada, Heishiro Matsuyama and Kojiro Ebisuzaki.

In November 1955 the Sangha initiated the Fall Bazaar, a highlight of the Toronto Buddhist Church calendar every year. It features baked goods, white elephant items and Japanese meals all at reasonable prices. Annually, the bazaar attracts so many that it has become an institution in the Japanese Canadian community.

The Sangha also formed a Sangha Women's Division to aid the Fujinkai in their work. The group would eventually separate and become the Dana.

Also in 1950 the Continental Family Co-operative was formed with the assistance of the church in order to facilitate the buying of Japanese groceries. Issei-bu leaders like Eikichi Kagetsu, Shinkuro Kozai, Zentaro Shin and Sukegoro Mori organized the operation. Each new member was required to lend the Co-op a sum of no less than $20 for a period of 20 years without interest. In such manner the store front at 618 Dundas St. West opened and offered staples of Japanese cuisine: *shoyu*, rice, *ajinomoto*, canned goods and *nori*. The profits were generally donated to the church treasury.

> I remember one time that Mr. Kawasaki was more or less the manager of this co-op. He was from the start. They purchased one ton of rice but they had no warehouse so they piled them into the hallway at Huron Street. The building and that darn floor were tilted so we had a hard time trying to close the doors.[18]

The Co-op eventually was privatized and became the present Japanese food store Furuya, located in Toronto's burgeoning Chinatown at Dundas and Huron Streets.

The final organization to be formed during those critical first years was the Asoka Society, an English speaking group of *nisei* and non-Japanese interested in Buddhist studies. They held philosophical discussions and delved into the spiritual aspects of the religion. They translated Japanese *sutras*, sponsored lectures on Buddhism and wrote articles on several topics of interest. Their first publication was the **Asoka Review**.

> We started the Asoka Society because there were some non-Japanese who became very interested in Buddhism and we felt that they wanted a more scholarly pursuit. They were more analytical, they weren't coming to the Buddhist Temple because of certain cultural and racial ties. They wanted to study the essence of the Buddha *Dharma*. So we had some very important discussions along those lines. In the meantime we had very dedicated Buddhists come in, people like Richard Robinson... Howard White...There were quite a few of those as well as some Japanese Canadian university students.
>
> I think it was Thursday night we used to meet, about six or seven of us. Our last project was translating the Tan Nisho into English...it must have taken about two years to do that because we would study each sentence and each word, how to translate it and so on, but we completed it and published this little tract.[19]

The Asoka Society remained active until Rev. Tsuji left for the United States in 1958. Soon thereafter the individuals went their own way. Dr. Richard Robinson, for example, left for the University of Wisconsin, eventually establishing the Buddhist Institute there. He died in an accident in 1971.

Toward a Permanent Home

In 1947 the senior Rev. Shinjo Ikuta came from the west to visit the Huron Street Church. He urged the congregation to find a way to retain Rev. Tsuji as a full time minister. The membership was growing steadily and the workload became extremely heavy for one part-time minister. By August of the following year, the church officials offered Rev. Tsuji a full time position at $120 a month. The salary was substantially lower than his wage at the chemical plant, but Rev. Tsuji accepted willingly.

Life for the young Tsuji family was particularly hard at the Huron Street Church. The building functioned as a multi-purpose community centre. The Tsujis lived on the second floor. Weekly services and meetings were held on the main floor. Mrs. Tsuji acted as hostess to an endless variety of visitors that seemingly trooped through the house on a continuous basis. Privacy was at a premium.

> [Mrs. Tsuji] had to do all the cleaning up after the meetings and during the meetings she had to make tea and so forth. She really worked hard. After a certain time there...she moved out and went to her mother's place. But Rev. Tsuji thought that being the minister, since it was a residence as well as a church, he stayed there for about six months.[20]

The Tsujis also contended with weddings and one funeral.

> The wedding ceremony was okay there. But we had a funeral once. They brought in a casket in the day-time and I guess that more or less aroused the neighbourhood.[21]

The Japanese Language School began on Sept. 11, 1949 at the Huron Street Church. Many believed such a move was taken at considerable risk since 60 such schools were closed down at the outbreak of the war. The *issei*, however, feared for their children losing their heritage and the ability to communicate with them. Therefore the Church approved in 1948 the formation of an Education Department that looked into the feasibility of a Japanese Language School. The leaders, Shinkuro Kozai (former principal of the Nanaimo Language School), Sasuke Nakagawa (supervised the Skeena school) and Sadamu Sato (organizer of a school at Comox, Vancouver Island), worked hard to open the school in 1949.[22]

> As the first Japanese language school to reopen in Canada following World War II, indeed the first ever east of Alberta, the event was hardly memorable or inspiring.
>
> Since they could be accommodated in one session, the 60 students, mainly children of the congregation, were taught in three shifts, two evenings a week, and

> on Saturday mornings. Utility tables instead of classroom desks, poor lighting, little room for coats and boots in the winter and a single washroom shared with the minister's family, all contributed to the makeshift atmosphere.[23]

Perhaps fortunately, the neighbours complained about the noise the students made outside the church, prompting city officials to intercede. They told the administrators that since the house was on a residential street it could not be used for gatherings on an on-going basis.

The Buddhist members faced the fact that the building would no longer serve their needs. Japanese language lessons and services had be held somewhere else. The school moved to the Canadian Legion Hall as an interim measure. A building committee headed by Zentaro Shin was formed in October 1950 and after much consideration placed an offer of $24,000 for a 17 room house at 490 Jarvis St. The plan was to use the house's facilities temporarily until a back addition could be built for the *hondo*. With 490 members (170 Bukkyo Kai, 120 Fujinkai, 60 Sangha and 140 TYBS members), the downpayment of $12,000 was easily raised. The final amount donated was $23,000.[24] Interestingly enough, the Huron Street house was not put on the selling block to generate funds. Probably the Sonen Kai thought it wise to leave the property for a future building fund or to allow the house to be used by a future young people's group within the church.

However, the building committee decided, after careful study, the cost of the addition was prohibitive ($50,000) and recommended selling the property. They subsequently sold 490 Jarvis Street for $27,000.

Shortly thereafter (Feb. 1951), a church on Shaw Street near College and Shaw came on the market. Motohito Yanagisawa, a real estate agent, checked into the property on behalf of the church. A deal was subsequently made with the resident minister.

The members decided to hold the Hanamatsuri Service in the new church to celebrate. Rev. Kono visiting from Chicago agreed to give the sermon. When everyone arrived, however, members of the African Canadian congregation barred the entrance. It seemed the minister had negotiated the sale without the approval of his entire congregation. The church, in the end, did not belong to the Buddhists.

The immediate problem was to find another location for the Hanamatsuri Service. Fortunately the Legion Hall was available and everyone moved there.

The Toronto Buddhist Church was incorporated in July 1952 under the Ontario Companies Act. With a new constitution and by-laws in place, the Central Executive Board (Riji-kai) was formed in March of the following year at the AGM with representatives from the TYBS, Sangha, Fujinkai and the Bukkyo Kai. One of the first decisions was to instruct the building committee to build a new church rather than to find an old one especially in light of the Shaw Street church incident (the building committee had forfeited the downpayment).

The *issei* membership found a large lot on Queen Street, ideal for them since it was affordable and most lived in the area. The *nisei*, however, did not like it since the location was considered run down. They found a property on Bathurst Street north of Bloor. The lot was $23,000; to build the church was an additional $40,000. The *nisei* lobbied for the purchase and won. The church established a fund raising committee and hired an architect.

Fund Raising

Again, differences of opinion split the *issei* and *nisei* into opposing camps. The Issei-bu wanted to follow the Japanese custom to raise the money: the directors of the Central Board would call individuals to ask for donations. The Sangha, on the other hand, consulted a professional fund raiser who advised choosing fund raisers from the membership and not from the directors. They took that advice. The old system was felt to be self-serving, adding to the stature of the directors rather than building a sense of togetherness. Everyone worked toward a common goal.

Another point of contention was how the donations were to be recognized. The *issei* felt that the head of each family should decide how much his family would donate totally. All the money from every family member then would be accredited to one name. The *nisei* wanted every adult, regardless of marital status, to be recognized separately for their donations.

> We had to get a certain amount from the general membership otherwise we could never realize $75,000 ($45,000 to build plus another $30,000 for furnishings). Just because [I was] chairman of the building committee, they probably thought that [I] should donate $5000 and if you belong to the general membership you can donate only about $50 or $100. We thought that we had to change this idea...So we figured, with about 300 total membership at about $150 a head, that would be about $45,000 for three years. That's a dollar a week...so everybody would put in a dollar's worth of coins a week.
>
> We wanted to find out how they felt about this $150 pledge towards the building because they hardly come to church meetings and services yet we know that they are Buddhists. So we went to the general membership first...They all pledged $150.[25]

With $45,000 pledged by the membership over a three year period, the debate between the two factions subsided and the building went as planned.

918 Bathurst St.

The Toronto Buddhist Church, the first Japanese Canadian-built centre in Toronto, was designed by George Yamazaki and Roy Matsui and built by the N & S (Nakamura-Sakaguchi) Construction Co. Employing triangles throughout the structure, the church took on the appearance of a postwar suburban Christian church. Both architects, however, felt the design "[was] in keeping with the spirit of Buddhism, depicting the harmony of man with nature."

The building was 40 by 100 feet; its *hondo* with a seating capacity of 450 held the *naijin* and sanctuary for the ashes of the deceased. The floor plan contained a library for Buddhist literature, social centre, kitchen, rooms for Sunday school, administrative offices, and "minister-ready" rooms.

> The dedication service [March 1955] included ritual offerings of incense by representatives of the Japanese Canadian Citizens Association, the Japanese [Language] School, the Buddhist Churches of Canada, and the East

Coast Young Buddhist League, a bilateral organization that had held annual conferences since 1946. Individuals in attendance included Rev. Gyodo Kono of the Midwest Buddhist Church of Chicago, who gave a sermon, and the Vice-Consul of the Toronto Japanese Consulate which had just opened in May 1954. Church groups participating included the Club Ami, a teenage club, the Toronto Young Buddhist Society, a group of young unmarried *nisei* numbering 125 - 150, the Sangha, a group for older married *nisei*, consisting of about 65 - 70 couples, the Fujinkai, and the Asoka Society, a philosophical group of largely white students of Buddhism.[26]

TBC archives

Toronto Buddhist Church, circa 1955. 918 Bathurst St.

Rev. Gibson and members of the Church of Ascension donated funds to put in a front lawn.

A unique feature of the temple is the original, handcrafted *Onaijin*. The altar was designed by architect and interior designer Nobuo Kubota with Rev. Tsuji as consultant.

> The recessed concave steps from the incense burner up to the *naijin* floor is an invitation of continuing sensual progression toward the main or principal object of reverence Gohonzon...a standing figure of Amida Buddha later replaced by the scroll with six

> character calligraphy *Namu Amida Butsu*, a treasured gift presented to the Toronto Buddhist Church, written by the spiritual head Gomonshu...
>
> Side walls of the *naijin* are also concaved to the back wall giving a feeling of progression into the inner *naijin*. Plastered white walls are warmly covered with drapes held by swinging metal arms which curtain and close the *naijin* area when the *hondo* is used for non-religious activities...
>
> Situated on each side of the Gohonzon (hung on a separate structure about three feet in front of the back wall) are scrolls of Saint Shinran and Saint Rennyo... hung in an enclosure, side altar, each with the three element arrangement of flower vase, incense burner and candle stand.[27]

Church Leadership

Rev. Tsuji was key to the establishment and growth of the Toronto Buddhist Church and Buddhism in Eastern Canada but he could not do it on his own. Kakuei Tada, *nisei* — son of Rev. Kakusai Tada, arrived in 1951. He had expressed a desire to become a Shin Buddhist minister and contacted Sukegoro Mori for church sponsorship. After receiving $500, he came as a student at the University of Toronto. He was first taken in by UnosukeTakenaka. Later he moved to the third floor of the Huron Street church in order to earn an honorarium for assisting Rev. Tsuji. In 1956 he became a part-time minister for the Montreal Church. After three years, he was ordained in Chicago and served as the second minister under Rev. Kono of the Chicago Midwest Buddhist Church. In the San Fernando Valley, he initiated a building program for the San Fernando Valley Hompa Hongwanji. Finally he went to the Seattle Church as a full time minister.

Elders such as Eikichi Kagetsu (former President of the Hompa Bukkyo Kai in Vancouver) and Sukegoro Mori (former President of the Fairview Bukkyo Kai) served as advisors in the early days of the Toronto church.

Through the co-operation of the BCA Bishop Shigefuji and the Hongwanji, four members were ordained as *hokkyoshi* or lay ministers: Kanjiro Yoshida, Sasuke Nakagawa, Kamezo Kawaguchi and Matsujiro Ohashi. They helped Rev. Tsuji administer to the needs of the three churches in Eastern Canada.

Perhaps the most interesting of the lay leaders was Richard Robinson. Educated at the University of Alberta, he came to Toronto to further his studies in economics in the late 1940s. He later moved to London, England, to complete his Ph.D. He brought to the Toronto temple a solid grounding in Buddhism and invaluable connections.

> At that time [early '50s] we all went to the Zen Institute on Riverside Drive in New York City. Richard, who was instructed in a number of things at the Zen Institute, acted as our guide.
>
> He learned Chinese and Japanese and went to the University of London to study Chinese with Arthur Whalen.[28]

He also possessed a keen insight into the true nature of Buddhism within an institutional context (see Chapter 23).

Other leaders of the church were recognized for their pre-war reputations in British Columbia. Hayato Kono served as President in 1955 with Shinkuro Kozai as Vice-President. Moreover, Zentaro Shin (as mentioned before) held the Chairmanship of the Building Committee.

All members whether *issei* or *nisei* dedicated much time and effort to getting the church off the ground. At times they met twice a week and on weekends, a very difficult regimen for families trying to establish themselves in a new environment.

Rev. Tsuji must have known that the sincere and deep devotion of the membership would carry the temple through as he announced his impending departure from Toronto for the United States at the January 1958 Annual General Meeting. In July 1958 Bishop Shigefuji formally appointed Rev. Tsuji Director of Buddhist Education in San Francisco, California. Ten years later in May 1968, Rev. Tsuji became Bishop Kenryu Tsuji, the first *nisei* Socho of the Buddhist Churches of America.

> At the present time, his [Rev. Tsuji's] departure date is still uncertain as he is awaiting approval of his visa. Not only will Rev. Tsuji's departure be a great loss to Buddhists, but to all the Japanese in Toronto. Through his constant personal appearances as guest

speaker and lecturer at innumerable groups, churches and events throughout Metropolitan Toronto, Hamilton and Montreal, he has been a good will ambassador gaining many friends and spreading good will and understanding for the Buddhists and Japanese in general.[29.]

A Period of Transition

Rev. Kenryu Tsuji - Rev. Newton Ishiura

Chapter 20

Bukkyo Tozen

The Toronto Buddhist Church:
A Period of Transition

Reverend Kenryu Tsuji - Reverend Newton Ishiura

The Toronto Buddhist Church on strong recommendation from the late Bishop Shigefuji of the Buddhist Churches of America has appointed the Rev. Newton Ishiura of Honolulu, Hawaii, to succeed Rev. T. Tsuji as the residing minister of the Toronto Buddhist Church. The Rev. Ishiura will be coming to Toronto as soon as his visa to enter Canada meets with final approval from the Dept. of Immigration in Ottawa.

The Rev. Newton Ishiura was born in KILAUEA, KAUAI, HAWAII, on October 15, 1918. He received his elementary, grammar and high school education in Hawaii and his Japanese Education at the KYUSHU GAKUIN in Kumamoto, Japan. He entered the RYUKOKU University in 1938 and received full ordination in 1941. After his ordination, he attended YALE Graduate School, the Union THEOLOGICAL SEMINARY in New York and was a lecturer at YALE UNIVERSITY. He has been attached to the LOS ANGELES HONGWANJI BETSUIN, BAKERSFIELD BUDDHIST CHURCH, FRESNO BUDDHIST CHURCH, and at present the HONPA HONGWANJI HAWAII BETSUIN where he is the Director of Buddhist Education (English).

Latest report according to the **Continental Times** (Sept. 19) says that the Rev. Ishiura has already left Hawaii and is in Berkeley where he was a guest

> speaker at the Berkeley Buddhist Church last Sunday.
>
> Rev. Ishiura is married and they have three small children.
>
> With all his qualifications and experience, we are sure the Toronto Buddhist Church made a very wise move in appointing the Rev. Ishiura as the successor to the Rev. Tsuji.[1]

With the announcement of Rev. Tsuji's successor, the church seemed to step back a moment to take stock. Despite its bright new home on Bathurst Street, the church in the late 1950s was a hodge-podge of organizations, generally not working at cross purposes but acting in a haphazard manner so as to make progress difficult.

Administering the church's affairs was very complicated and thus too much for one minister to handle by himself. Therefore, the church was divided into departments:

> Up until the time the Bathurst Street church was built, the TYBS was running the religious services. There was no separate board for the Sunday School. Rev. Tsuji used to look after it but it was getting to be too much for him so they put it in the religious department and we looked after all the Sunday School programs.[2]

Members who shared a language or an interest quickly gathered themselves into well-defined groups. The Goho Kai (formerly the Bukkyo Kai) and the Fujinkai were solidly entrenched in their status at the church but were not growing significantly in numbers. The Goho Kai in particular, wholly made up of *issei* men, had lost a great deal of influence in administering the church especially with the building of the Bathurst Street temple. Not to be taken for granted, however, they still represented the Japanese speaking segment of the congregation. The Fujinkai too continued their "background role" by participating in various events like the inaugural ceremony of the new church (sod turning), the Bon Odori at Christie Park (1961) and the North American and Eastern Buddhist Women's Leagues.

Membership in church organizations was in theory determined by age. In practice it depended on association, cultural preferences and friendship. In other words, the senior clubs were not growing in number because eligible members simply refused to join. Instead, new groups were formed.

To serve the needs of the teenagers, a group calling themselves Club Ami[3] was formed in the early '50s (circa 1954). The club endeavoured to bring Japanese Canadians together strictly on a social basis (dances, picnics, bowling and informal discussions).

> It was a social group, supervised or promoted by young people (TYBS), like Ed Tsuji, Charlie Shimizu, and Kaz Tatebe. They came to all our meetings, supported us, helped us, and chaperoned everything.
>
> The other club that was comparable to Club Ami was a dance club, but it was respectable because we were with a church. Religion, however, was the last thing in our minds. We were just trying to get these people together. I remember taking Don Tsuji (second President of the group) to Montreal to a conference but other than that it was mostly to have a good time. No central point.
>
> It was really great for us to be able to get together and to share our heritage, our common background. Because we all led very active lives in school, it gave us an opportunity to talk to other people with similar backgrounds, to have some sense of history and pride in our heritage.
>
> We began to break up when we had to go to the United Church to hear sermons by Reverend Yoshida. We were non-denominational in a sense even though the Buddhist Church sponsored us. We encouraged everybody to join but pretty soon we were flooded by United Church members. The main purpose was achieved I guess.[4]

Once the activities petered out in about 1958, the members did not move up to the TYBS. Instead, they became the Junior Young Buddhist Association (Jr. YBA). The first executive was elected in January 1959. At the same time the Sangha women created the Dana. The church officially recognized both organizations on January 27, 1959.

With the formation of the Sangha, many members left the TYBS thus leaving the young adults group with a small number. It managed to survive until 1962 when the TYBS was officially disbanded (marking also the demise of the Eastern Canada Young Buddhist League).

> For the past few years the Bussei has suffered from steadily declining membership and interest. It has become obvious that this trend cannot continue beyond this year. The Bussei must either make some radical changes to strengthen themselves or the club must cease existence.
>
> In order to help achieve the continuation of the Bussei we recommend that the basis of club membership and financial support be altered. We feel that everyone should belong directly to the Church and their financial support for the church should also be direct. The clubs would be without financial responsibilities on either the paying or receiving end. All church members would be assigned membership in one of the groups. Those between the ages of 18 and 30 who are unmarried would be given to the Bussei.
>
> In addition we feel that certain activities such as the picnic and *Dharma* classes should be the responsibility of the church rather than the Bussei alone.
>
> We feel if these reforms are carried out it will be possible to continue the Bussei, but if not it may be necessary to wind up the society at the next annual meeting.[5]

Terence Beresford's membership concerns went unheeded and the affairs of the TYBS indeed wound up by the next annual general meeting. The trend to form groups based on friendship continued into the early 1970s when the Taruna was formed to resist joining the Jr. YBA.

> So now we should be in the Sangha.
>
> Our older sisters are there.
>
> You can't argue with them. I've argued with my sister and I never get anywhere so why should I want to join Dana.
>
> We said that we just have to move up or if you don't want to join the Fujinkai, we'll form our own group.
>
> I said at a general meeting, don't try to force a younger group to come into Sangha or you're going to have problems. Try to work with the Goho-kai, try

> to, just like Fujinkai, come in together with the Dana. That is the way we should do it because after all, 30 years, close to 40 years of history, you just can't have young people come in...[6]

At the Crossroads 1958 - 1960

> I recollect all that has happened in the past ten years. There were glorious achievements and heartbreaking failures, but the experience we have gained is vitally important. Let us make use of and take advantage of that experience.[7]

The sentiment expressed by the President of the TYBS in the above passage indicates that the Toronto Buddhist Church and its members faced a crossroads in 1958. A survey of the **Guiding Light**, printed from 1958 to 1960, revealed the self-evaluation that took place in the church in an effort to discard the anachronistic and to prepare the foundation for the future.

> This is a candid appeal to all young Buddhists to follow the lead of Mr. and Mrs. Charlie Shimizu who kindly donated recently, in honour of their daughter, a sum of $25.00 toward the Young Buddhist Building Fund.
>
> The Young Buddhist Building Fund is not to be confused with the fund previously set up to finance the building of the temple we now occupy. The Young Buddhist Building Fund owes its beginning to the proceeds from the sale of property at 134 Huron St.; also to the resolution put forward by Sangha and carried unanimously by the assembled members at the 1957 General Meeting of the Toronto Buddhist Church, to appropriate it for a future specific building project.
>
> March 10, 1958

> The Asoka Society held its last meeting on Thursday, June 12. During the past few months the Society has been meeting every two weeks in order to make a complete study of ACVAGHOSHA'S DISCOURSE on the AWAKENING OF FAITH.
>
> Although the attendance was generally small, there was certainly no lack of enthusiasm shown by the

members who took part. The discourse was studied very thoroughly and at times it was discussed and debated sentence for sentence in order that nothing of importance would be overlooked.

In the evening of the last meeting the members were very fortunate in being able to listen to a recorded lecture given by Dr. T.D. Suzuki, the world authority on Zen Buddhism...[8]

...Mrs. Jean Reoch spent a great deal of time and effort in preparing and typing the forty-three page manual which formed the basis of the Studies.

July 3, 1958

It was in January of 1958 that the Buddhist community of Toronto learned that it would have to purchase a permanent residence for a new minister, as Rev. Tsuji had been assigned a new post in San Francisco. (No parsonage had been acquired previously as Rev. Tsuji had purchased his home out of his earnings.)

The Church groups met and decided to purchase a parsonage. The home had to meet the following conditions:

1. It must be in a central location, not too far from the Church and reasonably close to the majority of the congregation. A home in the suburbs was considered too inconvenient due to transportation and traffic problems.
2. The total price should not exceed (approximately) $20,000.
3. It must not be located in a district that would be considered unhealthy, especially for the sake of the Minister's children.
4. An old home was considered undesirable as it would be constantly needing repairs; its value would depreciate to zero in short time; and it would be uncomfortable.
5. It must be a nice home, a livable home, where our new minister and his family will be able to live in comparative comfort.

A Housing Committee was set up consisting of the following: TYBS - Mr. Charlie Shimizu; Sangha - Mr. Harry Yonekura;

Goho Kai - Mr. Yonekichi Kondo; Fujinkai - Mrs. Moto Taguchi.

The Housing Committee undertook an extensive search for the suitable home, and inspected some thirty houses. They found out that invariably, if the home was suitable, (that is not too old, well constructed, centrally located, and "livable"), then THE PRICE WAS TOO HIGH. When the price was right, the defects in the house or its location were too much.

Therefore, the Housing Committee concluded that if a suitable lot could be found, it would have N&S Contracting Co. build a brand new modern home on the lot, provided the total price did not exceed $20,000. Mr. Nakamura and Mr. Sakaguchi were able to meet these conditions. (This same firm built the modern Toronto Buddhist Church.)

The lot is located on Fenwick Ave., near Logan Ave. just south of Danforth Ave. It is twenty feet by one hundred and twenty feet. A house and a frame garage will be built on this lot.

The home will be a two storey brick building with basement, twenty feet by thirty feet, containing a living room, dining room, kitchen, recreation room in the basement and three bedrooms. In spite of the limitations and restrictions placed upon the house by the narrowness of the frontage, the house will be modern in design, relatively spacious inside, and provided with as much convenient ideas and devices as the budget will allow. The facade will show brick, timber and coloured glass.

Architect Mr. Sada Sato advised N&S Contracting Co. in the planning and provided the blueprints.

November 23, 1958

The Young Ladies Organization, which was formed recently, has chosen DANA for their name. As you know, Dana, a Sanskrit word, is the first of the six Paramitas which teaches the perfection of man and are among the noblest aspirations of man. Briefly, Dana means giving in all forms - that is, charity - giving in the form of material alms and also in the mental and spiritual giving.

> The Dana Group will hold its first General Meeting at the Toronto Buddhist Church on Friday, the 30th of October...All ladies are requested to attend. As an added attraction, Mrs. Y. Noda will give a cooking demonstration.
>
> October 26, 1959

> Continental Co-op (the church's Japanese food store) has purchased a store building on Dundas Street West, just east of Spadina Avenue.
>
> November 23, 1959

Perhaps the most revealing of articles came from the TYBS in late 1959 as a rumination on the possible direction the Buddhist Church was to take in the 1960s. The emotional tone of the piece is remarkable considering most Japanese Canadians chose not to mention, let alone publicize, their feelings about the wartime experience until the mid 1980s.

> There were many problems facing the Toronto Busseis of 1946, and a few general problems are summarized:
>
> 1. One hundred percent of its congregation had suffered a crushing economic blow when the Canadian Government, even while promising to keep their assets in trust, broke its pledge and sold everything belonging to the Japanese Canadians at fire-sale prices.
> 2. The economic position of the Buddhist Congregation was rough to say the least. In 1946, all *isseis* and *niseis* worked at whatever job they could find: i.e., eighty dollars a month at housekeeping, twenty-five dollars a week in garment factories, twenty a week dish-washing. The low earnings combined with a pressing need for every family to re-establish a home (starting from scratch) confronted the Buddhists of that by-gone era with formidable difficulties. Rev. T. Tsuji worked, among other places, in a spaghetti house on Danforth Avenue.
> 3. The entire congregation had suffered a physical, emotional and spiritual shock during the war years when they were sent to concentration camps. There was a fantastic hatred directed against them. This campaign of hate had come from all levels, the

Federal Government, educators, newspapers, employers, the tramp on the streets, school children, religious leaders, etc. (Rabbi Feinberg, the well known Jewish leader, will always be remembered by the *niseis* because he vehemently criticized the treatment accorded the Canadians of Japanese ancestry.)

4. *Niseis* themselves had become hyper-sensitive of their physical features and cultural background, and consequently, many *niseis* were almost pathologically opposed to anything remotely connected with Japan, the nation which had brought shame and misfortune on them.

5. There was a painful shortage of qualified religious leaders among the Busseis. There was only one *nisei* priest in all of Canada. As for good books, equipment, materials and facilities - there were none.[9]

The *nisei* felt by 1960 to have overcome most if not all of these aforementioned problems. Proof for them lay in the accomplishments of the Toronto Buddhist Church and the TYBS specifically.

1. The Busseis set up a program of religious education and practice which is more suited to native born Canadians.

2. They, along with other church groups, built the fine church on Bathurst Street.

3. They have probably been the most active *nisei* organization in Toronto, what with their many activities such as holding Sunday Services, Sunday Schools for the children, *Dharma* classes, speaking to other religious groups, entertaining old folks, printing pamphlets, books and news bulletins, charitable donations, sports activities, social activities, concerts, *kabuki*, etc.[10]

Certainly the *nisei* worked hard to overcome the financial setbacks experienced during the war but they dealt with the psychological damage inflicted by the government only partially through religion. Again, the *nisei* in 1960 saw the church's problems in specific, narrow terms:

The Sunday service could no longer generate the funds necessary through the use of the offertory plate to sustain the church because the *issei* congregation was dwindling. The church finances also depended on assessment of church organizations. Again with the decline of the *issei* congregation, a new system was needed to generate income from every member.

The younger *nisei* age group (between twenty and thirty years old) did not seem interested in Buddhism thus endangering the future of the church with the lack of new leadership.

There was a lack of communication among the various church organizations. The members did not participate in another group's activities, and they did not wish to join groups according to the age requirements.

The Japanese Canadian congregation was wholly Japanese. In order to prevent competing Buddhist organizations in Toronto, the Toronto Buddhist Church had to evolve into a "liberal Buddhist movement" including all people in the congregation.[11]

Fortunately, the Toronto Buddhist Church found in Rev. Newton Ishiura and his wife Mary the vision, boundless energy and progressive attitude necessary to overcome the residual wartime scars and the generational and cultural struggles to lead the congregation into an era of great activity and significant work.

Rev. Newton Ishiura

1958 - 1977

Chapter 21

The Toronto Buddhist Church:
Reverend Newton Ishiura 1958 - 1977

Rev. Ishiura and his wife Mary walked into a frenzy of activity from the start. The Fujinkai celebrated its tenth anniversary in October 1958 with the staging of a *kabuki* play. The following month, the (Gomonshu) Lord Abbot Kosho and Lady Yoshiko Ohtani paid the Toronto Buddhist Church a visit while on the way to South America to mark the 50th Anniversary of Japanese immigration to Brazil. During his stay, Rev. Ishiura performed a confirmation service at the TBC. The following year two new groups, plus a choir, were formed: the Jr. YBA and the Dana. In September 1959, the TBC celebrated its Tenth Anniversary with Bishop Shinso Hanayama as guest speaker. That same year the Eitaikyo (Perpetual Memorial Service and Fund) was created.[1] Rev. Ishiura also arrived in time to oversee preparations for the 700th Memorial Year (1961) observances for the passing of Shinran Shonin.

The 1960 Board of Directors indicates the growth of the church and its structure:

President	Sadamu Sato
Vice-President	Mamoru Nishi
Vice-President	Charlie Shimizu
Secretary	Hatsujiro Ejima (Japanese)
	Teruji Goto (English)
English Recording Secretary	Shizu Ebata
Treasurer	Izo Ebata
Chairman	Iwazo Sugiman
Religious Committee	Sakuhei Izukawa (Japanese)

	Yosoya Hayashi (Assistant)
	Iyo Nishikawa (Assistant)
	Toshio Hori (English)
Juvenile Education	Kaz Tatebe
Finance Chairman	Ty Ebata
Special Project	Tom Shimizu
	Fumiyo Mizuno (Assistant)
Library	Jack Shimizu
Membership	Harry Yonekura
Welfare[2]	Zentaro Shin
	Yonekichi Kondo (Assistant)
	Waki Hashizume (Assistant)
	Eda Shin (Assistant)
Social	Kunio Suyama
	Yae Ebisuzaki (Assistant)
	Moto Taguchi (Assistant)
Publicity	Otokichi Onishi
Public Relations	George Tahara

The Board of Directors held a delicate balance of *issei* and *nisei*; all decisions were made following consultations with both sides even though discussions sometimes turned heated. The church still supported the language school with church members as teachers and administrators though it was becoming more and more autonomous since its departure from the Huron Street building. All financial links were severed in 1952. Private interests too bought out the TBC's interest in the Continental Family Co-op during the early 1960s. Finally, the Japanese Canadian Cultural Centre provided space for community socials beginning in 1965.

Still the church incorporated a Religious Committee, an Education Department (for the Dharma School[3]), Library Committee and Special Projects.

The individual organizations as well contributed their time to worthwhile activities.

Fujinkai

The women's organization contributed much to the church during Rev. Ishiura's tenure. Perhaps the most enduring was the Obon Odori. At first, the Obon dance was included in the program for the TYBS picnics at Greenwood Conservation

Park in the early 1950s. In 1961 Chiyo Seko instructed the Fujinkai women in various Japanese folk dances and the church held the summer celebrations at Christie Pits, a city park just west of 918 Bathurst St. She continued to do so until 1965. Susie Yoshikawa was also one of the first teachers.

The popularity of the event grew so quickly that the Obon Odori moved first to Dufferin Park and then to Toronto City Hall. By then the community gathering featured several dancers (*issei, nisei* and *sansei*) from the Toronto Buddhist Church, Sakura Kai and Ayame Kai (formerly Haruyagi Kai) of the Japanese Canadian Cultural Centre, Hamilton Buddhist Church and Hamilton's Suzuran Kai. Kunio Suyama, one-time president of the TYBS, was the congenial and distinctive emcee.

Courtesy of Hedy Yonekura

Obon Odori, Christie Pits, Toronto, 1960.

Many demands were made of the dance group thereafter. Requests to perform came in from such diverse places as the New York Obon, which coincided with the 1964 World's Fair, to the Quincy Ethnic Festival in Belleville, Ontario. Most trips, especially to the smaller venues, were financed by the dancers and their families.

In 1967 Archie Nishihama wrote the words and music to **Canada Ondo**, a catchy tribute to his adopted country. Irene Tsujimoto from the Sakura Kai choreographed a dance for the Obon Odori group. It became their honour to perform the piece with dancers from Montreal and Hamilton at Montreal's Expo '67.

Similarly, Mrs. Chiyoko Hirano (Tatsumi-Ryu, Richmond, B.C.) choreographed **Wonderful Canada** (written by Tsuchiya Tada) in 1977 with the maple leaf as a dance motif. The Toronto Buddhist Church Obon dancers became an integral part of the local and national versions of the Nikka Festival Dancers, a dance troupe composed of Japanese Canadian *sansei* from across the country. The troupe gave concerts nationwide during the Japanese Canadian Centennial year 1977.

The Fujinkai also participated in the 1965 World Buddhist Women's Federation Convention in New York City. In 1972 with the support of its 229 members, they donated $5000 to the new residence for Rev. Ishiura and family in Don Mills, a Toronto suburb. Finally, the Fujinkai donated a Yamaha piano to the Toronto Buddhist Church in memory of their beloved advisor Fumiyo Mizuno who had died in February 1974.

The Dana

As mentioned before, the Dana began as a seven woman auxiliary group to the Sangha. Primarily, they were to help the Fujinkai in their activities without having to join the older women's group. In April 1959 six women met at Mary Ishiura's home on Palmerston Avenue in Toronto's west end to talk about a new women's organization. That summer, 39 members met and elected Terrie Komori (nee Sugiura) as the first President.

> Purpose of forming Ladies' Auxiliary - "We, lay women of the Toronto Buddhist Church, realizing our unique importance in the Church and community, do hereby organize ourselves in order to serve the church better as well as enhance our religious convictions and

promote mutual fellowship."[4]

The membership fee was set at a mere 25 cents. During October's clothing drive for the Nagoya Relief Fund, the group adopted the name Dana (meaning "to give to others") and separated from the Sangha.

The Founding Members included:

Nancy Ariza, Hisa Baba, Chiyo Ebata, Shizue Ebata, Yaeko Ebisuzaki, Asaye Ejima, Mary Hamazaki, Mary Ishiura, Hannah Katsura, Toshiko Katsura, Matsuyo Kawano, Mary Kawasaki, Waki Kiyonaga, Terrie Komori, Kazue Koyanagi, Miyo Nakamura, Yukiye Nakamura, Ann Nekoda, Fumi Ono, Kazuko Shimizu, Suzie Shimizu, Kiyoe Sugiman, Dorothy Tahara, Mary Tanabe, Sally Tanaka, Aki Tateishi, Yasuko Tsuchiya, Jane Tsuruoka, Kay Tsuruoka, Alice Uyeda, Kyoko Yamamoto, Fumi Yasuda, Hedy Yonekura, Masa Yoshida.

The activities of the new organization were varied as the need arose. In 1960 the Dana and the Fujinkai organized the first memorial service for Takeko Kujo, founder of Asoka Hospital in Japan.[5] The Dana observed her passing until the early '80s when they began holding memorial services for Eshinni-sama, consort of Shinran Shonin.

That same year, they staged the first fashion show, a popular community event performed annually until the mid 1970s. The Dana also began their annual two-day rummage sale that continued until the mid '80s. In 1962, the Dana further organized a Fooderama with the Fujinkai.

Two years later, they started to raise money for a scholarship fund. Miyo Nakamura was the first Chair of the committee. In order to give the fund a kick-start, the executive invited the visiting Abbot and Lady Ohtani to be honourary patrons of the fund. They graciously accepted and signed the table linen to start the campaign. Members with donations followed and signed the cloth. Dana volunteers then painstakingly embroidered the signatures as a tribute to their generosity. Kaz Hamasaki, noted *nisei Nanga* painter, gave the scholarship fund a boost in 1965 by donating the proceeds from his art show. That same year, the TBC Dana Scholarship was announced at the Hanamatsuri Tea, a social gathering that was started in 1964 for new members. Over 150 guests, including the Public School teachers of the *Dharma* students, attended.

By 1966 the fund had reached $4000 and the TBC Board suggested the first scholarships be awarded the following year during Canada's Centennial. It was also during that year that the Dana first sent members to join the community in *odori* practices in preparation for the Centennial celebrations.

The first three honourees of the TBC Dana Scholarship were Ross Yoshida, Elizabeth Ishida and John Maemura. The scholarship continues to be awarded annually on Scholarship Sunday, the third Sunday of September, followed by a celebratory luncheon served by the younger Dana members.

The Dana in 1968 adopted a Tibetan orphan, Karma Dorji, who was the first of three. They maintained a good level of life for these children until the mid 1980s.

In 1970 the Dana split into three groups: the Maya (over 45 years of age), Sila (between 35 and 45) and Metta (under 35). The system was developed in an effort to encourage younger women to join. It remained in effect until 1976 when it was abandoned, the result of a lack of membership.

The Dana, always interested in the education of the young Buddhists of the church, decided to offer a travel grant. Dr. and Mrs. Ted Izukawa generously pledged to donate over a ten year period $10,000 in order to fund the Bishop Ishiura Travel Grant. The recipient was required to give a presentation about his or her trip after the Sunday Scholarship luncheon. The first to benefit from the grant was Linda Akaye who visited Switzerland.

The Dana created a committee to oversee the fund and the scholarship. Included were the minister, TBC Board members, the Sangha President, a Sangha member as Treasurer, Youth Department members and professional Dana members. A Dana representative was always the Chair.

With money from the New Horizons Program, a provincial funding organization for Senior Citizens' programs, the Dana started the Fujinotomo group in 1972 in an effort to demonstrate their gratitude to the elderly members of the church. They also organized craft projects, workshops, and many excursions to Niagara Falls, Mennonite Festivals and Wasaga Beach (for *warabi tori*, fiddlehead picking) for the once-a-month meeting of the group.

The next year, Jean Furukawa headed the committee to create the Dana cookbook, **Itadakimasu**. It sold out quickly and generated a profit. The Dana earmarked the proceeds for a leadership training program in 1974. The program consisted of Buddhist study sessions with the ministers, St. John's First Aid courses and a series of Japanese cooking lessons.

For several years, Dana members were deeply concerned with communicating with Buddhist members across Canada. With the slogan "Buddhist Women Across Canada", Terrie Komori headed the 1975 task of uniting women of the Buddhist faith in every province. To raise funds, the committee initiated the "Talent Project". Each member began with $5.00 and tried to multiply the sum four or five times by using their skills, talent and expertise. Some knitted or crocheted garments, some baked cakes and cookies, some organized their own rummage sales. In any event, the project was a huge success. Terrie Komori was then able to travel across the country to promote unity. The Dana too donated $500 from the proceeds to the Buddhist Churches of Canada.

In 1976 the Dana organized a weekend retreat at Camp Lumbini. Mary Ishiura and Nami Moriki led the Prajna weekend program of early morning exercise, vegetarian meals and the chanting of *sutras*. Discussions of the *Dharma*, the life of Shinran, and the Tan Nisho also took place. These retreats have recurred occasionally. With about 10 to 15 women in attendance, they had met, by 1991, three times at Lumbini, once in High Park as a day trip, once at Toronto's Centre Island and once at the Ecology Retreat Centre in Hockley Valley.

In the early 1970s, the Dana considered moving its older members (those over 60) to the Fujinkai. One or two had made the move but now 25 were eligible. Unfortunately, the Fujinkai members objected vehemently to the mass influx of members. They cited cultural differences (especially language) that would make the mix untenable. The suggestion was dropped and not considered again until 1994.

The Youth Department

With the demise of the TYBS in 1962, the Jr. YBA carried on with a largely social program. The group, for instance, continued to organize the Miss Valentine Dance and Pageant until the mid 1970s. An activity that survived after the Jr. YBA folded (continued by successive Bussei groups) was the Jr.

Bussei Baseball team. A Japanese Canadian Hardball League was formed and played at Greenwood Park in Toronto's eastend, comprised of teams representing several Japanese Canadian organizations.

In May 1964 Tom Allen and Albert Nishimura started the Boys Club to keep the boys, aged 9 - 14, in the Dharma School from dropping out of the church altogether. They organized several activities for them. Similarly, Amy Murabayashi and June Katsura formed the Girls Club in 1966 allowing girls 9 - 14 to participate in craft workshops, sports and day trips.

In December 1966 a gathering of *sansei* between the ages of 13 and 15 met at the home of Joe and Miyo Nakamura to start a new Buddhist youth group called the Taruna (a Sanskrit word suggested by Mary Ishiura). Again, its purpose was social, but it filled the gap between the younger Boys and Girls Clubs and the university aged Jr. YBA. The first executive consisted of Gary Tanaka, President; Garry Kawasaki, Vice-President; Amy Nakamura, Secretary; Irene Ebata, Treasurer; Laurie Kondo and Steve Seko, Social Convenors; and Carolyn Nishikawa, Religious Convenor.

> The young people at that time had no place to congregate and were left out in the Church, being too young to join the Busseis and to form yet another organization within the Church was somewhat questionable, but as a means of social get-together and to discuss contemporary issues socially and religiously as amongst young people, we felt it was a good idea to consolidate into a group under an official name.
>
> It was still in the formative stages and the parents of the children were rather reluctant to have young people congregate at the Church, thinking that ultimately it would mean social dances and group contacts which they wanted to avoid, and there were some opposition and criticisms against the venture.[6]

Under the guidance of advisors Mary Ishiura, Sue Michibata, Miyo Nakamura and Tom Allen, the Taruna enjoyed trips to the CBC studios, Camp Lumbini and the Bloorview Children's Hospital. They performed for children, held parties at private homes and met with teenagers from the B'nai B'rith Jewish Youth of Toronto, the United Church and the Unitarian Group.

In 1970 Mary Ishiura and Miyo Nakamura asked Gloria Sumiya to help out. Most of the older members had moved on to the Jr. YBA, but several 12 and 13 year olds wanted their own club. Sumiya joined Nakamura and another advisor, Doug Fujiwara, in supervising Taruna activities. By the next year their numbers had swelled to over thirty.

That summer 32 members camped out at Lumbini (see **Camp Lumbini** this chapter) for seven days enjoying such activities as football, volleyball, swimming and talking with each other late into the night. Counsellors and cooks included Mary Ishiura, Gloria Sumiya, Yae Ebisuzaki, Misao Nishikawa, Jeanne Akaye and Sakae Goto.

In the meantime, the Jr. YBA delved into the connection between Buddhism and current world issues with folk-rock Sunday services and multi-media theatre presentations, all with the support of Rev. Ishiura and the reluctant blessing of the Board of Directors and Religious Department.

Eventually, the number of youth group members grew to the point where the Board of Directors felt it should be involved. Thus the Youth Department came into being (about 1975). The department solicited funds from the Board and encouraged participation. The chairpeople in succession - Roger Tanaka, Dr. Ted Izukawa, Jerry Kawaguchi and Tak Kushida - brought innovative programming in an effort to instill in the young an understanding of the Buddha *Dharma*.

The Dharma School

During the Labour Day Weekend of 1958, the Toronto Buddhist Church under the purview of the TYBS hosted a series of workshops on Sunday School education. Delegates from the Chicago Buddhist Church, Chicago Midwest Sunday School, Cleveland Sunday School, Montreal Church and Hamilton Church attended the first series of teaching workshops held by a Buddhist organization in eastern North America.

> From Saturday morning to Sunday night, program after program of intense teaching, training, learning and practice were enthusiastically carried out by the hosts, delegates and guests. No social event was

> allowed to waste the delegates' valuable time. The entire operation was comprehensive, well-planned and executed with a sense of purpose. A Cleveland delegate noted that he had come over a hundred miles for the purpose of obtaining some good ideas and instructions, and had, surprisingly enough, been successful. The Chicago delegate felt that this Seminar had provided a"basketful" of ideas.[7]

Seminars included "Teaching Children to Sing Gathas" by Rev. M. Nakagaki of Detroit, Michigan, and "How to Set Up a More Efficient Education System" by Val Scott, Education Director of the Toronto Unitarian Church.

The organizers included: Tak Yoshida (Chairman), Charlie Shimizu, Tin Goto, Ed Tsuji, Jack Shimizu, Kaz Tatebe, Nancy Shimoda, Harry Yonekura (Chair of the Toronto Dharma School), Rev. Tsuji, Sakaye Tsuji, Sakae Goto, K. Tada and Sue Michibata.

The Sunday School was well organized and underway when Rev. Ishiura arrived. Eight grades accommodated about 200 pupils. Classes expanded to occupy the entire basement of the church. During a special general meeting in April 1962, the membership adopted a resolution to construct three classrooms, expanded kitchen facilities, a library room and a minister's lounge. The budget was set at $30,000. The Building Committee included Ty Ebata as Finance Chairman and Hideo Yoshida, Construction Chairman. The church then hired Yamazaki and Matsui, Architects and N & S Construction. The project was completed in March 1963.

Twenty teachers came under the authority of the Religious and Juvenile Education Departments of the church. Teachers included Misao Nishikawa, Fumi Ono, Masa Yoshida, Molly Watanabe and Morgan Harris.

Rev. Ishiura saw the need for a link between the school and the minister and therefore instituted the supervisor system. At least then the school had a mechanism to approach the minister easily for religious guidance. The supervisors in succession were Kaz Tatebe, Tin Goto, Ed Tsuji and Jack Shimizu.

Throughout Rev. Ishiura's stay, the Sunday School enjoyed a multitude of activities. The children made flowers for Hanamatsuri beginning in 1950. They also commemorated

Mother's Day. The last Saturday in December the school held a turkey dinner for all the students and teachers. The teachers attended annual conferences in Chicago, Cleveland, Seabrooke and New York to learn new teaching methods.

> I was the teacher of the senior group, age 11 to 13 or 14, and often conducted *Dharma* discussions with Mrs. Robinson, and had them write compositions on Buddhism, and their thoughts on how individually it was important for them to be Buddhists.
>
> I took over a Grade 5 group at one time, and youngsters, like Karma Ishiura, Danny Tsujiuchi, wrote compositions on one particular theme of Buddhism, and there were many humorous childish thoughts on these.
>
> We took them on excursions, such as the tour of the **Toronto Telegram**, the Dunlop Observatory, the Ford Plant. We also visited the McKenzie House during Christmas time and the new City Hall. These visits were arranged before Sunday School began at 10:30 so you can imagine the preparation and arrangements that went into the group outings. We also conducted an oratorical contest, the winners being Gordon Yoshida and Ms. Koyata. The judges were recruited from prominent members of Toronto communities at the time, Richard Robinson and Rev. Tsuji.[8]

All in all, the Dharma School supervisors and teachers took to heart Kakuei Tada's advice given at the end of that workshop series held in 1958:

> You had before you the challenging task of teaching to the children the true meaning of Buddhism, and concurrently, to work diligently on the greatest challenge, their own Enlightenment.[9]
>
> K. Tada

The Sangha

The men's group remained remarkably cohesive from 1958 to 1977. The members seemed united in their conviction to maintain and develop the church. Even though an age limit was set (50 years old), the members, as with the other organizations within the church, did not move readily. The 1963 constitution read: "The membership shall consist of single individuals and married couples between the ages of 30 and 50. In the case of wives not members of any other group, they shall be considered unit members."[10] Still some advised, "it is not wise to have clearcut policies re membership requirements and age limits - elasticity is needed".[11]

Generally, the Sangha oversaw the main activities of the church: from fund raising to social events. Thus, meetings concerned themselves with Bingo Nights to raise money for a church organ, Hanamatsuri socials, joint services and conferences with Montreal and Hamilton Sangha (see **Eastern Sangha/Dana League**, Chapter 16), the Fooderama and Bazaar (members volunteered as dishwashers), youth co-ordination, Sangha Bowling, ballroom dance lessons, and Keirokai concerts.

Perhaps the most significant contributions of the Sangha come to light in the special projects of the Toronto Buddhist Church.

Special Projects

Camp Lumbini

Two years after the completion (1958) of his own cottage at Wasaga Beach, Sam Baba and his wife Hisa came across a one acre lot nearby that was for sale. He inquired and found the price was $1500. He had in mind a youth camp for the Toronto Buddhist Church since he frequently passed the Father Francisca Youth Camp just up the road. He immediately took his idea to the next board meeting and met resistance.

> Unfortunately at that time, this was early 1960, most people thought it was too extravagant for a Toronto Buddhist Church to have a camp site. So at the meeting we were turned down.[12]

Undaunted by the mainly *issei* objections, Baba led a campaign to buy the land.

> So the board told us if you young people feel strongly enough that you do it on your own...so I think we approached the Dana and the Fujinkai [for support]. After a few meetings, we [the Sangha] tentatively

> agreed to buy this property and share in the expense. I think it was $500 from each organization [Sangha, Dana and Fujinkai].[13]

The project got underway in 1964. Kay Kawano and Yukio Koyanagi agreed to head the development of the campsite. Even then opposition came from the older members and some factions of the young people. Despite it all, a small group of enthusiastic people travelled the 100 miles north to Wasaga to clear the land on weekends.

> When the project started getting underway, it seemed like everybody got very enthusiastic about it and we had more and more volunteers going up there and using our place as a kind of headquarters. We had a lot of Dana ladies coming up and preparing lunches for the men working on the construction.[14]

Abbot Ohtani and Lady Yoshiko visiting Canada on their way home from South America officially opened the camp with a ribbon cutting ceremony in July 1964. The work team completed the main building, including running water and electricity, by the fall. The deed was transferred to the TBC shortly after completion.

Initially, many youth programs took place at Camp Lumbini usually during weekends. The Boys and Girls Clubs went up for *Dharma* lessons, swimming and cookouts (largely organized by Mary Ishiura). In 1967 the Taruna were the first to stay at the campsite for a week.

Eventually, the Lumbini Camp Site Committee was formed to oversee the programs and the maintenance of the grounds. On April 16, 1966, the Sangha passed a resolution to build two rental cottages, additions to the main cottage. The estimated cost of $5000 was raised by borrowing $100 each from 50 members, returnable in ten years.

> Kay Kawano and Harry Koyanagi were instrumental again in building this place. We started the work and completed it in 1967. So this was another way of making available additional space for the members, plus the fact that it might bring in some income as a rental unit towards the expense of the camp site. That was our main purpose.[15]

By 1977 Camp Lumbini offered church members an excellent respite from the busy city. Its three cottages were in constant use throughout the summer by individuals, families and organizations. Wasaga as well saw a surge of Japanese Canadian inhabitants. Besides the Babas, the Otsus, Fujiwaras, Soras and Fujibayashis bought cottages along or near the waterfront. With guests and extended families of these owners, a Japanese Canadian community flourished by the shores of Wasaga Beach at least for the summer.

The Youth Building Fund

With the $14,000 profit realized from the sale of the Huron Street Church, Ed Yoshida proposed the Sangha establish the Toronto Buddhist Church Youth Building Fund. Ty Ebata became the custodian of the fund that was to be used strictly for the purpose of purchasing a building where religious, sports, craft and social programs for the young of the church could be developed.

The amount grew to over $17,000 by the 1960s when a committee under Harry Yonekura began looking in earnest for a site. The members searched in vain for three months. The apartments next to the church were ideal but the property was not for sale.

The quest stopped and the fund went dormant. No reports were filed since no activity had taken place, but concerns developed amongst the ranks of the Sangha. After a stormy meeting in which Ty Ebata, Izo Ebata and Harry Yonekura came under heavy criticism by the Sangha President, Tom Ohara, the three decided to hand over the custodianship of the fund to the Sangha.

> It was a strong word he used and Ty was shocked when he heard it, so after the meeting, Ty was depressed and said he wanted to quit. I said, "Ty, he's Sangha President. Why doesn't the Sangha look after it; after all, it's Sangha's children that we're talking about." So that's how Sangha became custodian of the Youth Building Fund from then on. And Sam Baba, Tosh Hori and Tomio Nishikawa were custodians.[16]

The fund still remained dormant, however, until 1974 when again questions about the fund arose. By then $20,000 had accumulated. Some felt it should be used to purchase the property adjacent to the church. Others felt obligated to use the money for its original purpose: to find property for a youth building.

> There was about $90,000 they were asking [for the property next door]. We didn't have that kind of money but we had enough for a down payment I thought in those days.[17]

Instead, the Sangha gave up the property and let the money sit, probably because of procrastination or a reluctance to be committed to another mortgage (they had just paid off the church's second mortgage). In any case, the money stayed idle.

In order to build the fund again despite its lack of purpose, the Sangha began holding the Momiji Ball (beginning in 1974), an annual formal dinner/dance. The dance, chaired by Harry Yonekura for three years and then Tosh Hori, continued into the 1980s.

When the final decision came in 1984 to send the Youth Building Fund to the Central Treasury, it had grown to over $150,000. In the end the fund helped to initiate the FAMAC program in the late 1980s.

Project '71

Perhaps the most controversial of the TBC activities was Project '71. When the Central Board was created in 1952, no one actually belonged to the Toronto Buddhist Church as a member. Instead, people came from church organizations: Sangha, TYBS, Fujinkai or Bukkyo-kai. The Central Treasury's main revenue was derived from an assessment of contributions for each affiliated group. The amount caused many of the groups to hold special fund raising events to meet the assessment. Many of these pet projects overlapped with other events causing a strain on the pocketbook and divided loyalties.

> When I became the church president [1952], it became quite clear that we had to make a change [to the makeup of the membership]. We had a tough time forming a budget since the members were responsible first to their affiliate groups, then to the church. For instance, if the *issei* group did not go along with some proposed project, they could withhold funds from

> their treasury. An example was the offertory gathered from the Shotsuki service [memorial]. The Goho-kai felt that it was theirs. The Fujinkai felt that every food project would be under their control. When the Sangha decided to hold a bazaar, they had to ask their wives to help in the food area. The Danas were not organized as yet, but they acted as a group of Sangha wives. I would keep on bringing this membership topic to the General Meeting without let up. I had an idea behind it all. I was looking toward a pledge system.[18]

Yoshida's idea had merit. If the church decided to institute general membership then membership fees would become an issue. Instead he planned to introduce a system whereby each member would pledge a yearly donation to the church.

The *issei* objected vigorously. They felt that since each pledge was to be published, comparisons would arise and cause some hard feelings. Another reason for dissension lay in the clash between generations. As with other issues, the *issei* wished to maintain the old distinctly Meiji Japanese traditions within the church. Donations should be given freely, any amount at any time. A pledge to donate meant the members were tied into an obligation. The *nisei,* however, felt the Pledge System ensured the future existence of the church by eliminating the dependence on donations by only those who attended the church regularly.

The debate continued well into the 1960s. Finally during the May 1969 General Meeting, the membership passed a resolution that called for the creation of a General Membership System for the TBC through a pledge system. It also provided for a committee, co-chaired by Harry Yonekura and Fred Kotani, to implement the system. Unfortunately, the committee met massive resistance from the *issei.*

> I was co-chair with Fred Kotani and my first meeting I remember the late Mr. Baba was president of Goho-kai and he told me point blank, before I could even start the discussion, how do you think these projects are going to succeed without Goho-kai support? You know how his voice carries. So I suggested to him it's not your generation, we're talking about future generations. So I'm going to go ahead with or without

> Goho-kai. Then Fujinkai backed me up. That's how he quietened down.
>
> After Mr. Baba, Mr. Amemori became the Goho-kai President; Mr. Baba was nothing compared to Mr. Amemori. Oh what a time he gave me. He won't even listen to reason - just no! He even told me I was a Hitler.[19]

In May 1969 the Riji-Kai or Central Board authorized the Co-Chairmanship of Fred Kotani and Harry Yonekura to head the Project '71 membership drive. The working committee included:

Advisors:	Reverends Ishiura, Watanabe and Miyaji
Publicity, Publication & Printing:	Representatives from the Membership and Finance Departments
Secretaries:	Lillian Ebata (English) Masakazu Shimoda (Japanese)

Difficulties persisted, but with help from key members of the church, the campaign proved successful.

> Harry [Yonekura] gave up. He came to the Director's meeting and said this is not going to work. I remember I was Board Chairman at the time, so I said, well Harry, last general meeting we passed this thing and we're going to put it into the machinery and this is no time to give up. I think he had strong opposition from Mr. Amemori. So I said, if he started the following general meeting with nothing being done, this is going to be cancelled altogether. Let's concentrate on the four organizations, their directors. Sign them up before the general meeting.[20]
>
> I did not give up. I had Goho-kai, Fujinkai meeting. Now Mr. Amemori called me a Hitler. That did it. From here on, if I push any more, it's going to be a fight with Mr. Amemori. So I called an Executive Board meeting and I told them, if I'm going to push any further, there's going to be a fight in this church. Somebody has to get in and tell Mr. Amemori to shut up because I was pretty upset about his statement.

> This was in front of all the people and I was really insulted. From here on it's going to be a fight. There's no way I could carry this on so I asked them, "Do you want that or not?" But I don't want any fights so rather than that I'm going to resign. Rather than have a split in the church, I'm going to resign. So Ryotaro Nakamura, at that time he was President of the Toronto Buddhist Church, said, "I'll tell Amemori to quiet down." I started in 1969 and I planned two years. From '70, we're going out to the public. The groundwork was done.[21]

The objective was 800 members 18 yrs. and over with a pledged amount of $30,000. All the executive members of the Goho-kai, Fujinkai, Sangha and Dana were to be canvassers. The number of volunteers increased with the need.

With 32 team captains and 170 canvassers covering 36 districts, the goals were set for two Pledge Sundays - Hanamatsuri and Obon of 1971. By November 1971, 803 had registered as members, pledging to donate $33,786. The following year the number rose to 1180 members.

> When the pledge system did finally come into effect, most of the pledges were made individually, but the *issei* still preferred family pledges. With the introduction of the general membership, the members were able to make a choice. A person may wish to be an affiliate group member only or he could be a member of the church but not belong to any group. Often, they became a group member first. Then in a couple of years he would be approached to become a church member.[22]

Church Leadership

The duties of the minister evolved into a rather complex job with a heavy workload. The Toronto Buddhist Church then petitioned for more ministers and got them. Rev. Takamasa Moriki arrived in 1976 and stayed until 1978. Rev. Fumimaro Watanabe served for five years (1964 - 1969) and then was replaced by Rev. Fumio Miyaji who performed his duties until 1975. Rev. Ishiura and his wife Mary, however, remained the heart and inspiration of the Toronto Church throughout the period.

> Once we came to Toronto, it was new territory for us. We [Rev. and Mary Ishiura] discussed a lot of things. She liked music, so music should play a very important part in church life. In my case, I liked to be involved in various civil rights movements. One day I met Rabbi Abraham Feinberg of the Holy Blossom Church. Rev. Tsuji had mentioned him. I got a call from him and went to Holy Blossom to meet him. In the budding days, we were discussing forming an inter-faith committee in Toronto - all religions. I got involved in that and from that evolved other movements working with the Indians, Inuits, the Ainu people from Japan, and the Hiroshima Peace Day. Of course my wife was all for it. During the Vietnam Era, there were many kids coming from the States, underground, AWOL, 18, 19 year old kids. There was an office on Yonge Street; they'd come in penniless, no home, no job, bewildered. So I was involved in helping them.[23]

Rev. Ishiura brought with him his own agenda for his new placement. The 1960s were a chaotic time, but a great era for change. The young learned minister saw the period as an opportunity to effect change and inspired all at the church to become "involved" with society at large.

> Remember the Chinese invaded Tibet. Do you recall in 1958, '59 other atrocities were going on. I heard one broadcast about the Dalai Lama making an escape into India and I felt with this, there would be lots of kids misplaced and sure enough, I got the news that in Dharamsara, they started a nursery, getting the infants together. With the Church [TBC] as a base, I collected money and sent it to the nursery school. I did it for about five years. And it so happened that when I moved to Berkeley, the Chancellor's office at UC Berkeley called me saying that the Dalai Lama was coming to give a lecture. He wrote that his sister was operating the Dharamsara nursery and that there was a Buddhist minister who was supporting the nursery and to invite him. I got a call to the luncheon, sat near his table and talked with him. He mentioned the Toronto Buddhist Church. He remembered all those things.[24]

The Dana adopted three Tibetan children. The Sangha held a conference with a Chinese Canadian community organization and the Japanese Canadian Citizens Association (JCCA) and sponsored a panel discussion about the "Black Experience in Canada". It was the youth, however, who explored most the interrelation between religion and society.

> Music-wise, we wanted to break the normal pattern, to bring others into the church. Once we had Terry Watada involved, playing folk music in a family service that was really quite different. We had Roy Sato and others in the YB movement and people who were artists but were not recognized in a place where they could exhibit their art work. These are things in which my wife and I were quite involved in trying to open the church.[25]
>
> There were two different occasions. One was an actual service; we just took over the whole service and asked Rev. Ishiura to do the religious chants. The other was a play, sort of multimedia play. We had slides and movies, singing, acting, dancing, all going on at the same time. I remember the *issei* men and women were shocked by what we did.[26]

Both Reverend and Mrs. Ishiura came under criticism from the conservative elements of the church for their involvement in human rights activities and for projects that were seen as sacrilegious or, at the very least, disrespectful. Very few for example approved of turning the *hondo* into a multi-media theatre featuring strobe lighting, three performance stages, bizarre images projected onto various screens and rock music.

> After the war, I was assigned to Fresno. I didn't last too long there. My idea was not acceptable. I got into trouble there. But now they tell me, "You were about twenty years ahead of us. We wish you were here now." Same thing happened in Hawaii. Then all my involvement in civil rights came out. They said, "Oh, we don't want that kind of minister here." Hawaii is still the same about those things.[27]

Still, Rev. Ishiura followed his conscience and joined several inter-faith committees for political action and protest groups over human rights violations.

> We went into civil rights, the Inuit Movement and all that. In fact, I remember they were saying about Quebec where all Canadians lost their civil liberties [the 1970 FLQ Crisis]. I was involved with Pierre Burton getting a petition out. It was a police state. I was sick of the whole thing. And someone told me when my family marched against Vietnam that our picture was taken. We were passing the American Consulate Office where the camera was taking a picture.[28]

Such publicity did not endear the minister to the same conservative elements in the church. Eventually the criticism was to the point where Rev. Ishiura offered his resignation to take effect June 1969.

What then drove this man to shun conformity and act with his heart? His wife's support was a great factor but not the entire story. In 1935 he found himself travelling from Hawaii to Japan with his family. His father had become custodian of the family Buddhist temple.

He found the going rough until he was offered a position in the church school office.

> I jumped at that. So he [the principal] taught me how to type and to file. Soon we needed a church newspaper so I was editor just at the time of the New Deal. FDR came into [political] office. I used to write about all this stuff in the church paper. But he [the principal] told me you're too young to write political news... that's how I got interested in politics.
>
> In Japan, I went one day to town near a Christian Church. I went in and there was a man known as an Evangelist. He really struck me. I met Toyohiko Kagawa and my mind was in the area to work in a slum district and help people. Kagawa convinced me that he needed young men like me in the ministry, so I went to a Lutheran School. My mother went crazy. But my father was neutral. They [the school] offered me a scholarship to Amherst. But I had other problems; political problems, theological problems and many problems the seminary left un-answered. Whenever I was perplexed I

> spoke to my father. He was always understanding and gave me good answers. I think it was my father's understanding that brought me back to the [Buddhist] church again. When I finished high school, I thought I'd go to Kyoto to study. I went into the life to become a Buddhist minister.[29]

Armed with political understanding and a fervent desire to help the needy, Newton Ishiura entered Ryukoku University and met an equally energetic and progressive young man, Takashi Tsuji.

> Rev. Tsuji and I were real pals. Every time we met we'd talk about when we went back what we were going to do, big dreams. Dreams about the present church. It's got to change into real Canadian and American. We had big dreams. In Kyoto we formed a Sunday School. We [also] planned this church service to make it interesting. We did a lot of things, a new innovation [Sunday School]. We were close friends.[30]

Ishiura returned to the United States in July 1941 to his first assignment. After a month, he started at the Los Angeles Buddhist Church and then moved to Bakersfield.

> One day, the Bishop [San Francisco headquarters] says, "Let's go for lunch. I have some business downtown I have to take care of." The first place he parked his car was in front of a men's shop. He went in, I followed. He said to pick any suit you want as long as it's black. I had no money. He said, "Don't worry about payment, just get your black suit." So I got my first black suit. They all wear black. That's how I started in the early days.
>
> One day, he [Bishop Matsukage] called me to his office. "I'm giving you the first choice of a church that's vacant." Well being a naive guy, I said, "Sure, anything you say - I'll go." So I hopped on the first train and went to Bakersfield. Hot place. I carried all my stuff and found 1707 M Street, old frame Buddhist temple. It was about 5 o'clock and nobody was there to greet me. Towards dusk, an old man came, "You the new *bonsan*?" He was the church president. That's how I started my church. And that church was known to kick the ministers out.[31]

The elders of the Bakersfield Church enjoyed meeting in a refrigerator room in a produce company owned by a Mr. Nakamoto, talk about the minister and then dismiss him. Such was the church's reputation. However, the members did not have the chance to dismiss Rev. Ishiura because the war started.

He was immediately assigned to the Los Angeles area. Thirteen ministers had been arrested and the Bishop mustered his reserves.

> I left all my stuff in Bakersfield. I was on my way to Los Angeles and was stopped by the Highway Patrol. They said, "Get out. Put up your hands." They searched me. "Where's your passport?" It's a funny question to ask. So I asked him, "Do all Americans carry passports?" He said, "Hell no, we don't carry a passport." "Why should I carry a passport?" I asked. "Oh, are you an American citizen?" So I got by.[32]

Rev. Ishiura held services through to March 1942 - remarkable since most churches closed down operations shortly after Pearl Harbor. During his stay at the Los Angeles Betsuin, he worked tirelessly to give comfort to the newly displaced. He invited the arrested ministers' families to stay at the temple. In the end, he slept on his office desk.

> I was up almost twenty hours a day helping them. So when I went to my first camp centre, I got sick. I got tuberculosis and went to a sanatorium in Wyoming.
>
> By four weeks, my whole cavity cleared. The doctor said, "Wow, this is a miracle!" And I said, "No doctor, it's not a miracle. The power of *Nembutsu*." "What's that?" So I sat with the doctor and talked about Buddhism.[33]

After the cure, Ishiura spent a short time in Arizona at the Gila River concentration camp before leaving for the east coast to pursue his illustrious academic and religious career.

At the Toronto Church, the Sangha talked Rev. Ishiura out of resigning his position in 1969. He then went on as Bishop of the Buddhist Churches of Canada and brought much good will to the Toronto Church through his work for human rights. In 1977 he was honoured with a charter membership of the Metro International Task Force on Racism and Human Rights. He was recognized in other ways as well.

> We received an invitation from the government to take part in the Canadian Centennial. They called Nishimura Sensei in Winnipeg. They wanted Buddhist participation. So I was called in and made my way to Ottawa. There is in the Centennial Book, the Buddhist Centennial Aspiration which I put in there. The Prime Minister's office called that they were going to have a big Centennial service at Westminster Abbey and wanted Canada to send four religious leaders: a Catholic, Anglican, United Church of Canada and a Jewish rabbi. He put my name in there too...a few days before departure the Prime Minister called me. The Queen's office had called. They were not ready to accept Buddhists yet. He was very apologetic and said he wanted to make it up to me somehow. So when the Queen came over to our Centennial service, he sat me close to the Queen. At the big reception, I was invited and introduced to the Queen.[34]

Mrs. Mary Ishiura

Mary Matsuura was born in 1922 into a Buddhist family in Guadeloupe, California, a small farming community north of Los Angeles. The third child of Rev. Issei and Mrs. Shinobu Matsuura, she attended high school in Santa Maria until 1942 when she and her family were exiled to the Gila River Relocation Center in Arizona. There she worked in a camouflage factory and met a tall and youthful minister - Rev. Newton Ishiura. They fell in love.

Unfortunately they were soon separated because she received a scholarship to Rockford College in Illinois having earned a B.A. in Sociology. Rev. Ishiura left Gila River as well and went to Minneapolis and Chicago before landing a position at the University of Michigan. So they were able to keep in touch.

After the war, they returned to the coast and settled in Berkeley. She worked with the underprivileged youth for the State Human Resources Dept. until her marriage to Rev. Newton Ishiura in Jan. 1953 and resettlement in Honolulu, Hawaii.

Almost from the moment she arrived in Toronto in 1958, Mary Ishiura became involved in every facet of the Buddhist Church.

> She gave of herself tirelessly. She would suggest how we (the Dana) might help a Tibetan child, a hurricane victim, the elderly...She took an active part and encouraged the members to become involved in peace movements and interfaith programs, to give moral support to struggling artists and writers... Through her guidance, invitations were sent out to all public school teachers of the Church's *Dharma* pupils, asking them to spend an afternoon at the Toronto Buddhist Church to see, to hear, and to become aware of the Buddhist religion.[35]

Mary Ishiura in fact advised the women of the church to start the Dana in 1959. She then initiated or acted as advisor to many of their projects: the Foster Child Program, the Dana Scholarship and the fashion shows.

For all of her and the Dana's effort, they were recognized at the World Buddhist Women's Federation Convention in New York, 1965.

> These things were done right here in Toronto. No other churches were doing that. The hospital in Tokyo, Asoka Hospital, the Toronto Dana and Fujinkai supported it for many many years. So when we went to Tokyo with a group, we got the royal treatment for the support we gave the hospital. This church has been going out of its own area to help in many ways. In fact, when the International World Buddhist Women met in New York, they talked about how Dana and our Toronto Dana Committee were helping internationally.[36]

Perhaps because of her elementary school background (she was a nursery school teacher in Honolulu, a supervisor of the Toronto YWCA Daycare Centre, and a mother of five), Mrs. Ishiura's main concern lay with the young. Besides her seminal work with the Dharma School, she formed a youth choir and remained the director for seven years. She also started the Dharma Children's Choir. She organized a youth orchestra and maintained keen interest in youth programs and summer camps at Lumbini. She encouraged and stood behind the activities of the Taruna and Jr. YBA no matter how outlandish.

Her attention also turned to senior members. She directed the Senior Citizens' Choir and was advisor to the Fujinotomo Group.

Even after she left with her husband and children in 1977, she held the Toronto Buddhist Church close to her heart.

> Throughout the 20 years, countless events took place. The pain and joy I shared with you enriched my life. When I cried with you and laughed with you during those eventful years, I realized Amida's presence. How could we have survived without the compassion and wisdom of Amida to guide us?[37]

On September 26, 1979, Mary Ishiura died in Berkeley, California. Bishop Kenryu Tsuji of the BCA officiated at her funeral on September 30. Bishop Seimoku Kosaka of the BCC, Rev. Izumi of Vancouver and all district ministers of the BCA attended. She was confirmed a Buddhist by the Gomonshu Ichijo-in Ohtani who gave her the Buddhist name Shakuni Myo-Jo.

To commemorate her memory and her love of music, the Dana with the approval of the church endowed a chair at Roy Thomson Hall. The scroll received by the Dana reads in part: "Be it known that the Toronto Buddhist Church Dana has endowed seat no. 17-010 in the Roy Thomson Hall to preserve her name in perpetuity."

On Sept. 29, 1991, the Dana donated to the church a Yamaha organ in Mary Ishiura's name to observe her 13th circuit memorial (Jusankaiki). Finally, the Buddhist Churches of Canada Women's Federation presented the Ishiura family with a Certificate of Commendation on June 26, 1994 for Mrs. Ishiura's dedication and good work.

> She was not just a minister's wife doing her duty, but almost from the day she arrived in Canada, she was committed. Her heart and mind cared not only for the welfare of her church members, but also for her community, for people across the country and even those across the seas.[38]

Spirituality and Decline

Chapter 22

The Toronto Buddhist Church: Spirituality and Decline

> Bishop Ishiura had very good news from his recent visit to the United States. Mr. Joe Fujino, Finance Chairman (BCA), mentioned that of all the Buddhist Churches in North America the Toronto Buddhist Church is the only church, he feels, that is living the Buddhistic life. He found real religious life here in the Toronto Buddhist Church.
>
> TBC Board Meeting Minutes
> Sept. 8, 1971

Despite the level of spirituality the Toronto Buddhist Church attained by the 1970s, the church experienced a slow decline from 1977 to 1995. Monetary concerns were no longer a major issue with the continued success of the annual bazaar (realizing nearly $30,000 in profit for a one day event), the highly effective Pledge System, plus other fund raising events. Each organization within the church saw falling numbers in its membership. Very few joined to replace those *issei* and *nisei* members who had died.

Perhaps one of the reasons for the decline was the inconsistent ministry. Both Rev. Tsuji and Rev. Ishiura had provided a stable presence by their longevity in Toronto.[1] After them came a long succession of ministers who by virtue of their short stays could not effectively establish their imprint on the church.

> Dr. Shigefuji's departure from Canada is instructive of the ministerial problems faced by the Buddhist Churches in Canada. From the time it was apparent that Canada

would be losing Rev. Newton Ishiura, one of the ablest ministers, to the time the Toronto Buddhist Church and the BCC were able to finally obtain a replacement, it took over two years. After only 18 months, Rev. Shigefuji had to return to Japan. In the meantime, two other ministers, Rev. Takamasa Moriki and Rev. Yujo Omori, both returned to Japan for reasons of health. During this period of instability, there was a period when Toronto's eight hundred or so members were being served by Rev. Omori alone, at a time when he was still going to classes to learn the English language.[2]

JCCC archives

Rev. K. Ikuta, Rev. O. Fujikawa and Bishop S. Tsunoda, Toronto, Ontario, circa 1982.

What follows is a list of the ministers who served the TBC 1976 - 1995.

Rev. Takamasa Moriki/Rev. Yujo Omori	1976-1978
Rev. Shinei Shigefuji/Rev. Yasuhiro Miyakawa	1978-1980
Rev. Shodo Tsunoda (Bishop of BCC 1981 - 1986)	1980-1985
Bishop Toshio Murakami (in Toronto)	1985-1988
Rev. Hisao Handa	1990-1992
Rev. Orai Fujikawa	1980-1994
Rev. Fukashi Nakatsumi (part time minister basis)	1980-1994
Rev. Grant Ikuta	1992-present
Rev. Yasuo Izumi	1994-present

Only Rev. Orai Fujikawa (1980 - 1994) served full time for any great length of time. When asked about the receding community nature of the TBC, Rev. Fujikawa felt perhaps it was better this way since the ministers and the membership could now concentrate on "pure religion".

Nevertheless, the *nisei* leadership were in fact alarmed by the falling numbers, principally because of the indifference of the *sansei* generation to the survival of the church. They decided to find ways to attract their children back into the fold.

Special Projects

FAMAC

Although his time was short at the TBC (he resigned for health reasons), Rev. Shigefuji initiated in 1979 a bold and innovative program called Financial Aid for Ministerial Aspirants of Canada (FAMAC). In co-operation with the BCC and the Hompa Hongwanji, FAMAC was designed to attract and train Canadian born Buddhists to the ministry. The scholarship offers the successful candidate $10,000 a year for five consecutive years to complete an MA at the Institute of Buddhist Studies in Berkeley, California, and to study at the Chuo Bukkyo Gakuin (Central Buddhist Institute) in Kyoto. After graduation the candidate is obligated to serve a minimum three year term with the BCC.

The Toronto Buddhist Church undertook the project to celebrate the 75th Anniversary of Buddhism in Canada and to counteract two of the contributing factors in the decline of the congregation: the ministers' problems with the English language and the perceived lack of relevancy in the church itself.

> We made a commitment, $10,000 a year. Then Doreen Hamilton sent in an application wanting to be a FAMAC candidate. The committee had a long discussion on that: whether the Toronto Buddhist Church could afford two candidates or not. We thought it was very important that Doreen Hamilton should be accepted in FAMAC because by that time, in 1989 - 90, we heard a lot of complaints from the young people that the Toronto Buddhist Church was getting too Japanese. Quite a few young members stopped coming to church, so maybe with Doreen Hamilton we might be able to overcome that.[3]

The BCC in addition to the TBC held much hope for the success of the program.

> This program will undoubtedly have very far-reaching effects on the Jodo Shinshu missions in all of Canada for many years...it seems abundantly clear that Canada must develop its own ministers. The parents should try to persuade their children to be ministers. Church leaders should develop programs that will encourage young scholars to be missionaries. I believe this problem is the most important problem facing all Canadian Buddhists today.[4]

Unfortunately no one applied until Doreen Hamilton did in May 1987 and Grant Ikuta in September 1987. Both were accepted in 1988.

Committee on the Future of the TBC

A committee of mostly *nisei* met in the early 1980s to discuss the future of the Toronto Buddhist Church in the face of a declining congregation. They decided in May 1984 to hire NRO Consulting of Halifax to design and implement a survey of the members and their children regarding their attitudes and opinions pertinent to future planning by the church.

Dr. Norman R. Okihiro of NRO enlisted the aid of committee members Dr. Ted Izukawa (Chair), Kunio Suyama (President, TBC), Rev. Orai Fujikawa, Mary Aoki (Secretary TBC), Fred Kotani, Doris Mito and Pam Yoshida (Research Secretary) in surveying *nisei* and *sansei* members.

The results published in the December 1984 report found:

> - The membership is dominated numerically by *nisei* between the ages of 55 and 69 years old. They have stable marriages.
>
> - 40% of the male members are retired.
>
> - The *sansei* are between 18 and 39 years old, single and generally live with their parents.
>
> - Three-fifths of the membership live evenly distributed outside the city.
>
> - Three-quarters found the location of the church convenient. Most *sansei* felt it inconvenient.
>
> - 20% of the membership attended church functions once a week, 25% never attended anything.

> Orientation to Japanese culture and the convenience of the TBC affected participation not only in regularly scheduled activities but also special religious services.
>
> - The *issei* (a substantial minority of the membership comprised mostly of women) favoured expansion of senior and religious activities. The *sansei* felt the expansion of social, cultural and sporting activities would attract them.
>
> - 89% of the regular church members and 83% of the *sansei* answering the main survey felt that the TBC should maintain a single church. The maintenance of tradition or continuity, convenience of location, nearness to the subway and costs were the most frequently cited reasons. Half wanted to maintain the church as is and half wanted to expand it. Establishing a satellite or new church or churches was supported by relatively few. However, persons feeling that the present church was inconveniently located or who were relatively dissatisfied with church activities were more likely to support satellites. They cited better transportation, parking and the appeal of a new facility.
>
> - Almost everyone cited the *sansei* or younger people as the most important group for the future of the Toronto Buddhist Church.[5]

Although never stating a recommendation himself, Dr. Okihiro concluded the report with suggestions by the membership about the survival of the church.

> Only expanding the present location or establishing satellites was thought to have a significant positive effect on the future attendance of groups felt to be important for the future of the TBC. A fairly low proportion of *sansei* (15%) indicated that relocating or establishing a satellite closer to their present location would result in more attendance at church functions. About the same proportion felt that relocating in central Toronto or expanding the present facilities and providing parking space would increase their future attendance.
>
> The uniform geographical distribution of both the regular church members and *sansei* about the downtown core suggests that there is no suitable location for

> a single satellite church. Two satellites, one in eastern Toronto and one in western Toronto, received support of those who felt the TBC should take this option.[6]

To date, the Toronto Buddhist Church is still in the throes of debate over the results of the survey, unable to decide on the most effective plan to continue.

Fujinkai and Goho-kai

As stated in the Okihiro report, most *issei* members were women and senior citizens. Both groups, however, continued through 1977 to 1995 to look after the needs of the Japanese speaking portion of the congregation. The Goho-kai with diminished numbers could not participate in the church as actively as in the past.

The Fujinkai, however, continued with great energy and enthusiasm. In 1978 the senior women's organization celebrated its 30th Anniversary. The following year they initiated with the Dana the Lady Eshinni Memorial Service, replacing the Lady Kujo Service. The Fujinkai, along with the Goho-kai, organized in January 1980 the annual Memorial Service for past members. They also continued to be involved with Japanese Canadian community activities: participation in the Japanese Canadian Cultural Centre's bazaar and Metro Toronto Caravan[7]; donations to the United Way; visitations to Castleview Wychwood Senior Care Home, Greenview Lodge Seniors Home and Nipponia Home.

In 1982 they sent representatives to the World Buddhist Women Federation Convention in Honolulu, Hawaii. Two years later in November, they welcomed the Gomonshu Ohtani and Lady Noriko at the TBC. They began a fund raising campaign in 1988 to help with the World Buddhist Women's Federation convention slated for Vancouver 1990.

The convention was a tremendous success. Nineteen Fujinkai members attended and met with the Honolulu Betsuin Church's Fujinkai representatives.

In 1990 the Fujinkai members turned their attention to the organization's future. They decided to ask the Dana to consider taking over the leadership positions. In 1991 however the executive still held strong with 24 directors including the offices of President, Vice-President, Treasurer, Membership, Social Convenor, Communication Officer and Welfare.

In 1993 the Goho-kai and the Fujinkai celebrated their respective 35th and 45th Anniversaries with a special service held in April. Rev. Y. Miyakawa, former TBC minister, came from Winnipeg to act as guest speaker.

The Dana

The Dana did not rest on their laurels after Mary Ishiura left for California. They continued their activities in the church and outside. In 1979 for example, they helped to put together three suburban services in an attempt to draw younger members and non-Buddhists to the church. They held services led by Reverends Shigefuji, Nakatsumi and Miyakawa at Don Mills Collegiate, Silverthorn Collegiate and Milneford Junior High. After each event the ministers fielded many questions of the students. The enthusiasm of the students encouraged the Dana in their attempts at outreach. Unfortunately other commitments forced the members to stop these visits at three.

They donated hundreds of dollars in successive years to the FAMAC Program, the Terry Fox Marathon of Hope, the Dana Scholarship Fund, Momiji Health Care and the TBC Youth Orchestra. Today the largest fund raising occurs during the concurrent "Hometown Fair" at Sherway Plaza in a west side suburb and at the Don Mills Centre in the east. The proceeds are ear-marked for FAMAC and the Dana's general funds. For the Scholarship Fund, the Dana conducted an art raffle, paintings donated by four well known artists including Kazuo Hamasaki. They then decided to raise the awards considerably. The Dana donated fabric for *happi* coats to the orchestra as well as a generous sum of money for their trip to the Ekoji Temple in the United States.

The 1979 passing of both Rev. Moriki's wife in Japan and Mrs. Mary Ishiura in California profoundly affected the Dana. They arranged memorial services at the TBC. Mary Ishiura, in particular, was remembered in several ways as the years passed.

In 1982 the Dana joined the World Buddhist Women's Federation. The twenty plus delegates to the Hawaii World Convention proudly watched as Terrie Komori, President of the first Buddhist Churches of Canada Women's Federation (BCCWF), formally accepted membership into the Federation. She thanked Bishop Tsunoda who acted as advisor throughout the process.

The 25th Anniversary celebration (1984) proved to be a gala event. The banquet held at the Harbour Castle Hilton featured Margaret Lyons, former head of the CBC, as keynote speaker. Mitsu Kamada of the New York Buddhist Temple spoke during the Sunday service. The Dana announced on this occasion the dedication of a chair at Roy Thomson Hall to Mary Ishiura.

The Dana headed the renovation plans for the church's kitchen in 1985. They worked closely with the TBC Maintenance Committee. Also in 1985 the Dana reorganized their administration. Instead of a single president, they decided to elect three district leaders who took turns chairing executive duties. The first and only triumvirate included Haru Baba, Yae Ebisuzaki and Bonnie Higashi. After that year, the executive chair was reduced to two.

The Dana's involvement with the World Federation increased in 1986 when Jean Furukawa, Eastern Director of the BCCWF, led a delegation to the convention in Kyoto. For the next four years, the Dana committed itself to fund raising and workshops in preparation for the 1990 Women's Convention in Vancouver. One such activity was the TBC Lottery.

In 1989 the Tanomoshi or Credit Union was discontinued and the remaining funds were turned over to the Dana. The following year, 51 delegates attended the 9th World Women's Convention in Vancouver. Jean Furukawa was the Executive Board representative. Participants as emcees for various events included Terrie Komori, Gloria Sumiya, Yuki Kondo, Doreen Hamilton and Sally Miyazaki. The panellists were Dorothy Kagawa and Marilyn Mori. Other workshop leaders were Misao Nishikawa, Hedy Yonekura and Toyo Hikida. At the convention, the Dana established a sister relationship with the Honomu Hongwanji in Pepeekeo, Hawaii. Presidents Hedy Yonekura and Shizuko Kishita of Toronto and Jane Ouye of Pepeekeo signed documents cementing the bond. In 1994, 35 Dana delegates headed for Anaheim, California, to attend the 10th World Buddhist Women's Convention.

Throughout the 1990s, Doreen Hamilton and Rev. Fujikawa led three Prajna Retreats for the Dana. They meditated, ate vegetarian meals and discussed issues in such pastoral locations like High Park in Toronto's west end, the Hockley Valley (north of the city) and Toronto's Centre Island.

The 1990s further saw the Dana reorganizing its priorities

since more and more of the Fujinkai's responsibilities were passed on to the younger group. Principally, the organization became involved in the 50th Anniversary Celebrations of the Toronto Buddhist Church. Many members participated in the research for the history project chaired by long-time Dana member Dorothy Kagawa.

Obon Odori

By the late 1970s, the Dana assumed the responsibility for the Obon Odori Group. Instruction within the various groups branched out to include classical *buyo*[8] in 1977 with the assistance of Yoshiko Kono who was the teacher until her death in 1990.

Every year from 1965 to 1989, the traditional dance brought the community together first to the waterfront Ontario Place at the site of the Japanese Canadian Centennial Bell and then to Toronto City Hall's Nathan Phillips Square. At its peak, 300 dancers from Hamilton, the TBC and the Japanese Canadian Cultural Centre participated. Hundreds of people formed the audience. Unfortunately City Hall officials for some unknown reason began double booking the space making the *odori* impossible to co-ordinate. In 1990 the Obon Odori moved to a more hospitable location, Mel Lastman Square in North York.

The Dana women acted as instructors for the young *sansei* dancers with Madam Tachibana from the United States coming to teach new dances from time to time. Yoshiko Kono, a dance teacher for the JCCC's Sakura-kai, often helped the church dancers as well. Throughout the years, several *taiko* accompanists enlivened the recorded music: people like Mrs. Doi, Fred Tsuji, Rev. Yasuo Izumi, George Fujita, Shingo Kono, Sho Wakabayashi, Aaron Aoki and Paul Aoki. The Dana and Sangha, parents of the *sansei*, took care of the finances. Involvement was on a volunteer basis. Venues like Buffalo University and shopping malls were not charged for the Odori group's performance. Other performances took place at Chateau Montebello, Quebec; Peterborough; Niagara Falls; Peach Festival, London; Queen's Park; old age homes; and hospitals.

The Odori program for Obon today still includes an appearance during the Peace Bell Ringing Ceremony at Ontario Place before the group heads to Mel Lastman Square.

The Sangha

In 1978 the Sangha recorded 185 paid members. These members along with the Dana (and the Fujinkai at times) planned, instituted and maintained the core activities of the church. These included the Keirokai (March), Hanamatsuri with dinner and concert (April), family banquets, family bowling, TBC Annual Picnic (June), Obon Odori (July), TBC Fall Bazaar (November), Bodhi Day and Year End Mochitsuki (December). The Sangha also took care of Camp Lumbini that traditionally opened in May and closed on the Thanksgiving weekend in October.

By the late 1970s, the Sangha became intrinsically involved with the Obon Odori. The choreography and *kimono* design were taken care of by the Dana and Fujinkai but the building of the stage at Nathan Phillips Square and then at Mel Lastman Square in North York was the Sangha's responsibility. The incomparable Kunio Suyama entertained the audience as emcee with his congenial banter and enthusiastic entreating of everyone to join the dancing.

Activities

When Rev. and Mrs. Shinei Shigefuji arrived to succeed Rev. Ishiura in 1978, the Sangha sponsored a welcome dinner at the Ports Restaurant. Later that year they established a *toban* (rotational shift) system for providing ushers for funerals at the church. Twelve teams of volunteers were allotted members selected somewhat geographically, each with two "co-captains". All teams came under the purview of the Welfare Chairman who would call each in succession when assistance was needed. Six volunteers also made themselves available to visit the ill and the hospitalized.

The Sangha on behalf of the church sold the parsonage on Fenwick Ave. in 1979 to generate money for the building of a possible addition to the Bathurst Street temple. They estimated the project would cost about $300,000 and take six months to complete.

The renovations were to consist of an addition to the side of the building between the library and the minister's office. It was to be an all-purpose room (mainly for meetings) named appropriately enough Ohtani Hall. The kitchen was also to be expanded and updated with modern conveniences from the

1963 renovations. The project was finished in 1985.

Like the Dana, the Sangha turned its attention to the youth of the church. They chaperoned and sponsored many activities of the various groups in the Youth Department. They encouraged the TBC Bussei Baseball Team, they accompanied the Jr. YBA and Boys and Girls Clubs on camping trips to Lumbini, and they led the Taruna on a canoe trip to Algonquin Park. They bought instruments for the youth orchestra. They also funded a seminar for the youth at Lumbini with Dr. Unno of California as leader. Finally, they sponsored a program to send interested youth (16 - 19 years old) to the Summer Program for Young People held at the Institute for Buddhist Studies in Berkeley, California.

In 1980 the Sangha celebrated its 30th Anniversary with a special service. President Tosh Hori offered *ohshoko* with all past presidents in attendance. Rev. Hiroshi Abiko from the San Jose Betsuin was the guest speaker.

For the next ten years the organization continued to oversee fund raising efforts, to work in the background at church events and services, and to support various church organizations to achieve their ends. They also attended and sponsored Eastern Dana/Sangha League Conferences as well as Eastern Buddhist League Conferences (including U.S. temples).

In 1990 the Sangha celebrated its 40th Anniversary which coincided with the TBC's 45th Anniversary. They held joint celebrations.

Future Concerns

At various times the Sangha pondered its own future. The organization itself remained fairly consistent throughout its existence. Most of the membership were former TYBS members; no younger members, however, came up from the Jr. YBA until the late 1980s, and only one at that. In 1986 the members considered forming a Junior and a Senior Sangha; in '87 the older members thought about moving up to the Gohokai; in 1988 they discussed the possibility of forming a younger men's group in the church. These suggestions, however, were not implemented.

At the same time, the Sangha turned its attention to the future of the church itself. In November 1980 they held an open discussion entitled "Concerns Over the Future of the

Toronto Buddhist Church". The conclusions of that forum were as follows:

- Buddhists comprise a minority among Japanese Canadians in Toronto and Ontario.
- survey indicates finances will increase, but activities by members of the Church will decrease.
- TBC budget is in the order of $100,000; deficit expected to be $45,000.
- pledges cover only 50% of the operation of the church.
- not enough young people attend church.
- need increased pledges from members.
- Church should not aim high for new or improved quarters.
- TBC's central location is good; *nisei* could contribute more to the Church.
- need to bring young people back to the Church.
- need more modern textbooks for Sunday School.
- facilities for youth needed but TBC has been backing off.[9]

From these discussions and the survey taken in 1984, the membership did not feel a change in location for the TBC was warranted. Still they needed to do something to ensure the future of the church.

In 1982 the Sangha and Dana went to Montreal to participate in the 35th Anniversary of the Montreal Buddhist Church. They again held discussions on the future. They concluded to seek ways to improve Sunday services to keep interest alive and to attract new members, to improve communications between the ministers and the congregation, to explore family religious education, and to relate Buddhist discourses to contemporary events and issues.

The effect of these conclusions became apparent among the youth of the church.

Youth Department

With the support of the various organizations above them in age, the Boys and Girls Clubs, the Taruna and the Jr. YBA activities flourished. With the numbers of youth swelling to a peak of 100 in 1979, the Dana and Sangha established and funded scholarships for post secondary education and travel. They also arranged canoe trips, field trips to various institutions and camp outings at Wasaga Beach. In 1979 the Sangha provided $1000 for a seminar on Buddhism at Camp Lumbini organized by the Jr. YBA for interested *sansei*. The church also arranged a talk in 1984 between the Gomonshu and the young members at the Prince Hotel in Don Mills.

Much of the planning and initiating of programs rested with Glen Kawaguchi, a *sansei* teacher and scout master. As Program Director for all youth groups in the church, he re-activated the Girls Club, with Yoshiko Tanaka, Sakae Goto and Shirley Kushida as advisors, and the Boys Club. Joyce Izukawa and Gloria Sumiya supervised the Taruna and Junior Y organizations. Kawaguchi also called on old friends to help as counsellors and activity monitors: Larry and Ken Matsuba, Karen Hikida, Geoffrey Ebisuzaki, Martin Kobayakawa and Yumiko Kobayashi.

Unfortunately by the mid 1980s, the Taruna and Jr. YBA members began losing interest in the church and turned their attention to the more immediate demands of education and career. The two groups fell dormant. An in-between group calling themselves the Mannaka flourished but for only a couple of years.

On the other hand, individuals like Mayumi Kumagai, Glen Kawaguchi, Larry Matsuba, Geoffrey Ebisuzaki and Pam Yoshida continued with or took on leadership roles with the younger members. The emphasis turned to sports to get the young involved. The Bussei Baseball team with distinctive powder blue uniforms was formed to play in a Japanese Canadian hardball league that came together every weekend at Greenwood Park in Toronto's eastend. In May 1979 the Bussei with 14 players stood solemnly as the Consul General of Japan threw out the first ball.

The Youth Department leaders rented the gymnasiums at Castle Frank High School and St. Alban's Boys Club to set up volleyball, ping pong and basketball games. They arranged ski trips, skating nights at City Hall and flag football tournaments.

They conducted educational tours of places like the Welland Canal, Hydro Electric Power Stations and museums. With the help of the BCC, the church offered an annual youth tour to Japan beginning in 1983. The focal point of the tour was the

Hongwanji and International Center in Kyoto, but the students also benefitted from a sightseeing component.

Perhaps the most ambitious group within the Youth Department was the Youth Orchestra started by Mary Ishiura in 1977 and led by Mayumi Kumagai. To buy instruments, the Dana donated 50% of the proceeds from their Bake Sale, the Fujinkai gave $1000 and the Sangha donated the profit from their annual Pancake Lunch to the Youth Department in 1979. The following year the Sangha gave a further $1000 for the orchestra and the Mary Ishiura Organ Training Fund.

Although the Youth Orchestra performed at various venues such as the 1977 EYBL Conference in Chicago and during Church events and services, the highlight must have been the tour to the Ekoji Temple in Springfield, Virginia. Approximately forty TBC members, led by Mayumi Kumagai and Gloria Sumiya, boarded the bus in April 1983 and headed for Rev. Tsuji's temple. Once there the orchestra performed while Pam Yoshida gave an interpretive reading at the temple.

The TBC Youth Orchestra stayed together until 1988. It began when a group of young would-be musicians from the Dharma School held a "jam session" in 1975 under the guidance of Mary Ishiura. The day proved so successful that the participants wanted more. Several more get-togethers took place before something more formal was organized.

In 1976 Mary Ishiura persuaded Mayumi Kumagai, a music teacher and church member, to head the new Japanese Youth Orchestra, a combination of traditional western instruments, the *koto* and *shakuhachi*. The Youth Department then decided to fully support the group in 1977. The orchestra became the TBC Youth Orchestra with 35 musicians.

By the 1980s, the orchestra started to lose members to universities or out-of-town work. The number was down to 13 by the last family service performance in May 1988.

Kumagai then took over the church choir until 1992 when a back injury prevented her from continuing. Dale Matsushige, a music teacher as well, took over the reins.

Today the Youth Department chairs are Elaine Wyatt and Bud Fujikawa. The trend too is the return of former members of the Taruna and Jr. Y and their young families.

I had fun in Sunday School and being a Taruna. I felt that I belonged. The friendships formed during those years will last throughout my life. I want the children to have the same experience.

Diane Mark (Tohana)
Taruna President 1971
sansei
TBC

The Dharma School

The departure of Rev. Ishiura also had implications for the Dharma School. Essentially, the responsibility for the school transferred from the minister to a supervisor selected by the Religion and Education Department from interested members of the congregation. The position was held by the following: Larry Matsuba 1978 - 1979, Dave Azuma 1979 - 1985, Gloria Sumiya 1985 -1988, Doreen Hamilton 1988 - 1991 and Elaine Takahashi 1991 - 1995.

At the end of his tenure, Larry Matsuba, a full time public school teacher, submitted a report that outlined several problems facing the Sunday School. He suggested the following:

1. The church must provide funds to hire professionals to teach Sunday School teachers methodology and technique.
2. The church must provide teachers with content like Buddhist history and philosophy.
3. The Sunday School administration should feature a Principal, Curriculum Advisor and Teacher Training Co-ordinator.

   The Principal will ensure there are enough teachers for the students. He will monitor student attendance. He will also handle school events like the picnic, year-end party and essay contests.

   The Curriculum Advisor will provide material to teachers about Buddhism. He will also design lesson plans and seek ways to keep Buddhist teachings as practical as possible.

   The Teacher Training Co-ordinator will provide pedagogy. He will seek out and make available reading material. He will also investigate college courses on teaching methods.[10]

Matsuba concluded "the solution lies in hiring a capable person to fulfil our needs. If the job is important then let us realize the need for a person who can devote the long hours required by the job. Let us consider hiring both principal and teachers."[11]

Dave Azuma became supervisor with the school suffering a fast decline in its number of students. Speculation on why centred on the fact that the *sansei* generation had delayed marriage and thus child rearing. Those who did marry and started a family moved to the suburbs too far from the church to commit themselves to Sunday School on a regular basis. The facilities were not conducive to learning. Quite often the classes were crowded into a corner while preparations were made for another church activity in the space provided for Sunday School. The rooms were usually used as storage space since the activities of the church had outgrown its building.

Azuma with the advice of Rev. Fujikawa approached the *shin ijusha* (new immigrant) parents at the Japanese Language School on Orde St. He encouraged them to send their children to Sunday School and many agreed. Twenty new students were more than half the enrolment.

He then turned to the innovations initiated by Mary Ishiura a decade before. He started a Parent-Teacher Association. Useful communication between the two groups took place on a monthly basis. One problem centred on the teachers' lack of experience. Several veteran teachers resigned and left a small group of young teachers who were themselves students during the week. Although the BCA Course of Studies proved adequate, the teachers simply lacked the wherewithal to teach. Azuma arranged through the TBC to send these teachers to seminars and workshops in the United States to improve their pedagogical skills. Each year two teachers attended these workshops.

Finally Dave Azuma introduced into the curriculum lessons on *taiko, ikebana, shodo, sumie* and Japanese cooking. He reasoned that through these endeavours the students would gain an appreciation of Japan and its cultural heritage. In turn the students would develop a well-rounded understanding of Jodo Shinshu Buddhism.

Gloria Sumiya as supervisor addressed the problem of space. The new kitchen installed in 1985 took away one Sunday School room. The kindergarten room was filled with unused tables, chairs and discarded boxes full of picnic and bazaar materials. The Dharma School books, records and teaching aids were scattered all over the church - in the library, office, work room and movable cupboards.

Sumiya first gathered staff. Added to the teachers during Dave Azuma's time were Yosh Tanaka, Myra Takasaki, Pamela Yoshida, Lisa Suyama, Kim Wakabayashi, Paul Aoki, Yoshiko Tanaka and Peggy Nishizeki. In the next two years, Karuna Sato, Kim Kushida, Kristine Tanaka, Elaine Takahashi and John Iwohara joined the staff.

Sumiya then started a monthly Dharma School newsletter which featured pupils' work and ministers' *Dharma* Talks. Finally, she led a work project to clean out the kindergarten room and paint it.

Teachers like John Iwohara, Elaine Takahashi, Yoshiko Tanaka and Pam Yoshida gave the church members reason to be optimistic about the future of the Dharma School. Iwohara, while studying for a Master's degree at Laurier University in Kitchener, travelled to Toronto to help the ministers every Sunday.

> He was young and got along well with the senior students, supervising their Youth Department activities. I asked the Church board if I could have him as one of the Dharma School teachers and was told - sure why not? He was the best thing that could have happened to the grade ten-and-up group. There were 12 or 13 in this group, and he had them in the palm of his hand. I would walk into their class sometimes and find them discussing religion heatedly and with obvious enjoyment. We were sorry that he could not stay another year. He obtained his degree, went to Japan, studied for several years and is now a *kaikyoshi*. He and Rev. Grant (Ikuta) were at Nishi Hongwanji at the same time.[12]

In 1988 the staff included Elaine Takahashi, Yosh Tanaka, Bud Fujikawa, Sari Fujikawa, Pamela Yoshida, Diane Hayashi, Sherri Nishimura, Richard Hayashi, Susan Takahashi, Kim Kushida and Marilyn Mori. Doreen Hamilton as supervisor worked out a new course of studies that included material from courses other than the BCA Curriculum. She felt the emphasis must return to religious education rather than cultural activities which apparently caused some tension within the teaching staff.

During Hamilton's tenure, the makeup of the students changed dramatically. The *shin ijusha* students had graduated. The *sansei* children dwindled to a few in number. However, two groups began emerging at the church: a small group of non-Japanese children and fourth generation children of mixed parentage. Slowly enrolment began to increase.

With Elaine Takahashi as supervisor in 1991, the Dharma School seemed to revitalize. In 1985 out of a student body of 50 (up to grade 10) only two students attended kindergarten. In the early 1990s, the number rose to fifteen who turned up on a regular basis. Much of the renewal can be accredited to the enthusiasm of Yoshiko Tanaka, the kindergarten teacher, and the advent of Rev. Grant Ikuta, the first *sansei* minister.

> Elaine showed much enthusiasm when she came on staff. She was and is a doer, with all kinds of ideas on how to make Buddhism enjoyable.[13]

In 1991 the TBC Dharma School Parent Group, replacing the old Sunday School PTA, became an integral part of the school. It has yet to be recognized by the Board of Directors but its value is obvious.

Activities

The Year End Party in appreciation of the Dharma School began in the '60s with the Dana women preparing the turkey dinners. With Dave Azuma as supervisor, the dinner was taken care of by the young parents of the Dharma School students. Gloria Sumiya decided to end the annual gathering since it was too close to Christmas (usually held the third Sunday in December). Instead, she and the staff chose to have a buffet lunch celebrating Bodhi Day. The children focused on Enlightenment and the Bodhi Tree. The luncheon continues to the present day.

The Dharma School always participated in the entertainment portion of the Keirokai and Hanamatsuri festivities. About one third of the Keirokai was devoted to a children's program. While the Jr. YBA and the Taruna helped with the formal concert on the eve of Hanamatsuri, the children performed after the Sunday service. The Hanamatsuri *Dharma* Program was discontinued in 1989.

One of the most popular annual events for the school was the Ho-onko sleepover (changed from Bodhi Day Eve in 1985).

> The pupils ate a *shojin* (vegetarian) supper and listened to stories of the young Shinran Shonin who entered the monastery at a tender age. Of course, the added attraction was a pizza snack at midnight and ghost stories and a McDonald breakfast the next morning.[14]

Over the years the church provided several workshops for Sunday School teachers. In 1983 Mrs. Etsuko Steimetz, a leader in the BCA's Dharma School Education system, conducted a workshop at the TBC. She eventually completely revised the BCA *Dharma* course that is still being used in Toronto. Bishop Murakami assisted in the 1986 two day workshop called the **Dharma Expo**. The next year Gloria Sumiya, Doreen Hamilton and Rev. Fujikawa attended a symposium in Washington, D.C., with a follow-up workshop in Toronto led by Rev. Fujikawa. The theme was the Six Paramitas (Perfections). Gloria Sumiya took charge of a Camp Lumbini retreat for teachers in the summer of 1988 where workshops on story telling and curriculum development were held. That same year John Iwohara, accompanied by thirteen senior students, visited five temples in Los Angeles and made several new friends among the American Buddhist youth. Finally in August 1993 the BCCWF (Women's Federation) and the TBCWF sponsored a Dharma School Workshop called **Enlightenment in the '90s**. Makoto Ikuta, retired B.C. educator, served as keynote speaker and Reverends Fujikawa and Grant Ikuta gave *Dharma* talks. Workshops given by Yosh Tanaka on story telling, Joyce Izukawa on lesson enhancement, and Elaine Takahashi on follow-up lessons proved invaluable for teachers new and experienced alike. Dale Matsushige led participants in a music workshop. Unfortunately, a familiar problem made itself apparent.

> The Workshop was a success but it brought one serious problem to the fore. We were unsuccessful in sparking interest in the younger generation. Over half the participants were TBC, Dana or Sangha members. Included in this group were two Dana members from

> Montreal and four from Hamilton. While we deeply appreciate the warm support from these people, we realize there is a problem we cannot overlook, and the TBCWF will endeavour to work closely with the minister and Religious Department to help address this situation.[15]

As an interesting sidelight to the Dharma School operations, the TBC in 1993 began two projects to attract young parents and seniors back to the church. A monthly Adult Study Group, led by Rev. Grant Ikuta and Dennis Madokoro, held discussions on current issues, aspects of Buddhism and religion in daily life. The second attraction was a series of seminars organized by Dr. Dennis Izukawa and given by several young professionals about various topics of interest: tax tips, estate planning and medical advice.

Religious Department

Beginning in 1963 the Religious Department provided leadership in spiritual matters and the manpower in staging services. By the 1970s the department also took care of the education of the young.

The committee led by Tak Yoshida assigned usher and chair duties to various volunteers, mostly from the Sangha, for morning services and funerals. They also continued the Lay Leaders Training Program.

In 1979 the Ministerial Association attempted to standardize funeral service procedures for all temples in Canada. The TBC Religious Department carried out the recommendations in February 1980.

In 1983 the department enlisted Rev. Fujikawa's help in importing family *butsudan* so that the congregation had the opportunity of obtaining one for their households. The program was very successful.

The Religious Dept. organized a *Chigo Gyoretsu* (Children's Procession) in order to celebrate the 40th Anniversary of the TBC. Other groups involved included the Dana, Sangha, Youth Dept. and Dharma School. The committee asked the Buddhist Churches in Vancouver and New York to lend them the elaborate ceremonial costumes for the children.[16] On the 29th of September 26 girls and 12 boys gathered at the TBC before following the ministers along Barton Avenue, up Bathurst, across the street at Wells, south on Bathurst and back to the Church. The parade then circled the altar inside and proceeded downstairs. Rev. K. Tsuji acted as guest minister.[17]

Church Leadership

As stated earlier, the ministry suffered from a lack of consistency. Rev. Shigefuji, Rev. Moriki and Rev. Handa resigned for health reasons. Rev. Tsunoda retired. Reverends Tsunoda and Murakami became Bishops during their stay in Toronto and thus performed their duties on a part-time basis. Several took time off to continue their studies. Rev. Fukashi Nakatsumi, a long term part time minister, decided for personal reasons to leave for Japan in late 1994.

Doreen Hamilton started her studies to become an ordained Jodo Shinshu minister in September 1987. With the help of FAMAC, she came under the tutelage of Bishop Murakami, Rev. Fujikawa and Toronto Buddhist Church leaders for three years. During her studies, she demonstrated a "sincerity of approach to Shin Buddhism, consistent effort put forth to deepen her faith and understanding, simple clarity of her presentation of Buddhism, and appropriate everyday examples to demonstrate Buddhist truths to the lay audience."[18]

Accordingly, Bishop Murakami declared her a ***kaikyoshi-ho*** (Assistant Associate Minister) to the TBC in 1990. The move to full ***kaikyoshi*** (Missionary Minister) status proved to be problematic. Unable to speak Japanese, Hamilton could not receive the full ***kyoshi - kyoshu*** (Missionary training) at the Hongwanji. There is a provision to train "foreign" ministers, but a minimum of five candidates is required. Unfortunately, such an avenue was closed to her because of that minimum.

In the meantime she participated in the TBC's Dharma School as supervisor, assisted and at times led Dana and Fujinkai activities, became involved in community outreach, assisted in various services, and created media items for the church. In 1991 Doreen Hamilton resigned as Assistant to the Minister of the TBC and applied for the Masters of Jodo Shinshu program at the Institute of Buddhist Studies in California. She was accepted but did not complete one year before returning to Toronto in June 1992 to pick up and continue her life there. For a time, she held two Jodo Shinshu evening study groups a week, one in Hamilton and one in Toronto. In the final analysis, she contributed a great deal to the TBC and was a great aid to the ministers of the church.

After Rev Ishiura, only Rev. Orai Fujikawa spent any length of time at the Toronto Buddhist Church as resident minister. The lay leadership remained strong, as exemplified by Tak Yoshida, and the many termed presidency of Kunio Suyama maintained a certain stability within the organizational hierarchy. Still, the ministry was the linchpin of the church. The mantle was passed to Rev. Grant Ikuta in 1994 when Rev. Fujikawa left after fourteen years of service in the Toronto area.

Rev. Fujikawa began life in Kisa, Hiroshima-ken on Oct. 30, 1941. His education at the Osaka University of Foreign Language and Ryukoku University led to his ordination and eventual assignment to Canada in March 1968. At first, he served the Buddhist Churches of Alberta. In 1970 he transferred to the Okanagan Buddhist Churches. After many fruitful years propagating Jodo Shinshu Buddhism, he left the Kelowna Buddhist Church and headed for Toronto in January 1980.

His contribution to the church was enormous. He offered a steadying force within the infrastructure. Not only did he serve the Toronto, Montreal and Hamilton Churches, he served as Buddhist chaplain at the University of Toronto (as did Doreen Hamilton) and at various Toronto area hospitals. Every organization within the church as well approached him for advice and participation. He never declined even though at times the stress was high.

> Handa Sensei and family took a leave of absence and left Toronto in February, so this left me alone as a full time minister in the Eastern District. Also the arrival of Rev. Grant was delayed and the Bishop requested I stay here. Thanks to the help of Nakatsumi Sensei and Mr. Tak Yoshida I was able to survive 'till October. I only found out recently that my blood pressure was at the borderline according to my family doctor.[19]

Late 1991 Rev. Orai (as he liked to be called) considered it was time to move on in his career. Although he and his wife enjoyed life in Toronto and their church, he approached Bishop Murakami for a transfer. Rev. Orai felt the timing was right since a *sansei* minister was assigned to Toronto in 1992.

Grant Masami Ikuta was born Sept. 1, 1964 in Vancouver. He

spent his childhood and youth in Kyoto and Calgary. He achieved his B.Sc. at the University of Alberta before going to Japan to study Japanese at the Ryukoku University. He then finished his *kyoshi* training at the Chuo Bukkyo Gakuin in May 1990. Finally, Rev. Grant Ikuta received his Master's degree in Theology from Ryukoku University in 1992. He came to Toronto as the first third generation Japanese Canadian Buddhist minister.

After much discussion, Bishop Matsubayashi granted Rev. Fujikawa's request to leave Toronto. In September 1994, he and his wife departed for Vancouver and Rev. Yasuo Izumi, long time minister of the Vancouver Buddhist Church, came as a replacement. Rev. Izumi left behind his wife Sachi and five children who preferred Vancouver's familiarity to Toronto's urban sprawl.

Rev. Izumi was born in Kawasaki City near Tokyo in 1944. He received his education from Taisho University, Ryukoku University and the Tokyo Bukkyo Academy. He was ordained *kaikyoshi* in 1969. After some orientation in Toronto by Bishop Ishiura, Rev. Izumi spent 1970 to 1977 at the Lethbridge Buddhist Church. In 1977 he transferred to the Vancouver Buddhist Church.

In Toronto, he states categorically his purpose was to propagate Buddhism and not to play the politician. Still he hopes for mutual co-operation with church members.

> As a matter of interest, many years ago before I became a minister, I lived in Toronto just for a short period perhaps about a month and a half. What was I doing then? I was studying English and helping with Sunday services at the TBC while working as a garden helper. I have fond memories of the time I beat a drum at Bon Odori. It was at that time that then Bishop Ishiura encouraged me to become a minister in Canada. Looking back on those days I cannot help but be amazed at the inconceivability of INNEN (causes and conditions).
>
> Let us work together, learn together and share our teaching with others.[20]

Epilogue

Chapter 23

Bukkyo Tozen: Epilogue

A *nisei* in Vancouver lamented recently that he was one of only a few who worked to maintain the temple. The young people simply were not coming out to help. Another *nisei* in Kelowna confessed that the *nisei* kept up the temple owing to an obligation to their parents, the *issei*. Unfortunately, the *sansei* felt no such obligation. In Toronto the membership, largely *nisei*, constantly fret about the future. Their children will not or cannot take part actively in church activities.

Mark R. Mullins in his 1988 paper sees the problem partially lying within the ministry.

> These churches have had difficulty securing qualified [bilingual] religious leaders to work with the acculturated generations. Interviews with priests and lay leaders across Canada, as well as responses to the organizational questionnaire regarding present and future problems, reveal that one of the most pressing concerns remains that of finding religious professionals to serve their congregations.[1]

He further sees the *sansei* and their unwillingness to accept the seemingly alien culture that Buddhism represents as reason enough for a pessimistic future.

> In addition to the language factor, *sansei* participation is discouraged by the "foreign-oriented" rituals which are central to the BCC.[2]

The *sansei*, Mullins opines, cannot retain Buddhism as their religion for geographical concerns (they live too far away) and for "exogamous" marriages. Once they outmarry, the family "will tend to discourage affiliation and active participation in an ethnic church."[3]

Sansei also may not be involved in the Buddhist church because as a whole the BCC had moved away from social relevancy. The Buddhist Church, once the centre of Japanese Canadian activity, now tends, consciously and adamantly, to avoid community issues. In 1983 the BCC advised all temples in Canada to abstain from involvement in the "Redress Action" movement, the single most important issue facing the Japanese Canadian community since the war, quite a different attitude from the "Golden Age" of the Toronto Buddhist Church when Rev. Newton and Mary Ishiura encouraged every organization to be "involved". Fortunately, individuals like Harry and Hedy Yonekura of the TBC carried on in that spirit and supported wholeheartedly the call for compensation for wartime incarceration and exile.

In general, the ministers maintain a *laissez faire* attitude. If in the end temples close and congregations disappear then so be it, Jodo Shinshu will flourish elsewhere. By and large, they agree, the church and its members should concentrate on the spiritual aspects of Buddhism. Rev. Grant Ikuta of the TBC believes members see involvement with the church on a par with their many other social activities. Religion is much more than merely another social organism revolving around the self; it is the hub of living itself. Therefore Toronto's Rev. Izumi feels his purpose is to share his knowledge of Jodo Shinshu Buddhism with others who demonstrate a genuine interest.

Despite the decline in community involvement, both the Toronto and Vancouver Churches are enjoying a slight if fragile return of younger members, especially in the Dharma Schools. Rev. Ikuta believes a careful nurturing of those members will yield a hopeful future but their presence is "fragile" at best owing to the various distractions in society today.

On the other hand, Mullins and the late Dr. Richard Robinson added another spin on the future of Canadian Buddhism. Both advised examining the true nature of Buddhism before any planning takes place.

As we enter the second and decisive half-century, we

> would do well to pause and consider the lessons of our history. The first lesson is that a purely defensive attitude will not preserve a faith. In the dynamic present-day world, only a growing, onward-going spirit can survive. Gone are the days when a temple in a quiet village can be handed down from father to son throughout the centuries. The old ways are gone or going, and we must find new words for the old message, and new ears to hear it...
>
> We live in an international age, and we have the honor to profess a universal religion.[4]

In any event, the BCC and concomitant churches stand at a crossroads. There are definite reasons to be pessimistic for the future of the church. Mullins finally recommends a "succession of goals".

> If Buddhist churches de-ethnicize their religious tradition and broaden their sense of relevance, organizational survival is a possibility.[5]

The church may also thrive if it again heeds the Ishiuras' entreaty to "get involved" and becomes the centre of a community, perhaps not one that is homogeneously Japanese Canadian but one that is largely but not exclusively Asian Canadian. Certainly, the Toronto Buddhist Church finds strength and commonality in the annual WESAK celebrations, a joining of all Buddhist organizations in the Toronto area to commemorate the birth of the Buddha. The programme includes musical performances, cultural dances and food from the East Asian representatives.

As it has demonstrated throughout its history, the Jodo Shinshu Buddhist Church in Canada will no doubt prosper through the perseverance of the congregation, sustained by an uncompromising faith in the Buddha *Dharma*.

Afterword

Hoshu Y. Matsubayashi, Ed.D.
Bishop
Buddhist Churches of Canada

The Essentials of Jodo Shinshu Buddhism

Hoshu Y. Matsubayashi, Ed.D.
Bishop
Buddhist Churches of Canada

I. The Title and the Founder

Jodo Shinshu, which is a branch of Mahayana Buddhism, was founded by Shinran (1173 - 1263) and is one of the largest Buddhist denominations in Japan today. The title of the denomination, "Jodo Shinshu," which means "True Pure Land," was coined by Shinran in his writings, and is often abridged as "Shinshu."[1]

Although Shinran was the first to use the words "Jodo Shinshu" in his writings, he never claimed himself to be the founder of the new denomination. In one of the poems in his **Koso Wasan**, he stated:

Our teacher Genku (Honen) appeared
Through the power of the Light of Wisdom,
And revealing the true Pure Land way (Jodo Shinshu),
He taught the selected Primal Vow.[2]

In this way, Shinran respected and considered Honen to be the founder of true Pure Land Buddhism. Yet the conditions for being an independent denomination were provided fully by Shinran. Those conditions were its title, its doctrinal characteristics, and the selection of the sutras and commentaries upon which the denomination depends. Shinran provided the above conditions as follows:

1. The Title, "Jodo Shinshu"
2. The Doctrinal Characteristics Revealed in the Theory of the Pair and Four Divisions
3. The Three Pure Land Sutras and the Selection of Seven Masters and their Commentaries

II. The Three Pure Land Sutras

The doctrine of Jodo Shinshu depends on the Three Pure Land Sutras which Honen originally selected. These sutras expound upon Amida Buddha and his land, and how to attain the Buddhahood. They are:

Muryojukyo (Larger Sukhavativyuha Sutra)

Kanmuryojukyo (Amitayurdhyana Sutra)

Amidakyo (Smaller Sukhavativyuha Sutra)

Shinran interpreted the Three Pure Land Sutras in two ways. First, he considered the **Larger Sutra** to be the only true teaching of Shakyamuni Buddha (c. 560 - 480), the founder of Buddhism, and states in his main writing, **Kyogyoshinsho,** that "to reveal the true teaching: It is the **Larger Sutra** of Immeasurable Life... Thus, to teach the Tathagata's Primal Vow is the true intent of the sutra; the Name of the Buddha is its essence."[3] Amida Buddha made 48 Vows in the **Larger Sutra**. Shinran explained that the essence of the **Larger Sutra** is embodied in the 18th (Primal) Vow, the **Kangyo** (an abridgment of the **Kanmuryojukyo**) expounds upon the 19th Vow, and the **Amidakyo** expounds upon the essence of the 20th Vow. Thus, he considered the **Larger Sutra** to be the true teaching, and that the others describe the means of understanding the true teaching.

Second, Shinran taught that all three of the Pure Land sutras expound on the true essence of Shakyamuni Buddha's teaching. The **Larger Sutra** teaches the truth of *dharma*, the **Kangyo** teaches the truth of human nature, and the **Amidakyo** describes *dharma*, human nature, and the praises of the Amida Buddha by various other Buddhas. Therefore, he considered that all three of the Pure Land Sutras teach the truth of Shakyamuni Buddha.

III. Seven Pure Land Masters

From India, China, and Japan, Shinran selected seven Pure Land masters and their commentaries on Amida Buddha and his Pure Land. With their instructions and guidance, he formulated the doctrine and established Jodo Shinshu. The seven masters are as follows:

India: Nagarjuna (Ryuju, c. 150-250)
Vasubandhu (Seshin or Tenjin, c. 320-400)

China: T'an-luan (Donran, 476-542)
Tao-ch'o (Doshaku, 562-645)
Shan-tao (Zendo, 613-681)

Japan: Genshin (942-1017)
Honen (1133-1212)

In addition, Prince Shotoku (574-622), who is considered to be the founder of Japanese Buddhism, was a great influence upon Shinran. He praised Prince Shotoku in "Kotaishi Shotoku hosan" (Hymns in Praise of Prince Shotoku) in his writing, **Shozomatsu wasan** (Hymns of the Dharma-Age).

IV. Shinran's Writings

The following are the important writings of Shinran that are available in English translation. The writings are listed chronologically and Shinran's age at the time of writing is given in parentheses.

1224 (52) **Ken jodo shinjitsu kyo gyo sho monrui** (A Collection of Passages Revealing the True Teaching, Practice and Realization of the Pure Land Way) This is the main writing of Shinran and is commonly called **Kyogyoshinsho**

1248 (76) **Jodo wasan** (Hymns on the Pure Land)
Koso wasan (Hymns on the Masters)

1251 (79) **Mattosho** (Lamp for the Latter Age: Letters of Shinran) The earliest letter is dated in 1251.

1255 (83) **Jodo monrui jusho** (Passages on the Pure Land Way)
Songo shinzo meimon (Notes on the Inscriptions on Sacred Scrolls)

1257 (85) **Ichinen tanen mon-i** (Notes on Once-calling and Many-calling)

Yuishinsho mon-i (Notes on 'The Essentials of Faith Alone')

1258 (86) **Shozomatsu wasan** (Hymns on the Right, Semblance and Last Dharma-Ages)

Writings of the Third Monshu Kakunyo (1270-1351), the Eighth Monshu Rennyo (1415-1499), Zonkaku (1290-1373), the **Tannisho**, and the **Anjin ketsujosho** are also important Jodo Shinshu scriptures.

V. The Doctrine of Jodo Shinshu

In order to be recognized as an independent denomination, a denomination has to declare its unique doctrinal characteristics. The unique characteristics of Jodo Shinshu can be traced back to the teachings of the seven masters and are of two types. The first type was originally presented by Nagarjuna in his writing, "Igyohon" (Chapter of Easy Practice). He categorized Buddhism into two paths; one is a difficult path, like walking on land, and other is an easy path, like traveling by boat. In the **Ojoronchu** (Commentary on Vasubandhu's Treatise on the Pure Land), T'an-luan expanded upon Nagarjuna's concepts of the Difficult and Easy Paths with his ideas of Self Power and Other Power. He states that to become the Buddha with one's own power is difficult, but to attain the Buddhahood with the Other/Buddha's Power is easy.

Tao-ch'o described the two divisions of Nagarjuna and T'an-luan as the Gate of Holy and the Gate of Pure Land. The time since Shakyamuni Buddha's passing has been divided into three periods: the Right Dharma period (the first 500 years), the Semblance Dharma period (the next 500 years), and the Last Dharma period (the next 10,000 years). In the **Anrakushu** (Passages on the Land of Peaceful Happiness), Tao-ch'o acknowledged that he was living in the Last Dharma period and that in this period the only way for ordinary people to become a Buddha was through the Gate of the Pure Land, using Buddha's Power. Jodo Shinshu falls in this category.

Shinran also adopted another type of doctrinal clarification that was presented by Shan-tao. In "Gengibun" in the **Kangyo-sho** (Commentary on the **Kangyo**), Shan-tao divided general Buddhism into two categories, the Sravaka (Hinayana) and the Bodhisattva (Mahayana). Shan-tao then divided Mahayana Buddhism into two more categories, the teachings of sudden and gradual enlightenment. Following Shan-tao's clarification, Shinran presented his doctrinal clarification of the Pair and Four Divisions (*Niso Shiju*).

Like Shan-tao, Shinran divided all the teachings of Shakyamuni Buddha into the Pair: Hinayana and Mahayana Buddhism. He further divided Hinayana into *pratyeka* (a self-enlightened Buddha) and *sravaka* (those who listen to the Buddha's teaching and attain enlightenment), and he divided Mahayana into *tongyo* (sudden enlightenment) and *zenkyo* (gradual enlightenment), thus creating the Four Divisions. Shinran explained that Jodo Shinshu belongs to the teaching of the sudden enlightenment in Mahayana Buddhism.

In Shinran's clarification, he also explained how easy it is for the followers of the Gate of Pure Land to become a Buddha with Amida's

Power with the concept of "crosswise leap." This is in contrast to the Self Power tradition, whose followers believe in the concept of "lengthwise" and "going around." He interpreted the passage of the **Larger Sutra** in the **Songoshinzomeimon** and showed the principle of absolute Other Power teaching as follows:

> One sunders crosswise the five evil courses and the evil courses close naturally (*jinen*). Crosswise: Laterally or transcendentally. This means that because a person entrusts himself to the power of the Tathagata's Vow -- this is the absence of calculation on the part of the practicer -- he cuts off and abandons the evil courses and becomes free of the four modes of birth naturally, by *jinen*; it signifies Other Power. This is the meaning of "crosswise leap." "Crosswise" is used in contrast with lengthwise, "leap" in contrast with going around. "Lengthwise" and "going around" characterize the self-power Path of Sages; the crosswise leap is the fundamental intent of the true teaching of Other Power.[4]

Shinran found the principle of absolute Other Power in "crosswise leap." The sense of suddenness points to the instantaneous aspect of salvation for Shinran, and he saw in it the operation of Amida's Primal Vow.[5] He gave a conclusive statement as to how Jodo Shinshu is superior to other teachings in the final volume of the **Kyogyoshinsho**.

> Among all the teachings that Shakyamuni Buddha taught during his lifetime, those that teach attaining sacred wisdom and realizing the fruit in this world are called the Path of Sages. They are termed the path of difficult practice... Attaining sacred wisdom and realizing the fruit in the Pure Land of peace is called the Pure Land path. It is termed the path of easy practice... "Transcending crosswise" refers to being mindful of the Primal Vow and becoming free of the mind of self-power; this is termed "Other Power of transcending crosswise." It is the true essence [of the Pure Land way].[6]

VI. Birth into the Pure Land by Amida's Primal Vow

In general Buddhism, the purpose of the Buddhist practice is to attain the state of enlightenment by self power. However, Pure Land teaches that sentient beings born into the Pure Land with the power of the Amida's Primal Vow attain the Buddhahood. The development of the Pure Land teaching can be traced in the historical development of the three types of learning in Buddhism: precept (*sila*), meditation (*samadhi*), and wisdom (*prajna*).

The practicing of the precepts, meditating, and gaining of wisdom form a cycle of learning. The Pure Land teaching developed primarily from *prajna*, the learning of wisdom. The method of obtaining wisdom also has three steps: hearing, thinking, and practicing. We listen to the teaching, think about what was heard, and practice the teaching in our daily lives. This is the process of obtaining wisdom.

The Eightfold Path is one of the basic teachings of Shakyamuni

Buddha. It is also practiced closely together with the three types of learning. *Right View* teaches the learning of wisdom; *Right Thought* (mind karma), *Right Speech* (verbal karma), *Right Conduct* (physical karma) and *Right Livelihood* (physical, verbal, and mind karmas) teach the learning of precept; *Right Effort* teaches all three types of learning; *Right Mindfulness* and *Right Meditation* teach the learning of meditation.

Practicing the three types of learning, we gradually realize the difficulty of practicing precept and meditation thoroughly. From this difficulty arose Mahayana Buddhism to provide more guidance in the path to enlightenment. Mahayana means "large vehicle," and Mahayana Buddhism is the teaching that can carry more people to the state of enlightenment. The Bodhisattva ideal became the important characteristic in Mahayana Buddhism, because Bodhisattva works primarily for others as one's own benefit. The Bodhisattva Dharmakara became Amida Buddha by fulfilling 48 Vows for the salvation of all sentient beings. Then, Amida Buddha established his Pure Land, where sentient beings are born to become the Buddha.

Jodo Shinshu is the teaching for ordinary people who realize the limitation of their capabilities to attain enlightenment and aspire for birth into the Pure Land to become the Buddha with the Other Power of Amida's Primal Vow.

VII. On the Tathagata, the Buddha

The term *Tathagata* can be defined two ways: *tatha-agata*, which means "to come from suchness", or *tatha-gata*, which means "to have gone to suchness." In either case *Tathagata* generally refers to "one who was awakened to the truth of suchness." In Jodo Shinshu, the term *Tathagata* is used as a synonym for "Buddha," and Shinran often used Amida Tathagata or Shakyamuni Tathagata instead of Amida Buddha or Shakyamuni Buddha in his writings. The doctrine of the *Tathagata* became one of the principal teachings in Jodo Shinshu because the absolute power of Amida Tathagata/Buddha is the essence of the Primal Vow.

The expression of the absolute and perfect *Tathagata* is often described in negative forms. For example, Shinran states that the *Tathagata* of Inconceivable Light (*Fukashigiko Nyorai*) is beyond praise (*fukasho*), inexplicable (*fukasetsu*), and inconceivable (*fukashigi*), etc. On the other hand, Shinran attributed Amida Tathagata/Buddha with a personality and called it the "Vow Power," "great compassionate mind," and "one who has wisdom." Thus, Shinran's view on Amida Tathagata/Buddha has two aspects: negative expressions and personification.

The Buddha has been divided into three bodies: the essential body (*dharma-kaya, hosshin*), the fulfilled body (*sambhoga-kaya, hojin*), and the accommodated body (*nirmana-kaya, ojin*). The *dharma* body of the Buddha is colorless and formless. Amida Tathagata/Buddha is the fulfilled body and Shinran interpreted that Amida Tathagata/Buddha is the dharma-body as compassionate means and Shakyamuni

Tathagata/Buddha is the accommodated body.

In order to provide a historical perspective on Amida Buddha, Shinran expounded that the attainment of Buddhahood was in the infinite past and in order to explain the perfection of Amida Buddha in quality, Shinran expounded Amida Buddha as the dharma-body as compassionate means.

The **Larger** and **Amida Sutras** state that Amida Buddha attained Buddhahood ten kalpas ago. However, since Amida Buddha is perfection in time, Shinran expounded that Amida Buddha attained Buddhahood countless ages ago in the **Jodo Wasan** as follows:

It is taught that ten kalpas have now passed
Since Amida attained Buddhahood;
But he seems a Buddha more ancient
Than kalpas countless particles.[7]

Amida, who attained Buddhahood in the infinite past,
Full of compassion for foolish beings of the five defilements,
Took the form of Shakyamuni Buddha
And Appeared in Gaya.[8]

Shinran's interpretation of Amida Buddha as having attained Buddhahood in the infinite past assured that Amida Buddha was perfect historically. His explanation of Amida Buddha as dharma-body as compassionate means assured the perfection of Amida Tathagata/Buddha in quality. His clear statement on dharma-body as suchness and the manifestation of dharma-body as compassionate means appeared in his **Notes on 'Essentials of Faith Alone'** as follows:

> There are two kinds of dharmakaya in regard to the Buddha. The first is called dharma-body as suchness and the second, dharma-body as compassionate means. Dharma-body as suchness has neither color nor form; thus, the mind cannot grasp it nor words describe it. From this oneness form was manifested; this form is called dharma-body as compassionate means.[9]

On the manifestation of dharma-body as compassionate means, Shinran expounded that Bodhisattva Dharmakara, who became Amida Buddha, was not a Bodhisattva for the first time to attain Buddhahood, but he was a Bodhisattva who manifested from dharma-body as suchness in order to establish the 48 Vows for the salvation of sentient beings. He describes why Bodhisattva Dharmakara manifested from dharma-body as suchness (oneness) as follows:

> From this treasure ocean of oneness form was manifested, taking the name of Bodhisattva Dharmakara, who, through establishing the unhindered Vow as the cause, became Amida Buddha. For this reason Amida is the "Tathagata of fulfilled body." He has been called "Buddha of unhindered light filling the ten quarters." This Tathagata is also known as Namu-fukashigiko-butsu (Namu-Buddha of inconceivable light) and is the "dharmakaya as compassionate means."

> "Compassionate means" refers to manifesting form, revealing a name, and making itself known to sentient beings. It refers to Amida Buddha.[10]

Since dharma-body is inconceivable for sentient beings, dharma-body as compassionate means manifested as a form and its name. Shinran expounds on the relation between these two dimensions of dharma-body by quoting the passage from T'an-luan's **Ojoronchu** (Commentary on Vasubandhu's Treatise on the Pure Land):

> [A]ll Buddhas and bodhisattvas have dharma-bodies of two dimensions: dharma-body as suchness and dharma-body as compassionate means. Dharma-body as compassionate means arises from dharma-body as suchness, and dharma-body as suchness emerges out of dharma-body as compassionate means. These two dimensions of dharma-body differ but are not separable; they are one but cannot be regarded as identical.[11]

Shinran expounded that Amida Buddha, dharma-body as compassionate means, manifested from dharma-body as suchness and these two are not separate, the quality of Amida Buddha was one with dharma-body as suchness.

In Sanskrit, Amida Buddha has two meanings, *Amitabha* (infinite light) and *Amitayus* (infinite life). Therefore, the meaning of Amida Buddha is the Buddha of Infinite Light and Life. The **Larger Sutra** characterizes Amida Buddha with two Vows; 12th Vow of infinite light and 13th Vow of infinite life. In regards to the infinite light, Shinran states:

> Reverently contemplating the true Buddha and the true land, I find that the Buddha is the Tathagata of inconceivable light and that the land also is the land of immeasurable light. Because they have arisen through the fulfillment of Vows of great compassion, they are called true fulfilled Buddha and land.[12]

Shinran stated that the true Buddha is the Tathagata of inconceivable light and the true Pure Land of the Buddha is the land of immeasurable light. Both Buddha and Pure Land are described with inconceivable and infinite light. Amida Buddha's infinite life and light are bases for the activities of Amida's great compassion and wisdom.

VIII. On Human Nature

The analysis of human nature in Jodo Shinshu is very serious and profound. Shinran established his thought on human nature based on his keen observations and deep reflection. He wrote:

> Ordinary people...we are full of ignorance and blind passion. Our desires are countless, and anger, wrath, jealousy, and envy are overwhelming, arising without pause; to the very last moment of life they do not cease, or disappear, or exhaust themselves.[13]

Among the seven masters of Jodo Shinshu, we find the early masters are not so serious in their views of human nature, but fourth master Tao-ch'o did feel that human nature had degraded in the Last Dharma period. Therefore, he thought that ordinary people are not able to become the Buddha unless they rely on Amida Buddha's Primal Vow in Pure Land teaching.

Fifth master Shan-tao was praised by Shinran in the **Shoshin-ge** because "Shan-tao alone in his time clarified the Buddha's true intent."[14] Shinran quoted Shan-tao's two aspects of deep mind in his **Kyogyoshinsho**. Shan-tao first states the deep mind of human nature as follows:

> One is to believe deeply and decidedly that we are foolish beings of karmic evil caught in birth-and-death, ever sinking and ever wandering in transmigration from innumerable kalpas in the past, with never a condition that would lead to emancipation.[15]

Then, Shan-tao presented the second aspect of the deep mind of the dharma as the function of the compassionate heart of Amida Buddha as follows:

> The second is to believe deeply and decidedly that Amida Buddha's Forty-eight Vows grasp sentient beings, and that allowing ourselves to be carried by the power of the Vow without any doubt or apprehension, we will attain birth.[16]

Shan-tao expounded that Amida Buddha directed his compassion to sentient beings who are incapable of emancipation.

Shan-tao used a historical analysis to describe the incapability of sentient beings to attain Buddhahood from beginningless to future. In addition to Shan-tao's historical analysis, Shinran further extended his observation to all beings horizontally as follows:

> I find that all beings, an ocean of multitudes, have since the beginningless past down to this day--this very moment--been evil and defiled, completely lacking the mind of purity. They have been false and deceitful, completely lacking the mind of truth and reality.[17]

Then, Shinran, like Shan-tao, described the effects of Amida Buddha's compassion which extended to all living beings:

> Thus, when the Tathagata, in profound compassion for the ocean of all sentient beings in pain and affliction, performed bodhisattva practices for inconceivable millions of measureless kalpas... With this pure, true mind, the Tathagata brought to fulfillment the perfect, unhindered, inconceivable, indescribable, and inexplicable supreme virtues. The Tathagata gives this sincere mind to all living things...[18]

Amida Buddha's sincere mind takes as its essence his Name, Namo Amida Butsu. Shinran expounded that the source of our enlightenment is Amida Tathagata/Buddha's Primal Vow. He reflected on the five kalpas' contemplation of Bodhisattva Dharmakara and expressed his joy on the accomplishment of Amida's Primal Vow as follows:

> When I carefully consider the Vow which Amida brought forth after five kalpas contemplation, I find that it was only for me, Shinran, alone![19]

IX. The Directing of Virtue of Amida Buddha's Name, Namo Amida Butsu

One of the important teachings in Jodo Shinshu is the directing of virtue (*eko*) from Amida Buddha to sentient beings. This teaching is originated in the Bodhisattva practice which benefits others as one's own benefit. It is also a type of *dana* (offering), the first of the Six Paramitas (perfections).

Shinran describes the content of virtue that Amida Buddha directs to sentient beings in the following poem:

The directing of virtue embodied in Namu-amida-butsu
Is, in its benevolent working, vast and inconceivable;
Through the benefit of the directing of virtue for going forth,
We enter the directing of virtue for returning to this world.[20]

Amida Buddha directs his name, Namo Amida Butsu, to sentient beings for the attainment of enlightenment and also for the returning to this world. Shinran further expounds the directing of virtue in his **Kyogyoshinsho**:

> I see that Amida's directing of virtue to sentient beings has two aspects: the aspect for going forth to the Pure Land and the aspect for our return to this world. In the going forth, there is the true teaching, practice, shinjin, and realization.[21]

Thus, Namo Amida Butsu embodies the two aspects of going to the Pure Land and returning from the Pure Land. In the aspect for going forth, there are the true teaching (*kyo*), practice (*gyo*), faith (*shinjin*), and realization of enlightenment (*sho*). The main reason that Shinran wrote the **Kyogyoshinsho** was to explain this concept.

Amida's name, Namu-amida-butsu, is a Japanese transliteration of *Namo Amitabha* (Infinite Light) and *Namo Amitayus* (Infinite Life) in Sanskrit. *Namu* is a transliteration of *namas*. When a Sanskrit word which ends with "as" is followed by a word which begins with a vowel, "as" changes to "o." Therefore, Namu-amida-butsu is commonly spelled as Namo Amida Butsu in English. Shinran wrote:

> The word *namu* means "to take refuge." In the term "to take refuge" (*kimyo*), *ki* means "to arrive at"... *Myo* means "to act," "to invite"... Thus, *kimyo* is the command of the Primal Vow calling to and summoning us.[22]

Amida's name, Namo Amida Butsu, has also another two aspects. First, it embodies all good acts and all roots of virtue for going to the Pure Land and for returning to this world. Second, it is Amida's calling to sentient beings. Shinran expounds that receiving Amida's call is essential for the attainment of enlightenment. By quoting Shan-tao's commentary, Shinran further expounds on the meaning of Namo Amida Butsu:

> *Namu* means "to take refuge." It further signifies aspiring for birth and directing virtue. *Amida-butsu* is the practice. Because of this import, one necessarily attains birth.[23]

Amida's name, Namo Amida Butsu, manifests from Amida's Primal

Vow. In other words, when the power of Amida's Primal Vow works for us, it manifests itself as Amida's name, Namo Amida Butsu.

When we receive Namo Amida Butsu without any doubt or calculation, our wholehearted acceptance is called the awakening of faith, or *shinjin*, in Jodo Shinshu. When we are awakened to faith in Amida's Primal Vow, Amida's name, Namo Amida Butsu, appears verbally as our recitation (*shomyo*). Shinran states that the great practice in Jodo Shinshu is to recite Amida's name, Namo Amida Butsu. This great practice embodies all good acts and possesses all roots of virtue. Thus, Amida's name, Namo Amida Butsu, will certainly lead us to enlightenment.

X. The Awakening of Faith or Shinjin in Jodo Shinshu

Faith in Amida Buddha is the most important doctrine in Jodo Shinshu, because it is the right cause for the birth in the Pure Land. Shinran states in the **Kyogyoshinsho** that "reverently contemplating Amida's directing of virtue for our going forth, I find there is great *shinjin*."[24] This great *shinjin* means "faith" in Jodo Shinshu.

The **Larger Sutra** describes the Forty-Eight Vows and among them, the 18th Vow is the Primal Vow. The Primal Vow is the expression of Amida's compassion which he extends to all sentient beings. The 18th Vow states:

> If, when I attain Buddhahood, sentient beings in the ten directions who, with sincere mind, joyfully entrust themselves to me, aspire to be born in my land, and call my Name even ten times, should not be born there, may I not attain perfect enlightenment. Excluded are those who commit the five grave offenses and those who slander the right dharma.[25]

The 18th Vow states that three minds are necessary for birth in the Pure Land. These are "sincere mind," "entrusting," and "aspiring to be born." Faith will be awakened to one who, with sincere mind, entrusts himself to Amida Buddha and aspires to be born in the Pure Land. Those who are awakened to faith will stay in the definitely assured state (*shojoju*).

Honen, Shinran's teacher, followed the teaching of Shan-tao, whose teaching was based mainly on the **Kangyo**. Both Shan-tao and Honen also taught the importance of the three minds for birth into the Pure Land. However, they emphasized the recitation of Amida's name, because the 18th Vow states "call my Name even ten times" along with the three minds. Thus, Honen's teaching summarized that "the Nembutsu is the foundation of the right act to be born into the Pure Land." On the other hand, Shinran emphasized the importance of the three minds and taught that "faith is the right cause for birth into the Pure Land and recitation of Amida's name will be an expression of gratitude."

As the most significant characteristic in Jodo Shinshu, Shinran expounded that faith was obtained by the directing of virtue from Amida Buddha. Shinran reversed the traditional way to obtain faith in the Buddha and he expounded that Amida Buddha directs all his accumulated merit and virtue through the Nembutsu to all sentient beings for their birth into the Pure Land. He further expounded that the three minds in the 18th Vow would be embodied in one mind of faith, because the three minds of sincerity, trust, and aspiration to be born into the Pure Land are one mind without any doubt in Amida's Primal Vow. Shinran explained why three minds are one mind in his **Kyogyoshinsho**:

> We see clearly that sincere mind is the mind that is the seed of truth, reality, and sincerity; hence, it is completely untainted by the hindrance of doubt. Entrusting is the mind full of truth, reality, and sincerity...the mind of delight, joy, gladness, and happiness; hence, it is completely untainted by the hindrance of doubt. Aspiration for birth is the mind of wish, desire, awakening, and awareness...hence, it is completely untainted by the hindrance of doubt... We find that the three minds are the mind of truth and reality, free of any taint of falsity... This is called *shinjin* because it is untainted by the hindrance of doubt. Shinjin is the mind that is single. The mind that is single is shinjin that is true and real.[26]

Thus, Shinran stated that the three minds are the true mind, which is completely untainted by the hindrance of doubt, and the true mind is one mind of true faith.

Shinran also stated that the three minds are all Amida Buddha's property, because the three minds are not innate in sentient beings. Those three minds are only accomplished thoroughly by Amida Buddha. Therefore, Shinran stated that the three minds are directed from Amida Buddha as the directing of virtue. The sentient beings can only have one mind of faith with no hindrance of doubt that is free from any calculation.

The **Larger Sutra** describes that one mind of faith is directed from Amida Buddha as follows:

> All sentient beings, as they hear the Name, realize even one thought-moment of *shinjin* and joy, which is directed to them from Amida's sincere mind, and aspiring to be born in that land, they then attain birth and dwell in the stage of non-retrogression.[27]

Based on the above passage, Shinran explained that the way to obtain faith or *shinjin* is by listening. Those sentient beings who hear Amida's name, Namo Amida Butsu, are able to obtain *shinjin*. Therefore, "to hear" is an important practice in Jodo Shinshu. Hearing is just to receive what is given, with no calculation. The phrase "hearing of Amida's name, Namo Amida Butsu, is believing" is essential in Jodo Shinshu teaching.

XI. The Definitely Assured State (Shojoju)

Shinran expounds that one who is assured birth into the Pure Land by obtaining faith receives the benefit of being grasped by Amida's Vow Power and will be placed in the definitely assured state, which is the stage of non-retrogression. This is another unique characteristic of Jodo Shinshu Nembutsu life, because the sentient beings who obtained faith in Amida Buddha will be guaranteed the attainment of enlightenment in this life. This assurance will be given to the sentient beings at the moment of the awakening of faith. This was originally promised in the 11th Vow in the **Larger Sutra**:

> If, when I attain Buddhahood, humans and *devas* in my land should not dwell in the Definitely Assured State and unfailingly reach Nirvana, may I not attain perfect Enlightenment.[28]

The 11th Vow states that humans and devas (heavenly beings) who are born in the Pure Land reside in the definitely assured state. Shinran interpreted to mean that since those who obtained faith are assured birth into the Pure Land by Amida Buddha, they are already in the definitely assured state in their present lives.

Shinran's interpretation of the 11th Vow led to the peaceful mind and lifestyle of the Nembutsu followers in the accomplishment of attaining enlightenment in ordinary life (*heizei gojo*). This is the truth and vitality of the Nembutsu faith that Shinran expounded upon in Jodo Shinshu.

Shinran expressed his gratitude for the rare opportunity for having been able to listen to the teachings of Shakyamuni Buddha and the subsequent Pure Land masters in the preface of his **Kyogyoshinsho**:

> How joyous I am, Gutoku Shinran, disciple of Shakyamuni! Rare is it to come upon the sacred scriptures from the westward land of India and the commentaries of the masters of China and Japan, but now I have been able to encounter them. Rare is it to hear them, but already I have been able to hear.[29]

In the **Kyogyoshinsho**, Shinran provided the true Pure Land way to attain enlightenment for all sentient beings.

XII. Postscript

Buddhism was founded in India by Shakyamuni Buddha in the sixth century B.C., and was transmitted to Chinese soil in 67 A.D. Buddhism, then, was introduced to Japan through Korea in 552 A.D. Jodo Shinshu Buddhism was founded by Shinran in 1224, the year that he completed his main writing, **Kyogyoshinsho**. Jodo Shinshu has become one of the largest Buddhist denominations in present-day Japan.

Dr. Daisetz T. Suzuki states that "of all the developments Mahayana Buddhism has achieved in the Far East, the most remarkable one is the Shin teaching of the Pure Land school. It is remarkable chiefly for the reason that geographically its birth-place is Japan, and historically it is the latest evolution of Pure Land Mahayana, and therefore the highest point it has reached."[30]

After Japan opened its doors from the isolation policy in 1854, it was rapidly introduced to western culture and knowledge. With the beginning of the Meiji era in 1868, the Japanese gradually began to immigrate into new lands for new opportunities. Along with the

Japanese immigrants, Jodo Shinshu Buddhism was brought to Hawaii and the first Jodo Shinshu minister, Rev. Soryu Kagai, came to Hawaii to begin the propagation of Jodo Shinshu in 1889. Ten years later in 1899, with urgent requests from Jodo Shinshu followers, the Hongwanji in Kyoto dispatched two ministers, Rev. Shue Sonoda and Rev. Kakuryo Nishijima, to the mainland of the United States to begin the propagation.

In 1905, Rev. Senju Sasaki, the first official minister from the Hongwanji, arrived in Vancouver to begin the Jodo Shinshu propagation in Canada. Jodo Shinshu was propagated in the west coast of Canada, mainly in British Columbia and partially in Alberta, where the Japanese immigrants were living before World War II. With the outbreak of the war, Jodo Shinshu was forced to move into central Canada and gradually to the east coast along with the Japanese immigrants and their descendants. After the end of World War II in 1945, Jodo Shinshu spread to major cities across Canada. The Toronto Buddhist Church was established at the end of the war in 1945.

Buddhism has continually been moving eastward for the past 2,500 years. The Jodo Shinshu organization was also established in Brazil and other areas in South America after the end of World War II. Jodo Shinshu was also introduced into certain countries in Europe, Mexico, and Australia. Whether Jodo Shinshu Buddhism is flourishing or declining in Canada today is certainly of great concern for Jodo Shinshu Buddhists. But it is certain that the true teaching of Amida Buddha and his name, Namo Amida Butsu, will continue to spread for the peaceful welfare of all sentient beings.

The Essentials of Jodo Shinshu Buddhism: Bibliography

Bloom, Alfred. **Shinran's Gospel of Pure Grace**. Tucson: The University of Arizona Press, 1965.

Inagaki, Hisao. **The Three Pure Land Sutras: A Study and Translation**. Kyoto: Nagata Bunshodo, 1994.

Jodo Shinshu Seiten - Chushakuban - [Jodo Shinshu Scriptures - An Annotated Edition]. Kyoto: Hongwanji Shuppan-bu, 1988.

Kiritani, Junnin. **Shoshin-ge ni kiku** [Listen to the **Shoshin-ge**]. Tokyo: Kyoiku Shincho-sha, 1975.

Matsubayashi, Hoshu Y. **The Sukhavativyuha Sutra**. Union City: Samgha Press, 1985.

Shinshu Shogyo Zenshu [Collected Shinshu Scriptures]. 2 vols. Kyoto: Oyagi Kobundo, 1964-65.

Suzuki, Daisetz T. **A Miscellany on the Shin Teaching of Buddhism.** Kyoto: Shinshu Otaniha Shumusho, 1949.

The Tanni Sho [Notes Lamenting Differences]. Translated and Annotated by Ryosetsu Fujiwara. Kyoto: Ryukoku University, 1962.

Ueda, Yoshifumi. gen. ed. **Hymns of the Dharma-Ages** - A Translation of Shinran's **Shozomatsu wasan**. Kyoto: Hongwanji International Center, 1993.

Hymns of the Pure Land - A Translation of Shinran's **Jodo wasan**. Kyoto: Hongwanji International Center, 1991.

Hymns of the Pure Land Masters - A Translation of Shinran's **Koso wasan**. Kyoto: Hongwanji International Center, 1992.

Letters of Shinran - A Translation of **Mattosho**. Kyoto: Hongwanji International Center, 1978.

Notes on 'Essentials of Faith Alone' - A Translation of Shinran's **Yuishinsho-mon'i**. Kyoto: Hongwanji International Center, 1979.

Notes on the Inscriptions on Sacred Scrolls - A Translation of Shinran's **Songo shinzo meimon**. Kyoto: Hongwanji International Center, 1981.

Notes on Once-calling and Many-calling - A Translation of Shinran's **Ichinen-tanen mon'i**. Kyoto: Hongwanji International Center, 1980.

Passages on the Pure Land Way - A Translation of Shinran's **Jodo monrui jusho**. Kyoto: Hongwanji International Center, 1982.

The True Teaching, Practice and Realization of the Pure Land Way - A Translation of Shinran's **Kyogyoshinsho**. 4 vols. Kyoto: Hongwanji International Center, 1983-90.

Ueda, Yoshifumi and Hirota, Dennis. **Shinran**. Kyoto: Hongwanji International Center, 1989.

Yamaoka, Seigen H. **Jodo Shinshu**. San Francisco: Buddhist Churches of America, 1990.

History of Jodo Shinshu Buddhism in Canada

Footnotes, Bibliography, Appendix and Glossary

Footnotes

Introduction, Footnotes:

1. Publication Committee. Preface. **The History of Buddhist Churches of Canada**. (Vancouver BC: BCC, 1980). p. 1.

Chapter 1, Footnotes

1. Buddhist Churches of America, **Buddhist Churches of America:** *75 Year History - 1899-1974*, Volume One (Chicago: Nobart Inc., 1974), p. 29.
2. Japanese Buddhist sect founded by Saicho in the early 9th Century on Mount Hiei near Kyoto. Followers emphasize the importance of meditation.
3. Yoshiko Ohtani, **The Life of Eshinni:** *Wife of Shinran Shonin*, trans. Taitetsu Unno (Kyoto: Hompa Hongwanji, 1970), p. 93.
4. Buddhist Churches of America, p. 30.
5. ibid. p. 30
6. ibid. p. 30
7. Ohtani, p. 91.
8. Kannon (Avalokiteshvara): The Bodhisattva of Infinite Compassion (Mahayana Buddhism)

   Bodhisattva (Buddha): The spiritual ideal of Mahayana Buddhism. The Enlightened One who motivated by compassion decides to remain within the cycle of rebirth in order to further the liberation of all living beings.
9. Ohtani, p. 16.
10. ibid. p. 91
11. ibid. p. 15
12. The Hongwanji in Kyoto uses the term "Gomonshu" to denote the spiritual leader of Jodo Shinshu Buddhism. "Lord Abbot" is a westernization that is not officially recognized.
13. Ohtani, p. 12.
14. ibid. pp. 92 - 93
15. Rev. Gendo Nakai, **Shinran and His Religion of Pure Faith**, (Kyoto: Hyakka-en, 1961), p. 145 - 148.
16. George Sansom, **A History of Japan:** *1334 - 1615*, (Stanford CA: Stanford University Press, 1961), p. 283.

Chapter 2, Footnotes

1. Daikichi Irokawa, **The Culture of the Meiji Period**, Translated by Marius B. Jansen, (Princeton, NJ: Princeton University Press, 1985), p. 7.
2. Joseph M. Kitagawa, **Religion in Japanese History**, (New York: Columbia University Press, 1990), p. 184.
3. Mikiso Hane, **Modern Japan:** *A Historical Survey, Second Edition*, (Oxford: Westview Press, 1992), p. 107.

4. ibid. p. 107
5. Irokawa, p. 31.
6. ibid. pp. 31 - 32
7. ibid. p. 17
8. "The way of the Shinto gods."
9. Kitagawa, p. 201.
10. Literally meaning "Expel the Buddha, destroy the teaching."
11. Kitagawa, p. 202.
12. ibid. p. 226
13. ibid. p. 227
14. Ironically, the concept of *minken* inspired peasant protests in prefectures like Echizen against Western thought and influence.
15. Kitagawa, p. 229.
16. ibid. p. 230

Chapter 3, Footnotes

1. Louise H. Hunter, **Buddhism in Hawaii:** *Its Impact on a Yankee Community*, (Honolulu, HI: University of Hawaii Press, 1971), p. 45.
2. Literally meaning "Expel the Buddha, destroy the teaching."
3. Hunter, p. 45.
4. Buddhist Churches of America, **BCA 75 Year History - 1899-1974**, Volume One (Chicago: Nobart Inc., 1974), p. 43.
5. ibid. p. 44
6. Toyo Takata, **Nikkei Legacy:** *The Story of Japanese Canadians from Settlement to Today*, (Toronto, ON: NC Press, Ltd., 1983), p. 12.
7. Ken Adachi, **The Enemy That Never Was**, (Toronto, ON: McClelland and Stewart, Ltd., 1976), p. 9.
8. Takata, p. 16.
9. Literally meaning "Thinning out of the rice seedlings."
10. Adachi, p. 14.
11. ibid. p. 16
12. ibid. p. 16
13. ibid. p. 16
14. Takata, p. 13.
15. Adachi, p. 24.
16. ibid. p. 35
17. Takata, p. 57-58.
18. Ordained in the United States, Kaburagi was the first Japanese minister in Canada.
19. Norio Tamura, **Japanese Newspapers of Canada**, trans. Deirdre Tanaka - "Japanese Canadian Newspapers of the Pioneer Days", (Tokyo: PMC Publishing, 1991), p. 1.

20. Adachi, p. 111.
21. ibid. p. 112
22. Hunter, p. 44.
23. Adachi, p. 113.
24. Tamura, p. 2.

Chapter 4, Footnotes

1. Messenger (minister) of Tathagata for the Nembutsu Sangha and propagating the teaching of Jodo Shinshu.
2. One interpretation of the name is "1000 elephants".
3. Rev. Takamichi Takahatake, "The Identity of a Pioneer: Rev. Senju Sasaki, the First Buddhist Minister in Canada", **Canada Times**. Nov. 20, 1984.
4. Rev. LaVerne S. Sasaki, "Eshinni-Sama Shinobu Hoyo". Talk given on June 2, 1990 at the Ninth World Buddhist Women's Convention in Vancouver.
5. Literal translation: "Person in the rear", "person within the room", "protector of the temple".
6. Ken Adachi, **The Enemy That Never Was**, (Toronto, ON: McClelland and Stewart, Ltd., 1976), p. 65.
7. ibid. p. 73
8. ibid. p. 74
9. Takahatake, p. 4.
10. ibid. p. 4
11. ibid. p. 4
12. Toyo Takata, **Nikkei Legacy:** *The Story of Japanese Canadians from Settlement to Today*, (Toronto, ON: NC Press, Ltd., 1983), p. 51.
13. The "Heaps" Church is often referred to as the Albert Street Church because Franklin St. continues as Albert St. after the P.N.E. grounds.

Chapter 5, Footnotes

1. Natsume Soseki, **Kokoro**, trans. Edwin McClellan (Chicago: Regnery, 1967), p. 245.
2. Ken Adachi, **The Enemy That Never Was**, (Toronto, ON: McClelland and Stewart, Ltd., 1976), p. 94.
3. Mikiso Hane, **Modern Japan:** *A Historical Survey* (Boulder: Westview Press, 1992), p. 185.
4. Adachi, p. 94.
5. Rev. Takamichi Takahatake, "The Identity of a Pioneer: Rev. Senju Sasaki, the First Buddhist Minister in Canada", **Canada Times**. Nov. 20, 1984, p. 3.
6. Jinshiro Nakayama, **Kanada-doho-hatten-taikan**, (Tokyo, 1921), p. 1320.
7. Rev. Shinjo Ikuta, **History of Buddhist Churches in Canada**, ed. Shoken Yamasaki, various translators, (Vancouver, BC: Buddhist Churches of Canada, 1977), chapter 12.

Chapter 6, Footnotes

1. The Buddhist Assembly Hall.
2. The inaugural Buddhist Hall.
3. Mikiso Hane, **Modern Japan:** *A Historical Survey*, Second Edition, (Oxford: Westview Press, 1992), p. 237 - 238.
4. Rev. Yutetsu Kawamura, **The Home of the Cowboy Song**, trans. TBC History Committee, (Kyoto: Dobosha), p. 17 (trans.).

Chapter 7, Footnotes

1. Ken Adachi, **The Enemy that Never Was:** *A History of the Japanese Canadians*, (Toronto ON: McClelland & Stewart, 1976), p. 146.
2. ibid. p. 148
3. Renamed the Kitsilano Buddhist Church in 1935.
4. Father of Kakuei Tada, Toronto Buddhist Church 1951 - 1956.
5. Toyo Takata, **Nikkei Legacy:** *The Story of Japanese Canadians from Settlement to Today*, (Toronto ON: NC Press Ltd, 1983), p. 84.
6. A Buddhist celebratory parade led by children.
7. **Tairiku Nippo**, July 1941.
8. **Tairiku Nippo**, August 1941.
9. Taken from the files of Ed Yoshida, Toronto Buddhist Church, 1994.
10. ibid.
11. ibid.
12. ibid.
13. Representation of the Amida Buddha.
14. Adachi, p. 32.
15. Rev. Zesei Kawasaki, **Straight from My Memories**. Memoirs written for the Toronto Buddhist Church History Committee by Rev. Kawasaki, Nov. 1992.
16. Adachi, p. 114-115.
17. Most temple histories were lost because of the war but information contained in the **Hokubei Kaikyo Enkakushi** and the **Raymond Buddhist Church History** provided insight into the history of the Royston Bukkyokai - one that was typical of smaller temples outside the Lower Mainland.

Chapter 8, Footnotes:

1. Ken Adachi, **The Enemy that Never Was:** *A History of the Japanese Canadians*, (Toronto ON: McClelland & Stewart, 1976), p. 116.
2. Interview with Rev. Tsuji. Conducted by Jesse Nishihata and Terry Watada, Toronto Buddhist Church, June 7, 1993.
3. Interview with Rev. Tsuji, June 7, 1993.
4. Interview with Rev. Tsuji, June 7, 1993.
5. Interview with Rev. Tsuji. Conducted by Jesse Nishihata and

Harry Yonekura, Toronto Buddhist Church, Sept. 20, 1990.

6. Interview with Rev. Tsuji, Sept. 20, 1990.

Chapter 9, Footnotes:

1. Akira Ichikawa, **Canadian Treatment of Jodo Shinshu Ministers During World War II**, (Dept. of Political Science, University of Lethbridge: Lethbridge AB, 1993), p. 2.
2. ibid. p. 13-14
3. ibid. p. 8
4. ibid. p. 8
5. ibid. p. 8
6. ibid. p. 9
7. The term "Evacuation" is considered today a government euphemism for the forced removal of all Japanese Canadians from the British Columbian coast during World War II.
8. Ichikawa, p. 17.
9. Interview with Terrie Komori. Conducted by Jesse Nishihata and Harry Yonekura, TBC, August 1990.
10. Interview with Rev. Tsuji. Conducted by Jesse Nishihata and Harry Yonekura, TBC, Sept. 20, 1990.
11. The detention centre for all those Japanese Canadians outside Vancouver. "The Pool" was located in the horse barn of the Pacific National Exhibition.
12. Interview with Terrie Komori, August 1990. Terrie Sugiura became Terrie Komori when she married in Toronto after the war.
13. Ken Adachi, **The Enemy that Never Was:** *A History of the Japanese Canadians*, (Toronto ON: McClelland & Stewart, 1976), p. 256.
14. Interview with Terrie Komori, August 1990.
15. Veronika Pellowski, **Silver, Lead and Hell:** *The Story of Sandon*, (Prospectors' Pick Publishing: Sandon B.C., 1992), p. 121.
16. ibid. p. 122
17. Interview with Terrie Komori, August 1990.
18. The use of the Welfare Committee still exists today although the purpose of the committee is to provide comfort to the ill and grieving.
19. Interview with Toshio Mori. Conducted by Hideo Yoshida and Gloria Sumiya, Toronto Buddhist Church, August 1991.
20. Interview with Rev. Tsuji, Sept. 20, 1990.
21. ibid.
22. Barry Broadfoot, **Six War Years:1939 - 1945***: Memories of Canadians at Home and Abroad*, (Doubleday Canada Ltd.: Toronto ON, 1974), p. 112.
23. Harry Yonekura in conversation with Alex Johnson, Steveston B.C., August 1991.
24. The Buddhist hall and its shrine were hand-built by the devout

Nembutsu followers during the internment period. It still stands today and is part of the Nikkei Internment Memorial Centre in New Denver B.C.

25. Ichikawa, p. 10 - 12.
26. Interview with Toshio Mori, August 1991.
27. Interview with Rev. Tsuji, Sept. 20, 1990.
28. Ichikawa, p. 20 - 21.
29. Interview with Toshio Mori, August 1991.
30. Interview with Terrie Komori (nee Sugiura), August 1990.
31. ibid.
32. Interview with Rev. Tsuji. Conducted by Jesse Nishihata and Terry Watada, TBC, June 7, 1993.
33. Name withheld upon request.

Part 2
Chapter 10, Footnotes:

1. Rev. Yutetsu Kawamura, **The Home of the Cowboy Song**, translated by the TBC History Committee, (Kyoto: Dobosha, 1988), p. 1.
2. Ken Adachi, **The Enemy That Never Was**, (Toronto ON: McClelland and Stewart, Ltd., 1976), p. 20.
3. ibid. p. 21
4. Akira Ichikawa, **Canadian Treatment of Jodo Shinshu Ministers During World War II**, (Dept. of Political Science, University of Lethbridge: Lethbridge AB, 1993), p. 22.
5. Kawamura, p. 6.
6. ibid. p. 2
7. ibid. p. 4
8. ibid. p. 2
9. ibid. p. 3
10. ibid. p. 3
11. Ichikawa, p. 23-24.
12. Kawamura, p. 8.
13. ibid. p. 8
14. Ichikawa, p. 24.
15. RCMP, Alberta Division "K", Lethbridge Sub-Division, June 21, 1946. Section 10 - Report RG 36/27/30/F1613.
16. ibid. Section 10
17. ibid. Section 9

Chapter 11, Footnotes:

1. See Chapter 12 "The Alberta Problem" for the continuation of Coaldale's history.
2. Dealt with in Chapter 12.
3. Letter to Bruce Kimura, Calgary Hoyu Kai, from Bishop Newton

Ishiura, BCC, June 12, 1970.

4. Press release to the membership and general public regarding a meeting to discuss the merits and problems of the Calgary Buddhist Church entering into a commercial business operation, July 1972.
5. Progress Report No. 1, Calgary Buddhist Church, Nov. 1972.
6. Preamble to the BFA Constitution.
7. Akira Terashima, "History of Buddhist Federation of Alberta", Lethbridge AB, May 1994, p. 1.

Chapter 12, Footnotes:

1. Interview with Rev. Yutetsu Kawamura. Conducted by Dorothy Kagawa, Jesse Nishihata, and Harry Yonekura. Lethbridge, Alberta - May 6, 1992.

   Rumours abound about the motives behind the death threats. It seems far fetched to believe congregation members threatened violence over a fund raising campaign for a Japanese Garden. However, since there is obstinate resistance to talk about the situation, Rev. Kawamura's word is taken at face value.

   The gardens later became a Lethbridge Centennial Project known as the Nikka Yuko Garden.
2. Letter to Bishop Ishiura concerning his article "Harmony Through Brotherhood" in **The Canadian Buddhist**. Author's name withheld. Dec. 12, 1970.
3. In 1967, the BFC became the Buddhist Churches of Canada (BCC).
4. Letter to Bishop Ishiura from Rev. O. Fujikawa. Nov. 23, 1969.
5. Letter to Bishop Ishiura concerning his article "Harmony Through Brotherhood" in **The Canadian Buddhist**. Author's name withheld. Dec. 12, 1970.
6. Letter to Mr. J. Colville, Government of Alberta, from Rev. Leslie Kawamura, Raymond Buddhist Church. Dated Nov. 9, 1965. Anonymous source.
7. Letter from Rev. Kawatsuki, Nishi Hongwanji, to Rev. Nishimura, Head Office, BCC. Translated by S. Kounosu PhD, Lethbridge University. Feb. 23, 1967.
8. Letter from M. Terakita, President Lethbridge Buddhist Association, to J. Colville, Director, Division of Vital Statistics, Edmonton Alberta. Anonymous source. December 18, 1968.
9. Resume of the Minutes of the Nov. 1, 1967 BCC Ministers Meeting Held in Winnipeg, Manitoba. Item 4, **The Relationship Between BCC and BCA**.
10. Excerpt from a study of The Bishopric, Kyodan Conference Minutes, Raymond, Alberta. March 9, 1965.
11. Letter to M. Takeda, Chairman of Honpa Buddhist Churches of Alberta from Bishop Ishiura concerning a Honpa request for a minister to replace Rev. L. Kawamura who was about to take a leave of absence to continue his studies.

12. Letter to Bishop Ishiura...Name of author withheld. Dec 12, 1970.
13. Letter to Bishop Ishiura from Rev. Chitoku Takeda, Head, Department of Overseas Mission, Jodo Shinshu Hongwanji-ha, Honzan. April 8, 1971.
14. See Lethbridge Buddhist Church history in Chapter 11.
15. **Lethbridge Buddhist Church Newsletter**, November 1986, p. 1.
16. Appeal made to Harry Yonekura (Toronto Buddhist Church) in a personal letter from the Lethbridge Buddhist Church for "support in curbing this inquiry". Name withheld by request.
17. Observations made by a *nisei* from the Honpa Buddhist Church of Alberta. Name withheld. December 1970.

Chapter 13, Footnotes:

1. Interested B.C. temples met in Kelowna in August 1952 to organize the activities of the BCBCF.
2. See Chapter 17, "The Buddhist Churches of Canada", for more details.
3. Letter from the Vancouver Buddhist Church and addressed to G.M. Nakashiba, Chairman, Buddhist Churches of Canada, Toronto ON. June 4, 1976.
4. Open letter to the membership from the Vancouver Buddhist Church President G. Yada. September 21, 1976.
5. Sakura Torizuka, "Rev. Kiribayashi of Steveston Buddhist Church ordered to leave Canada because of handicapped daughter", **The New Canadian**, Vol. 58 No. 22, May 26, 1994.
6. Open letter to Sergio Marchi from Tatsuo Kage, **Nikkei Voice**, Vol. 8 No. 5, June 1994.
7. Sakura Torizuka, "Rev. Kiribayashi and his family receiving more support", **The New Canadian**, Vol. 58 No. 24, June 9, 1994.
8. By 1957, the Dharma School enjoyed such an increase in enrolment that the church had to provide transportation as well as additional materials and audio-visual equipment.

Chapter 14, Footnotes:

1. Reyko Nishiyama, "History of the Raymond Buddhist Church", Raymond, Alberta, August 1992.
2. See Chapter 12, "The Alberta Problem".
3. Robert Hironaka, "History of the Lethbridge Honpa", Lethbridge, Alberta, Oct. 1992. p. 2-3.
4. ibid. p. 5
5. ibid. p. 6
6. Fredrich Ulrich, "History of Jodoshinshu in Edmonton", Edmonton, Alberta, 1992. p. 3.
7. ibid. p. 9

Chapter 15, Footnotes:

1. Yutetsu Kawamura, **Song of the Cowboy**, translated by TBC History Committee, (Kyoto: Dobosha, 1988), p. 16.
2. Ken Adachi, **The Enemy That Never Was**, (Toronto, ON: McClelland and Stewart, Ltd., 1976), p. 280.
3. ibid. p. 283

Chapter 16, Footnotes:

1. Bonnie Blake, "Jodo Shinshu Buddhism", speech given at Lakehead University during a symposium on Buddhism, November 1991.
2. **Hojo:** *50th Anniversary of Buddhism in Canada*, "The Next Fifty Years", Rev. Takashi Tsuji, (Toronto: BCC, 1955), p. 7. For more information, see "Eastern Canada Buddhist League" section at the end of this chapter.
3. Letter to F.Y. Okimura from Howard, Cate, Ogilvy, Bishop, Cope, Porteus and Hansard, Advocates, Barristers and Solicitors, January 17, 1966.
4. Quebec Civil Code, Article 42.
5. Interview with Rev. Newton Ishiura, conducted by Jesse Nishihata and Terry Watada, Toronto ON Sept. 27, 1991.
6. George Imai, "Remarks on the Entrenchment of the Bill of Rights", **The New Canadian** (Vol. 45, No. 21), March 20, 1981.
7. TYBS Minutes Book (1947 - 54). Entry under August 3, 1950 Executive Meeting.
8. Gloria Sumiya, Report to the TBC History Research Committee, Toronto 1995.
9. "Eastern Canada Sangha Dana League Education Fund", application form.
10. Minutes of Executive Meeting of ECSDL, Montreal Buddhist Church, May 22, 1983.
11. Minutes of joint Board of Directors meeting between ECSDL and ECBL, Toronto Buddhist Church, March 10, 1984.
12. Quoted in a letter from Harry Yonekura, ECBL President, to Bishop Tsunoda, March 30, 1986.

Chapter 17, Footnotes:

1. See Chapter 10, "Southern Alberta: The Struggle to Survive".
2. Minutes of the Eastern Canada Buddhist Church Conference held on December 23, 1967, at the Toronto Buddhist Church.
3. Minutes of special "A" and "B" Board Meeting, Toronto Buddhist Church, April 17, 1968.
4. ibid. May 9, 1968
5. Report of the Chairman of the National Board of the Buddhist Churches of Canada, March 24, 1976.
6. Minutes of the First Annual Meeting of the BCC, Toronto

Buddhist Church, March 1976. Note: Bishop Kosaka succeeded Bishop Ishiura in 1976.

7. Minutes of the BCC AGM held at the Toronto Buddhist Church March 26 - 27, 1976.
8. Special Delivery letter to George Nakashiba, Chairman Buddhist Churches of Canada from Genji Yada, President B.C. Buddhist Churches Federation, Feb. 22, 1977.
9. **BCC Board of Directors, Organizational Set-Up and Operations**, BCC report, (author unknown) 1977.
10. Minutes of BCC National Board Meeting #34, Nov. 8, 1977.
11. Minutes of the Third Annual Meeting of the BCC, March 24, 1978.
12. ibid.
13. Letter from Kimi Nakamura, President VBC Fujinkai, to Harry Yonekura, BCC, March 31, 1978.
14. In the spring of 1958, the World Federation of the Jodo Shinshu Hongwanji-ha Buddhist Women's Association was formed with Lady Yoshiko Ohtani as the honorary president. The convention is held every four years in various parts of the world.
15. Although the name changed in 1981, the organization is still known as the Buddhist Churches of Canada Women's Federation.
16. The Bishop's salary had been paid by his resident church until 1980.
17. 5th Annual Meeting, Buddhist Churches of Canada, Kamloops, B.C. March 1980.
18. **BCC 1981 Budget Proposals**, Schedule 4 - Notes.
19. Minutes of BCC Meeting No. 75, Feb. 1980.
20. Chairman's Report, Buddhist Churches of America, 1971.
21. The committee comprised Bishop Tsunoda, Reverends K. Ikuta and G. Abe, and Directors R. Akune, R. Inouye and C. Saimoto.
22. **Report on the Search for the Bishop of the BCC**, January 19, 1985.
23. For more information, see "Special Projects: FAMAC", Chapter 22, "Spirituality and Decline".
24. FAMAC brochure, January 1979.
25. Mark Mullins, **The Organizational Dilemmas of Ethnic Churches:** *A Case Study of Japanese Buddhism in Canada*, Sociological Analysis 1988. p. 225.

Part 3
Chapter 18, Footnotes:

1. John Armstrong, **Japanese Canadians in Toronto:** *Assimilation in the History of a Community 1940-1965*, MA Thesis (Los Angeles: U.C.L.A., 1991), p. 8.
2. **The New Canadian**, December 6, 1947.
3. Armstrong, p. 92.

4. Personal interview, name withheld by request, Toronto ON, 1991.
5. Armstrong, p. 95.
6. ibid. p. 98
7. ibid. p. 98
8. Rabbi Abraham Feinberg of the Holy Blossom Synagogue was also a dedicated supporter of the community.
9. Armstrong, p. 99.
10. ibid. p. 99
11. ibid. p. 100
12. Interview with Charles Shimizu. Conducted by Dorothy Kagawa, Toronto Buddhist Church, November 21, 1993.

    Roy Sato wrote another take on the above incident. It appeared in the **Guiding Light**, February 29, 1960.

    This article should be read carefully by all members of the Congregation. It is evangelical in tone, and prejudiced in its statements and conclusions. The article was written by Mr. Eddie S. Yoshida of the Canadian Japanese Mission at Northeast Biblical Institute in Sagawa City, Japan. We do not know how often Canadians of Japanese ancestry will be provided such Anti-Creed literature. We Buddhists should try all the harder to be better Buddhists and therefore better Canadians.

    *...when an influential ethnic organ (**The New Canadian**) publishes articles which give comfort to the majority (Christian Canadians of Japanese ancestry) and attacks the religion of a minority (Buddhism), the result is not mere religious pressure. It is religious persecution.*

    *We feel from the bottom of our hearts that there is something wonderful about Buddhism. Even the images (heathen idols according to **The New Canadian**) appear to radiate peace, wisdom, a transcendent serenity. Although we know that these images are merely wood, bronze, or clay works of artists, they serve to remind us of the ideal of Infinite Wisdom and Infinite Compassion.*
13. Interview with Tin Goto. Conducted by G. Shikatani, Multicultural History Society of Ontario, Toronto, Ontario, February 19, 1978

Chapter 19, Footnotes:

1. Interview with Rev. Tsuji. Conducted by Jesse Nishihata and Harry Yonekura, Toronto Buddhist Church, September 20, 1990.
2. Also known as the Issei-bu during the Huron Street Church days. In 1959, the organization became officially known as the Goho-kai.
3. Interview with Rev. Tsuji, Sept. 20, 1990.
4. ibid.
5. ibid.
6. **The New Canadian**, September 1946.
7. Interview with Rev. Tsuji, Sept. 20, 1990.

8. ibid.
9. See Chapter 17, "The Buddhist Churches of Canada".
10. Anonymous, "New Problems Confronting the Busseis and the Church", **Guiding Light**, (Toronto: TBC, Dec. 14, 1959), p. 3.
11. Minutes Book, **History of TYBS**, Sept. 15, 1946 to Nov. 16, 1947.
12. Committee members included Peggy Harada, Fumiye Maeda, Toshiko Maeda, Tsuruye Koyanagi, Nancy Kido, Mamoru Nishi, Masao Nakamura, Charlie Nekoda and Toyoaki Takata.
13. Interview with TYBS members. Conducted by Dorothy Kagawa and Harry Yonekura. TBC, November 2, 1993.
14. Gloria Sumiya, **The TYBS History,** Sept. 15, 1946 - Nov. 16, 1947.
15. Harry Kondo, "Establishment of the Toronto Buddhist Church", (Toronto: 1989).
16. Harry Kondo, "Establishment of the Buddhist Church", (Toronto: 1988), p. 3.
17. Onishi, one of the first to arrive in Toronto, owned a dry cleaning store at Ossington and Dundas. Rev. Tsuji had first met him in Victoria in 1942.
18. Interview with Goho-kai members. Conducted by Ed Yoshida, Dorothy Kagawa and Harry Yonekura. T.B.C., June 18, 1993.
19. Interview with Rev. Tsuji. Conducted by Jesse Nishihata and Terry Watada, Toronto Buddhist Church, June 1993.
20. Interview with Goho-kai members, June 18, 1993.
21. ibid.
22. Toyo Takata, **Ayumi:** *Toronto Japanese Language School Fortieth Anniversary 1949-1989*, (Toronto: TJLS, 1990), p. 11.
23. ibid. p. 9. The first staff of the school included: Shinkuro Kozai, Principal; Kiyomi Okuda, Haruko Kobayakawa and Kay Kikue Azuma, teachers.
24. Based upon the traditional and patriarchal method of donation, the approximately 100 directors of the various organizations within the church gave $18,000. The general membership donated $5000. In the ensuing years, this practice came into question. Many felt the members were not giving in the true spirit of the religion. A new method had to be found.
25. Interview with Hideo Yoshida, conducted by Gerry Shikatani, Multicultural History Society of Ontario, Toronto, Ontario, June 1993.
26. John Armstrong, **Japanese Canadians in Toronto:** *Assimilation in the History of a Community 1940-1965*, MA Thesis (Los Angeles: U.C.L.A., 1991), p. 106-107.
27. Tak Yoshida. "T.B.C. Altar". (Toronto: TBC, March 1995.)
28. Interview with Rev. Tsuji, Sept. 20, 1990.
29. "Rev. T. Tsuji to Leave Toronto Buddhist Church", **Guiding Light**, (Toronto: TBC, Sept. 22, 1958), p. 1.

Chapter 20, Footnotes:

1. "Rev. Newton Ishiura to succeed Rev. Tsuji as the Minister of The Toronto Buddhist Church", **Guiding Light**, (Toronto: TBC, Sept. 22, 1958), p. 2.
2. Interview with Tak Yoshida. Conducted by Dorothy Kagawa and Terry Watada, TBC, June 13, 1993.
3. A coincidental discovery of "Ami" taken from the French for "friend" and "Ami" as in "Amida Buddha".
4. Interview with several Club Ami members. Conducted by Dorothy Kagawa and Harry Yonekura, Toronto Buddhist Church, December 12, 1993.
5. Terence Beresford, President TYBS, on behalf of the Directors of the TYBS to the Board of Directors TBC, 1961.
6. Interview with former Bussei members. Conducted by Dorothy Kagawa and Harry Yonekura. TBC December 12, 1993.
7. Kunio Suyama, "TYBS President's Message", **Guiding Light**, (Toronto: TBC, April 14, 1958), p. 1.
8. Dr. Daisetsu Suzuki gave a lecture to the Toronto Buddhist Church congregation during the Hanamatsuri Service of 1956.
9. Anonymous, "New Problems Confronting the Bussei and The Church", **Guiding Light**, (Toronto: TBC, December 14, 1959), p. 3.
10. ibid. p. 4
11. ibid. pp. 4-5

Chapter 21, Footnotes:

1. The Eitaikyo Fund was created to ensure the veneration of the columbarium. The Religious Department with representatives from the Goho-kai and the Sangha took care of the fund until February 1971 when the money ($8260) was turned over to the Central Treasury.

   The Department itself was formed in February 1963. The executive consisted of Tak Yoshida, Chairman; Misao Nishikawa, Secretary; Charley Shimizu, Treasurer; Kunio Suyama and Bob Bentley, Hosts; and Tom Shimizu, Head Usher.
2. The Welfare Department was responsible for visiting ill members and aiding bereaved families within the church.
3. The Juvenile Education Department was established in February 1958 to transfer administration of the Dharma School from the TYBS to the TBC.
4. Minutes of Sangha Meeting, Toronto Buddhist Church, April 1959.
5. The Asoka Hospital was sponsored by the Nishi Hongwanji. The great earthquake of 1924 devastated Tokyo causing 240,000 dead and wounded and rendering 2,000,000 homeless. The Hongwanji immediately set up emergency clinics at Hibiya Park. Lady Kujo, daughter of Abbot Koson Ohtani, personally aided and comforted the victims.
6. Sue Michibata, personal letter, July 6, 1993.

7. "Sunday School Workshop Report", **Guiding Light**, (Toronto: TBC, Sept. 3, 1958), p. 2.
8. Personal letter from Sue Michibata, July 6, 1993.
9. Closing statement of the Sunday School Workshop, August 31, 1958.
10. Minutes of Sangha meeting, Toronto Buddhist Church, Feb. 3, 1963.
11. ibid.
12. Interview with Sam Baba. Conducted by Dorothy Kagawa, Toronto Buddhist Church, Sept. 1991.
13. ibid.
14. ibid.
15. ibid.
16. Interview with Harry Yonekura. Conducted by Dorothy Kagawa and Terry Watada, Toronto Buddhist Church, June 1993.
17. ibid.
18. From the files of Hideo Ed Yoshida and Church Minutes.
19. Interview with Harry Yonekura, June 1993.
20. Interview with Ed Yoshida. Conducted by Dorothy Kagawa and Terry Watada, TBC, June 1993.
21. Interview with Harry Yonekura, June 1993.
22. From the files of Hideo Ed Yoshida.
23. Interview with Rev. Ishiura. Conducted by Jesse Nishihata and Terry Watada, Toronto ON, Sept. 27, 1991.
24. ibid.
25. ibid.
26. Interview with Terry Watada. Conducted by Jesse Nishihata, TBC, Sept. 1991.
27. Interview with Rev. Ishiura, Sept. 1991.
28. ibid.
29. ibid.

    Rev. Ishiura adds: "When I was in Japan studying at an institute, I saw a billboard advertising a revival meeting featuring Toyohiko Kagawa, a renowned social gospel evangelist. Kagawa was known for his work in the slum district not only for bringing the gospel but for his work in founding cooperatives. I was very impressed with his zeal and refreshing faith."
30. ibid.
31. ibid.
32. ibid.
33. ibid.
34. ibid.
35. Terrie Komori, **A Tribute to Mary Ishiura**, Souvenir Booklet, (Toronto: TBC, 1990).
36. Interview with Rev. Ishiura, Sept. 1991.

37. Letter of congratulations from Mary Ishiura on the 20th Anniversary of the Dana, April 1979.
38. Terrie Komori, **A Tribute to the Late Mary Ishiura**, Dana 35th Anniversary Address, TBC, June 1994.

Chapter 22, Footnotes:

1. So too did Presidents Shinkuro Kozai and Sumiye Watanabe who held terms of more than five years each.
2. Harry Yonekura, Chairman's Report to the BCC, Kamloops BC, March 1980, p. 6.
3. Interview with Harry Yonekura. Conducted by Miyo Nakamura, TBC, 1994.
4. Harry Yonekura, Chairman's Report, p. 6.
5. Dr. N. Okihiro, **Report on the Survey on the Future of the T.B.C.**, (Halifax: NRO Consulting, 1984), pp. 16 - 17.
6. ibid. p. 18
7. A nine day commercial festival of singing, dancing, merchandise and food. About fifty ethnic groups participate.
8. Japanese dance seen as formal as ballet.
9. Sangha Minutes Book, November 15, 1980.
10. Larry Matsuba, **Sunday School Report**, TBC, 1979.
11. ibid.
12. Gloria Sumiya, **Toronto Buddhist Church Dharma School**, TBC, 1994.
13. ibid.
14. ibid.
15. **Guiding Light**, (Toronto: TBC, Oct. 1993), Vol. 41 No. 9.
16. Children were dressed to represent heavenly beings. They wore the *kariginu*, a robe with long, wide sleeves worn over a *hakama*, a wide skirt. It is the official garb of the Heian nobility. Boys wear a stiff hat of lacquered gauze called the *eboshi*. Girls wear the crown of a phoenix and bright metal pendants called *tenkan*. Both wear the ancient markings of the nobility called *kugemayu*, two black dots just above the space between the eyebrows.
17. Personal diaries of Tak Yoshida, Vol. 2 1971 - 1985.
18. Letter to Bishop Toshio Murakami BCC from Taitetsu Unno, Jill Ker Conway Professor of Religion, July 3, 1990.
19. Report from Rev. Orai Fujikawa, TBC General Meeting, Nov. 29, 1992.
20. Rev. Yasuo Izumi, "Greetings", **Guiding Light**, October 1994.

Chapter 23, Footnotes:

1. Mark R. Mullins, **The Organizational Dilemmas of Ethnic Churches:** *A Case Study of Japanese Buddhism in Canada*, Sociological Analysis, 1988, p. 223.

2. ibid. p. 226
3. ibid. p. 227
4. Richard Robinson, Editorial, **Hojo:** *50th Anniversary of Buddhism in Canada*, (Buddhist Churches of Canada, 1955), p. 3.
5. Mullins, p. 229.

Afterword, Footnotes:

1. Yoshifumi Ueda, gen. ed., **The True Teaching, Practice and Realization of the Pure Land Way**, 4 vols. (Kyoto: Hongwanji International Center, 1983-90), 1:63.
2. Yoshifumi Ueda, gen. ed., **Hymns of the Pure Land Masters** (Kyoto: Hongwanji International Center, 1992), p. 77.
3. **The True Teaching, Practice and Realization of the Pure Land Way**, 1:63-64.
4. Y. Ueda, gen. ed., **Notes on the Inscriptions on Sacred Scrolls** (Kyoto: Hongwanji International Center, 1981), p. 37.
5. Alfred Bloom, **Shinran's Gospel of Pure Grace** (Tucson: The University of Arizona Press, 1965), pp.50-51.
6. **The True Teaching, Practice and Realization of the Pure Land**, 4:502-503.
7. Y. Ueda, gen. ed., **Hymns of the Pure Land** (Kyoto: Hongwanji International Center, 1991), p. 49.
8. Ibid., p. 73.
9. Yoshifumi Ueda and Dennis Hirota, **Shinran**, (Kyoto: Hongwanji International Center, 1989), p. 265.
10. Y. Ueda, gen. ed., **Notes on Once-calling and Many-calling** (Kyoto: Hongwanji International Center, 1980), p. 46.
11. **The True Teaching, Practice and Realization of the Pure Land Way**, 3:376.
12. Ibid., 3:395.
13. **Notes on Once-calling and Many-calling**, p. 48.
14. **The True Teaching, Practice and Realization of the Pure Land Way**, 1:165.
15. Ibid., 2:213.
16. Ibid.
17. Ibid., 2:229.
18. Ibid., 2:229-230.
19. **The Tanni Sho** [Notes Lamenting Differences], Trans. and Annot. by Ryosetsu Fujiwara (Kyoto: Ryukoku University, 1962), p. 79.
20. Y. Ueda, gen. ed., **Hymns of the Dharma-Ages** (Kyoto: Hongwanji International Center, 1993), p. 41.
21. **The True Teaching, Practice and Realization of the Pure Land Way**, 1:63.
22. Ibid., 1:111.
23. Ibid., 1:109.

24. Ibid., 2:203.
25. **Shinshu Shogyo Zenshu** [Collected Shinshu Scriptures], 2 vols. (Kyoto: Oyagi Kobundo, 1964-65), 1:9.
26. **The True Teaching, Practice and Realization of the Pure Land Way**, 2:228-9.
27. Y. Ueda and D. Hirota, **Shinran**, p. 195.
28. Hisao Inagaki, **The Pure Land Sutras: A Study and Translation** (Kyoto: Nagata Bunshodo, 1994), p. 242.
29. **The True Teaching, Practice and Realization of the Pure Land Way**, 1:58-59.
30. Daisetz T. Suzuki, **A Miscellany on the Shin Teaching of Buddhism** (Kyoto: Shinshu Otaniha Shumusho, 1949), p. 1.

Bibliography

Adachi, Ken. **The Enemy that Never Was:** *A History of the Japanese Canadians*. Toronto: McClelland and Stewart, 1976.

Broadfoot, Barry. **Years of Sorrow, Years of Shame:** *The Story of the Japanese Canadians in World War II*. Toronto: General Publishing, 1979.

Buddhist Churches of America. **Buddhist Churches of America:** *75 Year History 1899 - 1974*, Volume One. Chicago: Nobart, Inc., 1974.

Hane, Mikiso. **Modern Japan:** *A Historical Survey*. Second Edition; Oxford: Westview Press, 1992.

Hunter, Louise H., **Buddhism in Hawaii:** *Its Impact on a Yankee Community*. Honolulu, HI: University of Hawaii Press, 1971.

Ikuta, Rev. Shinjo. **History of Buddhist Churches in Canada**. Ed. Shoken Yamasaki. trans. TBC History Committee. Vancouver BC: Buddhist Churches of Canada, 1977.

Irokawa, Daikichi. **The Culture of the Meiji Period**. trans. Marius B. Jansen. Princeton, New Jersey: Princeton University Press, 1985.

Kawamura, Rev. Yutetsu. **The Home of the Cowboy Song**. trans. TBC History Committee. Kyoto: Dobosha, 1988.

Kitagawa, Joseph M. **Religion in Japanese History**. New York: Columbia University Press, 1990.

Nakai, Rev. Gendo. **Shinran and His Religion of Pure Faith**. Kyoto: Hyakka-en, 1961.

Nakayama, Jinshiro. **Kanada-doho-hatten-taikan**. Tokyo, 1921.

Ohtani, Yoshiko. **The Life of Eshinni:** *Wife of Shinran Shonin*. trans. Taitetsu Unno. Kyoto: Hompa Hongwanji, 1970.

Pellowski, Veronika. **Silver, Lead and Hell:** *The Story of Sandon*. Sandon BC: Prospectors' Pick Publishing, 1992.

Powell, Andrew. **Living Buddhism**. New York: Harmony Books, 1989.

Raymond Buddhist Church. **First Fifty Years:** *Raymond Buddhist Church, 1929 - 1979*. Raymond AB: Raymond Buddhist Church, 1979.

Sansom, George. **A History of Japan:***1334 - 1615*. Stanford, California: Stanford University Press, 1961.

Shibata, Yuko, Shoji Matsumoto, Rintaro Hayashi, Shotaro Iida. **The Forgotten History of the Japanese Canadians:** *Volume 1*. Vancouver BC: New Sun Books, 1977.

Soseki, Natsume. **Kokoro**. trans. Edwin McClellan. Chicago: Regnery, 1967.

Takata, Toyo. **Ayumi:** *Toronto Japanese Language School Fortieth Anniversary 1949 - 1989*. Toronto: TJLS, 1990.

Takata, Toyo. **Nikkei Legacy:** *The Story of Japanese Canadians from Settlement to Today*. Toronto: NC Press Ltd., 1983.

Tamura, Norio. **Japanese Newspapers of Canada**. trans. Deirdre Tanaka - "Japanese Newspapers of the Pioneer Days". Tokyo: PMC Publishing, 1991.

Vancouver Buddhist Church. **75th Anniversary:** *New Temple and Complex Dedication*. Vancouver BC: VBC, 1979.

Articles and Periodicals

Armstrong, John. "Japanese Canadians in Toronto: Assimilation in the History of a Community 1940 - 1965". MA Thesis, UCLA, Los Angeles CA, 1991.

Blake, Bonnie. "Jodo Shinshu Buddhism". Speech given at Lakehead University during a symposium on Buddhism, Nov. 1991.

Guiding Light. editions: March 10, 1958; April 14, 1958; July 3, 1958; Sept. 3, 1958; Sept. 22, 1958; Nov. 23, 1958; Oct. 26, 1959; Nov. 23, 1959; Dec. 14, 1959; Dec. 1966; Oct. 1993; Oct. 1994.

Ichikawa, Akira. "Canadian Treatment of Jodo Shinshu Ministers During World War II". Dept. of Political Science, University of Lethbridge, 1993.

Imai, George. "Remarks on the Entrenchment of the Bill of Rights", **The New Canadian**. ed. March 20, 1981.

Kagawa, Dorothy. "Growing Up in the West Coast, Namely, Vancouver B.C." unpublished.

Kage, Tatsuo. "Open Letter to Sergio Marchi". **Nikkei Voice**. ed. June 1994.

Komori, Terrie. "A Tribute to the Late Mary Ishiura". Dana 35th Anniversary Address, TBC, June 1994.

Komori, Terrie. "A Tribute to Mary Ishiura". Souvenir Booklet, Toronto: TBC, 1990.

Matsuba, Larry. "Sunday School Report". TBC, 1979.

Mullins, Mark. "The Organizational Dilemmas of Ethnic Churches: *A Case Study of Japanese Buddhism in Canada*". **Sociological Analysis**, 1988.

The New Canadian. editions: September 1946; December 6, 1947.

Okihiro, Dr. N. "Report on the Survey on the Future of the TBC". Halifax: NRO Consulting, 1984.

Robinson, Richard. "Editorial". **Hojo**:*50th Anniversary of Buddhism in Canada*. BCC, 1955.

Sasaki, Rev. Laverne S. "Eshinni-Sama - Shinobu Hoyo." Talk given on June 2nd, 1990 at the Ninth World Buddhist Women's Convention in Vancouver, B.C.

Tairiku Nippo. editions: July 1941, August 1941.

Takahatake, Rev. Takamichi. "The Identity of a Pioneer: *Rev. Senju Sasaki, the First Buddhist Minister in Canada*". **Canada Times**. ed. Nov. 20, 1984.

Torizuka, Sakura. "Rev. Kiribayashi and His Family Receiving More Support". **The New Canadian**. ed. June 9, 1994.

Torizuka, Sakura. "Rev. Kiribayashi of Steveston Buddhist Church Ordered to Leave Canada because of Handicapped Daughter". **The New Canadian**. ed. May 26, 1994.

Tsuji, Rev. Kenryu. "The Next Fifty Years". **Hojo:** *50th Anniversary of Buddhism in Canada*. BCC, 1955.

Area Reports

Ebata, Lillian Shizue. "Skeena Bukkyokai: *1934 - 1942*". 1995.

Hayashi, M. "Thunder Bay Buddhist Church History". Thunder Bay ON, 1992.

Hironaka, Kaisuke. "Brief History of Rosemary Buddhist Church". Rosemary AB, July 1970.

Hironaka, M. "Rosemary Buddhist Church". Rosemary AB, 1993.

Hironaka, Robert. "History of the Lethbridge Honpa". Lethbridge AB, October 1992.

Honkawa, F. "Fraser Valley Buddhist Temple". Bradner BC, August 1992.

Izumi, Rev. Y. "Taber Buddhist Church: 1942 - 1945". Lethbridge AB, date unknown.

Nagai, Jack. "Taber Buddhist Church: 1947 - 1992". Taber AB, 1992.

Nakano, George. "History of the Montreal Buddhist Church: *1947 - 1987*." Montreal PQ, April 1995.

Nishiyama, Reyko. "History of the Raymond Buddhist Church". Raymond AB, August 1992.

Oga, Takumi. "Picture Butte Buddhist Church History". Lethbridge AB, Nov. 1992.

Okazaki, Rose. "History of the Vernon Buddhist Church". Vernon BC, 1993.

Okimura, F.Y. & J.Y. "History of Montreal Dana-Fujinkai", "History of Montreal Sangha Society". Montreal PQ, 1993.

Suenaga, Tomi. "History of the Hamilton Buddhist Church". Hamilton ON, Dec. 31, 1993.

Terada, Yosh. "Footprints of the Bukkyo Kai: *Kelowna Buddhist Church History*". Kelowna BC, 1993.

Teramura, Ken. "Record of Events, 1947 - 1991: *Manitoba Buddhist Church*", Winnipeg MB, 1992.

Teramura, Richard. "The Coaldale Buddhist Church". **Coaldale and District History Book**. Published in 1983.

Terashima, Akira. "History of Buddhist Federation of Alberta". Lethbridge AB, May 1994.

Terashima, Fred A. "History of the Lethbridge Buddhist Church". Lethbridge AB, Jan. 1993.

Tsukishima, Tom. "Report on the Coaldale Buddhist Church: *1982 - 1992*". Coaldale AB, 1992.

Ulrich, Fredrich. "History of Jodoshinshu in Edmonton". Edmonton AB, 1992.

Yoneda, K.C. "A Brief History of the Calgary Buddhist Church". Calgary AB, 1992.

Other Sources

Buddhist Churches of Canada, Meeting Minutes and Reports: 1950 - 1976.

Buddhist Churches of Canada, Meeting Minutes and Reports: 1977 - 1990.

Calgary Buddhist Church files, 1970 - 1979.

Eastern Canada Sangha/Dana League - Eastern Canada Buddhist Church League, Meeting Minutes and Reports: 1980 - 1990.

FAMAC: 1979 - 1992. File of Meeting Minutes and Reports compiled by Harry Yonekura.

Ishiura, Bishop N. Files and records, Buddhist Churches of Canada and the Toronto Buddhist Church, 1968 - 1976.

"Kamloops Buddhist Church History". trans. Dorothy Kagawa and Yae Ebisuzaki. TBC, Jan. 20, 1995.

Kawasaki Rev. Zesei, "Straight from My Memories". Memoirs, November 1992.

Kondo, Harry. "Establishment of the Toronto Buddhist Church". Memoirs, 1989.

Michibata, Sue. Memoirs, July 6, 1993.

"Oratorical Contests of the Bussei Renmei". The magazine "Buddha", from the files of Hideo Ed Yoshida.

Project '71: 1970 - 1972. File of Meeting Minutes and Reports compiled by Harry Yonekura.

Report on TBC Youth Dept. Activities - 1980 - '83. Compiled by Ken and Steve Motomura.

RCMP, Alberta Division "K", Lethbridge Sub-Division. Section 10 - Report RG 36/27/30/F1613. June 21, 1946.

"Royston Buddhist Church". trans. Ed Yoshida, 1994. From **Hokubei Kaikyo Enkakushi** and **Raymond Buddhist Church History**.

Sangha History. Meeting minutes, major events and decisions compiled by Fred Kagawa.

"Steveston Bukkyo-kai". trans. Ed Yoshida and Gloria Sumiya, 1994. From a handwritten manuscript by Konosuke Nishikihama, Jan. 1967.

Sumiya, Gloria. "Toronto Buddhist Church Dharma School". Memoirs, 1994.

Sumiya, Gloria. "The TYBS History: 1946 - 1947". Memoirs, 1994.

Sumiya, Gloria. "TBC Youth Orchestra: 1977 - 1988). Memoirs, 1995.

The Teaching of Buddha, Bukkyo Dendo Kyokai, Tokyo, 1984.

Toronto Buddhist Church Dana: 1959 - 1992. Highlights of the history compiled by Gloria Sumiya.

Toronto Buddhist Church. Meeting Minutes and Reports: 1960 - 1969.

Toronto Buddhist Church. Meeting Minutes and Reports: 1970 - 1979.

Toronto Buddhist Church. Meeting Minutes and Reports: 1980 - 1989.

Toronto Young Buddhists Society. **History of TYBS:** *Minutes Book Sept. 15, 1946 to Nov. 16, 1947.*

Toronto Young Buddhists Society. **Offical Record:** *1947 - 1954.*

"Vancouver Buddhist Church: 1951 - 1958". trans. Ed Yoshida and Gloria Sumiya. From the files of Genichiro Yada.

"Young Buddhist League, 1928 - 1941". From the files of Hideo Ed Yoshida.

Hideo Ed Yoshida. Personal files.

Tak Yoshida. Personal Notes and Diaries: 1963 - 1985.

Tak Yoshida. "T.B.C. Altar". Informative article written for the book. March 1995.

File on "The Alberta Problem". Raymond, Alberta. Anonymous source.

File on the "Quebec Situation". Montreal PQ. Anonymous source.

Interviews

Sam Baba. Conducted by Dorothy Kagawa, TBC, September 27, 1991.

Goho-Kai Session. Conducted by Dorothy Kagawa, Harry Yonekura, Ed Yoshida and Terry Watada, TBC, June 18, 1993.

Tin Goto. Conducted by Gerry Shikatani, Multicultural History Society of Ontario, Toronto, Jan. 19, 1978.

Rev. Newton Ishiura. Conducted by Terry Watada and Jesse Nishihata, Toronto Buddhist Church, Sept. 27, 1991.

Alex Johnson. Conducted by Harry Yonekura, Steveston BC, August 1991.

Rev. Yutetsu Kawamura. Conducted by Dorothy Kagawa, Jesse Nishihata and Harry Yonekura, Lethbridge AB, May 6, 1992.

Terrie Komori. Conducted by Jesse Nishihata, TBC, date unknown.

Toshio Mori. Conducted by Hideo Yoshida and Gloria Sumiya, TBC, August 1991.

Rev. Ensei Nekoda. Conducted by Hideo Yoshida, TBC, date unknown.

TBC Bon Odori Members. Conducted by Dorothy Kagawa, TBC, June 13, 1993.

Toronto Young Buddhist Society Members. Conducted by Dorothy Kagawa, TBC, Oct. 31, Nov. 2, Nov.21 and Dec. 12, 1993.

Rev. Kenryu Tsuji. Conducted by Jesse Nishihata and Terry Watada, Toronto Buddhist Church, June 7, 1993.

Rev. K. Tsuji. Conducted by Jesse Nishihata and Harry Yonekura, TBC, Sept. 20, 1990.

Harry Yonekura. Conducted by Miyo Nakamura, TBC, 1994.

Harry Yonekura. Conducted by Dorothy Kagawa and Terry Watada, TBC, June 1993.

Hideo (Ed) Yoshida. Conducted by Jesse Nishihata, Toronto Buddhist Church, June 14, 1991.

Hideo (Ed) Yoshida. Conducted by Gerry Shikatani, Multicultural History Society of Ontario, Toronto, date unknown.

Tak Yoshida about the Religious Department. Conducted by Dorothy Kagawa and Terry Watada, TBC, June 13, 1993.

Tak Yoshida. Conducted by Gerry Shikatani, Multicultural History Society of Ontario, Toronto, June 6, 1968.

Appendix

Buddhist Observances

Shusho-e: January 1st. New Year's Day is a day of dedication. With renewed resolution, Buddhists dedicate themselves to the way of the Nembutsu.

Ho-onko: January 16th. Ho-onko is a service held in memory of Shinran Shonin, the founder of Jodo Shinshu (True Pure Land Sect).

Nehan-e: February 15th. The day commemorates the passing of Sakyamuni Buddha into Pari-Nirvana.

Higan-e: March 21st. Higan, meaning Other Shore, is a service conducted in the spring on or about the equinox day. At this time, harmony rules throughout the universe. Buddhists gather to devote themselves to the realization of this harmony within their inner lives.

Hanamatsuri: April 8th. Hanamatsuri is held to commemorate the birth of Gautama in Lumbini Garden. During the service, a flower shrine known as Hanamido is set up in front of the main shrine as a symbol of Lumbini Garden. The sangha offers flowers and pours sweet tea over the image of the infant Buddha.

Gotanye: May 21st. Buddhists observe the birth of Shinran Shonin in Kyoto on May 21, 1173.

Obon: July - August. Obon is a Buddhist Memorial Day. It is an occasion for rejoicing in the enlightenment offered by the Buddha. It is also referred to as a "Gathering of Joy". The day is celebrated with the Bon Odori or Bon Dance as an expression of gratitude.

Higan: September 23rd. The sangha gathers twice a year during the spring and autumn to recall the practices of the Six Paramita.

BCC Day: October 12th. On October 12, 1905, Rev. Senju Sasaki arrived in Vancouver from the Hongwanji in Japan to serve as the first Jodo Shinshu minister. BCC Day celebrates the official introduction of Jodo Shinshu to Canada.

Bodhi Day: December 8th. Gautama meditated under the Bodhi Tree (Tree of Enlightenment) and became a Buddha, perfect in Wisdom and Compassion.

Joya-e: December 31st. On New Year's Eve, Buddhists meditate on the countless blessings they have received throughout the year and express their gratitude to parents, nation, all beings and Amida Buddha.

Glossary

Amida Buddha	"Amida" is a Japanese/Chinese transliteration of the Sanskrit "a-mita" meaning Infinite. Amida Buddha is the Buddha of Infinite Life and Boundless Light. Life symbolizes "compassion" and Light "wisdom".
Betsuin	A branch temple. According to Hongwanji rules, the temple must carry the name "Hongwanji" and has as its head minister the Gomonshu.
Buddha Dharma	A Sanskrit term for Buddhism. Religion (Dharma) of the Enlightened One (Buddha).
Bukkyokai.	Buddhist Temple.
Bukkyo Seinenkai	Young Men's Buddhist Association.
Bussei (also Bussei Renmei)	An abbreviation of Bukkyo Seinenkai.
Chigo	A celestial child in a Shinto or Buddhist ceremonial procession or parade.
Dharma	The Teaching of the Buddha.
Eitaiko	Sutra chanting for the perpetual memory of the deceased. In North America, it is generally held in November.
Fujinkai	Buddhist Women's Association.
Gakuen	Literally meaning a garden of learning, a campus, an education institution. Generally used for Japanese Language Schools in North America.
Gohonzon	The principal image enshrined in a temple or family altar. The Gohonzon could be a statue, a portrait of Amida Buddha or a scroll featuring the six characters for Na-Mu-A-Mi-Da-Butsu.
Gomonshu (Monshu)	The spiritual leader of the Jodo Shinshu sect of Buddhism, Nishi Hongwanji.
Hondo	The main hall of a temple.
Honzan	The denominational head temple. Also referred to as the Mother Temple.
Kaikan	(Multi-purpose) assembly hall.
Kantoku (also Socho)	Literally, a supervisor. Conventionally translated to "Bishop" in North America.
Keirokai	A "respect-for-age" party or association popular among Buddhists.
Nembutsu	Literally, a meditation upon Amida Buddha. The recitation of Amida's name in the form of Namu (or Namo) Amida Butsu is called the Nembutsu. It is an expression of gratitude to the Amida Buddha.

Nyu Butsu Shiki	A special service to newly enshrine the statue or portrait of Amida Buddha or scroll of the Nembutsu in the worship hall of a temple or family altar.
Onaijin (Naijin)	The inner sanctum, close to the Gohonzon, of a temple separated from the outer section where the general congregation is seated.
Prajna	The highest state of wisdom. One of the two great concepts of Mahayana Buddhism. The other is Karuna (Compassion).
Renshi	Title given to the brothers of the Gomonshu.
Sangha	A Buddhist community or assembly. Eastern Canada temples use the term as the title for their adult men's group.
Sensei	Teachers. Thus ministers are referred to as "Sensei".
Six Paramitas	The perfection of six practices for reaching Enlightenment. The first is Dana (offering).
Socho	Abbreviation for Kaikyo-socho (Bishop).
Sutra	Discourses of the Buddha usually recited in the form of a chant.
Tan Nisho	Important Jodo Shinshu scripture.
Tripitaka	The three scriptures preserved by the Theravada tradition (early Buddhist school in Sri Lanka).

See **Afterword** by Bishop Matsubayashi for a full discussion about Jodo Shinshu Buddhism.

Terry Watada is a playwright, poet, musician, educator and fiction writer living in Toronto, Ontario. His published works include **The Tale of a Mask** (play), **A Thousand Homes** (poetry) and **Daruma Days** (short stories). He has been a member of the Toronto Buddhist Church since he was a child.